THE SINEWS
OF AMERICAN
CAPITALISM

AN ECONOMIC HISTORY

The Sinews of American Capitalism *is one in a group of new books dealing with American history. The purpose of these topical histories is to present in brief compass the author's interpretation of the subject. Aïda DiPace Donald is consulting editor.*

THE SINEWS
OF AMERICAN
CAPITALISM

AN ECONOMIC HISTORY

by

Clark C. Spence

HILL AND WANG • NEW YORK

Manufactured in the United States of America
by American Book–Stratford Press, Inc.

To
MARY LEE

ACKNOWLEDGMENTS

THE AUTHOR wishes to thank the following for permission to use materials appearing in this book:

Brandt & Brandt, for the quotations from "Clipper Ships and Captains" by Stephen Vincent Benét, from *A Book of Americans* by Stephen and Rosemary Benét (New York: Holt, Rinehart & Winston, 1933), copyright, 1933, by Rosemary Carr Benét; The Macmillan Company, for the quotation from "Bryan, Bryan, Bryan, Bryan," from *The Collected Poems of Vachel Lindsay* (New York: 1925); The Johns Hopkins Press, for the information in the chart "Generation of Electricity, Compared with Total Energy Consumption for Selected Years, 1902–55," from *Energy in the American Economy, 1850–1975* by Samuel H. Schurr and Bruce C. Netschert, *et. al.* (Baltimore: 1960), published for Resources for the Future, Inc.; Chain Store Publishing Company, for the information in the chart "Growth of A & P Stores and Sales, 1859–1961," from *Chain Stores in America, 1859–1962,* 3rd ed., by Godfrey M. Lebhar (New York: 1963); Four Star Sales Company, for the quotation from the song "Don't Let Them Take It Away," words by Robert Sour, music by Bernie Wayne.

CONTENTS

TABLES

THE SINEWS
OF AMERICAN
CAPITALISM

AN ECONOMIC HISTORY

I

THE COLONIAL ECONOMY

THE OBJECT of this volume is to describe the development of
the American economy, its causes and consequences, and to explain in some measure the emergence of a nation in which roughly
6 per cent of the world's population produces some 40 per cent
of the world's goods and services. This transformation from a
simple agrarian-based economy to a complex modern industrial
one was both gradual and phenomenal and its impact profound.
The dominant thread of the story is that of technological change,
with increasing complexity of economic institutions and through
them the development of national productive capacity and a rising
standard of living. Tied closely to Europe in the colonial era,
American commerce, agriculture, transportation, financial agencies, and manufacturing were deeply and radically affected by
far-reaching "revolutions" in the nineteenth century—revolutions
based directly or indirectly upon expanding technology. As the
American economy matured, new institutions and relationships
emerged—labor unions, complex modes of business and financial
organization, shifting population patterns, and an extension of the
role of government in regulating and directing economic matters.
It is with these intricate and momentous changes over more than
three centuries that these pages are concerned.

The discovery and settlement of the New World was closely

1

tied to intellectual, political, and economic changes taking place in the Old. The European transformation, which began long before the sixteenth century, was responsible for the development of the Western Hemisphere in an economic manner not otherwise possible.

Beginning with the Crusades late in the eleventh century, Europe experienced a revival of commerce and of the capitalistic spirit, a revival that accentuated the rise of the Italian city-states, which became the great middlemen of Europe. Elsewhere, fair and market towns, located strategically for purposes of transportation, grew into thriving mercantile centers—London, Bristol, Antwerp, Hamburg, Lübeck, and others. In these centers wealth accumulated and surplus capital was available for further commercial ventures. There emerged a new class of artisans, tradesmen, merchants, and, later, lawyers and commercial officials—all men of wealth, all capitalists of a new commercial era.

At the same time came substantial developments within the world of commerce as merchant bankers learned to transfer funds by letters of credit or bills of exchange; indeed, exchanges developed in such centers as Bruges and Antwerp for the purpose of trading in such media. Ship insurance reduced the risk in trading and gave it an added inducement. Where ventures were too risky or too large for a single merchant, regulated companies or joint-stock combinations made possible a pooling of resources and a division of individual responsibility. Meanwhile, an expanding and flexible supply of money, first from the mines of Bohemia and Germany, then from the wealth of America, helped make for inflated prices and gave an additional incentive for trade.

The era from 1200 to 1600 saw the emergence of a number of integrated political states in Europe. In England, France, Spain, Portugal, and Holland powerful rulers broke down the old feudal structure based on a galaxy of competing nobles and managed to consolidate a fairly compact territory under a central government, at the same time infusing their people with a national, rather than a local, spirit of patriotism—patriotism based on similar tradition, language, and heritage. In general, these new nation-states looked to the west: they bordered on the Atlantic and they sought a better place for themselves in the trade with the Near East and the Orient. Their efforts to reduce competition and to eliminate Greek, Arab, and other middlemen helped stimulate the search for new trade routes. Their subjects pushed explorations for "God and Spain" or for "God and England," and in general the new states openly encouraged and even subsidized trade and commerce, providing protection and security under a system later known as mercantilism.

Add to these changes others that accompanied the Renaissance, that period of substantial cultural and intellectual achievement from about 1300 to 1600 which brought a return to the study of the classics and of science, with many practical applications. The Renaissance helped open the minds of men and created a growing interest in problems of natural philosophy, art, and literature. It brought a revival of ancient theories of the earth, and subsequent important advances in astronomy, navigation, and shipbuilding, with emphasis on larger, better sailing craft, rather than oared vessels. Concern for metallurgy, mining, and various types of industry went hand in hand with a popular interest in travel, which in turn stimulated commerce. With the development of printing by Gutenberg about 1450 the travels of men like Marco Polo were publicized more readily before a wider audience. Columbus carried with him to America a dog-eared copy of Marco Polo's *Travels,* its description of the Indies well-thumbed. And, as the Crusades had done before, the Renaissance fostered tastes for foreign goods encountered by travelers; it nourished the desire for comforts and the love of luxury and ostentation—all of which had an economic base.

Soon came a tremendous upheaval in religious beliefs, stimulated in part by the development of the integrated political state, in part by the spread of vernacular reading. During the Reformation, with the Bible printed in the vernacular, some of the more traditional limitations on natural science and business activity were broken down; nobility and middle classes sought to free themselves from the jurisdiction of the clergy and from the payment of tithes and fees. During the course of the struggle, the breakdown of the Holy Roman Empire helped bring forth strong national monarchs. Further, the Protestant Reformation led to direct persecution and a series of bloody religious wars which caused thousands to flee.

Such broad movements—the disruptive influence of the Reformation, the new impetus given science and the concern with natural phenomena in general fostered by the Renaissance, the emergence of the nation-state, the revival of commerce and the capitalistic spirit—provided the backdrop against which the great drama of American discovery, exploration, and settlement would be played. In the fifteenth century European sea captains, led by the Portuguese, seeking to eliminate Arab and Italian middlemen by opening new routes directly with the Indies, gradually probed southward along the African continent. They finally succeeded in 1498, when Vasco da Gama broached the Cape, tapped the luxuries of the Indies, and made a handsome profit in the process. Others, convinced that the world was round, set out to reach the Orient by sailing west, and in 1492 Christopher Columbus, a Genoese sailing under the Spanish flag, by chance discovered a new continent on his westward search for the Indies. This touched off a series of explorative voyages: Cabot for England (1497), Verrazano and Cartier for France (1524, 1534), the Corte-Real brothers for Portugal. Spain and Portugal immediately divided the New World into closed spheres of interest for themselves, while others, like Francis I of France, grumbling something about wishing to see the clause in Adam's will bequeathing the world to France's two rivals, took a lively interest but were in no position to present a serious challenge. There followed a century and a half of competition for routes to the Far East and for claims in the New World, but Spain took the lead both in exploration and colonization. When Hernando Cortes and his band of adventurers marched into Mexico City in 1619 and found great riches and excitement, they touched off a wave of conquest and plundering which ultimately took Spanish conquistadores through much of South and Central America and into the area that ultimately became the southwestern United States. The Spaniards found substantial wealth only in Mexico and Peru, but in their quest for treasure they explored a vast wilderness and created an immense empire, complete with universities and thriving seats of culture, before the English had established a single permanent colony in the New World.

Like England, France was late in planting successful colonies. French Huguenots made abortive efforts in Brazil (1555) and in Florida (1564), but not until 1608 did Champlain establish the first permanent settlement farther north. Religious conflicts at home and the Italian wars absorbed much of France's energy in the sixteenth century. If the Dutch and the Swedes enjoyed a fleeting moment in the New World early in the next century, their footholds were brief and were more footnotes than leading chapters in history.

It was England of all the nations seeking a place in the western sun who ultimately achieved the greatest success. Isolated from the continent, protected from foreign invasion, her defenses rested on naval strength, itself a prerequisite to an aggressive imperialism. A series of naval victories culminating in the defeat of the Spanish Armada in 1588 gave British merchants the additional security needed to exploit America. After the Wars of the Roses, major feudal disturbances ended and the strong Tudor line brought forth a new nobility and an English church-state and continued to play, and to play well, the balance-of-power game, allying itself against whichever continental nation seemed at the time the greatest challenge. Thus England, by the beginning of the seventeenth century, was in an advantageous position to exploit and maintain a far-flung colonial empire.

British imperialism developed as a creature of the nation, not merely of the Crown, and its justifications reflected broad and varied motives. These displayed an anti-Spanish, anti-Catholic cast: treasure from America supported the despised Spanish monarch; by seizing or diverting it the British could at once swell their own coffers and at the same time "singe the beard" of the Spanish king. Settlement offered bases from which English sea dogs might operate, and it posed a potential block to expansion of the Spanish empire. The salvation of Indian souls was not forgotten, though little was accomplished in this field. But at the beginning, even to managers of the Virginia Company, the "Principal and Maine Endes" of the enterprise "were first to preach and baptize into the Christian Religion, and by propagation of the

Gospell, to recover out of the arms of the Divell, a number of poore and miserable soules, wrapt up unto death, in almost invincible ignorance." Most dreamed of wealth and of a shorter route to the Indies. Authors wrote facetiously of Virginia as a land where "gold is more plentiful than copper with us," and where "for rubies and diamonds they go forth on holidays and gather 'em by the seashore to hang on their children's coats," and undoubtedly, in the back of many an Englishman's mind, this was more than mere imagination. A little actual experience in the New World soon punctured such dreams and a more realistic emphasis came to be placed on the possibilities of America as a source of raw materials, a market for manufactured goods, and as a refuge for the many "rogues, vagabonds, and sturdy beggars" set adrift in England by the breakdown of feudalism, the dissolution of the monasteries, and the enclosure of much arable land.

It is significant that the first permanent British settlements in America came in the form of business endeavors. The luckless experiences of Raleigh and Gilbert late in the sixteenth century underscored the futility of colonization by individual enterprise; corporate support seemed vital for so large an undertaking. In 1606 a royal charter created the London and Plymouth Companies and granted to them a region on the coast of North America running from southern Virginia to southern Nova Scotia. These were companies of stockholders, backed by merchant capital, who, among other incentives, hoped to find gold, to trade with the Indians, and to discover the elusive water passage to the wealth of the Orient.

Efforts of the Plymouth group to settle a colony on the Kennebec River in Maine proved fruitless; but because of better leadership and a milder climate, the settlement planted on the James River in Virginia by the London Company managed to survive. Even so, it would be years before Jamestown, as it was called, was on any but a precarious footing. An unhealthy location, inadequate financial support, misplaced emphasis on the search for immediate wealth rather than on production of foodstuffs brought what the Virginians called "the starving time"—a period of sickness, misery, and short rations. Captain John Smith reported a few years later:

Nay, so great was our famine, that a Salvage we slew, and buried, the poorer sort tooke him up againe and eat him, and so did divers one another boyled and stewed with roots and herbs: And one amongst the rest did kill his wife, powdered [salted] her, and had eaten part of her before it was knowne, for which hee was executed, as hee well deserved; now whether shee was better roasted, boyled or carbonado'd, I know not, but of such a dish as powdered wife I never heard of.

A new charter of 1609 separated the two companies and made Virginia into a joint-stock enterprise. Par value of stock was £12 10s.—the cost of equipping and transporting one settler—and all stockholders were entitled to a land grant and to dividends. With capital thus raised, settlers were to be sent to Virginia to labor for the company for seven years, at which time all improved land was to be distributed equally among the shareholders on the basis of a hundred acres for each share of stock. Meanwhile, the company was to retain control of natural resources and of the levying of duties within certain restrictions. But even this plan failed to bring in adequate capital, and a third charter (1612) permitted the raising of additional funds by means of lotteries. In the final analysis, however, migration was induced primarily by breaking down the corporate nature of the undertaking and giving land to settlers or to those who would outfit and transport others at their own expense.

A second permanent colony, Plymouth (1620), originated under different circumstances, but was also organized as a business enterprise. The Separatists, or Pilgrims, were extremists who would brook no interference from the Church of England in their religious beliefs. They had settled in Holland, but unsatisfied there, they had determined to migrate en masse to the New World in order to worship as they chose and to seek greater economic opportunity. From the Virginia Company, then under the influence of Sir Edwin Sandys and other Puritans, they received a charter but no funds. Financing was forthcoming from seventy London merchants who subscribed a total of £7,000 under the terms outlined in the "Articles of Agreement of Plymouth Plantation." Each emigrant to Plymouth was counted as holding one share of £10, and could purchase as many more as he desired. For a term of seven years, all products yielded in the colony were to go into a common supply. These, aided by provisions sent out from England, were to meet the needs of the settlers until, at the end of the prescribed time, "ye capitall & profits, viz. the houses, lands, goods and chatles, be equally divided betwixte ye adventurers, and planters; wch done, every man shall be free from other of them of any debt or detrimente concerning his adventure."

This was probably a more liberal plan than that attending Jamestown, where settlers were mere company servants, to receive only their freedom at the end of seven years. In neither case, however, did backers win a return from their investment. The Virginia colony was a heavy financial drain, which led to bankruptcy and a loss of the charter by 1624. At Plymouth the communal organization, according to William Bradford, governor of the colony:

> was found to breed much confusion and discontent and retard
> much employment that would have been to their benefite and com-
> forte. For the yong-men that were most able and fitte for labor and
> service did repine that they should spend their time and streingth
> to work for other mens wives and children, with out any recom-
> pence. The strong, or men of parts, had no more in divission of
> victails and cloaths than he that was weake and not able to doe a
> quarter the other could; this was thought injuestice. The aged and
> graver men to be ranked and equalised in labours and victails,
> cloaths, etc., with the meaner and yonger sorte, thought it some
> indignite and disrespect unto them. And for mens wives to be com-
> manded to doe service for other men, as dressing their meate, wash-
> ing their cloaths, etc., they deemd it a kind of slaverie, neither
> could many husbands well brooke it.

With the abandonment of this common stock system in favor of individual land allotments within a few years and with aid from the Indians, the Pilgrims managed to avoid a "starving time" comparable to that of the Virginians, but despite a limited profit from furs and fish, their enterprise was not a financial success. When Plymouth settlers made arrangements in 1627 to purchase the interests of London shareholders, the latter were happy to relinquish all their claims for a total of £1,800.

In time, Plymouth was absorbed by the Massachusetts Bay

Company, chartered in 1629. When Charles I put increasing pressure on his opposition, which included many leading English Puritans, the latter decided to retreat to Massachusetts. Buying up the stock of the company, they migrated, taking charter and corporation with them, to be followed by a mass migration of some twenty thousand persons between 1630 and 1640. Massachusetts Bay was organized as a corporation and has been compared to a modern business concern: its governor, deputy governor, and eighteen assistants would roughly correspond to the president, vice-president, and board of directors; its freemen, who moved to Massachusetts also, were comparable to shareholders of a contemporary business concern.

Despite their commercial failure, these early efforts provided the basis for the first permanent planting of English people on the North American continent. They endured hardships not encountered by later settlers, who profited from their experience. Subsequent colonies founded on the Atlantic seaboard were organized on different bases and for different reasons: Rhode Island and Connecticut, for example, emerged as offshoots of Massachusetts Bay, settled by religious dissenters or those attracted by rich, fertile land. Beginning with the grant of Maryland to Lord Calvert in 1634, the Crown discharged numerous obligations by handing over vast wilderness tracts in America to individuals or groups of proprietors. New York, captured from the Dutch, went to the Duke of York; Pennsylvania to William Penn; New Jersey to Sir George Carteret and Sir John Berkeley; the Carolinas went to a group of eight proprietors, who promptly engaged John Locke to write an elaborate, unworkable, and somewhat feudal frame of government for them. Eventually the proprietary colonies, and also Georgia, which was founded in 1733 as a buffer against the Spaniards and as a haven for British debtors, came under direct royal supervision, but, save for Georgia, which received a very limited amount of government aid, these were settled by the initiative of individual proprietors, who sought to attract population by liberal political and economic concessions. It should be remembered, however, that the thirteen mainland colonies were but part of a far-flung empire, which by the middle of the eighteenth century included nearly fifteen million people living under some thirty-one governments, all owing allegiance to the British flag.

The economy of the mainland colonies was at first predominantly agricultural, though in the long run diversification prevailed, with the extractive industries quickly assuming prime importance. Even in New England at least 90 per cent of the population was engaged in agriculture; elsewhere the proportion was even higher, and in the South a dualism developed with plantation proprietors using slave labor to produce export crops, while the great mass of small farmers sustained an economy largely based on self-sufficiency.

The colonial farmer, provincial, optimistic, versatile, and industrious, found his activities tempered by environment: by an abundance of fertile land and a corresponding shortage of labor, by new crops and techniques, and by markets which were either distant or exceedingly small. His existence was a matter of constant adjustment from the beginning. At first, lacking capital for adequate implements and livestock, his techniques were little more advanced than those of the Indians. Indeed, without the crops and methods of the Indians, he would have found survival impossible during the early years. Maize, or Indian corn, became a staple; it yielded well per acre with reasonable certainty and with a minimum of labor. Especially adapted to virgin soil, it was easily transported in liquid form or on the hoof and made excellent food for man or beast. Cotton, pumpkins, potatoes, and tobacco were also among the products borrowed from the natives.

At first the settlers adopted primitive farming methods from the Indians. According to Frederick Jackson Turner, the wilderness temporarily conquered the settler, causing him to revert to primitive ways of living. He learned to girdle and burn trees, or to plant between them using a sharp stick. Oxen and horses came in to provide power; additional machinery was added, but implements showed no real advance. Even in the eighteenth century, plows were heavy and cumbersome, though by no means as scarce as in the early years.

European crops, too, played an important role. Wheat, rye, oats, and other small grains throve after the ground had been broken and planted to corn. The fertile Connecticut Valley of

New England has been described as the "first wheat belt of America," and wheat was so important in the Middle Colonies that these became known as the "bread colonies." The harvesting of grain, however, was not too far removed from that of biblical description: reaping was done with the sickle or, by 1790, with the cradle; threshing was by tramping out with horses in the Middle Colonies or by flail in New England, with subsequent winnowing as of old.

Few domestic animals, apart from the dog, were native to North America. Livestock had to be imported and was scarce during the early years. Moreover, lack of indigenous forage plants led to the importation of traditional plants such as bluegrass, clover, and timothy from England. The method of raising livestock remained primitive for many years. Common pasturing in New England, the mingling of "everybody's son with nobody's daughter," made it difficult to improve breeds. Even by the mid-eighteenth century, little shelter was provided for animals in the winter, except in New England, parts of New York, and in Pennsylvania among the thrifty, advanced German farmers.

If labor and capital were scarce, land was abundant, though ordinarily not free. The mode of its distribution in different areas would affect the course of settlement and have an impact on future land policy of the United States. In Virginia, Maryland, the Carolinas, Georgia, and in parts of New Jersey, the headright system prevailed in one form or another. In essence, this involved the granting of a "headright" of a specified amount of land (usually fifty acres) to any person transporting another to America. In time the headright became a convenient vehicle for distributing colonial lands in general, and headrights were granted freely, with considerable laxity. Thus, in practice as much as two hundred acres might pass into private hands for each person crossing the Atlantic: a merchant sending an indentured servant, for example, might claim fifty acres; the captain of the ship providing passage another fifty, the Virginia planter who purchased the servant's services an additional fifty; and finally the servant himself might ultimately acquire fifty acres. Sizable estates were thus built up, especially by sea captains, and much good headright land passed into the hands of speculators, forcing bona fide settlers to push farther into the interior. By 1705 in Virginia the sale of headrights was made legal and they were peddled at a rate of five shillings for fifty acres. Under the system, land could be located anywhere not yet occupied and the registrant had to apply for survey, in some colonies to pay a nominal quitrent, and to "seat his grant," that is, to make some semblance of improvement upon it. Occasionally southern colonies attempted to parcel out land to encourage settlement in western areas for defensive purposes, as in 1645 when Virginia offered grants of six hundred acres each to individuals who would establish and maintain forts along the western fringe of the Tidewater. Again in 1701, after this and other means of encouraging border defenses had proved unfruitful, Virginia proposed giving land grants of from ten thousand to thirty thousand acres to groups of settlers, each of whom was to be a "warlike Christian man between sixteen and sixty years of age, perfect of limb, able and fitt for service"; but such proposals were not important in the process of settlement.

In New England both the system of land distribution and the westward advance were different than elsewhere. Whereas in the South individuals taking up the best lands under the headright system or through purchase from speculators had pushed out onto the frontier, then cleared their fields as quickly as possible for the production of staples, in New England the advance was more often by groups, closely regulated, and more evenly spread over poor lands as well as good. Greater co-operative effort and a more diversified agriculture were evident.

New England legislatures made two types of grants: early and relatively unimportant ones to favored officials, ministers, teachers, or veterans; and those to groups for the establishment of new frontier towns. After a number of families had petitioned for a "Plantation Right"—an authorization for settlement—and had been found of the proper religious and moral stamp, and after the contemplated site had been found fertile, defensible, and contingent to other settlements, and arrangements had been made for extinguishing Indian claims, the General Court authorized an orderly settlement, laying out a township measuring six miles square, although grants were often irregularly shaped because of rough terrain. The proprietors owned the land in fee simple, but were responsible for subdividing, constructing roads, gristmill, church, and school, and locating a minister and permanent settlers. To entice millers, blacksmiths, and ministers, land was offered free to them, and even in one case to a midwife, "in answer to the town's necessity, which at present is great."

Under the New England township system, house lots were apportioned, as well as marsh lands for pasturage. Large fields were divided into rectangular strips and distributed by drawing, those with wealth receiving more than those without. Proprietors retained control of undivided land and common pasturage. No doubt the system spared settlers many of the discomforts of individualistic pioneer life, and the frontier advanced gradually, with a greater degree of security. Joint, not individualistic, enterprise cleared the land and life proceeded on a community basis almost from the beginning. A relatively short growing season, thin, hilly soil, and a minimum of navigable streams focused the efforts of these settlers on diversified agriculture instead of any single cash crop. Newcomers lacked a voice in government and were at the mercy of proprietors for land and often were forced to move on. The system in general made for controlled settlement, fewer boundary disputes, and because of diversified crops, small units of cultivation. But in time, as secular breezes swept across New England, the control features tended to break down: in the eighteenth century veterans of the Indian Wars were being granted whole townships; by the 1760's both Connecticut and Massachusetts were auctioning off western townships. Speculators and land jobbers now loomed large.

Land systems of the Middle Colonies blended somewhat those of their northern and their southern neighbors. New York had a combination of the township plan and the Dutch patroon system of large land allotments, with rampant speculation superimposed over both. New Jersey combined the township and headright systems, while Pennsylvania, like most of the "Old West" beyond the coastal frontier, had chaos. At first, William Penn, reserving the proprietary tenth for himself, had sought to dispose of the remainder either in blocks of five thousand acres for £100 and a small quitrent, or two hundred acres sold outright, or fifty acres for each servant brought in and fifty more to the servant when

free. Later, in parts of central and western Pennsylvania a modified township system developed, and then in the eighteenth century a flood of Scotch-Irish poured in, appropriating unoccupied
farm land on the basic assumption that "It was against the laws
of God and Nature that so much land should be idle while so
many Christians wanted it to labor on and to raise their bread."
When the Scotch-Irish spilled over on Indian lands, as in the
valley of the Juniata, for example, the Penns first tried futilely
to eject them, then bowed to the inevitable and purchased the
region from the Indians. By this time, 1754, the Penn land office
was recognizing squatters' rights, which entitled the squatter to
purchase unappropriated land at normal prices where he had
made improvements on it. This recognition of the right of pre-
emption would be carried from Pennsylvania to other parts of
the frontier and would ultimately—for half a century or so—become a fundamental part of American land law.

Differences of climate, geography, and soil combined with land
systems to determine the peculiar economic growth of the various
colonial regions. Farming in New England assumed definite characteristics of its own, as apart from those of the so-called Middle
Colonies, while the South hewed to a totally independent line.
Yet, taken together, with the pattern of intercolonial and foreign
trade that developed, they worked in complementary fashion as
part of an integrated structure of production and distribution.

As has been mentioned, New England was predominantly a
land of small diversified farms. The rocky coastal belt was poor:
the soil was thin, the summers short, and the winters rigorous.
Thus agriculture tended to develop more on a subsistence basis
than elsewhere, though by mid-seventeenth century, grain, beef,
and orchard products were being exported. The black stem rust, or
the "blast" as it was called, devastated small grains about 1660,
"whether naturell, or a blasting frō heaven we know not," according to John Winthrop, Jr. Probably after the early 1680's, New
England no longer shipped out grain, except as a re-export from
her neighbors to the south.

New York, Pennsylvania, New Jersey, and Delaware—the
Middle Colonies—were more blessed with fertile soil, and apart
from a few sections like the pine barrens of southern New Jersey,

this region soon became highly important as a producer of grain, beef, pork, and horses for export to New England and to the West Indies. Here in the "bread colonies," a mixed population had brought in a variety of strains of livestock and crops; they farmed holdings generally larger than those of New England, and often employed superior farming techniques to produce remarkable yields.

The colonial economy of much of the South—Virginia, Maryland, and northern Carolina particularly—was said to have been built on smoke, "the blacke stinking fume" of tobacco, the all-important cash crop. So popular was the growing of the "weed" that cultivation had to be limited at first to assure the growth of an adequate food supply and later to prevent the glut of the market. By volume, tobacco exports rose from some 27.8 million pounds in 1665 to over 100 million pounds on the eve of the Revolution. From time to time the bottom fell out of prices, bringing disaster to small operators; however, for planters using slave labor and large-scale planting, tobacco generally returned a profit. But tobacco required careful cultivation and a large labor force, and it quickly exhausted even rich soil, thus continually requiring fresh land. The ease of acquiring land in the South promoted the rise of large plantations; slave labor came to be substituted for indentured; and since the crop was mainly for export, the land along the rivers, giving access to water transportation, was taken up first. Even so, the typical Southern farmer in colonial times operated on a moderate scale and emphasized a variety of products for his own consumption, rather than for sale abroad.

Below the tobacco belt, the production of coffee and sugar was largely experimental, but rice was being profitably grown in the moist lowlands of South Carolina by the end of the seventeenth century. Together, South Carolina and Georgia exported more than 27.4 million pounds of rice in 1750 and nearly 84 million pounds in 1770. A bounty of six pence a pound stimulated some raising of indigo, which because of its growth and labor schedule could be grown simultaneously with rice, using the same labor supply. Cotton production was limited, and centered primarily in South Carolina. Not until the waning years of the eighteenth century would this commodity take on importance in the export market to serve the powerful new demands of the British textile industry.

Colonial America presented an abundance of land and natural resources but a decided shortage of labor. The natives could not be counted upon to help as in the Spanish colonies of Central and South America. Indians were often enslaved, especially in the Carolinas, and sold in the West Indies; more civilized Indians in New England often were heavily fined for breaking the law, then put to work or sold as indentured servants to meet their fines; but never did the Indian figure as an important part of the colonial labor supply. Emphasis was on other sources.

Family labor was basic. White inhabitants of the thirteen colonies numbered about 1.6 million in 1760; a decade and a half later they numbered approximately 2.5 million, their numbers having been swollen both by domestic increase and by immigrants. Despite a high infant mortality rate, families were large: Ben Franklin was one of fifteen children. Early marriage was encouraged, widows remarried promptly, and large families were deemed economic assets since all members were expected to contribute labor. Morover, common fields and pastures and other forms of co-operation were labor-saving devices.

Young, energetic Europeans made the colonies from the beginning something of a melting pot. While the stock remained basically English, it was modified by important foreign elements such as the "Pennsylvania Dutch," the sturdy Germans who comprised some 6 per cent, and the pugnacious Scotch-Irish, who made up about 7 per cent by 1775, and who not only brought whiskey distilling but also provided the cutting edge of the frontier movement. Other groups included Swedes, Dutch, French, Irish, Welsh, and Swiss. With the Negro slaves included, almost 40 per cent of the colonials at the time of the Revolution were non-English in background; indeed, eighteen of the fifty-six signers of the Declaration fell in that category and eight of these had been born outside the Colonies.

The supply of free labor was increasing but was limited. High wages and excellent work conditions did not offset the westward drain prompted by cheap land. But the free labor which was available was usually important far beyond mere numbers because it was often skilled. It was not unusual for a businessman to bring over skilled masons, carpenters, tanners, or others under contract. Peter Hasenclever in 1765 brought 535 men and their families from Germany and England for employment in his iron, potash, and dye establishments in New York and New Jersey.

In the seventeenth century, probably the most important source of labor was the indentured servants, both voluntary and involuntary. Some signed articles of indenture before they left Europe; others, the so-called "redemptioners" or "free-willers," contracted to sell their labor once in America to repay money spent on their passage. Voluntary indenture provided a means whereby those lacking capital might gain a start in the new world by agreeing to work for a stipulated period of service in exchange for their passage.

Colonial agents in England and on the Continent seduced many into making the trip with glowing promises, but not all came willingly. "Crimps" and "newlanders" sometimes relied on fraud and misrepresentation, sometimes on more drastic methods. How many unfortunates were "spirited" away from waterfront dives or how many children were "trapanned" (kidnaped) and sold into indentured servitude in America is impossible to say. A report of the Privy Council in the mid-seventeenth century called this practice "a thinge so barbarous and inhumane, that Nature itself much more Christians cannot but abhore it." A tract published in London early in the eighteenth century caught the disillusionment of a young girl thus transported to Maryland:

> In weeding Corn or feeding Swine,
> I keep my melancholy Time.
> Kidnap'd and Fool'd, I thither fled,
> To shun a hated Nuptial Bed,
> And to my cost already find
> Worse plagues than those I left behind.

Increasing numbers of convicts—"His Majesty's Seven-Year Passengers"—were sent to relieve pressure on the prisons at home, a practice described by Ben Franklin as "an insult and contempt, the cruellest that ever one people offered another." At first, mainly paupers and beggars were sent, but with over 300 crimes in England punishable by death, more serious criminals were also sent: 655 migrant convicts (111 of them women) banished to one county in Maryland included many convicted of thievery, murder, and rape, not to mention those described glibly as "lewd." This, in general, was the background for Samuel Johnson's famous remark on Americans: "Sir, they are a race of convicts, and ought to be content with anything we allow them short of hanging."

After horrible voyages under conditions which many failed to survive, indentured servants were put on sale at port towns. About a hundred "Healthy Servants" were advertised at Leeds, Virginia, among them, "many Tradespeople—viz. Blacksmiths, Shoemakers, Tailors, House Carpenters and Joiners, a Cooper, several Silversmiths, Weavers, A Jeweler, and many others." If not sold at the port, redemptioners might then be taken inland by "soul drivers," who herded them along "like cattle to a Smithfield market" to be auctioned off at public fairs.

Treatment of the indentured servant no doubt varied. A Maryland servant in 1659 wrote:

> The Servants of this Province, which are stigmatiz'd for Slaves by the clappermouth jaws of the vulgar in England, live more like Freemen than the most Mechanick Apprentices in London, wanting for nothing that is convenient and necessary, and according to their several capacities, are extraordinarily well used and respected.

On the other hand, many examples of harsh, inhumane treatment might be cited, despite colonial laws to the contrary. Such laws stipulated that masters must provide a minimum in terms of food, clothing, shelter, and medical care, giving the servant the right to sue for breach of contract. The servants, on their part, were to labor at whatever work their master desired, and at the end of their time (four to seven years) were to be released with perhaps a few tools and clothes and, in some colonies, with fifty acres of land. Servants could be transferred by sale or bequest; their personal life was subject to regulation and they could not buy liquor, stay out late, or marry without permission. If they committed infractions, they could be punished by shipping or by having their term of bondage extended. At least one colonial report indicated that bastardy, even involving the master, was used as an offense to hold servant girls longer. "Late experiments show," said the report, "that some dissolute masters have gotten their maides with child, and yet claim the benefit of their services."

The many runaways and instances of corporal punishment would indicate that the indenture system was generally harsh. But for all that, it did provide a beginning for the poor in America. Once free, the servants often worked for wages or settled as small farmers. Many achieved distinction: two were even listed among the signers of the Declaration of Independence.

In 1619 Negro slavery was introduced and after mid-century gradually became more and more important in the Southern economy. Portuguese, Dutch, and ultimately English traders were responsible for the traffic from the African slave coast. Packed in infamous vessels in chains below decks, wretchedly overcrowded, many slaves fell prey to tropical heat or disease before completing the voyage. Many spent several years of "seasoning" in the West Indies before being sent on to the mainland colonies. Even the New Englanders had no moral scruples against the use of slaves, but the small diversified farming was not particularly suited for slave labor, shipbuilding and navigation were too specialized occupations, and the rigors of winter fishing too severe. Thus slavery spread more in regions where climate did not demand expensive winter clothing and housing and where gang labor could be used under general supervision for specialized crop production.

By 1775 there were an estimated 400,000 slaves, at least, on the mainland, of which only 15,000 were in New England and 32,000 in the Middle Colonies. Most prevalent in the South, the "peculiar institution" was not yet the all-important force it later became when cotton became king, but it was there, could not be ignored, and was part of a social pyramid. Slaves were at the absolute bottom level; above them came indentured servants, then lesser tradesmen and wage laborers, then a fairly broad group of yeomen farmers who owned their own land. Near the top came a relatively small category of officials, clergy, lawyers, and merchants, while at the pinnacle were the aristocrats—the more successful professional people, crown officials, merchant princes, or landed gentry.

But the labor shortage and the ease of acquisition of land

rendered this social structure fluid. Movement upward was possible for everyone, except for the Negro slaves. If colonial governments made efforts to regulate workers' activities, often setting maximum wages—especially for skilled artisans—or even attempting to prescribe the dress of the worker, such laws in the face of labor shortages were impossible to enforce.

With the labor supply limited, lacking the deposits of precious metals that stimulated the Spanish, without immediate extensive markets, British economic development in America proceeded more slowly, required a greater input of manpower and capital, and resulted in a more diversified base, with a wide variety of enterprises prevailing.

If agriculture predominated, other extractive industries quickly assumed importance. The French had successfully carried on fishing in the New World even before 1600; before long New Englanders gave stiff competition and by the early eighteenth century were dominating Newfoundland waters. Haddock, cod, mackerel, and hake were all significant; high quality fish went to Catholic Spain or Portugal; inferior fish to feed West Indian slaves. By 1700, New England was annually exporting over five thousand tons of fish—more than England herself shipped abroad. Since 1614, when Captain John Smith had visited the New England waters "to take whales and make trials at a mine of gold and copper," whaling had also become part of the New England way of life. Pursued for their oil, their whalebone, their spermaceti for candles, and ambergris for perfume, the great aquatic mammals gradually became scarcer and had to be hunted farther and farther away at sea. From about 1730, the oil began to be extracted aboard ship, and by the Revolution some 360 colonial vessels were involved in the occupation, ranging the seas from Nantucket, New Bedford, Sag Harbor, and other well-known ports. Only in the nineteenth century would the peak be reached.

Shipbuilding was a natural corollary of fishing and whaling, and the industry was most important in New England, although the Middle Colonies were also involved. Most New England towns had their noisy "Bedlam" or "Knockers' Hole," usually located on a sloping beach, where the sound of hammers and caulkers' mallets echoed incessantly. Occasionally a small vessel would be built close to timber and rolled to the water on tree trunks; later some were even constructed inland and floated downriver to the sea. Vessels were small, ranging between ten and four hundred tons. At the end of the eighteenth century the average gross weight of all vessels putting into England was but 176 tons. Small vessels were a matter of practical necessity, designed to reduce risk from pirates, privateers, or shipwreck. Attending shipbuilding were the kindred industries of iron manufacture, sailmaking, and rope manufacture, usually located near the shipyards, although ropewalks were frequently restricted to outside the town limits because of danger from fire. By 1676 at least 730 vessels had been built in Massachusetts alone; by 1776 an estimated 2,000 ships (apart from fishing vessels) were owned in New England, and nearly one third of those in the commerce of Great Britain had been built in the Colonies.

Associated with the maritime industries were those of the forest—lumbering, production of naval stores, manufacture of potash and pearlash, and even the fur trade. New England was noted for its cedar, spruce, and white pine, as well as for its rapidly moving streams, which provided easily harnessed and adequate water power. By the early 1700's, the Piscataqua River alone was turning at least seventy sawmills producing over six million board feet a year. At first this work was done with a single straight saw, given its up and down motion from a crank actuated by a water wheel; later came gang saws—several parallel straight saws set in a frame to cut several boards at once. Not until the nineteenth century did the familiar circular saw come into use.

Many farmers conducted their own small-scale lumbering operations, but larger enterprises were usually operated by partners, frequently backed by British capital in the form of advances of credit or goods in exchange for lumber. In the eighteenth century merchant investment and speculation combined to create more than one lumber king. There were few restrictions except on removal of tall trees marked with the broad arrow as potential masts for the Royal Navy, and even this restriction was almost impossible to enforce. The Admiralty was also interested in naval stores and placed bounties on masts, tar, pitch, hemp, and other commodities, hoping to make Britain independent of other, especially Baltic, sources. In the North, many of the naval commodities were used at home, thus North Carolina led in the export of supplies, largely from her pine forests.

Potash and pearlash, both wood products, were used for bleaching, for fertilizer, and for the manufacture of soap and glass. Made from the ash of burned timber, they were often manufactured by an individual settler and his family, either for home consumption or for an initial cash "crop" early in the process of settlement. By the time of the Revolution an estimated fourteen thousand barrels a year were being exported. Another forest product, oak bark, was highly valuable for its use in tanning leather. Tanyards were found in all parts of the country, usually relegated by law to the outskirts of towns because of their offensive odors.

All colonies engaged in the fur trade to one extent or another, but Virginia, South Carolina, New York, and Pennsylvania were most important. It was the Virginia traders who ultimately penetrated the mountains to tap the trade with the Cherokees in eastern Tennessee, until South Carolina competition put an end to it. And in South Carolina, the trade was primarily in deerskins, rather than furs or pelts. In the first fifteen years or so of the eighteenth century, the colony exported on the average of 54,000 deerskins a year to England, most of them obtained directly from the Indians. In New York the fur trade centered around Albany, which controlled the Mohawk route into the Great Lakes region and the West and at the same time guarded against the French coming down from Canada via Lake Champlain, Lake George, and the Hudson. Albany, moreover, was in a position to exploit the Iroquois Indians, who soon became aware of the advantages of trading with the British there. In the seventeenth century, Indians paid five beaver skins for a musket at Montreal, only two at Albany. A more advanced manufacturing nation, Britain provided cheaper, generally superior goods than France, except for gunpowder. The Iroquois were aware, too, of the desire of the English to use them in the collection of furs while the French did more of their own gathering. The fur trade of Pennsylvania came later and would be of significance because it brought the British traders up against the French line of empire in the Ohio Valley and ultimately precipitated a clash that would end in the ousting of France from North America, with a few minor exceptions. Hard on the heels of the first traders came land speculators and a new French "get tough" policy of establishing a series of forts in the West. The aggressive reaction of Virginians, interested in land companies in the West, led to an open clash and "the volley fired by a young Virginian in the backwoods of America that set the world on fire"—the beginning of the French and Indian War, which despite its flare-up in the wilderness of Pennsylvania was more broadly based in questions of global imperial rivalry.

Properly speaking, the thirteen mainland colonies did not constitute a manufacturing region; yet their isolation and the desire for goods not available at all or available only at high prices made it inevitable that manufacturing industries should develop. Usifacture—manufacturing in the home by the family for its own use —predominated, and the average family displayed remarkable versatility in meeting its own wants. Foodstuffs such as butter, cheese, lard, and hominy were produced at home as a matter of course. Candles were made from mutton fat or possibly from bear grease or bayberry. The same sheep that provided the mutton fat had earlier provided wool, which when carded, spun, woven, fulled, dyed, and dressed, often in the home, clothed the entire family. More commonly, several of the processes, especially fulling and dyeing, were done elsewhere, but much home-dyeing, using indigo, berries, hickory, or oak barks, was common. Likewise leathermaking, shoemaking, the manufacture of furniture and of a thousand and one everyday items were accomplished at home.

Substantial manufacturing in the Colonies, as apart from usifacture, was hampered by a shortage of skilled labor, by scattered domestic markets and inadequate transportation, by British restrictions on manufacturing of certain commodities, and by the fact that capital tended to flow into more immediately lucrative pursuits—commerce, trading, or tobacco planting. Yet, despite barriers, industries of one kind or another gradually developed and assumed importance if only for domestic consumption.

Manufacturing linked with agricultural products was among the first. Flour milling was basic and fell into two categories: small local gristmills which ground for individual farmers, taking grain in exchange; and larger, more complex mills which produced for the retail or for the export trade. A few were powered by the wind but most were water-operated. More than one miller attempted to corner the market or to boost prices by not purchasing grain, and more than one colonial legislature acted to regulate this all-important basic industry. The distilling of liquor was also a by-product of agriculture. Much liquor was consumed in the Colonies, and rum, especially after the late seventeenth century, was highly important as an international trade commodity. By 1750 Massachusetts was exporting two million gallons of rum a year and by the time of the Revolution there were at least sixty-three distilleries in the colony. But except in New England and New York, distillation was mainly for home consumption.

Such towns as Lynn, New Haven, Philadelphia, and Newark early became centers for the manufacture of boots, shoes, harnesses, and saddles on a commercial basis. Hats at first were made at home, but their production soon became also a shop industry, using such material as wool, beaver, and raccoon. The Hat Act of 1732 prohibited the export of hats to other countries and even the other colonies and prohibited the use of Negroes in the trade, but these limitations were largely ignored. Most colonies did their best to encourage the woolen industry.

Early efforts were made to establish blast furnaces in Virginia, but these were abandoned after an Indian attack in 1622. In 1641 John Winthrop raised capital and skilled workers in England to exploit bog iron deposits at Lynn and Braintree, Massachusetts. Although British investors put in at least £11,500, and although the enterprise was in operation for several decades, it was never a complete success, partly because of regulated prices, exhaustive litigation, and a failure to solve technical problems. There were a few other ironworks of the seventeenth century, but not until the eighteenth did real progress occur. By the time of the Revolution there were ironworks in every colony except Georgia and more forges and blast furnaces in the Colonies than in England and Wales combined; roughly one seventh of the world's iron supply was being produced on the western side of the Atlantic. Concentration was heaviest in southeastern Pennsylvania, where ore deposits, water power, and timber for charcoal were located in close proximity. There were a number of sizable "iron plantations"—self-contained units where food supplies were also raised—some using slaves, some indentured servants, but most utilizing free artisans, often imported from abroad. Since the iron plantation represented considerable capital outlay of from £7,000 to £12,000 for land, houses, furnaces, forges, mills, and other equipment, most were partnership arrangements, with one partner personally supervising operations. A large operator, like the well-known ironmaster Peter Hasenclever, however, might own as many as six blast furnaces and seven forges, plus a stamping mill. Parliament, by the Iron Act of 1750 and other acts which followed, had regulated the production of refined grades of iron, but had permitted the production of bar and pig iron. It prohibited the erection of new steel furnaces and slitting and plating mills, but permitted those already established to continue in operation. Such laws meant little; the iron produced was utilized in the Colonies and not meant for export.

Other metal industries did not flourish to the same extent. There was a little brassworking, as for warming pans; but brassworks were rare, because although copper was available, all zinc used in the alloy had to be imported. Much of the pewterware had to be imported for a similar reason; the copper was available, but the tin was not, though after the 1750's lead was often used as a substitute. No silver was found in the Colonies and little was imported from England, but silver coins from the West Indian trade were often converted into silver sets until the introduction of banks and of Sheffield plate prompted a decline of individual silversmithing in the nineteenth century.

Some glassmaking was done at Jamestown as early as 1609 and in Salem in 1639, but mainly for the production of beads for trading with the Indians. More important was the glassworks established across the Delaware from Philadelphia in 1739 by Caspar Wistar. With specialists imported from Holland, this plant for more than forty years produced window glass, pitchers, bottles, and an assortment of other items. In 1763, Heinrich Steigel established near Lancaster, Pennsylvania, a glassworks so large "that a coach and four could turn around within the brick dome of its melting house." Here all types of glass, including a beautifully colored variety, were produced, but Steigel died in poverty, the victim of speculation and high living. Small pottery plants developed and New York produced some stoneware of importance; indeed, just prior to the Revolution the growing number of potteries in the Colonies alarmed British manufacturers, including Josiah Wedgwood.

Other miscellaneous manufactured products included: candles, particularly those made by the spermaceti chandlers, who in the 1760's sought to gain a monopoly by setting prices and rigorously controlling members and processes; rifles, especially after 1730, when the fine craftsmanship of the Pennsylvania Germans made both their guns and their wagons famous; watches and clocks, manufactured in number in New England by the late eighteenth century, which rapidly replaced sundials and hourglasses; bricks; books; metal items; and paper.

In many different ways, local government attempted to stimulate industries. Colonies or even towns encouraged wool raising by giving special pasture rights or prohibiting the export of sheep: Connecticut exempted sheep from taxation. Iron, raccoon skins, and hides were also banned from export by law by a number of colonies, while some placed an export tax on such goods to discourage shipment. Early statutes in Virginia and Connecticut required the planting of flax and hemp; Virginia required each country to establish at least one public tannery; some, like Virginia, the Carolinas, and New Jersey, offered bounties for hemp and some for flax also; several gave bounties for woolen cloth made within the colony; after the British Woolens Act of 1699, only Rhode Island gave a bounty on wool, and only briefly, but several colonies resumed this policy in 1775 as a matter of direct revolt. There were bounties for linen, duck, and silk; for the building of small ships, and the manufacture of salt, tar, and wine. Land grants or monopolies were often given and loans without security made to help establish sailcloth factories or silk culture. Some colonies made certain local manufactured goods legal tender for payment of debts, partly because of a shortage of specie and partly to encourage certain industries, tar, wool, flax, hemp, and turpentine among them.

Local governments also undertook to regulate manufacturing in the public interest. Where special fire dangers existed, they sometimes required permits for the erection of buildings such as bakeries, potter's kilns, and chocolate mills; occasionally they limited or banned distilling to save grain or molasses; or as an encouragement to the manufacture of iron, they banned the sale of liquor near foundries. Most colonies regulated mill dams for the preservation of navigation and fish; most regulated the rate charged for grinding grain, usually permitting a sixteenth for wheat and a twelfth for maize in New England; higher tolls in the South, for example, a sixth in Virginia, indicated a relative scarcity of mills. Local authorities also inspected millstones and fined millers for poor work. In the British tradition, they regulated the weight and quality of flour, bread, beer, and packed meats, and often appointed an inspector, or "sealer," to check barrels of pork, tobacco, or potash; Connecticut and Massachusetts inspected shipbuilding to make certain that sound timber was used. Whether such controls and stimuli were ever very effective is debatable; industries were probably affected much more by the presence or absence of basic factors—labor, capital, and transportation.

Moreover, colonial industry was hemmed in somewhat by the limitations of mercantilist theory. Loosely defined, mercantilism was a system designed to enhance the power, prestige, and prosperity of the mother country, government, and people. It was predicated on the assumption that colonies, as part of the British Empire, would be made to yield wealth; that wealth, in turn, contributed to natural strength, which in turn augmented victory over Britain's enemies; and with victory came the acquiring of additional colonies to produce more wealth, the circle repeating itself. The theory subordinated the interests of the colonies to those of the mother country in several ways. The colony was to be considered as a source of cheap, noncompetitive raw materials —items not produced at home—silk, hemp, indigo, naval supplies. Moreover, these noncompeting goods must be carried in British vessels or those built in the colonies and must come to England as required by the series of Navigation Laws enacted between 1651 and 1663. The law of 1663 prescribed that most

European goods must also pass through England en route to the colonies. Enumerated items produced in the colonies such as sugar, tobacco, indigo, ginger, and ultimately molasses, furs, and naval stores could go only to England. However, fish, grain, and rum could be sent directly to any market until 1766, but after that only to nations south of Cape Finisterre. Such regulations were designed to strengthen the British merchant marine and to divert profits of the carrying trade from the Dutch especially, with whom England had fought three wars in the 1650–70 era.

Under mercantilism, colonies were designed not only to provide raw materials, and to enhance the carrying trade of the mother country, but also to provide ready markets for manufactured goods. In 1700 goods shipped to the mainland colonies made up 15 per cent of total British exports; by 1775, with 2.5 million whites between Georgia and the St. Lawrence, the percentage had risen to 33. Moreover, mercantilism presupposed a favorable balance of trade on behalf of the mother country. For England to export more to her colonies than she imported from them meant that the colonies made up the difference in cash. With this debt to British merchants, particularly on the part of mainland Southerners, specie drained from the colonies and its shortage was a constant plague. Money scarcity helped keep export prices low and imports high, to colonial detriment. Where specie was available, it was commonly in the form of the Spanish dollar, often clipped to "halves," "quarters," or even "bits." Inevitably barter became an important part of the colonial economy, with Indian wampum, corn, beaver pelts, rice, tobacco, or tobacco warehouse certificates being used in various colonies from time to time as mediums of exchange. When colonies issued paper money, redeemable by taxes within a specified period, depreciation set in, so that by mid-eighteenth century, paper issued by Massachusetts had sunk to less than 10 per cent of its face value. Despite numerous complaints from the colonies, Parliament stepped in in 1764 to forbid the issuance of paper money.

Direct trade with the mother country accounted for the bulk of colonial transactions: in 1769, for example, the thirteen mainland colonies sent more than one half of their recorded exports to England and received more than 60 per cent of their recorded imports from that source. Yet, because of the specie shortage, because of the desire to import more British goods than they could pay for with colonial produce, because the Colonies needed goods which England could not supply, or because Britain could not absorb all colonial goods, there developed a multi-sided international trade which involved a large part of the commercial world. It was this arrangement which enabled Pennsylvania, as Benjamin Franklin explained in 1766, to import some £500,000 worth of English goods annually, while exporting only £40,000 worth of goods to the mother country.

Although often referred to as the triangular trade, this facet of mercantilism was a good deal more complex than that. A hexagon with corners marking Newfoundland, the mainland colonies, and the West Indies in America, the British Isles, the Iberian Peninsula, and West Africa on the opposite side, formed the trade perimeter. Connection of each of these six points with the others within the perimeter gave the combination of possible oceanic trade routes for colonial and English vessels, although upon the British West Indies—the most important part of the eighteenth-century Empire—hinged New England's maritime success. These islands provided the tropical or semitropical products not grown by the mother country; while on the mainland, Georgia and South Carolina exported rice and indigo and Virginia and Maryland sent tobacco. To the West Indies went lumber, barrels, horses, or foodstuffs from the Middle Colonies, in exchange for sugar, molasses, silver, or transshipped English manufactured goods. New England fish went both to the West Indian islands and to southern Europe as a part of a variety of trade patterns, the most popular of which might involve food and rum to Newfoundland, fish to the Indies, and island cargo back to New England; or fish to Spain, rum to Africa, slaves to the Indies, and, again, island cargo home.

In all probability the administration of the mercantilist system on the mainland was not effective, especially during the long era of "salutary neglect" before 1763. The colonials benefited from bounties and from a virtual monopoly for the sale of such goods as tobacco, sugar, and tar in England, not to mention the advantages of protection by the British navy. Commerce and smuggling both seemed to thrive, and among the most influential men in the Colonies were the general merchants who conducted nearly all the functions of finance and distribution and were at once wholesalers, retailers, exporters, importers, bankers, insurance agents, and shipowners.

On the other hand, restrictions, even largely unenforced, were galling to the Colonies. Much more serious, however, was the growing imbalance within the Empire. The Northern service colonies—New England and the Middle Colonies—handling the shipping and distribution and producing the foodstuffs, grew faster than the Southern producers of staples, so that the North was forced to trade increasingly with the colonies of Spain and France. Any enforcement of the mercantile regulations which would restrict this outside commercial activity would, and did, create economic tension which contributed directly to the coming of the Revolution.

II

A NEW NATION

IN PART, mercantilism and a long series of Anglo-French wars set the stage for the American Revolution, but this drama was played against a background of a much broader nature. No single cause or even set of causes can explain the Revolution. Many of its roots went back throughout the entire colonial experience. "The Revolution was in the minds and hearts of the people," John Adams insisted in 1818. The colonial civilization was gradually growing apart from that of the mother country; poor communications, a breakdown of understanding, the impact of the frontier experience, an increasing racial heterogeneity—all pulled the Colonies in their own direction. A long era of "salutary neglect" on Britain's part permitted lax enforcement of the law and the development of a political structure with strong and effective local powers. The complexities of the Revolutionary situation preclude full treatment of all factors—social, political, and economic—here, but in dealing with those of an economic nature, we must recognize them as part of a more intricate whole.

So long as the rules governing British mercantilism were not rigorously applied, they had little effect. Despite regulations, colonials did whatever was profitable for them. Yet underneath was the gnawing realization in the Colonies that colonial interests were always secondary to those of England, that navigation laws boosted prices and freight rates adversely, and that the drain of specie worked to colonial disadvantage.

Then came change: beginning in 1763 Britain sought to tighten up the mercantilist system, to strengthen it and to weld the bonds of the Empire more closely. After a long series of global wars, England in 1763 had emerged triumphant over her traditional rival, France. Experience in the last of these conflicts, the French and Indian War, convinced British leaders of the need to unify the colonial structure and to force colonial financial support for their own defense. Save for Massachusetts, colonial contributions to the war effort had not been impressive. Indeed, William Pitt estimated that the war had been prolonged at least three years by American smugglers, who constantly frustrated the work of the Royal Navy. At the same time, Britain imposed restrictions upon settlement of the vast territory she had acquired between the Appalachians and the Mississippi River—territory taken from France. These restrictions remained until a workable policy for extinguishing Indian title and for an orderly advance could be evolved. This was the background for the tightening of British policy toward the Colonies between 1763 and the Revolution.

When the Royal Proclamation of October 7, 1763, forbade for the time being colonial grants or settlement beyond the crest of the Appalachians, it was part of an honest effort to solve the Indian problem rather than to usurp colonial prerogatives. The outbreak the previous May of the bloody uprising under Pontiac had hastened this action, but coming as it did at a time when American speculators were feverishly engaged in efforts to obtain large grants of land in the Ohio and Mississippi valleys, the Proclamation did not set well in the Colonies.

Neither did the new imperial policy of maintaining a standing army of ten thousand men in the Colonies at a cost of some £360,000 a year, especially since the French menace had been eliminated and since the colonials themselves were expected to pay the expense. English leaders and their already severely taxed constituents agreed that a heavier burden of colonial protection should be taken care of by colonial taxes. For effectiveness, these new tax measures would contain enforcement mechanisms and no longer would Royal officials wink at violations.

The Sugar Act of 1764, for example, was pushed through Parliament by the British sugar planters from the West Indies who could not compete with producers from other islands. While actually cutting duties on foreign molasses in half, it taxed important trade items such as sugar, coffee, indigo, and wines, and was no doubt an expression of subordination of the mainland colonial interests to those of the sugar planters. What rankled mainland colonials most was that machinery for enforcement was included: collection was to be done by British naval officers and smuggling cases were to be tried in Admiralty, rather than local, courts. Even a drastically reduced tax on molasses—if enforced —would drive out the cheaper, non-British product and upset trade, the Americans feared.

The year 1765 brought the famous Stamp Act, which levied a tax on newspapers, legal documents, pamphlets, diplomas, commercial paper, and like items, with the proceeds to be used in "defending, protecting, and securing" the Colonies. The immediate reaction was as vigorous as it was adverse: colonial spokesmen condemned the stamp tax as internal, sometimes with the thundering eloquence of Patrick Henry before the Virginia House of Burgesses; protests were forthcoming from the Stamp Act Congress in New York and from the Sons of Liberty at the local level, who demonstrated and intimidated stamp agents. American merchants joined together in pledging nonimportation of goods, and soon pressure from British merchants helped bring a repeal of the Stamp Act (1766) and a revision of the taxes of the Sugar Act downward, although Parliament still specifically retained the right to make all laws it saw fit for the Colonies.

Shortly thereafter, the illness of William Pitt, who had headed a coalition cabinet, threw leadership to Chancellor of the Exchequer Charles Townshend, a brilliant, if somewhat erratic, statesman noted for his sparkling addresses and his experiments in scientific agriculture. Townshend was responsible for the series of tax laws bearing his name and enacted in 1767 which put duties on numerous articles used in everyday living—glass, lead, paint, tea, and other items. At the same time the customs service was reorganized to expedite the handling of violations and to authorize the issuance of writs of assistance—general warrants for the search of private homes. Moreover, the law specified that the tax money so raised would be used to pay the expenses of civil government, thus eliminating one measure of colonial control over Crown-appointed officials. In a number of colonies, the assembly had long voted the governor's salary and had often used this power of the purse strings to influence or even to coerce. One North Carolina chief executive is supposed to have been eleven years in arrears in pay because of his unwillingness to please the legislature.

Like the Stamp Act, the Townshend Acts were met with protest, nonconsumption and nonimportation in the Colonies. They produced almost no revenue: in one year they netted £295, while military costs ran £170,000. After three years, the acts were repealed, except for the duty on tea, which was retained as a matter of principle. During the controversies over the Townshend Acts, the colonials had raised the cry of "no taxation without representation." But when colonials questioned whether Parliament could "take money out of our pockets without our consent," they were ignoring the fact that they had been taxed from the beginning without a direct voice. What they really meant was "no taxation by anyone at any time," or at least no tax laws which were to be enforced.

With the repeal of the Townshend Acts, trade was resumed and business revived, although full prosperity failed to return. The quartering of troops in Boston in 1768 had brought first complaint, then friction and the so-called Boston Massacre in 1770. When the British government in effect granted the wavering East India Company a monopoly to sell tea in America tax-free, colonial merchants, fearing that other monopolies might be chartered bypassing them as middlemen, reacted vigorously with the Boston Tea Party of 1773, thus posing a direct challenge to British authority. In response, Britain closed the port of Boston until the destroyed tea had been paid for, drastically limited Massachusetts local government, and took officers charged with capital offenses out of the hands of colonial courts. At the same time, provision was made for the further quartering of troops, and the civilian governor of Massachusetts, Thomas Hutchinson, was replaced with General Thomas Gage, who also commanded all

British troops in North America. Unconnected with these actions was the Quebec Act (1774), which attached to Quebec the region lying between the Ohio River and the Great Lakes, thus applying French law and recognizing the Catholic Church, much to the distress of New England Puritans and of colonies with land claims in the Ohio country. Inspired by these so-called Intolerable Acts, the First Continental Congress met in Philadelphia in September, 1774. Its members adopted strong nonimportation and nonconsumption agreements, with a system of enforcement committees, and British imports fell from £2.6 million to £196,000 within a year.

With the air crackling with tension, with such agitators as Samuel Adams, Patrick Henry, and Thomas Jefferson at work, with a lack of understanding on both sides, Massachusetts was declared in a state of rebellion in March, 1775, and trade forbidden, an interdict which soon extended to most other colonies. Then came the first actual conflict at Lexington and Concord; Ticonderoga and Crown Point were taken by Ethan Allen and the Green Mountain Boys "in the name of the Great Jehovah and the Continental Congress," and in June, 1775, came the first formal engagement, the Battle of Bunker Hill. The Colonies were moving toward an open break—a break which would come fully a year later.

The war which followed lasted formally until 1783. It pitted thirteen disunited, ofttimes dispirited colonies against the strongest naval power on earth, a naval power which, fortunately for the Americans, was engaged in warfare with other European nations during much of the period, a naval power operating in many parts of the world and at great distance from her nerve and supply center. That the Americans won out was not only a result of the international situation, but also a tribute to the tenacity and the raw courage of a people waging a desperate battle under the most adverse of conditions.

Of course, any war is a disrupting influence, and American economic life was modified in numerous ways by the Revolution and its outcome. Agriculture was damaged by depredations by both armies, especially in the Middle Colonies and in the South, where slaves were confiscated. But farm prices were high and many a farmer waxed fat trading with both sides. George Washington was enraged when Pennsylvania and New Jersey farmers sold supplies to the enemy while patriot armies froze and ran short of food at Valley Forge. Blockade runners sped Southern cotton to Europe and indeed to England, although the last phases of the war damaged Southern agriculture. Certainly one effect of the war and the shutting off of imports was the stimulation of the growth of both cotton and wool for domestic uses.

Since the publication of J. Franklin Jameson's *The American Revolution Considered as a Social Movement* in 1926, much emphasis has been placed on transformation of the land system as a result of the war's outcome. Royal restrictions on settlement beyond the Appalachians naturally came to an end and feudal quitrents due the Crown and proprietary families were wiped out. According to Jameson, another by-product was a deathblow to the twin institutions of entail and primogeniture, which had worked to keep large estates intact. Beginning during the Revolution, Thomas Jefferson led the fight which resulted within the next fifteen years in the abolition of these practices in almost every state. Most important, in the eyes of Jameson, was a leveling process in land distribution due to the breakup of large estates by confiscation. Many such estates, held by Tory sympathizers, were seized by state action and broken into small farm holdings, with the British Parliament ultimately paying owners some $15 million.

On the other hand, more recent studies, while recognizing that the war undoubtedly did have its leveling tendencies, show that in many areas the prominent Tory aristocrats remained or returned after the war and prospered. Further, Robert Brown's research on Massachusetts indicates that most adult males there held the franchise and held land prior to 1776. If Jefferson thought primogeniture and entail highly important, recent investigations show that most estates in Virginia were not entailed and that primogeniture was mandatory only if the property owner died without making a will. Studies of land confiscation have not been made for all states, but those completed, especially for New York, show that some such land was broken up and passed into the hands of small holders but that the bulk of it was acquired by wealthy patriot families like the Roosevelts, the Schuylers, and the Livingstons. In Virginia, Maryland, South Carolina, and New Hampshire, at least, laws for distribution favored those who already had wealth.

In some ways the war stimulated industry and domestic commerce. Nonimportation prior to the outbreak of hostilities and the British blockade during the conflict served to protect infant industry. The new states sought to stimulate industry artificially through bounties: Connecticut early offered bounties on guns and on gunlocks, Rhode Island offered £60 a ton on steel manufactured within its limits, and Maine granted £450 for the establishment of a steel plant. Industries such as shipbuilding were no doubt hurt by the war, but in general manufacturing was quickened and a remarkable spirit of profiteering prevailed both in town and out. Flour speculators in 1779 were "as thick and industrious as bees, and as active and wicked as the devil himself," according to one observer. "Most people are engaged in getting and some in spending money as fast as they can," a friend wrote Samuel Adams during the previous year.

Once mercantile regulations were removed, American vessels had access to other parts of the world if they could penetrate the barrier thrown up by the British navy. With normal avenues of sea commerce often disrupted, ships and crews turned en masse to privateering, which despite the capture of 570 American vessels by the British between 1776 and 1779, proved so lucrative that it was widespread: some two thousand commissions were issued and, in all, an estimated ninety thousand men were engaged in it. Thus capital and skilled manpower were retained in the maritime industry and a nucleus was provided for a merchant marine that would seriously challenge British ocean commerce in the late eighteenth and early nineteenth centuries.

Privateering made sense at sea and it brought in goods for colonial markets, but it did little to help finance the war itself. In regard to financing, the American colonies were at a decided disadvantage. Leaders of the Revolution had based part of their arguments on tax grievances; hence raising funds by taxation was not without embarrassment. Besides, taxation presupposed prosperity and adequate specie in circulation. Specie was scarce and at least some sectors of the economy were suffering—the loss of the fisheries to the north and of West Indian markets to the south was felt adversely by New England, despite the possibilities of privateering. For a new nation—a poor one and a disunited one, at that—a lack of credit made borrowing difficult. The nation was not even recognized until 1778, after which France and Spain did give some aid. Some $8 million was borrowed abroad, mainly from France, while $67 million was borrowed at home, but the actual gold worth of the latter was only about one sixth of that figure. Congress could merely requisition support from the states and could not enforce these requests, so that the $6 million received from state loans and taxes was but a fraction of the total solicited. In the face of such difficulties, therefore, it is not surprising that the bulk of the war cost was met by the issue of paper money. Between 1775 and late 1779 Congress authorized forty-two such issues totaling $191.5 million; by 1783, eleven states had authorized even more—$246.4 million—all unbacked by specie of any kind. The result was rapid depreciation of this paper money, with the worth of the continental dollar falling to as low as 2.34 cents. Housewives paid as much as ninety dollars in paper currency for a pound of tea, and the expression "not worth a Continental" was coined to describe the situation. Yet this depreciation served its purpose: of the entire cost of the war—an estimated $104 million in gold—roughly one half was paid off by the Revolutionary War generation through depreciation of their paper money, with no individual bearing much of the loss.

With the Revolution came new forms of government, both on the state and national level. These changes at the state level usually moved in the direction of separation of church and state; many abolished the traffic in "black ivory" or even abolished slavery itself. As might be expected, new state constitutions gave strong powers to the legislature rather than to the executive and the judiciary. In addition, many retained property qualifications for voting and officeholding. At the same time, the national government, in a reaction to the colonial experience, clipped the powers of the central authority and did not even provide for an executive and a judicial branch at the national level.

The framework of government, the Articles of Confederation, was originally proposed in 1776, accepted in modified form late the following year, but not finally ratified by all the states until 1781, since Maryland withheld her assent until the other states had agreed to deed their lands west of the Appalachians to the national government. Under the Articles a loose confederation was created—"a firm league of friendship"—which reserved to the individual states the bulk of power: Congress might wage war or make peace, receive or send ambassadors, sign treaties, regulate coinage and weights and measures, establish post offices, handle Indian affairs, borrow money, raise an army or navy, and settle disputes between states. But state powers sometimes overlapped, and the national government was hamstrung through lack of an executive branch, lack of control over commerce and taxation, and lack of means of enforcement.

During the war years, this "government by supplication" hardly received a quarter of its requests for state aid; in 1782 and 1783, Congress received only 15 per cent of what it asked. Only by giving broad powers to financier Robert Morris, as superintendent of finance, did the government, by borrowing from abroad and from the newly created Bank of North America, manage to survive. It was with such a relatively weak framework of government, therefore, with limited powers at the national level, that the new nation got off to a shaky start once the Treaty of Paris settled the conflict with Great Britain in 1783.

Since the publication of John Fiske's popular account *The Critical Period of American History* in 1888, historians until recent years have emphasized the darker aspects of the immediate post-Revolutionary era, stressing the weaknesses of the Articles and the economic difficulties which seemed to stem from them. This point of view was not seriously challenged until mid-twentieth century, when Merrill Jensen and others reappraised the period; they have done much to re-evaluate it and to focus on its accomplishments, rather than its disappointments.

Undeniably the Articles were weak and there were economic dislocations. Immediately after the treaty British trading vessels swarmed in, glutting the market with manufactured goods. This, together with overextended credit and the usual scarcity of specie, precipitated a commercial depression, especially in the Northern seaport towns. Some of the war-born industry failed to survive, but much did and small-scale manufacturing continued widespread, as indicated in an address by Tench Coxe in 1787 in which he told Philadelphians that Americans were breaking away from dependence on British suppliers:

> How great—how happy is the change! The list of articles we now make ourselves, if particularly enumerated, would fatigue the ear, and waste your valuable time. Permit me, however, to mention them under their general heads: meal of all kinds, ships and boats, malt liquors, distilled spirits, potash, gun-powder, cordage, loaf-sugar, pasteboard, cards and paper of every kind, books in various languages, snuff, tobacco, starch, cannon, muskets, anchors, nails, and very many other articles of iron, bricks, tiles, potters ware, millstones, and other stone work, cabinet work, trunks and windsor chairs, carriages and harness of all kinds, corn-fans, ploughs and many other implements of husbandry, saddlery and whips, shoes and boots, leather of various kinds, hosiery, hats and gloves, wearing apparel, coarse linens and woolens, and some cotton goods, linseed and fish oil, wares of gold, silver, tin, pewter, lead, brass and copper, clocks and watches, wool and cotton cards, printing types, glass and stoneware, candles, soap, and several other valuable articles, with which the memory cannot furnish us at once.

Money was drawn off by an adverse balance of trade. The wartime paper issues of the central government were virtually worthless by 1783 and most states stopped their printing presses momentarily. However, heavy pressure in certain areas prompted seven states by 1786 to issue large amounts of paper, which depreciated rapidly. As hard times struck, debtors pressed for stay laws to postpone payment of debts or tender acts which would make lands or goods legal tender at fixed prices. In Rhode Island, where paper supporters were in control, the legislature made it mandatory for a creditor to accept paper at par value in payment of debt, although the courts refused to sustain such a law. In Massachusetts, debtors united under a veteran of Bunker Hill, Captain Daniel Shays, to prevent further judgment for debt, only to be crushed and dispersed by the militia.

The American merchant marine now found itself outside the pale of mercantilism and shut out of the British West Indies and the sugar trade. The loss of these markets no doubt hurt, but there were other outlets. Smuggling was not new to Americans and British regulations left loopholes "for emergencie," so some trade continued with the British Caribbean islands. The French West Indies were open, though the Spanish empire, except Cuba, was not; indeed the Spaniards even momentarily choked off the Mississippi River. Large merchantmen found an alternative in the lucrative China trade, and soon commercial treaties had been signed with France, Holland, Sweden, and Prussia, to the benefit of smaller shippers. Much trade with Britain continued, and the Dutch re-exported American tobacco for all of Europe. Statistics for the period are open to question, but there seems ample evidence that commerce recovered steadily after the Revolution; by 1787, Franklin, Washington, and others were optimistic about the state of the economy.

Agricultural output was increasing; tobacco export was up and its average price for the decade after the Revolution was higher than the price during the decade prior to the Revolution. Indigo would thrive momentarily, but withering competition from the British East Indies ruined the market in the 1790's. Grain production was up, with 1.1 million bushels exported in 1790, nearly four times as much as in 1771. Still, problems of transportation, debt, a lack of hard money, and inadequate marketing facilities worked to the detriment of the small farmer, especially in New England.

In their attempts to stimulate commerce and manufacturing at home and to retaliate against the British, individual states set up navigation laws of their own and enacted protective tariffs. Earlier historians made much of these regulations, emphasizing them as examples of interstate barriers to trade. They were not uniform, but in general, though not always, there was reciprocity between states. Confusion and discrimination existed but so also did mutual accord and co-operation. But did it necessarily follow that the inherent weaknesses of the Articles of Confederation were responsible for the economic ills of the period? Certainly a stronger central government would have been an advantage in dealing with foreign questions—in helping open the West Indies, forcing Britain to retreat from her chain of fur posts on American soil, pressuring Spain to open the mouth of the Mississippi, and combatting the demands of North African pirates for tribute. But might not economic troubles have been responsible for a poor working of government?

Propertied interests, commercial men, creditors, and speculators—an influential minority—believed at an early date in a stronger framework of government. Out of earlier meetings to discuss matters of commerce, notably at Annapolis in 1786, came the convention at the red brick statehouse in Philadelphia in 1787 "for the sole and express purpose of revising" the Articles of Confederation. The fifty-five delegates, selected by state legislatures, may not have been "an assembly of demigods," as Thomas Jefferson called them, but among them were some of the giants of the period—the august Washington, brilliant young Alexander Hamilton, slight, scholarly James Madison, and urbane octogenarian Benjamin Franklin. Missing were the radicals of the earlier era—Jefferson, Patrick Henry, Samuel Adams, John Hancock, and Thomas Paine. Some of the delegates had served in the Revolution, thirty were college graduates, two were future presidents, two future chief justices, six state governors. All were men of some substance—merchants, lawyers, shipowners, financiers, landowners, and speculators.

In his *Economic Interpretation of the Constitution of the United States,* written in 1913, Charles A. Beard made much of the identification of these delegates with the propertied, creditor class, with the implication that the Founding Fathers acted in drawing up the Constitution to protect their own economic interests. Recent historians, among them Robert E. Brown and Forrest McDonald, have questioned Beard's research techniques and his general thesis. Brown points out that a broader basis existed in selecting delegates than Beard implies; McDonald insists that the men assembled at Philadelphia represented much more than their own immediate interests, that lawyers, for example, represented various interests of clients and that landowners in essence represented agriculture in general. However that may be, one point is clear: these delegates believed that a stronger national government would be in the public good.

The constitution they wrote has been called a "bundle of compromises," but the compromises were mainly in matters of detail, not on the basic premise of a more powerful central government. Congress was given the power to lay and collect taxes, a competence which enabled the government to operate and to discharge the national debt—a far cry from the mere power to requisition accorded under the Articles. Congress was authorized to raise and support naval and military forces, which could be used to quell internal disorder and to guarantee each state a republican form of government, as well as to protect commerce or even pry open markets whether in the Sea of Japan or the Caribbean. Congress was given control over foreign and interstate commerce in broad general terms that subsequent interpretation would greatly enhance. The power to dispose of territories and make rules and regulations for them had implications for speculators in western lands interested in a rapid establishment of government and would be of grave significance in the slavery controversy that developed later.

Congress was granted the power to coin money and regulate its value, while the states were limited in certain functions, including coinage, the enactment of ex post facto laws or laws impairing the obligation of contracts. In addition, written into the Constitution were sanctions—enforcement mechanisms—that the Articles had lacked. A chief executive was provided, whose duty it was to enforce the laws of Congress. The so-called supremacy clause of Article VI clearly gave the federal law precedence over state:

> The Constitution, and the Laws of the United States which shall be made in Pursuance thereof; and all Treaties made, or which shall be made, under the Authority of the United States, shall be the supreme Law of the Land, and the Judges of every State shall be bound thereby, any Thing in the Constitution or laws of any State to the Contrary notwithstanding.

In addition, the "elastic" clause which accompanied the eighteen specifically delegated powers of Congress gave that body the right "to make all Laws which shall be necessary and proper for carrying into execution the foregoing Powers, and all other Powers vested by this Constitution in the Government of the United States or in any Department or officer thereof." This flexible article would in the future be used to justify everything from the first Bank of the United States to the Taft-Hartley Act and civil rights legislation. Thus, in one form or another, sanctions were included, and could only serve to strengthen the already broad powers accorded by the Constitution to the national government.

Ratification did not come easily, for a determined opposition fought the creation of a strong central government. These anti-Federalists stood for states' rights and drew considerable support from farmers, artisans, and debtors, although no clear-cut class, occupational, or even geographic lines divided those for or against the new constitution. Washington gave his support; Hamilton, Madison, and John Jay presented their arguments in favor in the *Federalist Papers,* a classic of political philosophy, and after a hard battle, with both sides resorting to questionable tactics, ratification was accomplished and a persistent minority triumphed.

As the new state was launched in 1789, Congress met in its first session in New York, a pleasant city of some 33,000 persons and 131 licensed taverns. Among its first acts were those levying a tariff and those creating executive departments, including a Department of the Treasury. The tariff, passed on July 4, averaged about 8 per cent, which was low, and was primarily for revenue, but at least recognized the principle of protection. To head the Department of the Treasury, President Washington first named financier Robert Morris, who declined the post, at which point thirty-four-year-old Alexander Hamilton was chosen.

Brilliant and captivating, Hamilton had served his apprenticeship in a counting house in the West Indies, had been educated in New York, and had served as Washington's private secretary during the Revolution. Essentially aristocratic in outlook, he believed in an ideal government controlled by "gentlemen." He had accepted the Constitution as "better than nothing," but was not satisfied by this "frail and worthless fabric." Yet he fought for its ratification and would try by his own means to strengthen it and make it workable by "increasing the number of ligaments between the government and interests of individuals," as he phrased it. His "individuals" were businessmen, merchants, large landholders, and others of substance, whom he would endeavor to bind to the national government.

At its first session, Congress requested Hamilton to prepare a master financial plan; subsequently he brought forth reports on public credit, the mint, excise taxes, a national bank, and manufactures—all part of his proposed course of action. Only on manufactures did Congress take no direct action.

Hamilton's report on public credit was read before Congress early in 1790 and suggested funding the entire national debt. All outstanding securities were to be redeemed at their full value and a new series issued in their place. The total involved was some $77.1 million and included $11.7 million of foreign debt owed mainly to Spain, Holland, and France; $40.4 million in domestic debt; and approximately $25 million of debts accumulated by the states in fighting the Revolution, which Hamilton believed should be incorporated into the national debt. By funding the whole, he believed popular support would be consolidated behind the new central government; by assuming state obligations, he hoped that creditors would look to the national, rather than the state, governments. He expected the issue of new securities to help relieve the shortage of currency for large-scale transactions.

The report was received in Congress with mixed emotions. Even before it had been read, word of its contents had leaked out, and public figures—even congressmen and friends of Hamilton—were busy buying up national securities at market rates, which was forty or fifty cents on the dollar, confident that they would soon be redeemed at full value. Even before the speculators went to work, a greater part of the securities had passed from their original owners into the hands of more prosperous individuals for a mere fraction, often 10 or 15 per cent, of their par worth. Opponents of the funding bill questioned the fairness of enriching already wealthy speculators at the expense of original holders. James Madison threw his influence against Hamilton, proposing a compromise funding plan that would split the payments between the original purchaser and the subsequent buyer. But in the end, the Hamiltonian funding program was adopted, and later it became known that twenty-nine of the sixty-four members of the House stood to profit personally by it.

The matter of assuming the $25 million in state debts caused even more controversy. Before the news of the proposed plan could penetrate into the back country, speculators were busy rounding up state securities. Many of them were Northerners and it was argued that they would accumulate all the Southern debt certificates in the North and that one section would be paying taxes to benefit a favored class of another. Moreover, state debts were unequal; some states had already liquidated most of their war debts. Why should they be taxed to help pay the obligations of less scrupulous states? "A number of drones are brought into society and the industrious bee is forced to furnish them with all the honey of its search," complained one Southerner. Patrick Henry of Virginia stood firm against assumption and saw "the subserviency of Southern to Northern interests written in capitals on its very front." When, after much debate, the assumption bill was beaten in the House by two votes, the speculators and "Hamilton's gladiators," as gruff Senator Maclay of Pennsylvania called the supporters of the measure, were deeply shocked. But Hamilton was not finished. Conferring with Thomas Jefferson of Virginia, he worked out an acceptable compromise: he—Hamilton—would support the establishment of the national capital on the Potomac, while Virginia would swing her weight behind the assumption bill. On this basis, assumption passed, and the state debts were added to the national obligations, to be funded along with the rest.

Funding of the debt called for additional revenue. Hamilton believed that a national debt was a national blessing, a bond of union, as was the public domain. But in order to maintain credit, the government must make some provision for retiring its debt. In addition, Hamilton was anxious to establish the right of the federal government to collect internal revenue. Already the tariff law was on the books; now Hamilton proposed an excise tax on spirituous liquors, a proposal which precipitated heated debate but which passed, much to the disgust of Senator Maclay, who thought "war and bloodshed—the most likely consequence."

Maclay was prophetic—and he knew the backwoodsmen of his home state. Before long, in 1794, they rose up in protest to the new tax. In central and western Pennsylvania, as in other frontier regions, specie was short and transportation poor. An easy means of transporting grain to market was to convert it into whiskey, which became a common medium of exchange. To tax such a commodity hit hard at the frontiersman, who had few luxuries and who enjoyed little protection from the national government, so when the Pennsylvania "Whiskey Rebels" rose up in complaint and manhandled a few tax collectors, their action was at least understandable. What they had not foreseen was that Washington, at Hamilton's urging, would send out a sizable army to quell the uprising and to serve notice that the national government intended to enforce its tax laws.

Hamilton's over-all program called for a national bank, patterned in part after the Bank of England, with the federal government acting as a substantial shareholder in an otherwise private institution. Such a bank, contended Hamilton, would provide a safe depository for federal funds, and its branches would facilitate the transfer of funds from one place to another; it would facilitate the sale of national bonds and issue a paper money that would remain stable throughout the land; it would create credit and help expand industrial and commercial enterprise; and—but the Secretary of the Treasury did not emphasize this—it would help concentrate more power into the hands of wealthy men and tie them more closely to the federal government.

As with Hamilton's other proposals, the bank bill provoked opposition. Some viewed it as a monopolistic combination of government and vested interests; states' rights advocates feared the growing power of central government and any elaborate fiscal and tax structure; many, including both Jefferson and Madison, believed that the Constitution did not contemplate a national bank and could not justify it. Using the "strict construction," they contended that unless the Constitution specifically empowered Congress to act, it could not. On the other hand, Hamilton argued on behalf of the bank, contending that the implied powers of the Constitution in effect gave Congress the right to do what was necessary and proper to carry out the powers specifically delegated to it. Since those powers included the regulation of commerce and the coinage of money and regulation of its value, the Bank, as a means of accomplishing these ends, was fully justified, insisted Hamilton, using the Federalist "broad" or "loose" interpretation. Hamilton prevailed and in 1791 the first Bank of the United States was chartered to run for twenty years.

Hamilton's accomplishments were impressive and he must be considered one of the great Secretaries of the Treasury. In splendid rhetoric Daniel Webster paid tribute to his genius in 1831: "He smote the rock of the national resources, and abundant streams of revenue gushed forth. He touched the dead corpse of Public Credit, and it sprang upon its feet." Certainly Hamilton's ideas of public finance put the nation's fiscal structure on a more orderly, efficient basis and strengthened credit at home and abroad. If the national debt was not paid, the young nation was given a breathing spell—time to get on her feet, so to speak— before major financial or foreign dislocations arose. An incidental by-product, the creation of a righteous opposition, no doubt contributed to the growth of a two-party system, a development not at all contemplated by the Founding Fathers.

Furthermore, Hamilton's policies did benefit a particular group and concentrated money power in Northern urban hands. Philip Freneau, "Poet of the Revolution" and vitriolic Jeffersonian, castigated Hamilton figuratively in this regard:

> And, Sir, 'tis true
> ('Twixt me and you)
> That some have grown prodigious fat,
> And some prodigious lean.

Hamilton did not benefit personally, though some around him, including his Assistant Secretary of the Treasury, took advantage of inside information to speculate wildly. Ironically, at one point, in order to protect his reputation for public honesty, Hamilton was forced to sacrifice his reputation for private morality by confessing a personal scandal involving his relations with a married woman and her blackmailing but not-too-irate husband.

Perhaps the most flattering commentary on the Hamiltonian measures were their continuance by subsequent administrations, who were practical enough politicians to recognize how ingrained the program quickly became. Observed Jefferson later, "We can pay off his debt in fifteen years, but we can never get rid of his financial system." And except for repealing the excise tax and gradually reducing the debt, the Jeffersonians did not modify the structure.

Ratification of the Constitution in 1789 officially joined the thirteen states into a nation, and Hamilton's financial program helped to cement the union. But the new nation would be truly welded together only as it developed a single economy, encouraged by the guidelines set down by the Founding Fathers. With tariff barriers forbidden between the states and with the central government in control of foreign commerce, the way was being opened for a thriving commercial growth over new trade routes as well as old.

III

NEW PATTERNS OF TRADE AND COMMERCE

THE IMMEDIATE post-Revolutionary period was one of readjustment and abnormality for American shipping and foreign trade. The new nation had to get used to the idea of being outside the protection of British mercantilism and she had to live through an exciting and profitable role as the leading neutral carrier in a series of Anglo-French Wars, into which she was ultimately drawn, before entering into a period of normality in 1815. The period 1815 to the Civil War was one of expanding overseas trade, with shipping reaching its peak in the 1850's, but with trade itself continuing to grow, increasing some 1,600 per cent between 1790 and 1860.

During the postwar readjustment after 1783, old markets— especially the British West Indies—were momentarily closed to American shippers, who sought alternatives elsewhere. Large vessels found the trade with the Orient lucrative when it began to open in the mid-1780's, but small shipowners could ill afford to tie up their limited capital for so long. Soon France, Denmark, Holland, and even Spain opened their Caribbean ports to American vessels, although not until 1830 did Britain reopen Jamaica, Barbados, and other of her West Indian islands. American trade soon gravitated back to British ports, with England and the United States destined to be each other's best customers during most of the nineteenth century. The French were less able to attract American trade, due to differences in language, systems of weights and measures, and less generous credit terms. Moreover, industry was further advanced in Britain and goods were cheaper.

Then in 1793 came war between England and France. The United States, as a neutral carrier, enjoyed a prosperous maritime boom until 1807, except for the temporary lull during the Peace of Amiens (1801), when earnings from the re-export and carrying trade fell off. Neutral vessels risked illegal seizure and British condemnation of American-owned goods more than once threatened to drag the United States into the conflict, while French confiscations in 1796 led to an undeclared sea war until 1800. But high ocean freight rates, price increases, and a rapid development of the re-export trade made profits worth the hazards. Some vessels plied the trade to British ports, even hauling sugar to England; others carried sugar from the West Indies to France, using the "broken-voyage" technique of technical re-export from American ports. With profits adequate to pay for a ship in a year or two, shipbuilding in America boomed, tonnage doubling, then tripling over the prewar level.

In 1807 came evidence that the belligerents were going to bring the American neutral role to an end. Napoleon's infamous Continental System and Britain's Orders in Council made trade all but impossible and ship seizures and impressment of American sailors were so great that President Jefferson's response was the Embargo (December, 1807), which closed off all foreign trade and consequently brought economic distress. Prices fell, unemployment grew, debtors' prisons overflowed, and bankruptcy, suicide, and crime rates all went up. In Federalist New England, which was particularly hard hit, there was much grumbling over Jefferson's "Damn-bargo":

> Our Ships all in motion,
> Once whiten'd the ocean;
> They sail'd and return'd with a Cargo;
> Now doomed to decay
> They are fallen a prey
> To Jefferson, worms, and EMBARGO.

So great was the adverse reaction to the Embargo that Congress was forced to repeal it in favor of the Non-Intercourse Act of March, 1809, which reopened trade with all nations except the two most important, England and France. This gave way to the ingenious Macon's Bill No. 2 a year or so later, which opened commerce with France and Britain but provided that if either repealed her obnoxious decrees against American shipping, the United States would close off trade with the other. France made a pretense, and nonintercourse was applied against Britain in the spring of 1811 at the expense of increased Anglo-American tension.

When the United States was drawn into the war in 1812, a tight British blockade sharply curtailed mercantile activity, though ironically permitted American ships to provision Wellington's army in Spain for some time. Fortunately, the war was brief and the year 1815 ushered in an era of peace for both the United States and Europe. Immediately the British dumped accumulated manufactured goods upon the American market, to the distress of local industries which could not yet compete. These American industries cried out for a higher protective tariff, which was duly passed in 1816. At the same time, the United States adopted a more affirmative navigation policy. Congress closed the coastal trade to foreign vessels, levied a heavy tonnage duty on foreign ships coming from ports closed to Americans, and sought agreements with other nations for a mutual removal of all discriminatory levies. In 1828, such an agreement was reached with Britain and two years later trade was reopened with the British West Indies on a legal basis. American commerce was then characterized by increasing trade with England, the rise of a significant commerce with Germany and France, the development of cotton as the major export, and the emergence of Cuba as the outstanding Caribbean market.

Tea from China and pepper from the "Salem East Indies" were part of a glamorous, exciting story, but in terms of volume and value the East did not compare with English, or even Cuban, trade. In 1821, 64 per cent of American imports came from Britain; by 1861, 61 per cent. South America in 1860 accounted for but 10 per cent, Asia for 8 per cent, and Canada for 6 per cent. The chief imports were manufactured items ready for consumption; even as late as 1855–59, nearly half (47.4 per cent) fell in this category, although the percentage of manufactured imports would gradually decline. Yorkshire woolens usually headed American import lists, but the growing cotton textile trade in Lancashire gained rapidly. Hardware from Birmingham, cutlery from Sheffield, and later iron rails indicated the superiority of British industrial techniques. After about 1840, trade with France, which had not gone well earlier, became more important for its silk, wines, and other luxury goods. From the old Hanseatic ports of Bremen and Hamburg came a steady flow of goods also, but French and German goods combined did not equal half the British total. Cuba generally ranked third behind England and France, her main export commodity being sugar. But increasingly the coffee imported from Brazil assumed significant proportions. Imports of foodstuffs came from all corners of the world, of course, some direct and some by way of re-export from such intermediaries as Holland.

Except for cotton, exports down to 1860 differed only slightly from those in colonial commerce. Europe took two thirds of our exports in 1820 and three fourths of the total by 1860. Products of the sea, of the forest and of agriculture, and small manufactured items dominated at the beginning of the period, but by 1860 more variety and more manufactured goods had begun to figure in American outgoing trade. American whalers provided oil for the lamps of China, as well as Europe and the Caribbean; by 1841 Boston ice was being shipped to every large port in South America and East Asia. Exports of flour tripled between 1821 and 1860, with Brazil, Canada, and the British Isles the leading customers, for Britain, by repeal of her Corn Laws in 1846 and her Navigation Laws in 1849, had thrown her markets wide open to all comers.

But after about 1820, due to the new demands for raw cotton in England and the growth of the American market for textiles, cotton overshadowed all other exports by a wide margin. By value, cotton in 1820 was worth over 3.5 times as much as the next most important export, tobacco; in 1830, it was worth nearly five times as much as wheat and flour, the runner-up; in 1840, six

VALUE OF GENERAL IMPORTS, BY COUNTRY OF ORIGIN, 1821–60
(in Millions of Dollars)*

Year	Total Value	Canada	Cuba	Mexico	Brazil	United Kingdom	France	Germany	China	Other
1821	55	—	5	—	1	24	4	1	3	17
1825	90	—	7	1	2	37	11	3	8	21
1830	63	—	5	1	2	24	8	2	4	17
1835	137	1	11	1	6	60	22	4	6	26
1840	98	1	9	1	5	33	16	3	7	23
1845	113	1	6	1	6	45	21	3	7	23
1850	174	5	10	1	9	75	27	9	7	31
1855	258	15	18	1	15	106	32	13	11	47
1860	354	24	32	2	21	138	43	19	14	61

* *Historical Statistics of the United States, Colonial Times to 1957, p. 553.*

VALUE OF EXPORTS, INCLUDING RE-EXPORTS OF U.S. MERCHANDISE, BY COUNTRY OF DESTINATION, 1821–60
(in Millions of Dollars)*

Year	Total Value	Canada	Cuba	Mexico	Brazil	United Kingdom	France	Germany	China	Other
1821	55	2	4	—	1	19	6	2	4	17
1825	91	3	5	6	2	37	10	3	6	19
1830	72	3	5	5	2	26	11	2	1	17
1835	115	3	5	9	2	52	19	4	2	19
1840	124	6	6	3	2	55	20	4	1	27
1845	106	6	6	1	3	45	12	6	2	25
1850	144	10	5	2	3	71	18	5	2	28
1855	219	28	8	3	4	92	29	9	2	44
1860	334	23	12	5	6	169	39	15	9	56

* *Historical Statistics of the United States, Colonial Times to 1957, p. 551.*

VALUE OF MERCHANDISE EXPORTS, BY ECONOMIC CLASSES, 1820–60
(in Millions of Dollars)*

Year	Total	Crude materials	Crude food-stuffs	Manu-factured foodstuffs	Semi-manu-factures	Finished manu-factures
1820	52	31	2	10	5	3
1830	59	37	3	10	4	5
1840	112	76	5	16	5	11
1850	135	84	8	20	6	17
1860	316	217	12	39	13	36

VALUE OF MERCHANDISE IMPORTS, BY ECONOMIC CLASSES, 1821–60
(in Millions of Dollars)†

Year	Total	Crude materials	Crude food-stuffs	Manu-factured foodstuffs	Semi-manu-factures	Finished manu-factures
1821	55	3	6	11	4	31
1830	63	5	7	10	5	36
1840	98	12	15	15	11	44
1850	174	13	18	21	26	95
1860	354	40	46	60	35	172

Historical Statistics of the United States, Colonial Times to 1957, p. 545.
† *Ibid.*

times as much as the same commodities, still the leading export contenders; in 1850, over seven times as much as the challenger (again tobacco), and in 1860 almost ten times as much. By 1860 Britain was buying three fourths (about a billion pounds annually) of the cotton produced from the United States and was taking three times as much as the American textile industry, leaving the Southern cotton producer dependent upon the foreign market. Cotton helped redress an unfavorable balance of trade, for in only five of the years between 1790 and 1860 was the value of exports as high as the value of imports, leaving a sizable deficit to be offset by various means. American control of the carrying of much of American foreign trade contributed to lowering this deficit, though the percentage carried in American vessels gradually declined from 92 in the abnormal year 1807 to 66 by 1866. Re-exports, especially in the period before 1815, brought in considerable wealth, so also did the sale of American ships abroad. Foreign loans, with American merchants borrowing from British banks or more importantly by the sale of American securities abroad, a moderate tourist trade, and the export of specie, particularly gold after 1849, all helped redress the balance.

Control of the shipping of cotton over the so-called cotton triangle also did much to stimulate the rise of New York over her rivals, Boston, Philadelphia, and Baltimore. New York, centrally located and served by the Gulf Stream with a deep, excellent, protected harbor, had the additional advantages of the Hudson, which was navigable 150 miles inland, and of the Erie Canal to tap the interior; as a result it outstripped its rivals quickly. Fine packet ships hauled the pick of European manufactured goods to her docks, and returned cotton to Europe, extracting commissions and profits that sometimes ran as high as 30 to 40 per cent of the value of the cargo.

UNITED STATES COTTON EXPORTS, 1795–1860*

Year	Quantity (in millions of pounds)	Value (in millions of dollars)
1795	6	—
1800	18	—
1805	38	9
1810	93	15
1815	83	18
1820	128	22
1825	176	37
1830	298	30
1835	387	65
1840	744	64
1845	873	52
1850	635	72
1855	1,008	88
1860	1,768	192

* *Historical Statistics of the United States, Colonial Times to 1957*, p. 547.

Northern ports in general were more interested in imports; Southern ports in exports. As the Cotton Kingdom pushed westward, New Orleans became the center for cotton shipping and by 1834 had surpassed New York in handling exports. Mobile also developed rapidly and displaced Charleston and Savannah to become the South's second leading port.

The American import trade, and to considerable extent the export trade, was largely financed by British credit. American importers usually bought from British exporters on twelve to fifteen months credit and sold to middlemen who in turn sold to retail storekeepers, who normally settled with their customers once a year, usually after the harvest. American cotton for export passed through the hands of several intermediaries, including factors, Northern buyers, British commission houses and brokers, with British banks providing the ultimate credit base for the transaction.

American shipping was given extra stimulus in the 1840's: first when the British Parliament, in response to industrial pressure, repealed the Corn Laws, throwing Britain open to grain from the United States, and then when the potato famine prompted a mass exodus from Ireland, mainly in Yankee square-riggers. Immigration from the Emerald Isle jumped from 52,000 in 1847 to 163,000 in 1851. Shortly thereafter, thousands of Germans flocked into the United States as a result of political and economic unrest on the Continent; 69,000 came in 1851, 176,000 three years later. In the same period, discovery of gold in California and in Australia, the opening of the Chinese trade, the Crimean War, and the Sepoy Mutiny all opened new possibilities for passengers, freight, mail, or bullion to be hauled in a hurry.

Despite the inherent romance of foreign commerce, domestic trade throughout the period was more important, whether the goods originated abroad or in the United States. When the eighteenth century closed, foreign trade was about one third of domestic in value; by 1850 it was roughly one seventh. Further, the Industrial Revolution had brought the consumption of far more American than imported merchandise.

In the early nineteenth century, such merchant capitalists as John Jacob Astor and Robert Bennet Forbes tended to dominate the economy and played a variety of roles in the distribution process. They were importers and exporters, wholesalers and retailers, commission agents, frequently bankers, and sometimes—through the putting-out system—even manufacturers. With time, and especially in response to the greatly increased volume of trade on the Atlantic shuttle between New York, Liverpool, and the cotton ports, specialization began to prevail and these functions were often separated, to be handled by individual specialists. Wholesale importers generally developed on the eastern seaboard before specialized exporters. Sales were often divorced from manufacturing by merchant capitalists: wholesalers were at first important in New York and as early as the Era of Good Feeling were handling, in addition to imports, domestic textiles, shoes, or groceries. At the same time, retail and wholesale functions were beginning to separate and by the mid-nineteenth century the line was clearly drawn. Of increasing importance were various middlemen—commission agents or jobbers who purchased from wholesalers, then resold in smaller lots to retailers, often helping the latter finance. By mid-century produce exchanges had been established in commercial cities to facilitate the wholesaling of flour, cotton, tobacco, coffee, and other commodities.

Throughout the first forty years of the nineteenth century, the auction was an important means of handling wholesale goods, and the auctions of New York City predominated on the eastern seacoast. The New York auctions went back to the period after the War of 1812, when British shippers had used that means to dump their manufactures on American markets. Low overhead and quick sale meant cheaper goods; moreover, in 1817 New York stipulated that goods put up for auction could not be withdrawn, no matter how low the bidding. As New York became the great center, this 1817 law presumably helped keep prices low; in fact, buyers flocking in tended to bid prices up. About 44 per cent of all imports into New York were handled by auction sales between 1821 and 1830, but the system, even then, was beginning to decline, primarily because merchants disliked the fluctuation in prices that was invariably a part of it.

The forms of retailing on the domestic scene changed from simple to increasingly complex. The public market, a form used from time immemorial, was the most unsophisticated, and at the end of the Revolution prevailed in nearly every village and town. Farmers brought their produce once or twice a week, and wives and servants came to buy. But as towns expanded, distance became a factor and producers found it simpler to sell to middlemen —wholesalers—who in turn sold to stores or butchershops within walking distance of the consumer. Public markets had declined gradually in importance by 1860, but many continued well into the twentieth century.

The greater part of the nation was rural and was remarkably self-sufficient until transportation broke down its isolation. People consumed their own products, swapped with their neighbors, and traded on a limited basis with itinerant peddlers or at the general stores which popped up wherever a few families settled. Because of the scarcity of specie in rural areas, the barter of goods was the only way extensive trade could be conducted. A traveler in Ohio decided to sell his horse in 1806. "I was offered in exchange for him," he related, "salt, flour, hogs, land, cast-iron salt pans, Indian corn, whiskey—in short, everything but what I wanted, which was money." The traveler took the highest offer, $130 worth of cast-iron salt pans, which he traded for some glass bottles. These he exchanged for tobacco in Kentucky, and this he finally sold in New Orleans for cash.

In backwoods country, the peddler was an important part of early American life. He went anywhere, roads or not, unabashed by man or wilderness. "He was never taken by surprise," wrote an early contemporary: "accidents never came unexpected, and strange events never disconcerted him. He would whistle 'Yankee Doodle' while his horses were floundering in a quagmire and sing 'Hail Columbia' while plunging into an unknown river!" With his wooden nutmegs and basswood hams, the Yankee peddler became a stereotype, as proverbial for his wit as for his sharp trading. Sometimes he operated strictly on his own; sometimes he was financed by New England capitalists or manufacturers who supplied his stock of goods and sent him out in the spring. Sometimes he specialized in a single commodity, such as clocks or pots and pans. But often he carried a marvelous variety of Yankee notions on foot, on horseback, or by wagon: cloth, pots and pans, knives, razors, jewelry, needles, pins, thread, dolls, and jew's-harps. Of necessity, he took farm goods in exchange when cash was not available. This meant that he had to carry such produce until he could rebarter it; moreover, he was limited by the necessity of keeping within distance of his supplies, though as time passed he often established depots at strategic spots.

But the peddler was not dependable: he did not always bring the desired goods at the proper time. His low overhead made him resented by local businessmen and he was heavily taxed in towns. Yet many prospered and, like James Fisk, laid the foundation of a mercantile or financial enterprise in this way. Even as late as 1860 there were still more than sixteen thousand of them in the country, but rapidly improving transportation was hastening their end.

There were also floating emporiums that plied their trade on the inland waterways west of the Alleghenies, their tin horns announcing their arrival at various points along the way. Zadok Cramer, in *The Navigator* (1814), describes how an aspiring merchant might procure a

> small square ark-boat, which he loads at the head waters, with various wares, liquors, fruits, dry-goods and small groceries, and starts his bark for the river traffic, stopping at every town and village to accommodate the inhabitants with the best of his cargo.
>
> This voyage performed, which generally occupies three months, and the ark sold for half its first cost, the trader returns doubly invigorated, and enabled to enlarge his vessel and cargo, he sets out again.

Often these floating stores returned such good profits that their owners could soon establish themselves as a general merchant in a small town. Those who had not settled down were put out of business by the growth of the railroads.

Throughout the period, undoubtedly the most important retail distributor was the general store, although in urban centers a trend toward specialization was gradually taking place. In rural regions, the general store was not merely a source of supply, it was at once an economic keystone and a highly important social center. Unlike the itinerant peddler, it was there when needed, it could more readily dispose of farm goods taken in barter, and it could carry heavy goods ranging from plows, saddles, and log chains to kegs of nails and bar iron. Operations were usually small, the average business per year running $10,000 or $15,000, but because of the varied needs of customers, the general store was compelled to keep a remarkably diverse stock of goods. Thomas Ashe described a typical general store in western Pennsylvania in 1806:

> These storekeepers are obliged to keep every article which it is possible that the farmer and manufacturer may want. Each of their shops exhibits a complete medley: a magazine where are to be had both a needle and an anchor, a tin pot and a large copper boiler, a child's whistle and a pianoforte, a ring-dial and a clock, a skein of thread and trimmings of lace, a check frock and a muslin gown, a frieze coat and a superfine cloth, a glass of whiskey and a barrel of brandy, a gill of vinegar and a hogshead of Madeira wine, &c.

Many general storekeepers personally bought fresh goods at the auctions in Philadelphia or New York once or twice a year, using long-term credit. Certain commodities—coffee, tea, iron, powder, and lead—were usually considered "cash articles," but much retailing was done on a barter basis and the goods thus received by the retailer sent either in payment to the wholesaler or to be sold by a commission agent. Such practices, except in isolated country areas, had largely disappeared by 1860. General store prices were high because the merchant gave credit, often at some risk, and because barter was fraught with uncertainty. A 50 per cent markup was fair; 75 or 80 per cent was not uncommon. Usually, however, there was no price competition in the local area, and prices might vary with the financial circumstance and bargaining ability of each customer. Thus coffee in a store in Missouri in 1818 sold to two different customers on the same day at 50 cents and $1.12 a half pound. A. T. Stewart, department store pioneer and the original proprietor of John Wanamaker's New York store, attempted to establish a one-price system on the eve of the Civil War, but the idea caught on very slowly.

As urban centers grew, specialized stores tended to replace general ones. In large cities specialization was evident by 1800 in groceries, hardware, and dry goods, but not until the 1830's was there a haberdashery in New York City and not until after 1850 were there furniture, jewelry, or shoe stores, even in the largest cities. Specialty shops developed for several reasons: the owner could be better informed about his specialty, he could carry a much greater variety, and he could buy more cheaply by dealing in larger lots. Indeed, in time, some of the larger specialized retailers cut costs even more by large-scale buying direct from the manufacturer. In the case of dry goods, specialty developed because ladies did not wish to shop in general stores where men were doing their drinking. In the cities, a few sizable retail outlets were beginning by the Civil War to move in the opposite direction, to expand gradually into department stores, though the major trend in that direction would not come until the 1870's and 1880's.

Advertising was limited usually to handbills and classifieds in local newspapers and generally did not mention prices nor praise goods. There were few brand names and almost no national advertising, except for the patent medicines. By mid-century, advertising was becoming more aggressive and more versatile, as that of Oak Hall, Boston clothiers, indicated:

> You may go to the West, you may go to the East,
> And the North and the South, till your eyes have a feast:
> But whatever you witness, you'll say from your heart,
> That Simmons' Oak Hall is the Principal Mart.

The pre-Sumter era also saw the beginnings of that American institution, the traveling salesman. Some of the collectors sent out by wholesalers to collect from storekeepers when bills fell behind occasionally made efforts to sell merchandise along the way; some of the peddlers carried samples and took orders. Others began as agents sent by wholesalers to meet retailers coming into New York to buy, and these persistent "borers" or "drummers," as they were called, soon extended their operation into the retailer's store.

In time wholesalers found it desirable to know something of storeowners' business standing—especially after the crash of 1837. In 1841 a New York merchant, Lewis Tappan, founded an agency to amass and provide such credit information to subscribers of his service. By 1851 his agency had branches in seven cities and had compiled huge ledgers on businessmen in all parts of the country. Eight years later, the firm became R. G. Dun & Company and in 1933 was combined with the Bradstreet Company, which had been founded about 1849 by a Cincinnati lawyer.

Thus by mid-century the structure and pattern of both domestic and foreign trade was changing. Distribution was becoming more intricate, more sophisticated, reflecting in its gradual maturing the fundamental forces at work in other sectors of the economy.

IV

THE WESTWARD MOVEMENT

GROWING COMMERCIAL ACTIVITY, particularly the demand for cotton to satisfy British textile operators, provided one of the prime stimuli for westward expansion. Other specialized staple crops also pushed westward and found ready markets, at first in the cotton-producing South, later in rising urban centers on the Atlantic Coast. Furs, precious metals, religious impulses had lured men across the little-known Far West by 1860, but the major incentive was based primarily on agriculture.

On the eve of Revolution, settlement had pushed into the valleys of the Appalachians and stood poised at the crest of the mountains, ready to sweep into the great basin drained by the Mississippi and its tributaries. Moving first through Cumberland Gap into Kentucky and Tennessee, then a little later along a variety of routes converging at Pittsburgh, the edge of the frontier moved across the mountains into the Old Northwest, ignoring hardship and danger, encroaching on Indian lands, and ebbing and flowing with the tide of circumstance. Settlers came on foot, on horseback, and later by wagon; or they floated down the Ohio by the thousands in crude, clumsy flatboats, rafts, and keelboats. Under such population pressure, the federal government, by treaty and by intimidation, broke the resistance of the Indians and took from them millions of acres of land. Soon a new project was conceived,

65

that of removing the tribes to a "permanent" home beyond the Mississippi, where they might live unmolested "as long as the sun shines and the waters run."

The reduction of the Indian menace, the advertising connected with the purchase of Louisiana, the Lewis and Clark Expedition, the travels of Pike to the Rockies, boundary disputes with Spain and England, and the War of 1812 all encouraged migration. By the end of the war, the great National Road was under construction and the first steamboats were beginning to appear on Western waters. Land bonuses to veterans put cheaper land on the market. Cotton pushed into the new South, the first commercial crop to move westward on a large scale. This growing emphasis on a specialized crop created additional demands in the South for corn, hogs, and other products to be grown in the Northwest. The overall result was the "Great Migration," which began with the end of the War of 1812 and reached its peak in 1818–19. Federal land sales topped a million acres for the first time in 1814 and climbed to a high of nearly 3.5 million in 1818. "Old America seems to be breaking up, and moving westward," wrote Morris Birkbeck, an Englishman who traveled the National Road in 1817. "We are seldom out of sight, as we travel on this grand track toward the Ohio, of family groups behind and before us." Sweeping across southern Ohio, Indiana, and Illinois, the Great Migration moved both northward and southward, following the Mississippi as well as lesser rivers. In the South, the "Alabama fever" filled in much of the rich cotton belt, while in the North a string of settlements cropped up along Lake Erie as far west as Detroit. By 1820, Ohio, the most populous state beyond the mountains, had nearly 600,000 people, and the entire transmontane region contained some 2.5 million, nearly a quarter of the country's total population.

If the flood of settlers ebbed after the panic of 1819, it began to rise again in the late 1820's and early 1830's, with land sales increasing to over 20 million acres in 1836. Growing at a rate almost twice as great as the rest of the nation, the trans-Appalachian region by 1840 had 6.4 million people. Here, according to her exuberant residents, was the land of opportunity, the land of

PUBLIC LAND SALES, 1800–60
(in Thousands of Dollars)*

Year	Acres	Year	Acres	Year	Acres	Year	Acres
1800	67.8	1815	1,306.4	1830	1,929.7	1845	1,843.5
1801	497.9	1816	1,742.5	1831	2,777.9	1846	2,263.7
1802	271.1	1817	1,886.2	1832	2,462.3	1847	2,521.3
1803	174.2	1818	3,491.0	1833	3,856.2	1848	1,887.6
1804	398.2	1819	2,968.4	1834	4,658.2	1849	1,329.9
1805	582.0	1820	814.0	1835	12,564.5	1850	1,405.8
1806	506.0	1821	782.5	1836	20,074.9	1851	2,055.9
1807	320.9	1822	710.0	1837	5,601.1	1852	894.8
1808	209.2	1823	652.1	1838	3,414.9	1853	3,787.1
1809	275.0	1824	737.0	1839	4,976.4	1854	12,823.0
1810	285.8	1825	999.0	1840	2,236.9	1855	11,959.8
1811	575.1	1826	848.1	1841	1,164.8	1856	5,247.0
1812	386.1	1827	926.7	1842	1,129.2	1857	4,220.1
1813	505.6	1828	965.6	1843	1,605.3	1858	3,663.6
1814	1,176.1	1829	1,244.9	1844	1,754.8	1859	4,011.7
						1860	2,543.4

* Historical Statistics of the United States, Colonial Times to 1957, p. 239.

homes, happiness, and security for all, without the drawbacks of the static, unprogressive East.

> And there's your Massachusetts,
>   Once good enough, be sure;
> But now she's always laying on
>   Taxation or manure;
> She costs you pecks of trouble,
>   But de'il a peck can pay;
> While all is scripture measure
>   In *Michigania*.

Since the publication of Frederick Jackson Turner's paper "The Significance of the Frontier in American History" in 1893, the impact and the characteristics of the westward movement have been of vital interest to American scholars. The European heritage, said Turner, accounted for only the similarities between European and American society; to understand the differences, we must look at the distinctive environment of the United States. "The existence of an area of free land, its continuous recession, and the advance of American settlement westward, explain American development," he wrote. There were successive frontiers, insisted Turner, limited by more or less natural boundaries: the Fall Line, the Appalachians, the Mississippi River, the Big Bend of the Missouri, and the Great Plains and Rockies. Differences existed as well, contended Turner, but each frontier displayed the same general pattern of settlement:

> Stand at Cumberland Gap and watch the process of civilization, marching single file—the buffalo following the trail to the salt springs, the Indian, the fur trader and hunter, the cattle-raiser, the pioneer farmer—and a frontier has passed by. Stand at South Pass in the Rockies a century later and see the same procession with wider intervals between.

Each frontier required modification of complex political, social, and economic ways to more simple forms as men battled to overcome their environment. The struggle won, complexity returned, but the net result was a new product—a new society, with new institutions and outlooks, molded by a peculiar environment. An American emerged with distinctive traits: he was more individualistic, self-reliant, and materialistic; more impatient, optimistic, and antipathetic to control; more nationalistic, democratic, and egalitarian. Turner also mentioned the frontier as a "safety valve" for discontent, but he neither emphasized nor explained this concept.

Turner's critics have been numerous and outspoken. They have objected to the omission from Turner's scheme of town builders, land speculators, and Spanish pioneers in the Southwest and have pointed out that he ignored important currents such as the European Enlightenment, Romanticism, or even the Industrial Revolution. These critics have disagreed with the contention that democracy sprang from the forest rather than from the *Mayflower,* noting the essentially undemocratic features of Indian tribal organization, the Mormon theocracy, and the slave system, and insisting that reform movements have all had their roots in Europe or in the East. They have been especially critical of the "safety valve" concept, or at least of the concept as they interpret it.

Perhaps the truth lies somewhere between the two extremes. Surely the conquering of three thousand miles of wilderness over a period of nearly three centuries must have left an indelible stamp on the American character. Yet the frontier was not the only force at work, and if a "new American" emerged, his traits were a blending of many influences, of which the westward movement was one important one.

People were drawn west for many reasons, but land hunger and high agricultural prices were among the most potent forces. Often the man in the vanguard, however, was a farmer only in an incidental way. Ignorant, sometimes disorderly, he continually tramped on the heels of the Indian and squatted on land without title. According to J. M. Peck's *A New Guide for Emigrants to the West* (1836),

It is quite immaterial whether he ever becomes the owner of the soil. He is the occupant for the time being, pays no rent, and feels as independent as the "lord of the manor." With a horse, cow, and one or two breeders of swine, he strikes into the woods with his family, and becomes the founder of a new county, or perhaps state. He builds his cabin, gathers around him a few other families of similar taste and habits, and occupies till the range is somewhat subdued, and hunting a little precarious, or, which is more frequently the case, till neighbors crowd around, roads, bridges, and fields annoy him, and he lacks elbow-room.

While the frontiersman moved on to repeat the process elsewhere, a new wave of settlers moving in held different values.

The next class of emigrants purchase the lands, add "field to field," clear out the roads, throw rough bridges over the streams, put up hewn log houses, with glass windows, and brick or stone chimneys, occasionally plant orchards, build mills, school houses, court houses, &c., and exhibit the picture and forms of plain, frugal, civilized life.

Then, says Peck, while a few of the first two classes remained and improved their lot, another wave rolled on, at least in Northern areas.

The men of capital and enterprise come. The "settler" is ready to sell out, and take advantage of the rise of property—push farther into the interior, and become himself, a man of capital and enterprise in time. The small village rises to a spacious town or city— substantial edifices of brick, extensive fields, orchards, gardens— colleges and churches are seen.

In the South, the pattern might proceed through the first or even the second stage, but close behind the settler who cleared a few acres came the larger planter, buying up farms, consolidating them, and replacing white labor with slave. Too often the third phase in the South, very different from the prosperous agriculture and budding industry and commerce of the North, was one of decline fostered by soil exhaustion, the product of repeated planting of cotton year after year. Soil depletion and a constant shifting westward in search of new land brought changes in the progress of the Cotton Kingdom.

In addition to the handling of the original occupiers, the Indians, each frontier experienced other common problems, especially those attending the distribution of land and those involving the political relationship of newly settled regions to the remainder of the United States. From cessions made by states to the national government between 1780 and 1802 came the creation of a public domain and the necessity to evolve some kind of land policy, for settlers were already pouring into the region north of the Ohio. By its Land Ordinance of 1785, Congress set down the fundamental outline of its future public land system, adopting a somewhat unwieldy compromise between making cheap land available for settlement and building up revenues through land sales. Requiring the extinguishing of Indian title and surveys prior to occupation, the law of 1785 prescribed a rectangular survey system based on townships six miles square, subdivided into thirty-six sections, an arrangement which with slight modification is still used. Setting aside portions of land for veterans, for school maintenance, and for the national government, the act provided that half the remainder be sold at auction in sections (640 acres) and half in townships (23,040 acres) at a minimum price of one dollar an acre.

Such units were too large, the price was too high, and the survey too slow. Little revenue was returned, but in 1787, a conservative Congress, beset by aggressive lobbyists, granted speculative companies a total of some 6.5 million acres in Ohio at prices which amounted to about eight cents an acre. Gradually over the next few decades the land laws were liberalized, with the minimum price and size of the unit shrinking until by 1820 eighty acres could be purchased outright for $100 cash. However, the elimination of credit provisions in that year hurt land sales, as did the depression of 1819, and not until 1829 did sales again reach a million acres.

By a general pre-emption law of 1841, legal protection was given to the right of the squatter to purchase his improved land at a minimum government price, thus obviating the need for the "claims clubs" or "honor associations" which were sometimes designed to protect squatters against outsiders when their lands came up for sale and which were also used as devices by land speculators to control the purchase of improved farms. Other modifications put into practice briefly, but which proved unworkable, were distribution of proceeds from land sales among the states and graduation—the progressive reduction in the price of land remaining unsold on the market.

After about 1820 the movement for free public land for bona fide settlers began to gain momentum under the leadership of men like Thomas Hart Benton of Missouri, Sam Houston of Texas, Stephen Douglas of Illinois, and Horace Greeley, editor of the influential New York *Tribune*. Land ownership was a natural and an uplifting right, they argued, from which liberty and democracy spontaneously flowed. To sell land as "mere merchandise, like molasses or mackerel," was both sinful and unhumanitarian, insisted Horace Greeley. Did not the Bible say, "The land shall not be sold forever; for the land is mine; for ye are strangers and sojourners with me"?

Opposition was voiced by the South and to a lesser extent by the Northeast on the grounds that free land would accelerate Western settlement, draw off population and depress land values in older areas, produce competitive farm crops, and raise the cost of labor and manufacturing. Moreover, Congress would be packed with radical Western representatives and the balance between North and South upset. Free land might also people the West with the overflow of European prisons and poorhouses, said Southern critics, and reduce treasury receipts, thus leading to demands for a higher tariff—anathema to the South. Although numerous homestead bills were introduced, they fared poorly, except for several limited to specific regions, for example, East Florida and Oregon, until their espousal by the Republican Party and the withdrawal of Southern congressmen during the Civil War. Only then, in 1862, was the public domain thrown open to all bona fide settlers, and the idea abandoned that land should be a federal income producer.

Almost as early as the first land law, Congress had also enacted fundamental legislation to provide future governments in Western regions, thereby encouraging settlement. Written in part as a result of a group of land speculators desiring government protection for property rights for a huge grant they were about to acquire beyond the Ohio, the Northwest Ordinance of 1787 included among its provisions the stipulation that the region north of the Ohio and east of the Mississippi was ultimately to be divided into three or five states, depending upon the need. Three stages of government were outlined, each giving a greater degree of participation in government than the last. At first the territory was to be administered by a governor, secretary, and three judges appointed by

Congress; when five thousand free males resided in the territory, it was allowed an elected legislature and a nonvoting delegate in the national House of Representatives; when population reached sixty thousand, it might be admitted to statehood on a basis of equality with the original thirteen. It was this principle of transitional government culminating with the casting off of "colonial" status in favor of full standing in the Union that made the Northwest Ordinance so important. Reapplied again and again, with modification of details, the idea became the basis for American expansion to the Pacific and even beyond. Since most settlers welcomed established government, law and order, and the protection of property rights, the Ordinance did much to encourage the westward movement.

By 1860 settlers had surged across the Mississippi River, peopling much of the first tier of states just west of the river and spilling over into Kansas and Nebraska. Far beyond lay pockets of population in the Far West or on the Pacific Coast. Already the story of the fur trade had been written: reckless, hardy trappers and traders had penetrated the streams and the mountains, risking their lives in search of beaver, and in the process becoming the true explorers and pathfinders of the trans-Mississippi West. Already the final chapter, the dominance of Astor's great American Fur Company, was nearly finished. Efficient and ruthless, the company had absorbed and squeezed out the opposition, but by 1840 the fur trade had been reduced to a mere trickle and an era was gone.

In the Southwest, the curtain had been drawn on another episode, the colorful Santa Fe trade, which commenced in the early 1820's and endured until the Mexican War. Across those wastelands came specie at a time when cash was scarce in the United States and the word that the Mexican hold on the Southwest was weak. Americans had already filtered into Texas in the twenties and thirties, attracted by generous land grants but never forgetting the land of their birth. Revolt, independence, and a period of republican existence preceded annexation to the United States in 1845, a move which set the stage for war with Mexico.

Meanwhile, the call "On to Oregon" had drawn thousands to the Pacific Northwest, then under joint occupation by England and the United States. Rich free land, the fur trade, a spirit of nationality, the pull of Christianity and the publicity of missionaries, and the work of the great popularizers like Hall Kelley and Nathaniel Wyeth were all attracting forces, and by 1846, when the Oregon boundary was settled, five thousand Americans resided there, their numbers increasing every year.

On the deserts of Utah the Mormons had founded a new Zion long before 1860. Harassed and harried in Ohio, Missouri, and Illinois over a decade and a half, they had followed Brigham Young in an orderly migration to the banks of the Great Salt Lake in 1847, there to build a new religious commonwealth where they could live and worship as they pleased. Industrious, practical, and inventive, the Mormons prospered and their communal experiment remained distinctive for its degree of success, although the practice of polygamy long brought Utah into disrepute with the federal government.

By 1860, too, a strong influx of population had swarmed into California. The discovery of gold in 1848, just a week before California changed hands as part of the Mexican War cession, touched off an excitement almost unparalleled in modern history. In 1849 approximately 25,000 gold seekers reached California by sea, either by way of Panama or around the Horn, while another 55,000 trekked overland, headed for picturesque camps like Humbug Creek or Shirt Tail Canyon, there to become part of a remarkably cosmopolitan conglomeration drawn from all quarters of the world. A few struck it rich, but most drifted into farming, business, or other occupations, while hundreds wandered on, pan in hand, seeking another elusive Eldorado in Nevada, Colorado, Idaho, or Montana.

By 1860, the army had already experimented with the use of camels for transportation in the Southwest; already there had been serious talk of a railroad to the Pacific and the survey of five possible routes had been completed. Beginning in April, 1860, the colorful Pony Express began carrying the mail between St. Joseph, Missouri, and Sacramento, and less than eighteen months later was superseded by a transcontinental telegraph line, flung across the largely uninhabited Great Plains, the Rockies, and beyond.

V

THE AGRICULTURAL REVOLUTION

THE UNITED STATES was still an agricultural nation in 1860. Urbanization was proceeding, but at a gradual pace. Twenty per cent of its people lived in towns of 2,500 or more, as opposed to about 5 per cent in 1790, and population density had increased from 4.5 to 10.6 people per square mile in the same period. Agriculture, like the rest of the economy, was in a state of transition. In the words of historian Louis B. Schmidt:

> Agriculture was transformed from a simple, pioneer, and largely self-sufficing occupation into a modern business organized on a scientific, capitalistic, and commercial basis; industry definitely underwent the change from hand labor in the home to machine production in the factory; and the local market was transformed into the world market. This threefold revolution in agriculture, industry, and commerce is the key to the study of the recent history of the United States.

Among the complexities of the agricultural revolution, three characteristics were outstanding: the vast extension of the farm domain into unsettled regions; the specialization and commercialization which developed; and the beginnings of scientific farming and the increasing application of labor-saving machinery.

Except for the fur trade and the mushrooming of mining camps, most of the westward expansion prior to the Civil War had an agri-

AREA AND POPULATION OF THE UNITED STATES, 1790–1860*

Year	Gross Area (Square Miles)	Rural Population	Urban Population	Total Population	Population per Square Mile
1790	888,811	3,727,559	201,655	3,929,214	4.5
1800	888,811	4,986,112	322,371	5,308,483	6.1
1810	1,716,003	6,714,422	525,459	7,239,881	4.3
1820	1,788,006	8,945,198	693,255	9,638,453	5.6
1830	1,788,006	11,738,773	1,127,247	12,866,020	7.4
1840	1,788,006	15,224,398	1,845,055	17,069,453	9.8
1850	2,992,747	19,648,160	3,543,716	23,191,876	7.9
1860	3,022,387	25,226,803	6,216,518	31,443,321	10.6

* Historical Statistics of the United States, Colonial Times to 1957, pp. 8, 14.

cultural base. The purchase of Louisiana in 1803 practically doubled the size of the country, and within the next fifty years the expansive force of Manifest Destiny and of commercial interests would again double the land area. By 1860, when agriculture had been extended into almost all of the vast Mississippi Basin from the Gulf of Mexico to the Great Lakes, improved farm land totaled 163.1 million acres, with about one and a half times as much unimproved land in reserve.

The flat, fertile prairie and lake plains north of the Ohio and the Missouri rivers became pre-eminently a region of corn, wheat, and livestock production and of early specialization and commercialization. The American farmer was traditionally a debtor: it took money to buy land, move, and sustain a family until the first crop was harvested. Only by raising what he needed and in addition something which could be sold for cash could the settler pay off his debts. But markets and transportation were essential before cash crops could replace mere self-sufficiency. In time, as these requirements were met, farmers in the Northwest made this transition to commercial agriculture and the production of staples—corn, wheat, or livestock—came to dominate the area. Ohio had reached this stage by 1830; Illinois, Indiana, Michigan, and parts of Wisconsin by 1850. And all the while, the center of production of these staples was shifting westward: in 1849 the leading wheat-growing states had been Pennsylvania, Ohio, and New York; a decade later they were Illinois, Indiana, and Wisconsin. By 1860 fully one half of the wheat in the United States was being produced by the five states carved out of the Northwest Territory.

Corn and hogs also became a major interest of farmers in a corn belt that extended from Ohio to Iowa and Missouri. Most early settlers maintained a few swine, usually of the lean, lanky "wind splitter" variety. In the towns they roamed up and down the streets as perambulating garbage receptacles and were rounded up only at slaughtering time. In the country they foraged precariously for themselves in the woods and were anything but attractive. But when fattened on corn, often by being turned into the fields to "hog it down," these "long and slim, long-legged and long snouted, slab-sided, large-boned, gaunt bodied, flat eared"

razorbacks became a marketable commodity. As hog raising became a more commercial enterprise, the animals were enclosed in
tight fences, regularly fed on grain and milk, and occasionally
their strain improved with imported breeding stock. By the fifties,
Ohio and Indiana had replaced Kentucky and Tennessee as the
leading producers. Much of the early pork went downriver to
Memphis, Natchez, and New Orleans, and early in the nineteenth
century overland drives to the East were not uncommon; as many
as five thousand pigs in a herd headed toward Philadelphia or
Baltimore at the rate of eight or ten miles a day. With the development of western packing centers, especially Cincinnati, Chicago,
and St. Louis, and with the extension of the railroads, such drives
passed into oblivion.

Cattle also followed the corn belt, and beef far outsold pork
on the Eastern seaboard and in New England. As was the case
with hogs, early critics frequently commented on the poor quality
and the neglect of beef animals, invariably likening them to the
lean kine of Pharaoh. Specialization in cotton made the South
dependent upon the upper Mississippi Valley for much of its beef
and pork; farmers in the East even prior to 1850 were turning
to dairy cattle, and thus the urban centers of the East also comprised an excellent market for beef from the prairies. Long before
the railroads penetrated, cattle were being driven from the Ohio
Valley eastward. Morris Birkbeck in 1817 noted a group of "fat
oxen" headed for Philadelphia for which the drover expected to
receive a premium of from $20 to $25 a head. Such cattle drives
were often difficult and the animals might lose from 150 to 250
pounds en route. Prior to the Civil War, a number of prairie
cattle kings had emerged in Indiana and Illinois, emphasizing the
feeder cattle business, fattening for the markets. Jacob Strawn,
of Illinois, for example, grossed $100,000 on cattle sales in 1854,
to justify his reputation as the "Napoleon of Cattle."

In the Northeast a greater degree of specialization and commercialization also came about. With such exceptions as the
Connecticut Valley, parts of Rhode Island, Pennsylvania, the
western counties of Massachusetts, and the Hudson and Mohawk
valleys of New York, colonial patterns of agriculture had lingered
in New England and the Middle Atlantic states until commercial

outlets began to appear beginning about the time of the War of 1812. To meet the needs of growing manufacturing towns, farmers began to specialize in market gardening, dairying, wool growing, or in production of hay for the horses in urban centers. At the same time, while this process of adaption was underway, the Northeastern farmer was forced by Western competition in staples to concentrate more and more on products which by their bulk or perishability could not be grown in the West for Eastern markets. Maine and Long Island came to specialize in potatoes; New York, Vermont, and southeastern Pennsylvania were all prominent in the production of milk, butter, and cheese; truck gardening expanded near all urban areas and orchards soon became important in the Mohawk Valley.

Of all sections, specialized agriculture came to the South first. Even before the Revolution, through the cultivation of rice, tobacco, and indigo, many Southern farmers had made the transition to commercial farming and had developed a more "advanced" civilization than their northern rural brethren. East Indian competition eliminated indigo as an exportable commodity and tobacco was hard pressed, due also to foreign competition and heavy duties—as high as 900 per cent in England at one time. But tobacco production survived, and, along with rice, sugar, hemp, and, of course, cotton, constituted one of the important cash crops of the South.

In the Upper South the chief staples were corn, wheat, tobacco, flax, and hemp, running in that order throughout the ante bellum period. In fact, corn was the chief staple of the entire South, in terms of acreage, amount, and value of the crop produced. In 1849 the South grew approximately 18 million acres of corn, 5 million of cotton, 400,000 acres each of sugar and tobacco, and 70,000 acres of rice. In 1855 the Southern corn crop was valued at $209 million, cotton at $136 million, tobacco at $17.5 million, sugar at $35.4 million, and rice at $10 million. Wheat grown in the South that year was equal to the combined value of the rice, tobacco, and sugar crops. Much of the corn was raised in the Upper South and shipped to the Deep South; much of the wheat was consumed locally and neither, though highly important, was closely identified with slavery and the intricate politics of the era.

Tobacco was long the problem crop. It gave a high rate of return, but thoroughly depleted the soil within three or four years, and so long as virgin land existed, the tobacco planter was unwilling to fertilize, diversify his crops, or rotate them at the expense of his cash crop. Prices fluctuated in keeping with the general level of business, unless crop failure or bumper harvest made for an abnormal year. Favorable prices prevailed from 1815 to 1819, 1833 to 1841, and 1849 to 1860, but high prices always brought increased production and the threat of oversupply. Efforts to limit cultivation and control markets were never successful and until the 1850's tobacco planters could prosper only by growing on virgin land. In the fifties a new mode of curing made possible the use of the bright yellow variety which grew best in parts of Virginia and North Carolina and which did much to revive production. Kentucky, Tennessee, and Maryland were also leading growers. Crop rotation came to be common as farming diversified in the fifties, so that by the end of that decade soil exhaustion was no longer a problem in Virginia. Tobacco in the nineteenth century went increasingly for domestic rather than foreign consumption, most of the crop going for plug tobacco for chewing, though parts of Virginia specialized in the manufacture of cigars and snuff.

Rice was grown mainly in Georgia and South Carolina, along the lower reaches of such rivers as the Savannah, the Altamaha, the Santee, and the Combahee. An exotic crop, it required considerable capital, much crude labor, and especially skillful management. Because of the large number of slaves needed, the high value of improved land, and the expense of threshing, grinding, and polishing machines, the total investment in a rice plantation might range from $50,000 to $500,000. Crop rotation was difficult on rice lands, which had to be flooded. Hurricanes, flood or tidal damage, and soil erosion were all perils, and the wet ricelands were unhealthy for valuable slaves. Competition from Oriental rice for the markets of Europe and the West Indies often kept prices to a moderate level, and in the 1850's the production of American rice declined noticeably, dropping from 215.3 million pounds in 1849 to 187.2 million pounds in 1859.

Sugar production centered along the lower Mississippi, the Lafourche, the Atchafalaya, and Bayou Teche in some two dozen parishes of southernmost Louisiana, having been introduced from Santa Domingo by early Frenchmen. Sugar, like rice, was not a poor man's crop. It made heavy capital demands for clearing and draining land, grinding cane, evaporating, crystallizing the sugar, and purifying the molasses. From $75,000 to $100,000 was needed to put into operation a 300-hogshead plantation which required from forty to fifty hands and highly technical skills at certain points of the refining process. The industry more than quadrupled between 1843 and 1853, concentrating more and more into the hands of a relative few, who were often absentee owners. Sugar prices varied, depending upon the weather, the size of the crop, the tariff rates, and the extent of competition from Cuba, and ranged from the 11.8 cents a pound received in 1820 to the 4 cents of 1840. Large planters sought to reduce operating costs by striving for self-sufficiency. Bishop Leonidas Polk, for example, on his great plantation on the Bayou Lafourche, attempted to raise food for his 370 slaves and numerous farm animals and even manufactured clothing and shoes for his workers, built wagons, and made implements.

"If sugar and rice were the aristocrats of Southern crops, tobacco and cotton were the commoners," says Paul Gates. As the eighteenth century ended, planters, impressed by Britain's rapidly expanding textile industry, saw the possibilities of cotton, but also realized the difficulties involved. A standard upland variety of cotton grew well over a wide region of the South, but its short fibers were difficult to separate from its fuzzy green seeds. A man could clean only a pound or two per day. The fibers of Sea Island cotton, another type, separated easily from its glossy black seeds, but the plant was so sensitive that it could only be grown in a limited region, mainly the islands off the coast of Georgia and South Carolina. Moreover, its average yield was low, its labor requirements high, but it brought premium prices, although less than 1 per cent of the total cotton crop was of this variety and it was unimportant in the Southern economy as a whole.

COTTON PRODUCTION, 1792–1859
(in Thousands of Bales)*

Year	Cotton Production
1792	6
1797	23
1802	115
1807	167
1812	157
1817	272
1822	439
1827	565
1832	816
1837	1,428
1842	2,035
1847	2,128
1852	3,130
1857	3,012
1859	4,508

* *Historical Statistics of the United States, Colonial Times to 1957,* p. 302.

If Sea Island cotton was not a solution, the gin invented in 1793 by a young Yale graduate, Eli Whitney, was. A simple device to comb seeds from the fiber, Whitney's cotton gin could clean a thousand or even two thousand pounds a day. The machine caught on quickly, as excited planters turned to the cultivation of upland cotton.

Cotton requires a growing season of at least two hundred days, which meant that its cultivation in normal years was limited to a large region (apart from the lowlands of the Tennessee River Valley) generally south of a line running along the northeast corner of North Carolina, across northern Georgia and Alabama, then northward to include western Tennessee. Most of the slave states, except Virginia and the border states, grew cotton on a large scale. But cotton, like tobacco, quickly depleted the soil and the need for new lands was constant, pulling the Cotton Kingdom steadily westward as production increased from 6,000 bales in 1792 to 4.5 million bales in 1859, when cotton made up half the value of all United States exports. When the depression of 1819 slowed down the movement into Alabama, over 200,000 people already lived on the Gulf Plains and nearly half the nation's cotton was produced there. The trickle of migrants of the 1820's reached flood proportions again in the prosperous thirties, when cotton producers sometimes reaped profits of as much as 35 per cent, though the market was soon glutted and prices fell to disastrous levels. Cotton grew too readily and too many came to depend upon it. When the price dropped to its nadir, about five cents a pound, as it did in 1842 and 1844, some planters sought to redeem their losses by planting more on better land, some adopted improved methods, and some attempted, usually with little success, to achieve self-sufficiency by reducing the purchase of foodstuffs and manufactures and producing more at home.

Along with new land, the Cotton Kingdom rested uneasily on a base of slave labor, for cultivation of the staple was well adapted to the "peculiar institution." Its culture was primitive and simple and extended over a large portion of the year. Little machinery and much labor was required, and the entire labor force—men, women, and children—could be employed under supervision. Plowing ordinarily commenced in February. Seed was sown by hand in March and covered by hoe; then came thinning and frequent cultivation. Picking started in late August and might be spread over four or five months, with each field being repicked several times. Dried in the sun or in gin houses, the cotton was then ginned to remove the seeds and pressed into 400-pound bales, ready for transporting.

The question of whether or not slavery was wasteful, inefficient, and increasingly unprofitable has long been controversial, but the viewpoint of such recent scholars as Kenneth Stampp is that slavery was generally profitable, though not always, and that, cotton planting not having reached its maximum development, the institution was not fated for an early extinction. With persuasive research and argument, Stampp repudiates the favorable view of the old plantation system popularized in another generation by U. B. Phillips, casting aside Phillips' overly sympathetic treatment of the slaveholder as well as his assumption of an innate Negro racial inferiority. If the South was saddled with a one-crop system, it was the greed of the planter, rather than slavery, that was responsible, insists Stampp. If the planter was "caught" in an endless vicious circle, buying more land and more slaves with which to produce more cotton, as is so commonly contended, so was the industrial capitalist of the same and later era who plowed back his surplus profits to improve his plant and expand his capital holdings.

In any event, given the tremendous expansion of cotton production and the lack of any real diversification of agriculture in much of the South, the enormous importance of the commodity is understandable. Understandable, too, is why the average Southerner echoing the sentiments of Senator Hammond of South Carolina in 1858 wholeheartedly believed that cotton made the South invulnerable, that world textile interests could not do without it. "No," said Hammond, "you do not dare to make war on cotton. No power on earth dares to make war upon it. Cotton *is* King."

Along with the extension of the farm domain and the accelerated shift to commercial farming, the Agricultural Revolution also brought the beginnings of the application of scientific techniques and mechanization. The way had been paved by European advocates of "high farming," but cheap land and an innate American conservatism retarded scientific farming in most parts of the United States. It was cheaper, Jefferson pointed out in 1793, to buy a new acre of land rather than to manure an old. Even at mid-century, an observer commenting on farming in Missouri described the process as a "regular skinning system," in which most farmers *"scratch* over a great deal of *ground* but cultivate none." Especially in the South where cash crops were not only important but were rapidly soil-depleting, it was difficult to convince a planter of tobacco or cotton of the desirability of fertilization or crop diversification and rotation when these techniques reduced the market crops and tied up slave labor. The more enlightened planters proved receptive, but the most common solution was to exchange the butchered lands of the Old South for the fresh, virgin soil of the New. Northern farmers often used methods that were no better, but few crops were as exhausting as the Southern staples. Even in the North, the more substantial farmers were the innovators. The average tiller welcomed laborsaving machinery, but tended to look askance at "book farming" and the application of newfangled science to the field.

Still, in many ways the nineteenth century, and especially the era from 1815 to 1860, was a period of continuous agricultural experimentation. Importation of pure-bred animals was not uncommon: the "Shorthorn fever" was at its peak in 1837–38, and by mid-century British buyers were beginning to buy Shorthorns at American auctions. Spanish and English sheep were popular in the 1840's; about the same time came a craze for rather exotic poultry from abroad—Leghorn, Cochin China, Brahma Pootra, and Chittagong hens were all the rage. Yet, in general, American poultry and livestock did not compare favorably with those in Britain, though there were many exceptions.

Much interest was evidenced in new seeds and species of plants, and seed salesmen, nursery firms, and even the federal government provided an interesting, though not always useful, variety of seeds, plants, and trees from foreign countries. The introduction of Mexican cotton early in the century has been called, next to the cotton gin, the most important development in fastening cotton cultivation upon the Deep South. Other new cotton seeds— Banana, Pomegranite, Sugar Loaf, or Accidental Poor-Land Cotton—commanded high prices from time to time, although some were outright frauds. The Chile potato was introduced in the 1850's and was found to be immune to many diseases. Perry's Black Squadron returned from Japan with a wide sampling of beans, rice, tea, soybeans, turnips, and other plants. The silkworm craze that burst upon the country in the 1830's was so severe that no fewer than seven journals devoted to sericulture were established between 1836 and 1839, before the bubble burst in the early 1840's.

A number of agencies were prominent in fostering interest in scientific farming methods or new products. By 1856 there were 912 local and state agricultural societies in the country, about 80 per cent of them in the North and West. These societies were successful in reviving the county fairs; they published statistics of crops and livestock, descriptions of new practices, and in general focused attention on scientific knowledge in agriculture. Many were followed by state boards of agriculture, and a national organization, the United States Agricultural Society, founded in 1852, existed for a time. Most such societies, however, as well as the fairs, tended to be dominated by large-scale or "gentlemen" farmers.

Beginning with Massachusetts in 1830, numerous states established bureaus or appointed experts to make detailed surveys of minerals and soils, and published volumes on soil analysis, the chemical composition of crops, or on injurious insects. States provided funds for research on remedies for plant and animal diseases: Massachusetts, for example, offered $10,000 in the early 1850's for a cure for potato blight and took drastic action to prevent the spread of pleuropneumonia among cattle a few years later. Through the Patent Office, which also distributed seeds, the federal government collected information and statistics on agriculture and published them in its *Annual Report,* which old John Quincy Adams found so intriguing in 1844 that he "was finally obliged to break it off so as not to lose the whole day."

Until the 1850's, agricultural education was limited to a few private or semiprivate vocational academies or isolated courses in agricultural chemistry here and there. But in the fifties came the creation of a number of agricultural colleges, namely Michigan State, Pennsylvania State, Iowa State, and Maryland, all of which would soon be receiving federal support under the Morrill Act.

Most weekly newspapers could be counted upon to dispense information about agricultural advances and increasingly they replaced the rural almanac. Outstanding in this respect was the semi-weekly edition of Horace Greeley's New York *Tribune* (subscription, three dollars a year), which carried detailed, up-to-the-minute intelligence of the newest happenings in farming. Even more important were the specialized agricultural periodicals. Beginning with the short-lived *Agricultural Museum,* the first to appear in the nineteenth century, over four hundred farm journals were published in the ante bellum period: on the eve of the war there were between fifty and sixty in circulation, with from 250,000 to 350,000 readers. Among the best were John Skinner's *American Farmer* (Baltimore), the *Cultivator,* edited in Albany by Jesse Buel, and Edmund Ruffin's *Farmers' Register* in the South. All borrowed freely from other sources; sometimes their advertisements were dishonest or even fraudulent, as some editors were also interested in the sale of fertilizer, livestock, or farm implements. But, good and poor alike, farm journals were a widely read medium which put information on better techniques, crops, and equipment before the American farmer.

At the same time, and more readily accepted, came one of the most original of American contributions to the Agricultural Revolution, the development of agricultural equipment. Emphasis in a developing economy where labor was scarce and land cheap naturally fell on the introduction of labor-saving machinery. Many farm implements were self-designed and self-made—or made by the local blacksmith—although ready-made machinery of a wide variety was available near cities. Expanding transportation widened the market for farm implements, if such machinery was practical and could raise production while reducing overhead. From the light, flimsy wooden plows and the very heavy, clumsy iron ones of the eighteenth century, 372 variations and changes had been patented by 1855. In the Era of Good Feeling, Jethro Wood of New York had perfected a cast-iron plow that was both cheap and efficient, though he lost his patent rights. But the cast-iron plow, light and simple though it was, would not polish or scour in the heavy, sticky soils of the Middle West; nor was it strong enough to break the tough prairie roots. It remained for John Deere, an Illinois blacksmith, to devise and manufacture a light plow of high-grade steel that met these requirements. After 1847, Deere's Moline factory became the leading plow producer in the upper Mississippi Valley. In 1856 his sixty-five employees turned out 13,400 plows, 2,100 of them for heavy prairie work.

Grain production methods improved, mainly by the replacement of hand sowing, the sickle, the cradle, the flail, and the technique of winnowing wheat from chaff. Hand rotary sowers were not successful, and a few English grain drills were imported before 1840, but continued tinkering had by 1860 produced a number of fairly workable American drills. In 1830 Cyrus McCormick had tried to bring out a practical reaper, but success eluded him for another ten years. Meanwhile Obed Hussey brought a better machine into production, but McCormick quickly met the competition. Moreover, in 1847 he shrewdly moved his plant to Chicago, soon to be the hub of the wheat-producing West. His reapers, and those of his rivals, saved an estimated labor of four men per day and, at the Paris Exhibition of 1855, one cut an acre of oats in twenty-two minutes, while the British entry took seventy-five. Many farmers now turned from corn to wheat and wheat acreage more than doubled, with the profits sending land prices upward. In the 1830's John and Hiram Pitts of Maine produced an effective thresher-cleaner, and by the 1850's threshing and winnowing were combined, but not until after the Civil War did steam power generally replace the horse-tread in their operation. Horsedrawn corn planters were on the market in the 1830's but were not practicable for another twenty years. Other inventions of note included the horsedrawn hay rake, the tedder, the baler, the horse fork for barn loading, improved cotton-seed planters, corn-shellers, and potato diggers. Steam power was used in the processing of rice and sugar, and optimistic Americans dreamed of its application to cultivation. By the late 1850's the Illinois Central Railroad and the Illinois State Agricultural Society were jointly offering an award of $3,000 for the invention of an effective steam-drawn plow.

By the time of the Civil War, improved farm machinery was contributing to remarkable change. Except in the South, where slave labor was often careless and where hand implements prevailed, agricultural machinery conserved labor and made tasks easier. Yet such advances did little to eliminate the wasteful cultivation methods of American farmers, and by increasing the capital requirements of the farmer, such advances made it more difficult for farm hands and tenants to become independent. Increasingly the farmer became a small, specialized capitalist, subject to the vicissitudes of the business world and dependent upon credit agencies and middlemen. As the economic structure grew ever more complex, so also did agriculture, which as time passed came to be tied more and more to developments in transportation and industry.

VI

THE TRANSPORTATION
REVOLUTION

IN THE FIRST HALF of the nineteenth century the greatly expanded demands for goods and for raw materials to meet those demands created new transportation needs and stimulated far-reaching changes in transport that were vital to the emergence of an industrializing economy. The period witnessed remarkable struggles for supremacy involving turnpikes, canals, railroads, and steamers, both inland and coastal. Not only did the era bring by the 1850's a basic shift in the commercial axis from a New York to New Orleans base to a New York to Chicago one, it produced a revolution in communications as well. In the end, the American public was the winner, with cheaper, faster, more flexible haulage of both passengers and freight and a broader, easier dissemination of the news.

When the new government was launched in 1787, travel in the United States was primitive and arduous. Along the coast in navigable waters it was poor enough, but inland conditions were abominable. Highways were often mere trails. Rutted when wet, dusty when dry, many had stumps left in the middle and in muddy weather the term "stumped" had practical meaning. In the absence of bridges or ferries, most rivers were forded, which made travel during spring thaws uncertain and hazardous. Even more unreliable was winter travel. A firm in Rhode Island, sending a shipment of yarn to a customer sixty miles away, could inform the buyer early in December, 1803, that the consignment could be expected to arrive "in the course of the winter."

There were exceptions. After 1794 numerous travelers were favorably impressed by the Lancaster Turnpike, which had been privately built between Philadelphia and Lancaster, a distance of sixty-six miles, to tap the rich agricultural regions just east of the Susquehanna. Costing $465,000, this macadamized pike was a model, "a masterpiece of its kind." Although only moderately successful financially, it ushered in an era of turnpike building which was to last three or four decades, with countless other endeavors encouraged by its fine initial showing. This turnpike fever raged throughout the East and the South, as well as the Northwest, once settlement pushed into the Ohio Valley. In New England and the Middle Atlantic states, except for Pennsylvania, financing came almost entirely from private investors. Elsewhere, probably because population was less and private capital not available, states provided most of the funds in the era of boom building before the end came in 1837.

In one notable instance the national government underwrote construction of an interstate project, the famous National Road, designed to link Baltimore with the Northwest. Congress authorized it in 1806, contracts were signed five years later, but the War of 1812 intervened and the first stretch was not completed until 1818. Gradually it pushed westward, bending north into Pennsylvania and out across Ohio to Columbus by 1830 and on across Indiana to Vandalia, Illinois, by mid-century. Congress refused to vote funds for maintenance, leaving President James Monroe to provide money under the federal power to establish military and post roads. Plans for extending the National Road to its logical terminal, St. Louis, were abandoned with the coming of the railroad, and it eventually fell into disuse, becoming part of U.S. Route 40 in modern times.

This one example of federal construction brought a flood of other proposals before Congress, but Jackson's dramatic veto of the Maysville Road Bill in 1830 on the grounds that the contemplated road was entirely within the state of Kentucky brought an end to such serious requests. While the West was enthusiastic about internal improvements, New England had a relatively good system of local roads and no desire to facilitate the exodus of her own sons to the West nor to aid the commerce of another region; Pennsylvania and New York favored aid only if the routes went across them alone; the South came to fear that internal improvements would create a need for increased revenues, to be gained by pushing tariff rates upward. In addition, as the slavery question became more prickly, a broad construction of the Constitution, such as was necessary to justify spending federal funds for roads, was entirely unacceptable.

Over the turnpikes or over the National Road—the best highway westward for emigration—went a variety of traffic, ranging from rattling Concord stagecoaches to the colorful red, white, and blue Conestoga freight wagons. While the turnpikes were undoubtedly a boon to passenger travel, their tolls, no matter how low, tended to discourage freighting except for local hauling, and many of them were defunct from a lack of business even before they were called upon to meet competition from canals and railroads.

The turnpike era also gave an impetus to important technical advances in bridge building, especially the improved truss and the suspension bridge. Toll bridges often proved more profitable than turnpikes, but public ownership gradually replaced private. In the 1830's and 1840's a new mania was added, that of the plank road, imported from Canada. Built of eight-foot planks, three or four inches thick and placed crossways on stringers, most were short, designed as feeders for canals or railroads. Initial costs were moderate, but as their owners sadly learned, upkeep and replacement were prohibitive and a plank road in disrepair was worse than no road at all. Few survived the panic of 1857.

Far more important than the plank roads, or even the turnpikes, were the countless miles of ordinary country roads, maintained, if at all, by counties. Essential for local commercial and industrial activity, they were generally shamefully kept and fitted Charles Dickens' ill-tempered description of American roads as a "series of alternate swamps and gravel pits."

Overlapping the turnpike era was the sensational development of the steamboat on inland waterways. Early America had depended largely on water transportation. It was said in 1818, not without some exaggeration, that two thirds of the market crops in South Carolina were raised within five miles of a river and the other one third within ten miles. Indeed, before steam brought great changes, a huge one-directional circle of some three thousand miles dominated commerce into the trans-Appalachian regions. Moving counterclockwise, Western foodstuffs—wheat, butter, or pork from Pennsylvania, Ohio, or Indiana, tobacco from Kentucky, cotton from the Tennessee Valley, lead from Illinois or Missouri—floated down the Ohio-Mississippi river system to New Orleans. From there, some of these products were distributed to the South, some went to Europe or the West Indies, but most went by ship to New York, Philadelphia, or Boston. Closing the circle, Eastern or European manufactured goods went west by laborious routes over the Appalachians from Philadelphia or Baltimore. The new changes would make the rivers usable upstream as well as down, and would bind the West, by turnpikes, canals, and railroads, closer and closer to the Northeast.

After the Revolution, and especially after the control of the Indians was assured following the War of 1812, the Ohio-Mississippi system provided the waterway on which an empire floated to a new home west of the mountains. On crude, clumsy flatboats, broadhorns, or even rafts—piled high with children, livestock, household goods, and farm equipment—families drifted downriver on the easiest route of western settlement. Farm produce went by flatboat (much of it by night, for rivermen believed that a boat floated faster after dark) to New Orleans, where it was sold, along with the lumber of the boat, leaving the crew to make their way upriver as best they could. Professional river-boat men carried both passengers and freight, expertly steering clear of shoals and snags and tooting their long tin horns incessantly in the fog.

But such traffic was downstream. By tacking, small ocean vessels could, under favorable winds, ply the lower parts of such rivers as the Mississippi, the Potomac, and the Hudson, but few vessels ventured up beyond Natchez, except for an occasional keelboat, which did so with extreme difficulty. Within a relatively few years, steam would change the pattern: it would make navigable streams into two-way thoroughfares and immeasurably speed up and cheapen the cost of water transportation.

The era was touched off by the ambitious painter-engineer Robert Fulton, who, with financial backing and a British-built engine, pushed his unique steamboat, the 160-ton side-wheeler *Clermont,* out into the Hudson River on an historic day in 1807. Later Fulton wrote in a letter:

> My steamboat voyage to Albany and back has turned out rather more favorably than I had calculated. The distance from New York to Albany is one hundred and fifty miles. I ran it up in thirty-two hours, and down in thirty. I had a light breeze against me the whole way, both going and coming; and the voyage has been performed wholly by the power of the steam engine. I overtook many sloops and schooners beating to windward, and parted with them. The power of propelling boats by steam is now fully proved.

Fulton was not the first: at least sixteen steamboats had been built prior to his, but he was fortunate in having a stout engine and equally stout financial support from wealthy Robert Livingston. Ironically, the Fulton-Livingston combination restricted the spread of river steamboats for a time through monopolies on steam navigation granted them by both New York and Louisiana until the Supreme Court under John Marshall declared such state-conferred monopolies void and upheld the right of Congress to regulate interstate commerce (*Gibbons v. Ogden,* 1824). This decision, plus important technical improvements in engine and hull, contributed much to the rapid expansion of steam navigation, first on Eastern, then on Western waters.

Steamboats in the East emphasized passenger service and increasingly became luxury vessels—"floating palaces"—striving to attract customers. Those in the West, especially in the Mississippi Valley, were of greater importance. The *New Orleans* had gone down the river in 1811; by 1820, sixty-nine steamboats were plying Western waters. At the same time, flatboat traffic remained significant until nearly the end of the 1840's. By 1855 there were 727 steamers, with a total tonnage of over 170,000. A few even made the trip around the Horn to California from the Atlantic Coast.

Western river travel was limited and hazardous: water levels fluctuated greatly; ice was a menace in the spring, as were the numerous rocks, sandbars, and "snags" (submerged trees) already present. About 30 per cent of all steamboats built before 1849 were lost in accidents, and of those lost, nearly 40 per cent hit snags. By mid-century, an estimated 1,070 vessels, costing over $7 million, had been lost, with 2,260 fatalities. No wonder one New York diarist looked upon steamboats as "a substitute for war in the philosophical plan for keeping down the superabundance of the human race . . . !" To natural river dangers were added others. The lighter, cheaper high-pressure boilers used in the West were more prone to explode, and the practice of tying down the safety valve or using pitch, tar, or turpentine to produce a hotter fire and consequently more speed only added to the peril. Racing may have been an exciting form of advertising but it was also risky, as numerous accidents indicated. The *Ben Sherrod,* for example, caught fire and exploded while racing another vessel upriver to Louisville early in May, 1837, and an estimated 120 to 175 passengers lost their lives. But the worst disaster in American inland waterways history occurred late in April, 1865, when the *Sultana* blew up in the Mississippi, just north of Memphis, killing 1,450, many of them Union soldiers en route home.

Gradually Western steamers were modified to meet existing needs. Hulls became broader and shallower, displacing remarkably little water. The *Orphan Boy,* a craft of 169 tons built in 1841, reportedly drew but twenty-two inches when loaded with forty tons of freight and eighty passengers, thus lending credence to the common saying among rivermen that Western steamers could travel in a heavy dew. Engines were placed above deck on an elaborate wooden superstructure, which included all living and carrying accommodations. Side-wheelers were not uncommon, but stern-wheel propulsion saved on weight and made shallow-water travel easier.

On the Mississippi and the Ohio a medium-sized vessel might cost about $20,000; larger, more elaborate ones might run three times that, and the luxury liners of the Hudson even more. But since no right of way had to be acquired, initial capitalization was lower than for turnpikes, canals, or railroads. Eastern steamers tended to be dominated more by company operation, whereas Western ownership was more often an individual or small group enterprise with local financing. Though their lives were short—an average of five years—many returned fabulous profits, some repaying their construction costs in a single year. Far less government aid was forthcoming than to turnpikes, canals, and railroads. There were almost no land grants or purchases of securities: Georgia's direct investment of $100,000 in a steamboat company was exceptional. If assistance was given at all, it was usually in the form of improved navigation facilities, but state and federal governments alike after 1838 showed an interest in enacting safety regulations, although not until 1852, after a growing number of accidents, were inspection laws strengthened to set any real safety standards.

Steamboating enhanced the use of Western rivers, speeded up transport, and lowered costs. In 1819 the passenger fare from New Orleans to Louisville was $125 cabin class, with the return downstream but $75; by 1832 the fare from New Orleans to St. Louis, which was about the same distance as Louisville, was $25, with the return $20, or deck passage either way was available for a mere $5. As charges decreased, speed increased. In 1817 the record run between New Orleans and Louisville was made by the *Enterprise* in just over twenty-five days; in 1853 the *A. L. Shotwell* made the trip in under four and a half days.

Beginning with the *Walk-in-the-Water,* which ran regularly on Lake Erie between Buffalo and Detroit from 1818 until wrecked three years later, steam vessels also operated on the Great Lakes, but their success came less rapidly than on the rivers. Sailing ships could still function without difficulty on the lakes, and even in 1860 two thirds of the tonnage on the Great Lakes was still powered by sail.

The height of the steamboat era came in the 1850's and 1860's. Thereafter, except in the carrying of bulky goods, the coming of the iron horse rapidly forced the romantic steamers to the wharves. Railroads could go more directly, swiftly, and dependably; they could operate the year round, while northern lakes and rivers might be closed from two to five months and low water might limit western navigation in the summer. Railroads could run any direction, could build spurs to shippers and consumers; rivers ran where nature put them, not always in a straight line. By river, the distance from Pittsburgh to St. Louis was 1,164 miles; by rail, 612.

If rivers were not flexible, why not bend them or run artificial waterways to connect them? Beginning with the Erie, which opened its first link in 1819, the canal madness began to sweep the United States and would last until 1837, thus paralleling part of the turnpike era and the rise of the river steamers. When the New York legislature in 1817 voted to construct a waterway to connect Lake Erie with the Hudson River at Albany, it was, in the words of a modern historian, undertaking "an act of faith, the demonstration of a spirit of faith by an organized government that has few parallels in world history." Perhaps a hundred miles of canal had been built in the United States prior to this, and the longest—the Middlesex Canal, which joined Boston with the Merrimack River—was but twenty-eight miles long. These few earlier efforts had not been particularly successful, canal engineering was all but unknown in this country, and the unclaimed wilderness of upstate New York hardly seemed the place for amateurs to gain experience. But with DeWitt Clinton, Governor of New York, pushing assiduously, construction of the $7 million project commenced in 1818.

"Clinton's Big Ditch" was planned and dug "by guess and by God," with men of legal background directing it, learning as they proceeded. And it was remarkably well built. When Governor Clinton symbolized the union of Lake Erie and the Atlantic by pouring a cask of lake water into New York Harbor early in November, 1825, the canal stretched over 364 miles, had eighty-four locks, and had cost considerably more than the original estimates. But it was immediately successful and paid back its cost within a few years. A decade after its completion, the work of enlarging it commenced, and despite panics and growing competition, traffic grew to a peak in 1880.

The Erie Canal had broad implications. The cost of shipping grain from Buffalo to New York City fell from $100 to $5 a ton, enabling the latter to tap upstate farmlands. By 1827 the Governor of Georgia could complain that wheat from central New York was underselling Georgia wheat on Savannah markets. The value of land along the route shot upward as such cities as Utica, Syracuse, and Rochester blossomed forth, while farther west the lake villages of Cleveland, Toledo, and Detroit would benefit immensely. Canal packets drawn by horses or mules on towpaths regularly carried passengers westward at three or four cents a mile, subject to wretched food, unventilated sleeping quarters, and other hazards. Tens of thousands of Yankees moving out over the Erie Canal settled the northern parts of Ohio, Indiana, and Illinois, offsetting the Southerners who moved up across the Ohio and helping bind the Northwest to the Northeast.

Moreover, the success of the Erie touched off an orgy of canal building in all parts of the nation. Some states, notably Pennsylvania, launched elaborate attempts to connect the Atlantic with the Ohio Valley in competition with the Erie. Pennsylvania's $10 million Main Line, completed in 1834, combined an intricate system of canals with inclined planes crossing the Alleghenies, but soon proved such a financial drain that the state disposed of it, along with the rest of its waterways. Others had less pretentious aims. Some sought merely to link the upcountry with the coast, and among the most successful were the private "anthracite canals" built in eastern Pennsylvania to move coal to Philadelphia and New York. Northwestern states made efforts to connect the Ohio-Mississippi river system to the Great Lakes at various points. Some, such as the Ohio and Erie (1833), linking Cleveland to Portsmouth, were well-planned, well-executed enterprises; others, especially feeder lines, had little justification apart from porkbarrel politics. Indiana commenced a mammoth canal network that was mostly abandoned when the state went bankrupt in 1839. Illinois was more successful in building the Illinois and Michigan Canal, tying Chicago to the Illinois River (1836–48). The expense was fantastic, but traffic grew rapidly and undoubtedly contributed to the phenomenal rise of Chicago.

Because of its heavy expense, canal building was financed mainly by federal and state governments. The former granted some four million acres for canal projects in the Northwest and subscribed more than $3 million to the stock of canal companies in the Middle Atlantic states. Even more important was the role of the individual states in supplying capital to private builders, or planning, constructing, and operating canals themselves, frequently ruining their credit in the process. Ohio and New York were especially hard hit and had to retrench drastically; Indiana and Pennsylvania went bankrupt after the 1837 and 1839 panics.

Between 1816 and 1840, 3,326 miles of canal had been built at a cost of about $125 million. Little mileage was added after that; by 1850 abandonments were exceeding new construction and the great boom was over, although some were enlarged and one of the most important, the Saint Marys Falls Canal (later the Sault Ste Marie), was not built until the mid-fifties. Several factors contributed to the collapse. Construction costs were higher than estimated: a macadam turnpike might cost from $5,000 to $15,000 a mile (the National Road cost $13,000); most canals ran from $20,000 to $30,000, and some even more—the Susquehanna and Tidewater cost about $80,000 a mile. Railroad building might well average higher (the Baltimore and Ohio ran $54,000 a mile), but canal maintenance expenses were more extreme, for depth had to be maintained and banks kept from crumbling. Floods might ruin them or a shortage of water close them down. Many were designed for small boats and were obsolete before they ever opened. Locks, portages, or inclined planes slowed traffic on some and poor management or speculation by their directors destroyed others. By 1840 most of the natural routes had been developed and the financial crises of 1837 and 1839, along with growing railroad competition, made canal builders and investors more timid.

The Erie and a few others were successful. Some were able to challenge coastal shipping for short distances, as between New York and Philadelphia, but all were too slow to take much passenger service from the turnpikes. Nor could they compete with the railroads, except in the hauling of bulky freight. The enlarged Erie—now known as the New York Barge Canal—handled nearly 4.5 million tons of such freight in 1957.

But the advantage generally rested with the railroad, which with its fast, cheap, reliable service, best met the needs of agriculture and industry. Developed first in England, steam railroad construction spread most rapidly in the United States, which had over 3,000 miles of line by 1840, compared with but 1,818 miles for all of Europe. Here the need was urgent, there were no legal or political restrictions, government was amenable to aid, and there were fewer powerful interest groups and only a superficial prejudice against railroads.

Opposition naturally came from innkeepers, stagecoach and freight line operators, and bridge or turnpike companies who stood to lose business. Farmers feared the loss of their hay and horse markets and canal backers were especially perturbed. One canal spokesman of the 1840's damned the railroads in no uncertain terms:

> Canals, sir, are God's own highway, operating on the bosom of the fluid that comes straight from Heaven. The railroad stems direct from Hell. It is the Devil's own invention, compounded of fire, smoke, soot, and dirt, spreading its infernal poison throughout the fair countryside. It will set fire to houses along its slimy tracks. It will throw burning brands into the ripe fields of the honest husbandman and destroy his crops. It will leave the land despoiled, ruined, a desert where only sable buzzards shall wing their loathsome way to feed upon the carrion accomplished by the iron monster of the locomotive engine.

Early legislatures sometimes penalized railroads by special taxes, but these were but temporary obstacles and opposition was not widespread. The average citizen welcomed the coming of the railroad, depended on it, and sometimes invested his money in it.

In 1825, the same year the Erie Canal was officially opened, the first general transportation railway—the Stockton and Darlington—went into operation in England, heralding the commencement of the Railroad Age. Americans watched trans-Atlantic developments eagerly, and commercial cities lacking inland water links enthusiastically sought to tap growing Western markets by pushing rail lines into the interior. By 1835, Baltimore, Charleston, and Boston had all moved in this direction and the beginning of a great railroad boom was evident. Pennsylvania led the way, mainly with short lines connecting her mines with canals and rivers; New York, where the Erie was doing so well, was a poor second. Despite fluctuations in the economy, railroad mileage jumped to 9,021 in 1850, and in

1860, just thirty-two years after old Charles Carroll, the last surviving signer of the Declaration of Independence, had turned the first spade for the Baltimore and Ohio, the country had 30,626 miles, mostly in the North. But there was as yet no solid, integrated system. Most lines were local, with more than three hundred independent companies in 1860, but with consolidation advancing slowly. Rails poked as far west as Chicago, that city of "magnificent pretensions," in 1853 and reached East St. Louis two years later. In 1856 the Illinois Central was completed, stretching from Cairo in the south, with one arm branching northwestward to Dubuque and another flung northeasterly to Chicago, and would be highly instrumental in opening up rich prairie farmlands.

RAILROAD MILEAGE, 1830–60*

Year	Miles of Road Operated (December 31)
1830	23
1835	1,098
1840	2,818
1845	4,633
1850	9,021
1855	18,374
1860	30,626

* *Historical Statistics of the United States, Colonial Times to 1957,* p. 427.

Early railroads were flimsy affairs which improved only with time. Roadbeds were cheaply constructed, with steep grades and sharp turns. Experimentation with materials ranging from granite blocks to piles driven into the ground eventually showed the superiority of wooden cross ties set in gravel and treated with a preservative. Most early lines used wooden rails capped with bar or strap iron, which sometimes worked loose and sent dangerous "snakeheads" curling up through the floor of passing coaches, a hazard which was eliminated early in the thirties with the adoption of the T rail.

The first locomotives were British built and Americans at first used the English, or "standard," gauge of 4 feet 8½ inches. But as individualists experimented with engines of their own, there came to be almost as many rail widths as manufacturers. The Hotel and baggage men violently resisted standardization at Erie for fear trains would no longer stop if the gauge were unified, and progress at the national level came slowly. At the time of the Civil War, a traveler going from Philadelphia to Charleston was compelled to change cars at least eight times because of the difference in gauges.

American manufacturers soon began to evolve their own engines, gradually improving them over the years. The first were so weak and unreliable that horses were often kept in reserve. The cowcatcher was added in the 1830's and in 1836 sand boxes were in use against grasshopper swarms in Pennsylvania. Engine cabs were a New England innovation and were first made of canvas, later of wood. Night runs on the Charleston & Hamburg were first accomplished by pushing a fire car ahead of the engine, but conventional kerosene headlights with tin reflectors came into use on most lines by about 1840. Engineers early added a swivel truck of four wheels to the fore part of the locomotive to spread the weight more evenly and to facilitate taking curves; the addition of an equalizing beam permitted the front wheels to rock without twisting the power plant and not only prevented much derailing, but also made for smoother riding on rough rails.

Outstanding among engine manufacturers was Matthias Baldwin of Philadelphia, one of the founders of Franklin Institute and a member of the American Philosophical Society. In the early thirties, Baldwin built "Old Ironsides," a 5.5-ton wonder which ran a mile in fifty-eight seconds, and prior to his death in 1866, his firm manufactured over 1,500 locomotives, many of them magnificent examples of workmanship which ran regularly for thirty or forty years.

Railway cars were at first modeled after horse-drawn carriages, even to the elevated seat for a coachman. Often uncovered, they were attached by several feet of chain, and provided rough, exciting riding. Live cinders menaced haystacks along the line, and after a short trip in 1836, Harriet Martineau found thirteen holes burned in her dress, but enclosed cars, the substitution of coal for wood, and the development of a "spark arrester" eliminated the hazards of fire. A link and pin coupling reduced jerks and passenger cars improved. A crude sleeper appeared on the Cumberland Valley Railroad in 1836, and in the following year the Philadelphia, Germantown & Norristown added several new cars which featured a middle aisle, a women's changing room at one end, and a male barroom at the other. By 1840 the Camden & Amboy was offering its commuters two fancy coaches equipped with rocking chairs!

"To lie like a timetable" became a common expression. Trains were invariably behind schedule and accidents were frequent. Boilers exploded, cars were derailed, and livestock constantly disputed the right of way. But great improvements would come by the time of the Civil War, with stronger boilers and engines, heavier wheels and rails, fenced-in right of way, double tracks, and telegraphic train dispatching.

Government construction aid was of utmost consequence. Between 1824 and 1838 the federal government was willing to bear the expense of running rail surveys, and between 1830 and 1843 it saved railroad builders an estimated $6 million by reducing the tariff on imported iron used for construction. After 1850 it provided land grants, benefiting some forty-five railroads in ten states, with the Illinois Central the most outstanding recipient.

Even more important were the contributions of state and local government. States often gave liberal charters conferring monopolies and sweeping rights on their public domain. They put few limitations on financing, exempted lines from taxation, sometimes granted lottery or banking privileges, or even required banks to purchase railroad stock as a prerequisite to incorporation. Some states, notably Indiana, Illinois, and Michigan, commenced their own ambitious railroad projects in the 1830's, but turned over many of them to private owners when hard times struck. Some states plunged deeply in debt to give direct aid to private companies: New York had advanced over $9 million to ten rail concerns by 1846, when a constitutional amendment barred further assistance; by the time of the Civil War, Virginia had poured about $21 million into railroads, both state and private, and Texas had loaned almost $2 million and had given five million acres of land. The city of Milwaukee, with a population of 45,000 in 1860, had loaned $1.6 million to rail concerns two years earlier. In 1853 the per capita railroad debt of Wheeling was estimated at $55; of Pittsburgh, $34; and Philadelphia, $20.

Public agencies provided a substantial share of railroad capital before Sumter, but private sources provided more. Local investors, as well as those in Eastern cities, were interested not merely in a direct return, but also in the indirect benefits that might accrue to their own businesses or municipalities, as well as to the nation and economy in general. There was a limited but significant sale of securities abroad, especially to the Swiss and the Germans immediately after the revolutions of 1848 and to the British in the early fifties. Investment banking prospered in helping finance railroads, and as a result of heavy railroad business in the 1850's this banking had centralized in Wall Street in New York.

Fraud, manipulation, and speculation sometimes characterized railroad financing and undeniably weakened both the railroads and the national economy. Powerful companies sometimes exerted an unwarranted political influence by distributing free passes, controlling newspapers, or, as James Buchanan complained in 1843, by maintaining shrewd, skilled lobbyists in Washington.

Yet Americans believed in railroads and supported them soundly. By 1860 the major technical troubles of rail construction had been overcome, resulting in the farming of the prairies and acceleration of the settlement of the West. Internal commerce was being stimulated and great cities began to emerge. Sandburg's Chicago—"the Big Junction," "Player with railroads and the nation's freight handler"—was one of the most obvious creations of the new transportational revolution.

As a result, people and goods were moved cheaply, more rapidly, and more readily. Between 1800 and 1819 land transportation rates ranged from thirty to seventy cents per ton mile, varying with the season, the amount of competition, the cost of labor, the condition of the roads, and the availability of a return load. A Senate report of 1816 complained that nine dollars, the cost of shipping a ton of goods across the Atlantic, would haul a ton only thirty miles by land. At such prices, only the most valuable products would bear shipping. With the coming of the

Erie Canal, the rate of shipping grain between Buffalo and New York had fallen from an average of 19.12 cents a ton mile in 1817 to .8155 cents by 1860. Railroad rates varied, but by the same date it was possible to ship wheat between Chicago and New York for about 1.2 cents per ton mile.

Steam speeded things up. Wagon freight and loaded canal-boats might average about two miles an hour if traffic was not heavy; stagecoaches might make from six to eight miles an hour on good roads at rates of from five to ten cents a mile. Mississippi River steamboats averaged close to ten miles an hour, with packet steamers doing fifteen and the Hudson luxury vessels making twenty by the end of the era. Railroad trains might average as much on short passenger runs, but with freight, including stops, they averaged only ten or twelve miles an hour. But because of their directness and the gradual increasing of their speed, they proved the fastest and, when competition flourished, also the cheapest. The immigrant trains of the 1850's charged only a cent a mile for their meager accommodations, less than any other mode of travel.

The railroads' chief competitors had been coastal and river steamers and their triumph had meant a shifting of the basic commercial alignment to a more East-West axis. This contest was dramatized in the courts as a result of the collision in 1856 of the steamer *Effie Alton* with the newly erected railroad bridge spanning the Mississippi River at Rock Island, a legal struggle the outcome of which was much less decisive than the symbolism of the East-West trestle. Henceforth, goods passed more and more by rail directly between New York City and Chicago, with much less dependence on water transport by way of New Orleans.

Meanwhile, ocean transportation was also being revolutionized. After 1820, sea-going vessels became larger. Whereas for reasons of insurance, limited capital, and the smallness of many ports, the average full-rigger had measured about 250 tons in 1800, by mid-century ships of 1,000 tons were frequently built and a few topped 2,000 tons. Most freighters were ungainly and sacrificed speed for maximum cargo capacity, but Americans also specialized in turning out fast, streamlined clipper ships of beautiful design, which after the middle 1840's were the pride of American mariners. With sharp, concave lines, towering masts, and magnificent clouds of sails, they set speed records wherever they went and returned remarkable profits on runs where speed was more important than carrying space.

> Stately as churches, swift as gulls,
> They trod the oceans, then——
> No man had seen such ships before
> And none will see again.*

They served the gold fields of California and Australia, rushed the first tea of the season from China to Western markets, and sped troops to put down the Sepoy Mutiny in India in 1857. But despite their beauty and their speed, they proved in the long run uneconomical. Expensive, they had small carrying capacity, and when the premium on swiftness was gone, they could not compete with the less romantic but more capacious and profitable iron steamers of the British.

Except for steamers and an occasional whaler, corporate ownership was rare. A few wealthy merchants like Stephen Girard or John Jacob Astor might own sizable fleets outright, but generally shares in a single vessel might be divided among a number of people—the shipbuilder, sailmaker, captain, merchants, even casual investors. In terms of operation, merchantmen fell into three categories: the tramp or transient, which roved the seas, waiting for or seeking cargo wherever it might be obtained; the "regular trader," which usually moved between specified ports, carrying her owner's cargo, but alert for additional lading if space permitted; and the packet, which sought to operate on a regular schedule and to cater to passenger as well as valuable freight trade. After 1818, when the first ships of the Black Ball line sailed from New York and Liverpool, the packets became highly important in the transatlantic runs and in the coastal trade, bringing cotton north for reshipment from New York and distributing imports to the South. By 1845 at least fifty-two packets were sailing regularly between New York and Europe and their relative dependability enabled them to skim the cream of freight and passenger service. Steam would give them even more regularity.

* From "Clipper Ships and Captains" by Stephen Vincent Benét.

Steam was one of the advances in ocean travel that Americans were slow to accept. True, the American steamer *Savannah* had crossed the Atlantic in 1819, pursued briefly by a British captain who thought her on fire, but she had used sail power most of the way. Not until 1838, when the *Sirius* and the *Great Western* (English vessels) put into New York Harbor at almost the same time, was regular transatlantic steam service inaugurated, and then not without skepticism from those who doubted the practicality of a ship "with a burning volcano in her bowels."

Yankee shipbuilders scoffed at the iron hulls which were necessary if steam-powered vessels were to withstand heavy battering at sea. The use of sea water in boilers was not satisfactory, and early steamers found difficulty in maintaining a profitable fuel-cargo ratio. The *British Queen,* making her first crossing in 1839, was designed to carry 750 tons of fuel and 500 tons of cargo. But steam and iron ships advanced slowly, the British leading the way. Steam packets, beginning in 1847, began to take over the best freight and passenger trade on all but the longest major sea routes where refueling was still a problem. With a subsidy from the British government, the Cunard Line opened a packet route between New York and Liverpool in 1848 and was quickly challenged by the Collins Line, which received a lesser subsidy from the United States government. But the Collins Line encountered difficulties, ultimately lost her subsidy, and Atlantic liner traffic came increasingly under foreign flags. Better engines, metal hulls, and screw propellers were being introduced, but Americans long remained contemptuous, even though Lloyds of London in 1854 set higher insurance rates on wooden Yankee ships than on British iron ones.

As with domestic shipping, the cost of ocean transportation fell and speed went up, with steam giving the added advantage of regularity. In 1816 the average time westward across the Atlantic from Liverpool to New York was 49.4 days and the eastbound run took about a third less time. Sailing packets averaged 37.9 days between 1818 and 1832, and 34.6 days for the 1848–57 period. Steamships made the same run in 1839 in seventeen days, and by 1860 the usual time was thirteen or fourteen days, with record crossings being made in under ten.

Passenger and freight rates varied, depending upon the service, but in general the trend was downward. Packet service by sailing vessel dropped from $186 in 1818 to as low as $75 in the 1840's for the Atlantic crossing. The first steamers charged $140 in 1838, but the fast Cunarders pushed the price up, though competition leveled it off in the 1850's. The cost of shipping a pound of cotton from New York to Liverpool fluctuated, but fell steadily between 1823 and 1855 from a halfpenny to about one third of that.

By 1860 American merchant shipping was receding from the peak of the early fifties; total tonnage was higher but profits were falling off. The clippers had been overbuilt and were not profitable for ordinary runs; the panic of 1857 had taken its toll; and Great Britain, basing her growth on steam and iron, was forging into the lead. The Civil War, with destruction of much Union shipping by Confederate raiders, only accentuated a tendency already well under way. Not for a full half century would the American merchant marine again become a serious challenger. American trade abroad would thrive, but it was not carried exclusively in American bottoms.

As transportation was revolutionized on land and on sea, so also were communications. The technical advances in transportation and in printing permitted a more rapid exchange of messages and dissemination of information; soon electrical impulses passed through wires would permit communication far more rapidly than a man might travel. Postal service and the circulation of newspapers were speeded up in keeping with improvements in transportation, though postal rates remained almost prohibitively high until 1845. Free city delivery did not come until 1863. Newspapers, however, received special treatment from the post office. They carried little advertising and little local news, but along with their editorials they reported verbatim much news from foreign correspondents and other newspapers. Circulation was limited and the cost of paper high, but with the 1830's came the wider use of the steam press, the advent of the penny paper, and a broader circulation.

One new technological improvement which would greatly modify newspaper work as well as communications in general was the development of the magnetic telegraph. If this instrument was the product of many minds, one man, Samuel F. B. Morse, did more to perfect and to publicize it than any other. Morse, who was also a painter of some talent, persuaded Congress to appropriate $30,000 for an experimental line of his "talking wires" between Washington and Baltimore. His initial message in 1844, "What hath God wrought," stirred many, but not the federal government, which declined to develop the new telegraph on the grounds that it would not pay. Private capital supported it and by 1860 over 50,000 miles of line had been built; a year later the continent had been spanned and the romantic Pony Express rider was technologically unemployed. Much of this expansion was concomitant with that of the railroads, the telegraph companies using the railroad right of way and in return granting the use of their telegraph facilities for railroad operations. Thanks to the persistence of a wealthy paper manufacturer, Cyrus Field, the first transatlantic cable was laid between Newfoundland and Ireland in 1858, but after wild rejoicing and an exchange of congratulations by Queen Victoria and President Buchanan the cable parted and not for another eight years was a newer, heavier one laid down.

VII

MONEY AND BANKING TO THE CIVIL WAR

TO MEET THE NEEDS of financing the movement of crops and the importation of finished goods over expanding transportation routes, specialized financial institutions developed in the early years of the new republic. Of particular significance was the growth of commercial banking and the role of the second Bank of the United States as a stabilizing factor in an era known for relatively few restraints on banking operations.

Organized primarily to receive deposits, make loans and transfer money and credit, commercial banks in the modern sense developed late in America. Because of the simplicity of the colonial economy, the legal restrictions imposed by the British, and the availability of merchant credit through English sources, there were no banks in the Colonies prior to the Revolution, apart from a few abortive land banks. But the severing of ties with Britain, the Constitutional relinquishment of state rights to issue bills of credit, and, above all, the growth of transportation and commerce soon gave rise to a growing number of banking institutions, appearing first in urban centers to provide short term commercial loans.

When the first Bank of the United States was chartered in 1791 as part of Hamilton's financial program, there were but three other banks in the country, with a fourth about to open its doors. By 1811, when enemies of banks in general combined with those who wanted unrestricted banking to block recharter of the Bank of the United States, the number had grown to 90 and within five years to 250. A single act of the Pennsylvania legislature in 1814 authorized the incorporation of forty-one new banks, of which thirty-five were in business within two years. Bank notes increased from $28 million to $68 million between 1811 and 1816, and loans expanded even more as the War of 1812 brought fiscal chaos that prompted Congress to charter a second Bank of the United States. Growth continued steadily, except during panic periods: by 1860 there were 1,562 banks, over one third of which had been set up since 1857. Bank capital rose from $102 million in 1820 to $442 million forty years later, and note circulation multiplied thirteen times in the same period.

Throughout the era the banking system was simple, though growing in complexity. Some of the earliest were unincorporated or "private" banks that developed from import-export ties with British mercantile houses, in the manner of Alexander Brown and Sons of Baltimore. Most, however, were chartered by state legislatures, at first by individual acts which often conferred special privileges on the banks and sometimes on the lawmakers as well.

State incorporated banks were most commonly financed by the issue of bank stock, requiring a small cash installment by the purchaser, who borrowed the unpaid balance from the bank on his personal note, using the stock as collateral and taking newly issued notes of the bank in exchange. The granting of the right of borrowers to draw checks against demand deposits was rare in the pre-Civil War era, except in the larger commercial cities; but in effect, banks created credit by printing their own notes and issuing them as money to borrowers.

Loose banking practices prevailed. Actual fraud was common enough and banking theory was but little understood in the days of amateurs. An anonymous pamphlet on banking observed in 1827: "The time was when to get a bank charter it was thought necessary to have money to put in; now men get a bank charter for the contrary reason—because they have no money and want some." In theory, perhaps, many bankers may have recognized the need for liquid reserves and for limitations on the expansion of credit and note issue, but the gap between theory and practice was a wide one. Often a bare minimum of capital went into the creation of a bank, and while men may have talked about the desirability of restricting note issue to one and a half or two times the capital or of maintaining specie reserves at from 20 to 25 per cent of note issue, not until the 1840's did the concept of legal reserves begin to prevail. Meanwhile, huge note issues were circulated on the flimsiest of bases. One of the most flagrant examples, the Farmers Exchange Bank of Glocester, Rhode Island, was probably the first bank to fail in the United States (1809). Because of negligent, inept, and totally unscrupulous management, at one point it had $580,000 worth of notes issued and only $86.46 in cash on hand for redemption.

At all times, but especially after the restraining influence of the second Bank was removed in the middle 1830's, the public was faced with a confusing and widely fluctuating array of currencies. Wildcat banks, short on reserves but long on "red dog" or "sick Indian" bills, set up business in the West, and "saddlebag" banks cropped up sporadically, leaving behind a sea of depreciated currency. Small denomination "shinplasters," issued by municipal governments, merchants, taverns, even bootblacks, circulated freely, usually at substantial discount. At Zanesville, Ohio, in 1817, over thirty kinds of paper money were in use. Some twenty years later a traveler reported his difficulties with a variety of currencies:

> At Wheeling exchanged $5 note, Kentucky money, for notes of the Northwestern Bank of Virginia; reached Fredericktown; there neither Virginia nor Kentucky money current; paid a $5 Wheeling note for breakfast and dinner; received in change two $1 notes of some Pennsylvania bank, $1 Baltimore and Ohio Railroad, and balance in Good Intent shinplasters; 100 yards from the tavern door all notes refused except the Baltimore and Ohio Railroad; reached Harpers Ferry; notes of Northwestern Bank in worse repute there than in Maryland.

By 1861 the more than fifteen hundred banks were issuing some ten thousand kinds of currency under the laws of thirty different states.

Even when the two Banks of the United States exerted some pressure, there was a noticeable lack of responsibility, a decided reluctance by state banks to pay out specie, and a wide fluctuation in the value of their notes. Not all currency was payable on demand: to delay redemption in specie, some notes were made payable at some future specified date; some were payable only at some point other than the place of issue; others were taken far from the issuing bank for exchange to borrowers. Because of the diversity of notes and of value, printed guides were essential to keep local businessmen abreast of the times. One such guide of early 1839 listed twenty fictitious banks with notes circulating, fifty-four banks that had failed, and the descriptions of 1,395 notes that had been counterfeited or altered.

The first banks specialized almost completely in short term commercial credit and were run by merchants for financing trade balances. As the business sector grew, the desire to finance improved farm lands, real estate speculation, and the construction of mills, canals, and railroads built up pressure for long-term credit that tended to break down this specialization. Legislatures sometimes sought to meet these demands by granting banking along with other powers to gas, canal, or rail companies, but such "industrial banks" proved financially unsound, although they did dramatize the need for long-term capital as the economy shifted to manufacturing and to specialized, more mechanized agriculture.

With the failure of "industrial banks," continuing pressure from industrial and farm interests forced commercial banks to lengthen maturities and grant almost automatic loan renewals. Many bankers went to an extreme, failing to recognize the need for greater reserves and for planned spacing if long-term replaced short-term loans. Many went into receivership, especially in time of panic, before they learned that the commercial banking structure could not hope to handle the entire demand for long term capital. As a result, new financial institutions arose—savings banks and insurance companies especially—and a direct investment market evolved.

Despite many differences in practice stemming from chartering under state laws that were often dissimilar, local American banking houses by 1860 showed many similar trends. Particularly in urban centers there was considerable unity. Many short term capital markets had been linked together by the movement of funds to Eastern banks into what approximated a national market. Most states by this time had "free banking," which helped make capital more readily available. New York, following the example of Michigan, in 1838 passed a Free Banking Act, under which bank charters were now granted to anyone who could meet certain general requirements. According to a modern banking historian, speaking facetiously, this meant "that it might be found somewhat harder to become a banker than a bricklayer, but not much." In Michigan, "free banking" had resulted in a wild orgy of fly-by-night banks which usually ended in abrupt receivership within a short time. In New York the results were not so extreme, for the area had sufficient wealth and credit to support an unreasonable number of banks. Although the courts ultimately disallowed both laws, "free banking" was widely adopted and its general principles would be written into the National Banking Act of 1863.

Moreover, by the time of the Civil War, bankers were more sophisticated and more practical when dealing with reserves and liabilities. In many areas regulation had done away with many of the worst features of unrestricted banking, giving a growing stability that permitted bankers to supply the economy with an increasing volume of short term credit. Most states made efforts to safeguard investors and limit wildcat banking, though not always with wisdom or with success. At one extreme, six states, beginning with Texas in 1845, constitutionally forbade the incorporation of banks, but concerns chartered ostensibly for other purposes managed to perform banking functions and bank notes poured in from outside, negating these prohibitions. Other states, especially in the South and West, provided banking by a state monopoly or near-monopoly. The Bank of South Carolina, for example, was one of the oldest and most honorable of these, having been active from 1812 through the Civil War. The Second State Bank of Indiana had a monopoly in that state during much of its life (1834–57) and worked reasonably well. On the other hand, state enterprises in Alabama, Illinois, Kentucky, and Mississippi were notoriously poor. And sometimes states, while not granting bank monopolies, invested in private banks, often with disaster.

Other attempts sought to stabilize or add safeguards by co-operation. One such effort, the Suffolk System in New England, proved fairly successful. Beginning in the early 1820's, many local New England banks kept sufficient cash in the Suffolk Bank in Boston to assure prompt honoring of their notes, which instead of being returned to their home bank were cleared at the Suffolk and retained their par value. Less workable was the so-called Safety Fund arrangement in New York (1829), which required banks to build up jointly a safety fund, administered by a board of commissioners, to meet the failure of any bank to redeem its notes or deposits. Despite weaknesses, especially the basing of the fund on capital rather than on note circulation, the system worked reasonably well until the 1840's, when a large number of bank failures depleted the fund and required the state to inter-vene directly, a situation from which the system never fully re-covered. A good deal more successful was the creation of the New York Clearing House in 1853. This made for daily settle-ments among banks, prompted better organized accounts, and was an influence in curbing speculation, as well as an example for Philadelphia and Boston, both of which adopted similar plans over the next few years.

Even the free banking laws of most states contained some pro-visions for regulation, usually by requiring legal reserves, though these were never closely observed. Much more important in a regulatory sense was the adoption by many states of the Louisiana, or Forestall, System after 1842. This ordinarily limited all loans of deposited funds (as opposed to loans of capital) to ninety days, with renewals prohibited, and required short term liabilities to be backed one-third by specie reserves and two-thirds by un-renewable short term commercial paper.

Another important stabilizing influence during the periods of their existence were the two Banks of the United States. Chartered in 1791, with one fifth of its capital of $10 million held by the federal government and the remainder subscribed privately in less than an hour, the first Bank prospered and returned about 8.5 per cent annually to its investors during its twenty-year life. Through its eight branches, it fulfilled the expectations of Hamilton and more, especially when it came to exercise a salutary influence over the indiscriminate issue of paper by state banks, forcing them to keep specie on hand for redemption of notes on demand.

The second Bank, chartered in 1816, ultimately came to exert even more powerful control functions, particularly as its policy came to be defined by its third and most important president, Nicholas Biddle. Like its predecessor, the second Bank was incorporated for twenty years, but its capitalization was higher— $35 million, of which $7 million was subscribed by the national government, which also selected five of the Bank's twenty-five directors. Early in 1817 it opened its doors for business at Carpenter's Hall in Philadelphia, but within a few years was moved to a classical building of its own on Chestnut Street, just a block east of Independence Hall.

But the new Bank was off to a poor beginning in an era of postwar prosperity. Under its first president, the inept and incompetent William Jones, the Bank followed a loose expansionist policy designed solely to return dividends. Branches were opened in other cities but little control retained over them; directors speculated in the Bank's own stock; and when a crisis arose in 1818, the Bank narrowly avoided bankruptcy by sharply contracting loans, which only made matters worse and helped bring on the panic of 1819. Jones was forced to resign and his successor, Langdon Cheves of South Carolina, did much to bring the Bank back to an even keel. But for two years depression prostrated the land. Farm prices were low, businesses and banks failed (including the Cincinnati branch of the Bank), estimates of unemployment ranged from 40,000 to 500,000, and, according to Mathew Carey of Philadelphia, the country exhibited "a state of things at which our enemies must rejoice—and our friends put on sackcloth and ashes!" Cheves' program of retrenchment, reduction of loans and note circulation, control over the branches, and collection of defaulted debts proved effective, and the Bank weathered the storm, although dividends fell and shareholders complained.

Opposition to the Bank's operation had already been manifested. The Illinois constitution of 1818 expressly forbade any but state banks. Others, notably Maryland, Ohio, Kentucky, and Tennessee, sought to tax "foreign" banks out of existence, but reckoned without the United States Supreme Court. Under John Marshall, the Court for thirty-four years after 1801 handed down a long series of nationalistic decisions which strengthened the federal government and the protection of property rights. In the case of *McCulloch v. Maryland* (1819), it upheld the constitutionality of the Bank, using Hamilton's interpretation of the implied powers, and insisting that any effort of Maryland to tax the Baltimore branch could not be maintained. "The power to tax involves the power to destroy," said the court, and no state may be permitted to destroy what the national government by constitutional laws has seen fit to create.

When Cheves resigned in 1823, he was followed by thirty-seven-year-old Nicholas Biddle, Princeton-trained scholar, writer, and legislator, in whose hands the fate of the Bank rested for the next dozen years or so. Under Biddle the Bank flourished. By 1830 it would have twenty-five branches throughout the country and would exert profound influence on the nation's commercial and financial life. Its notes expanded from $4.5 million in 1823 to $19 million in 1831—a quarter of the nation's paper money—and it helped create a sound currency, both by meeting specie demands on its own issue and by forcing state banks to do the same. Biddle stressed the importance of short-term commercial loans concentrated in the larger trade centers, especially Philadelphia, Boston, and New York. New York, an aggressive, energetic city of enterprise, rapidly developed as a leading port, surpassing Philadelphia (which controlled the Bank), and federal revenues, mainly from import duties, accumulated in the New York branch. Likewise, because of the expansion of the cotton trade, the New Orleans branch did a large volume of business, providing much capital and currency for the South and West, and dealing heavily in foreign exchange. Under Biddle, says Bray Hammond, the second Bank acted as the balance wheel of the banking system. It regulated the supply of money; restrained the expansion of bank credit; governed the exchanges; safeguarded the investment market; protected the money market from the disturbing force of Treasury operations and of payments of balance, inter-regional and international; and facilitated Treasury operation vis-à-vis the rest of the economy.

Biddle himself admitted that it could, if it chose, destroy practically any bank in the country. As to his own power, he said, "I have been for years in the daily exercise of more personal authority than any President habitually enjoys."

Controlled by a small, wealthy group of commercial aristocrats, the Bank could sometimes be autocratic. Biddle was not above using its funds to make influential friends. Loans went to important newspaper editors and to members of Congress, among them Daniel Webster, who also accepted annual retainers as counsel for the Bank. Unfortunately, however, when aggressive business interests made the Bank a political football in the Jacksonian era, Biddle lacked the political acumen and the flexibility to avoid a head-on clash, a clash which brought down the Bank around his head.

Jackson had sounded warnings in his messages to Congress in 1829 and 1830, when he disparaged the usefulness of the Bank. Though its charter did not expire until 1836, Biddle was unwisely persuaded to apply for a recharter in 1832. Henry Clay and other Whig politicians believed they could make political capital of this in the election of that year and that Jackson would lose support from some faction regardless of whether he accepted or rejected recharter. Congress passed the recharter bill, but Jackson chose to veto it with a resounding message, which Biddle said had "all the fury of a chained panther biting the bars of his cage." The Bank, said the President, was unconstitutional and conferred monopolistic privileges on the small handful of wealthy Easterners and foreigners who held its stock. He could not, he said, permit the "prostitution of our Government to the advancement of the few at the expense of the many."

With the gauntlet thus thrown down, the Bank became the central issue of the election of 1832. Despite the heavy opposition of the press and the thunderings of Clay, Webster, and to a lesser extent, John Quincy Adams, Jackson won re-election without difficulty and accepted this as a popular mandate in support of his anti-Bank war. Since the Bank would continue under its old charter until 1836, Jackson took action to scuttle it before then by ceasing to put federal deposits in its vaults and by allowing existing deposits to dwindle with their use for the regular expenses of government. To do so, he had to shift two un-co-operative Secretaries of the Treasury until he found one who would carry out the somewhat questionable policy. The Bank was dying and the editor of the Boston *Post* composed its epitaph: "Biddled, Diddled, and Undone." It survived to the end of its charter and a few years longer as a private concern under Pennsylvania law.

A standard version of the Bank struggle is that agrarian hostility was responsible—that the Bank was a grasping Shylock lending to impoverished farmers, then exacting its pound of flesh, when Andrew Jackson stepped in to destroy the Monster. Actually, when the final assault came, it came more from New York banking and business interests, with whom the Bank, dominated by Philadelphians, was in competition, but spokesmen for Wall Street interests shrewdly united several important elements behind them. States' rights politicians had long been hostile; businessmen preferred the easy credit of private banks without restraint from the B.U.S. The private banks themselves, of course, were usually unfriendly, though not always, especially to competing branches of the "Monster of Chestnut Street." In the popular mind the Bank was often identified with a business aristocracy or damned because it was a corporation as well as a bank, and agrarians were split, some preferring local banks of easy virtue, some being skeptical of all banks in general. Hard money advocates like Jackson and "Old Bullion" Benton of Missouri believed all banks and all paper money evil.

No doubt Jackson's Bank War and its ramifications were among the factors contributing to the financial dislocation in 1837. Without the restraining influence of the B.U.S., private banks could more readily over-extend their credit and note issues, and this, in turn, fostered inflation and speculation, especially in Western lands. The "pet" banks, state banks in which federal funds reposed, moreover, used government deposits as a basis for a wild expansion of credit. In 1836, Jackson, concerned over the situation, issued his Specie Circular, requiring that federal land payments be made only in gold or silver, a stipulation which dislocated Western banking somewhat and brought a drain in specie from Eastern banks just at a time when Great Britain was tightening credit and calling home loans. States had already borrowed heavily for internal improvements and Congressional distribution to them of much of the federal surplus in 1836 only increased their extravagance. Crop failure in 1835 had brought importation of grain and a high adverse balance of trade. The net result was pressure on New York banks, their suspension of specie payments in May, 1837, and panic and depression. Cotton prices fell alarmingly, banking and commerce were particularly hard hit, and numerous states repudiated their debts. The economy revived somewhat in 1838–39, but the summer of 1839 brought a severe relapse which was not overcome until 1843.

Beginning in the 1840's, the federal government withdrew from central banking. Under an independent treasury arrangement established in 1840, then repealed and re-established in 1846, it built its own depositories and stored its own funds, requiring all receipts in specie or United States Treasury notes and all outgoing payments in specie. The independent treasury stood until the Federal Reserve Act of 1913, but had the disadvantage of tying up too much specie in deposits, though this weakness was mitigated somewhat by several factors. Federal balances were often small, and the occasional purchase of government securities by the Treasury put specie in circulation. More important were the new gold discoveries in the West which put vast amounts of precious metal into the monetary system at a time when the economy was rapidly expanding.

New York City had clearly emerged as the leading commercial and financial center. Banks there did a heavy business in foreign and domestic exchange and country banks kept deposits there, against which drafts could be drawn. Moreover, since New York banks used these funds on the call-loan market, they drew interest. Such an arrangement had its advantages for exchange and for emergency reserves accumulating a slight profit, but it made for great vulnerability in time of crisis. This was the situation in

1857. A great railroad-building boom was on, land speculation was again on the increase, wheat production had overexpanded to meet the demands of the Crimean War, and a general aura of inflation and optimism ruled. When credit abroad began to tighten and when the Ohio Life Insurance and Trust Company, a New York concern, failed in August, 1857, country banks began a run on New York banks, which called in their loans. Security prices fell so fast that the loans could not be met and in the ensuing panic the majority of New York banks collapsed and most banks throughout the United States suspended payment. Recovery was rapid in banking, but the depression broadened, and general recovery came slowly over a period of nearly three years. That the South was not affected as severely as other sections of the country only confirmed the Southerners' belief in the invincibility of cotton.

On the whole, government participation in banking tended to decline before the Civil War; individual enterprise grew in importance and a greater degree of competition prevailed than before. The role of the Banks of the United States as instruments of control, especially the second one, was important, but the Bank's life was limited and its influences not all pervasive. The circulation of notes of the second B.U.S. was important—more so than the federal short-term Treasury notes issued during the War of 1812, during the depression of 1837, and again during the Mexican War. The first B.U.S. had kept from $3 million to $5 million of its notes circulating; the second B.U.S., some $10 million. But, after the War of 1812, state banks of issue ordinarily were responsible for one half to two thirds of the circulating medium. Banking systems tended to develop on a regional and sectional basis, as in New England, where the Suffolk System had five hundred members, or in New York, where even above average co-operation failed to stem the debacle of 1857. Banking by the time of the Civil War still had many weaknesses, but it had matured as it had expanded, and had managed by fits and starts to supply a good part of the capital and credit needed by an economy in transition.

VIII

INDUSTRIAL CHANGE IN AN
AGRARIAN ECONOMY

CLOSELY LINKED to the changing network of demand, supply, and transportation was one of the great transforming forces of the modern age, the Industrial Revolution, which commenced in the United States about the beginning of the nineteenth century. Such historians as John Nef and A. P. Usher have questioned the use of the term "revolution" and have quite properly pointed out that the bases of the industrial metamorphosis of both Britain and the United States went far back over earlier centuries, but were now speeded up tremendously. This so-called Industrial Revolution was characterized by the coming of the factory system, localizing all manufacturing operations under one roof, producing for general markets through the use of specialized power-driven machinery, and labor under skilled supervision working fixed hours for fixed wages.

Such a situation could develop only if certain basic prerequisites were met, as was the case in America by the early nineteenth century, and fifty years earlier in Britain. Essential were the basic ingredients of raw materials, capital, and labor; technological advances; a concentrated population or improved transportation; general confidence in a government inclined to encourage and protect mercantile and manufacturing enterprise.

121

The young nation was fortunate in having within easy reach the important natural resources—timber, iron, coal, and particularly water power. Gradually small, then larger amounts of capital appeared in the form of merchant capitalism, along with increasingly complex agencies for handling capital and credit. Population growth—with the population almost doubling between 1820 and 1840, for example—increased the available labor supply and simultaneously broadened the market for goods. Unable to compete with Western farmers tilling rich, virgin soil, younger New England farmers, or more frequently farmers' daughters, were often driven to work in the mills. On one hand, a shortage of labor prompted the invention of laborsaving machinery, which drove production costs down; as mechanization proceeded, profits were plowed back into expansion and improved techniques. Americans could build on technological innovations of the British—Kay's flying shuttle, Hargreaves' spinning jenny, Arkwright's water frame, Crompton's "mule," and the forerunners of Cartwright's power loom. Boulton and Watt's improvements on the steam engine and Wilkinson's new techniques of boring with close tolerance were necessary before steam could replace water power.

Government gave evidence of a kindly disposition in protection of property rights in the Constitution, in the adoption of the Hamiltonian economic program, and in the decisions of the Supreme Court under John Marshall. The Court's decision in the Dartmouth College case (1819) upheld the sanctity of corporate charters as contracts not to be modified by subsequent legislatures; in *Gibbons v. Ogden* (1824) state limitations on interstate commerce were denied and steamboat monopolies on the Hudson and the Mississippi were rejected; three years later (*Brown v. Ogden*) the court upheld the exclusive right of Congress to control both foreign and interstate trade.

From the beginning a certain measure of protection, either artificial or natural, prevailed. The dislocation of shipping and trade during the Revolution, during the period of the Embargo and Non-Intercourse acts, and during the War of 1812 no doubt encouraged domestic manufacturing, although this aspect is frequently overemphasized. A Philadelphia toast of 1808 proclaimed: "The Best Mode of Warfare for our Country—the artillery of carding and spinning machinery, and the musketry of shuttles and sledges." Some capital did shift from commerce and shipping to manufacturing during these disruptive war, or near war, years, though industry was hard put to compete with transportation, land speculation, and agriculture for capital at a time when a great many Americans distrusted industrial activity and believed wholeheartedly in the primacy of farming. Moreover, at the end of both the Revolution and the War of 1812, British shippers threw accumulations of manufactured goods on the American market at low prices, to the detriment of American producers. As the Englishman Henry Brougham told Parliament in 1816, "It was well worth-while to incur a loss on the first exportation in order, by the glut, to stifle in the cradle those rising manufacturers in the United States, which the war had forced into existence." Yet undoubtedly many of these local "war babies," such as the steel, gunpowder, and cut-nail industries, survived the postwar deluge.

With a rapidly growing domestic market becoming more accessible by virtue of an expanding and improving transportational network, government contributed first by underwriting parts of the transportation system and by placing few, if any, restrictions on the movement of goods over a vast area. In addition, states gave tax concessions, land grants, and liberal charters of incorporation, while at least mild tariff protection existed at the national level beginning in 1816. Tariff rates went up in 1824 as part of Henry Clay's American System to aid Eastern industry and finance Western internal improvements, and they rose again sharply four years later when the "tariff of abominations" became law more or less by accident. Amid the nullification controversy it was scaled down by compromise and subsequently by the Walker tariff of 1846 and a revision of 1857 which dropped rates to their lowest level since 1815 while still retaining the principle of protection.

In 1815 at least half of the clothing worn in the United States was the product of household manufacture; by 1860, except for food preparation, household manufacturing had largely disappeared, although its rate of decline differed with each part of the country. Household manufacture, using "mother and daughter power," gave way most rapidly where transportation was best; thus it lingered longest in the South and in newly settled areas of the West. As household manufacture declined, production for the market expanded enormously, with emphasis on larger shop operations, the spread of the domestic, or putting-out, system, and the factory system.

In this change, the merchant capitalist played a vital role. It was he who risked capital and found markets. More and more, individual craftsmen's shops became small production units rather than retail outlets, selling to the merchant capitalists instead of directly to the consumer. Hatmaking illustrates the trend. Originally hats had been made to the order of local customers; after about 1800, when wholesale merchants began to enter the picture, it tended to centralize in a few important towns, such as Danbury, Connecticut, where larger shops and more personnel helped meet market demands until the 1850's when power machinery and the factory system began to take over. The palm and straw hat industry, however, continued to be organized on the domestic basis well past the Civil War. Merchant capitalists distributed Cuban palm leaves to local homes, where the products were woven or braided by women or children, often in exchange for goods. The hats were then collected, bleached, pressed, and trimmed in central shops before marketing.

The boot and shoe industry, while not necessarily typical, also illustrates many of the basic changes at work, although it should be emphasized that all stages of development were contemporary, with no uniform sequence of progression. In pre-Revolutionary days and afterward on the frontier, shoes were generally made at home. But at the same time wandering cobblers did a better job and in addition brought news and information to isolated settlers or communities. Eventually the itinerants would settle in some thriving community, thus ending one phase and commencing another—the handicraft stage. The handicraftsman, in his own shop, made shoes to order and perhaps in lax times manufactured some additional, average-sized ones for trade. Ultimately, when the shoemaker no longer made his product for the customer directly, the handicraft stage had given way to the domestic. Now onto the scene came the middleman—the local merchant or someone with capital—who supplied leather to a number of cobblers in an area, collected the finished shoes from them, and distributed them over a fairly wide market region. But this putting-out system had its drawbacks: perhaps the individual cobbler, anxious to increase his income, speeded up his work by lowering his standards, often leaving simple, unskilled tasks in the hands of other members of his family. Perhaps he wasted leather or sold the scraps for his own profit. To meet this waste and to reduce costs, the merchant capitalist next established his own shop, where the leather was cut, then sent out to have the uppers fitted; these were returned, then sent elsewhere to have the soles attached, and so on until the product was completed. Time was lost and the quality of work varied and the putting-out system began to give way to the factory stage where all processes were brought into one building and where workers employed on a daily wage basis could be closely supervised. Here labor could be minutely subdivided, and unskilled workers introduced to handle certain tasks. A standardized and more refined product resulted. The old practice of making "straight" shoes with no distinction between the left and right foot gave way to the production of "crooked" shoes; the practice of packing a barrel full of shoes of all sizes gave way to the packing of sized shoes, a pair together. Mechanization came more slowly than in other industries, but the sewing machine was adapted in the 1850's although broad scale mechanization was not introduced until after the Civil War. In 1860 the American shoe industry employed some 123,026 persons and produced goods valued at nearly $92 million; in each case, Massachusetts accounted for approximately one half of these figures.

As might be expected in an economy that was basically agricultural, the food-processing industries were the first to feel the impact of the new revolution. Cincinnati, by virtue of a strategic location with access to markets, labor, and banking facilities, was by 1818 the center of the American pork packing industry and would remain so until mid-century. Here in "Porkopolis," using systematized butchering methods, five men could kill, cut up, and trim hogs at a rate of more than one per minute in the 1840's.

Harriet Martineau, though too squeamish to view the process for herself, compared the division of labor with that of the pin manufacturers in Birmingham. Pork preservation was usually done by salting and by smoking, or by heat sterilization and packing in airtight containers. In time, as the centers of grain and livestock production moved westward with improved transportation, St. Louis and especially Chicago—"Hog Butcher to the World"— became the most important meat packing centers.

Tanneries were present everywhere, usually on a small scale, as were tobacco factories in the South. The distillation of whiskey was always an important industry at several levels. In 1810 Pennsylvania had 3,594 stills and produced 6.6 million gallons of whiskey; North Carolina, which had more stills, 5,426—one for every 111 people—turned out only less than one fifth of that quantity. By 1850 several Ohio Valley cities, particularly Cincinnati and Louisville, along with New York stood high on the list of whiskey producers and shippers for the general market. In 1850, 14.5 million gallons were sent south from Cincinnati, via the Ohio and Mississippi rivers.

Flour milling expanded and, more than meat packing or distilling, profited from technological change. Late in the eighteenth century the versatile inventor Oliver Evans had devised an ingenious milling apparatus, which cut in half the manpower required by using power for lifting, cleaning, grinding, and sifting. A number of such mills cropped up quickly: by 1800 there were at least sixty of them along an eight-mile stretch of the Brandywine in Delaware and Pennsylvania. Gradually, with advancing transportation facilities, great milling centers arose. Baltimore handled grain from the Middle Atlantic states, and after completion of the Baltimore and Ohio Railroad, also from the Ohio Valley. By canal Richmond tapped the central Virginia wheat fields, while along the route of the Erie Canal farther north a series of mill towns pushed westward. Rochester was the most important of these in the 1840's and 1850's; Oswego surpassed it momentarily then fell behind again. By 1851 St. Louis was annually grinding and marketing over 400,000 barrels of flour, even though lacking the good water-power facilities of her competitors. At the same time, small gristmills scattered throughout the country were of extreme local importance: even in 1860, there were at least 13,866 of them. In that same year, the census returns showed that in terms of the value of the product, flour and meal stood first on the list of American manufactures and in terms of value added by the manufacturing process was fourth, being preceded only by cotton goods, lumber, and boots and shoes.

Both in England and in the United States, the cotton textile industry was in the forefront of the Industrial Revolution, with two distinct systems of manufacturing prevailing in America by the early nineteenth century. South of Boston, centering in the Providence-Pawtucket region, a system predominated which stressed mill villages under individual or partner ownership, producing comparatively fine, diverse cotton goods and using highly skilled labor. Samuel Slater, twenty-one-year-old Englishman who was familiar with textile machinery in his homeland, brought plans to America in his head and in 1791 had established a yarn factory at Pawtucket, "the cradle of the cotton textile industry." The enterprise prospered (Slater was worth some $625,000 when he died in 1836) and other small plants followed his lead, producing first for local, then broader, markets, with much weaving still done at home under the putting-out system. Soon, because of careless workmanship and irregular output, power looms were adopted and weaving came under the same roof as the spinning.

This first occurred at Waltham, when the industry spread north of Boston, with another distinctive mode of production. Francis Lowell, an importer, had paid an extended visit to England and had made a close study of a number of Lancashire cotton mills. On his return two years later, in conjunction with his brother-in-law Patrick Jackson, he proceeded to design his own machinery, organize the Boston Manufacturing Company, and at Waltham was highly successful in establishing the first integrated textile factory in the United States, combining spinning and weaving under one roof, and applying power, standardized processes, and mass production. After Lowell's death in 1817, Jackson founded the town of Lowell on the Merrimack, a center destined to become the hub of the early textile industry. Under the Waltham-Lowell system, generally prevailing north of Boston and in the upper Connecticut Valley, ownership was usually by corporations with large capital investment; with mass production techniques more goods were produced, but of generally inferior quality than those produced in the Pawtucket-Providence area. All processes —spinning, weaving, bleaching, fulling, and dyeing—were in a single plant and obsolete equipment quickly gave way to the most modern. Moreover, the Northern mills tapped a new source of labor—the daughters of New England farmers, who were attracted to the mill sites and sheltered in boarding houses under strict supervision.

Early visitors to the Lowell-Waltham type of cotton mills were either appalled or tremendously impressed. Some saw in them "the first germ of the Industrial or Commercial Feudalism that is to spread over our land." One described the work room at a New Hampshire mill in 1836:

> It is four hundred feet long, and about seventy broad; there are five hundred looms, and twenty-one thousand spindles in it. The din and clatter of these five hundred looms under full operation, struck us on first entering as something frightful and infernal, for it seemed such an atrocious violation of one of the facilities of the human soul, the sense of hearing.

Others, like Davy Crockett, who visited Lowell in 1834, were very favorably disposed. Crockett was impressed not only by the "mile of gals" and by the suit of clothes the management presented him, but also by "the power of machinery wielded by the keenest calculations of human skill" that enabled Northerners to "buy our cotton, and carry it home, manufacture it, bring it back, and sell it for half nothing, and in the meantime, be well to live, and make money besides." "I never witnessed such a combination of industry," he said, "and perhaps never will again."

The Northern mills, centered in Lowell and Waltham and in such towns as Manchester, New Hampshire, and Lewiston, Maine, quickly outstripped their competitors in production. Along with the Rhode Island region, another important district had developed in the Paterson-Philadelphia area, specializing in skill and high quality goods rather than on mass production. In the South mills were important in such centers as Richmond, Augusta, and Columbia, but were on a comparatively limited scale. In

1860, when the entire textile industry of more than five million spindles and 122,000 workers produced goods valued at $115.7 million, the city of Lowell alone had more spindles than all of the South combined.

As early as 1788 a woolen factory had been established at Hartford, but because of poor quality American wool and intense foreign competition it soon failed. Woolen textiles lagged behind cotton, in part because of stiff British rivalry, in part because machinery for handling woolen fibers was more difficult to devise. But gradually small fulling mills were established, new equipment contrived, and power adapted. New England's Middlesex Mills (Lowell) were producing the first power-woven wool fabric in 1840, but considerable time would elapse before any but coarse cloths or flannels could be produced to compete with the finer English goods.

A simple agrarian economy made relatively light demands on the metal industries, but with an increasing number of factories and the coming of steamboats and railroads, requirements were stepped up, especially for iron and steel, although the great demands would not come until after 1860. In 1810, according to the census of that year, 153 furnaces produced 53,908 tons of iron; fifty years later 987,559 tons were produced. Before 1840 most of this production was local and centered in New York, New Jersey, Pennsylvania, and Ohio, although bog iron deposits running from New England to Delaware were also worked. Cast iron and wrought iron were used most widely, since steel, though increasingly desirable for machinery, was expensive and difficult to produce. Cast iron, containing from 2 to 3 per cent carbon, was hard and brittle; wrought iron, with most of the carbon burned or pounded out, was softer, more malleable, and not so easily broken. Before 1840 the mode of manufacturing these products changed little, although Henry Cort's puddling process, first used in the 1780's, was slowly adopted and many of the impurities were burned out in furnaces while the molten metal was stirred with a long rod. Down to the early 1850's charcoal was the most common fuel used, partly because it was readily available and partly because it produced a more workable iron than did coal. Subsequently the industry would adopt on a widespread basis the Reverend Frederick W. Geissenhainer's patented means of smelting with anthracite, using a hot-air blast, but it can be argued that mass production of iron through the use of coal and coke was adopted only after the demands of railroads and industry created a need for iron of quantity, rather than of mere quality. Then came the first integrated iron mills.

The demand for wrought iron and for steel increased steadily, and cheap steel was on the horizon by the Civil War as a result of the discovery made independently by William Kelly in the United States and Henry Bessemer in England that cold air blown through molten iron would remove the carbon. Although litigation between the two tied up production for a number of years, the age of inexpensive steel was not far off.

Iron and steel production came to center more and more in Pennsylvania, but manufacture of iron goods was scattered and to some extent specialized. Except for the Tredegar Iron Works at Richmond, the South produced little; New England manufactured a variety of nuts, bolts, nails, wires, and metal buttons. The iron stove industry—in 1860 producing the most valuable single iron product—specialized early, its manufacturing concentrating mainly in New York, Philadelphia, Providence, Pittsburgh, Albany, and Cincinnati. The production of small items such as guns, clocks, cutlery, and tools centered largely in New York and New England, while Massachusetts produced the bulk of textile machinery, and almost all of the 110,000 sewing machines built in 1860 were made in Boston, Bridgeport, and New York. Philadelphia and Paterson, New Jersey, were the most important builders of locomotives.

As requirements for metals increased, local iron deposits were supplemented by vast new discoveries in the Marquette range on the north shore of Lake Michigan, which by 1857 were shipping ore at the rate of 1,000 tons a day. After the 1840's copper came in increasing amounts from the Keeweenaw Peninsula, west of the Marquette iron deposits: by 1860 this area was producing 60 per cent of the nation's requirements. The lead mines of the Galena-Dubuque region of Illinois and Iowa had been worked intermittently by Indians and by whites even prior to the Revolution, but reached their heyday in the period between 1835 and 1855, with the metal being used primarily for bullets and paint.

Hand in hand with and of primary importance to expanding manufactures was the growth of a machine-tool industry—an industry to produce the equipment which in turn produced consumer goods. In the manufacture of machine tools, the United States lagged behind Britain, but moved rapidly ahead in designing equipment to produce agricultural machinery and light goods such as wires, watches, and guns. British limitations on the export of textile machinery literally forced Americans to devise their own equipment. Americans, too, gradually began to adopt the idea of interchangeable parts. In 1789 Congress had appropriated funds for 50,000 guns during the undeclared war with France, and Eli Whitney, with a contract to produce 10,000 of these in fifteen months at $13.40 each, discarded the idea of a hand-made gun, each part manufactured individually, and set about making interchangeable parts by machine, a concept which had appeared earlier in France. Whitney's process moved too slowly and his delivery was after the war scare had vanished, but gradually the idea caught on. By the 1850's interchangeable parts were being used for locks, clocks, watches, sewing machines, and farm machinery. At the same time, better boring machines, the turret lathe, and the vernier caliper aided machine production.

Countless ingenious and talented inventors contributed technological improvements essential to the expansion of the factory system. Only three patents had been issued in 1790, and the annual number remained under a hundred until 1808, then grew to a peak of 1,067 in 1849, with an average of about 2,500 a year for the 1850–60 decade. The head of the patent office resigned in 1838 on the grounds that all inventions had been made and his work was complete. The year 1932 would see an all-time high of 56,856 patents issued. Technical improvement in production, either domestically inspired or borrowed from abroad, combined with cheaper transportation to spell lower prices: iron in 1860 was 50 per cent cheaper than in 1830; a clock in 1810 had cost from fifteen dollars up, while in 1860 it was on the market for as little as seventy-five cents. Usually mechanization led to the factory system, with the exception of the clothing industry, where the invention of the sewing machine in 1846 had the effect of stimulating home production, since women using the new machines could sew and perform the routine home tasks without difficulty.

The adaptation of power was part and parcel of the Industrial Revolution: the textile mills at Lowell, the flour mills along the route of the Erie Canal, the Baldwin locomotive works in Philadelphia, all depended upon power, either water or steam. Early water wheels were clumsy, expensive to construct, and slow in operation, but gradually they improved as dams were built to channel the flow and metal gears replaced wood. They might vary in type, from the simple float wheel set in the stream to run as fast as the current, to the more complex and effective overshot, undershot, or pitch-back wheels using elaborate tailraces. By 1850 the hydraulic turbine, even faster and more efficient, was beginning to come into comparatively widespread use.

Steam did not replace water power in manufacturing prior to the Civil War, though it made serious inroads. Of 421 manufacturing plants in New England in 1831, only about one tenth used steam, and these were mainly printing presses. Early steam engines were comparatively inefficient and expensive, even where coal was cheap. In 1839 steam power was four times as costly to produce as water power. Steam was used much more in transportation than in manufacturing and was more prominent in Western regions, where fluctuating water levels made water power less dependable than in the East. In 1859 42 per cent of the ironworks in the United States used steam power, while in the Ohio Valley, 72 per cent used it. Coal rapidly replaced wood as fuel, and as the cost of steam engines dropped and their efficiency increased, their use spread rapidly. By the time of the Civil War they were coming into their own, and perhaps the historian who underlined the importance of coal in industry during the middle era by using the term "Carboniferous Capitalism" had some basis for his emphasis. The use of power equipment greatly increased output per worker. According to Adam Smith, in his day ten men working together could produce 48,000 needles a day; by the middle of the nineteenth century one girl, operating four machines, could produce 600,000 a day.

The type and concentration of industry in early America was conditioned by several factors. New England was endowed with few raw materials, but had ample water power, an industrious, concentrated population, and an early capital market which was first built around foreign trade. The Middle Atlantic states had more varied resources, as well as capital and labor, and in addition easier access to the interior regions, an advantage in opening broader markets but a disadvantage by helping drain off labor to the agricultural West. Industries naturally followed shipping routes and available water power. Regional specialization developed, with the Northeast providing textiles, machinery, and finished metal goods, while the West specialized in lumber, the processing of food products, and agricultural machinery. The South sustained little manufacturing, partly because of the heavy competition of cotton for capital and labor, partly because of an inadequate transportation system.

Capital everywhere naturally gravitated to the most certain and profitable fields. Manufacturing had worthy rivals in agriculture, land speculation, turnpikes, canals, railroads, and commerce, both foreign and domestic. In the early years little European capital was available to manufacturing and direct state or federal aid was rare. Capital accumulation was private and came from a variety of sources. Small industrial plants commenced on a shoestring, with capital from craftsman or mercantile profits. Great merchant families like the Lowells and the Lawrences provided much capital for New England manufacturing and the linkage between commerce, manufacturing, transportation, and banking was significant. By 1850, fifteen Boston families controlled about 20 per cent of the nation's cotton spindlage, not to mention 30 per cent of Massachusetts' railroad mileage, 39 per cent of the state's insurance, and 40 per cent of Boston's banking. Capital accumulated in manufacturing increased from the $50 million estimated by the wholly inadequate census figures of 1820 to the $1 billion recorded in 1860. Reinvestment was undoubtedly the most important source; successful enterprisers plowed back their profits and built their holdings higher and higher. The Du Pont Company began operation in 1802 with $36,000; seventeen years later it had assets of $317,000, without an additional issue of stock. Frequently, profits from one field might be channeled into another. Earnings from Peter Cooper's glue and gelatin works provided the funds to found his great iron mill in Trenton.

But with few exceptions, working capital was short. Not infrequently manufacturers lacked distribution and marketing systems and this increased their capital need, for goods and capital both might be tied up for a considerable time until sale could be accomplished. It was not uncommon for early Connecticut clockmakers, for example, to halt production while they went out in the field to sell their ware.

Prior to the Civil War most manufacturing was done by partnerships and unincorporated joint-stock arrangements. It was possible to amass more capital in this way than individuals or family undertakings usually could, but these arrangements lacked permanence and individual members might be held liable for the concern's full debt, regardless of the extent of their own investment. The chartered corporation gave relief from these shortcomings in many instances, but only eight manufacturing concerns were chartered prior to 1800. In the next twenty-five years 557 more were authorized by eight states, their total nominal capital set at $72 million, but their actual capital was probably a third less. The number doubled in the decade of the 1850's, largely due to the relative ease of incorporation. Although New York adopted a seldom used general incorporation law in 1811, most chartering was done by special act of legislature. A Massachusetts law of 1830 established the principle of limited liability for corporate shareholders, and other states followed this example. But even though thirteen states had provided for general incorporation laws by 1861, charters were still most generally granted by special legislative acts, which tended to provide more liberal terms, often conveying monopolies on political favorites or granting special concessions. Early corporations were suspect and frequently damned as monopolies, as recipients of special privilege, and, ironically, as enemies of individual enterprise.

Everything considered, the revolution in industry had made an auspicious beginning by the time of the Civil War, but lagged behind the changes taking place in transportation. The real advances lay in the future. Yet the revolution in manufacturing was no doubt more fundamental than that in agriculture, where farming would remain essentially in small units, while in industry the coming of the factory system not only altered the size of the production unit, but brought entire new relationships, often substituting unskilled for skilled labor and divorcing the owner of machines from the workers who ran them.

IX

THE EARLY LABOR MOVEMENT

AMONG OTHER TRANSFORMATIONS, the factory system brought a
fundamental change in the relationship between capital and labor.
In the factory, the artisan no longer manufactured products from
his own shop for his own customers; now a middleman—the
merchant capitalist—entered the scene, and there followed increasing competition, with each merchant capitalist attempting to
undersell his rivals on expanding markets. Only by organizing in
shops for more efficiency and by reducing labor costs could price
competition be met. By hiring women, children, or unskilled
labor to do the simpler operations, labor costs could be cut and
a cheap, standardized product manufactured. But in the process
the skilled worker found his trade invaded by outsiders, his income reduced, and his standards of workmanship lowered. His
response was to organize in protest and to lament the passing of
his own trade into the hands of capitalists and speculators. Thus
it was not the factory laborer, but rather the skilled craftsman
who was the first to organize to protect his interest and improve
his condition.

Far back in the colonial era artisans had founded their own
craft associations, either for fraternal purposes or to facilitate the
establishment and maintenance of their apprenticeship systems.
Most of the early post-Revolutionary labor combinations came

136

into being to meet some particular grievance and dissolved when they had succeeded or had been defeated. The Philadelphia printers had struck as early as 1786. The Federal Society of Journeymen Cordwainers had a "turnout" in 1799 in an effort to raise wages for making boots: the organization's "tramping committee" stood watch in the shops to prevent "scab" or "dung" labor, and when the strike was won, the cordwainers demanded the discharge of those who had not co-operated.

But few of the early trade-unions enjoyed success. Employers reacted with their own organizations to combat and destroy them. They imported workers from other localities and generally had the backing of the courts in falling back upon British common law to declare labor associations conspiracies prejudicial to the public interest. The Philadelphia cordwainers, for example, were in 1806 found guilty "of a combination to raise their wages" and were disbanded. Four of the six separate conspiracy trials between 1806 and 1815 were decided against the workers. Strikes and associations continued, but most groups were too weak to make much impression or to survive any major depression: in the debacle of 1819, members forgot their problems of status and workmanship standards and concentrated on the struggle for mere economic survival.

Returning prosperity after 1822 brought a revival of union activity, now on a stronger, more aggressive basis. For the first time local craft unions began to unite into a few city-wide federations and to publish their own journals. At the same time many came to believe that prevailing abuses might be redressed only through political action, and in the late 1820's and early 1830's there appeared in some fifteen states a number of local workingmen's parties. Some, like that in Philadelphia, which elected enough candidates in 1829 to hold the balance of power, were reasonably successful at first, but were absorbed into the Jacksonian wing of the "Republican" Party and disappeared. Others, like the New York City Workingmen's Party, showed great promise in the beginning but were wrecked by extremist reformers with radical ideas. In this case, the party came to be dominated by such leaders as Thomas Skidmore, who called for cancellation of all debts and title to property and an equal division of all wealth;

Robert Dale Owen, who urged free public education and state guardianship of all children in national schools; and Frances Wright, the attractive and intelligent reformer whose ideas on education, religion, and marriage were so unconventional as to earn her the sobriquet "The Red Harlot of Infidelity" from her foes.

In general the workingmen's parties were interested in restoring status and, while concerned with questions of long hours, low pay, and poor working conditions, called for broader, more radical reforms. They urged free public schools, tax equality, separation of church and state, the direct election of public officials, and the elimination of chartered monopolies. Imprisonment for debt was decried, for the Boston Prison Discipline Society in 1829 estimated that there were 75,000 people in jail on debt charges. The parties sought mechanic's lien laws to protect the worker and assure him his wages; they urged revision of the state militia system, which took a man from his job for a time each year but favored the more wealthy who could afford to commute their service. Since many party supporters were anti-Bank, they supported Andrew Jackson, and while they tended to merge or vanish after 1832, they were modestly successful in making their ideas heard. Ohio eliminated imprisonment for debt in 1828 and by 1840 most other states had followed suit; Pennsylvania created a free, tax-supported public school system in 1834; mechanic's lien laws were widely adopted, and the basis of state militia service was modified as desired.

Following these political efforts, which at best were limited in accomplishment, the trade-union movement revived somewhat along British lines, with renewed emphasis on immediate gains in the form of higher wages and shorter working hours. In the period of prosperity between 1834 and 1837, the cost of living rose and real wages fell, and many new labor organizations were created, fifty-two in New York City alone.

This flurry of activity brought a rash of strikes in the mid-1830's, with an estimated 168 of them between 1833 and 1837. A Philadelphia general strike of 1835 won the ten-hour day, which Jackson also adopted in the naval yards. Ely Moore, head of the General Trades' Union of New York, was, with the aid of

Tammany Hall, elected to the national House of Representatives, the first spokesman of organized labor to sit in Congress. But employers gave way only when absolutely necessary and the courts repeatedly handed down opinions hostile to labor in the continuing struggle between "the house of Have and the house of Want," as George Bancroft called it. The panic and depression commencing in 1837 left in their wake a mass of tangled union wreckage. Wages were down from 30 to 50 per cent and hours were lengthened; union funds were depleted and federations collapsed. Once again men turned their full attention to economic survival, ignoring collective action for the time being.

By the early forties, another reform wave, reminiscent of the 1820's, was sweeping the country, touching labor as well as other segments of the economy. The utopian efforts of men such as Robert Dale Owen and John Humphrey Noyes and the land reform program of George Henry Evans attracted few working men, but did detract from more feasible reforms. A few producer's co-operatives and even fewer consumer's co-operatives achieved limited success before the movement tapered off. Under pressure, President Van Buren in 1840 had established a ten-hour day for federal workers on public projects and the movement spread, spearheaded by the Lowell girls and the Fall River mechanics. Beginning with New Hampshire in 1847, a number of states enacted ten-hour legislation, but the laws were practically unenforceable and useless.

Meanwhile, the trade-union movement, so hard hit in 1837, made a weak reappearance and once again gathered momentum in another era of rising prices (1843–47). By mid-century it had discarded many of the ideals of the humanitarian reformers and placed increasing emphasis on such day-to-day problems as higher pay, the closed shop, and the control of apprentices. The courts had tempered some of their earlier anti-union decisions. In the case of *Commonwealth v. Hunt* (1842), the Massachusetts Supreme Court held that labor unions per se were not illegal conspiracies if their methods were honorable and peaceful. As a precedent recognizing the right of union existence and operation within reasonable limits, this decision gave labor new hope.

But a recession of 1854 slowed up organization momentarily,

and the depression of 1857 again demolished much of what had been built up over the preceding twenty years, as workers concerned themselves with the bare struggle for survival and competed savagely instead of co-operating. Immigration also posed a general setback for unionization, although newcomers from England and Germany brought with them strong traditions of craft organization. The most numerous immigrants—the Irish—were unskilled, and like others, were willing to accept lower wages and a lower standard of living. Factory workers began to play more of a role in the union movement, but the craftsmen were still the innovators. And organized labor prior to the Civil War remained weak and ineffectual. The idea of an agrarian society was firmly rooted, and American farmers—the majority of the population— did not accept labor unions. The farmer wanted inflation; the wage earner, deflation. The farmer desired cheap manufactured goods, while the laborer wanted high wages, which could only add to the price of manufactured articles. Why should the farmer, who often worked from sunup to sundown, be sympathetic with the workers' drive for a ten-hour day? Probably even the bulk of the laboring class itself was apathetic toward union organization. Land was plentiful, class lines not clearly drawn, and labor generally conservative.

The factory system brought a new impersonality to economic life, for a corporation or a large unincorporated enterprise had neither a stern to be kicked, nor a soul to be damned, as the old saying went. "These artificial creatures," said an early report to the Massachusetts legislature, "unlike individual employers, are not chastened and restrained in their dealings with the laborers, by human sympathy and direct personal responsibility to conscience and to the bar of public opinion." Many early mill owners, it is true, prided themselves on their paternalism, and the great textile factories at Lowell and Waltham were often cited as model enterprises. To Anthony Trollope, Lowell was "the realization of a commercial utopia," where workers were "taken in, as it were, to a philanthropical manufacturing college, and then looked after and regulated more as girls and lads at a great seminary, than as hands by whose industry profit is to be made out of capital." Harriet Martineau, after a visit to Waltham in 1835, raptly described the "well-dressed young ladies" she saw at work there. Most were achieving financial independence under excellent circumstances; some had built houses with their own earnings, some had cleared mortgages from parental farms, others had educated a brother at college. In their small world, with a factory-built church, a lyceum similarly contributed, and an excellent library, they were healthy, happy, and contented. The popular "Song of the Manchester Factory Girl" presented life in the New Hampshire mills in the best possible light:

> O sing me a song of the Factory Girl
>   So merry and glad and free—
> The bloom on her cheeks, of health it speaks!—
>   O a happy creature is she!
>
> She tends the loom, she watches the spindle,
>   And cheerfully talketh away;
> Mid the din of wheels, how her bright eyes kindle!
>   And her bosom is ever gay.

Such descriptions were no doubt overdrawn. Orestes Brownson, writing in 1840 of the Lowell girls, showed the other side of the coin:

> The great mass wear out their health, spirits and morals without becoming one whit better off than when they commenced labor. The bills of morality in these factory villages are not striking, we admit, for the poor girls when they can toil no longer go home to die.

That conditions were not ideal was indicated in an impartial report tendered in 1849 to the American Medical Association by Dr. Josiah Curtis, after a visit to Lowell. "There is not a state's prison or house of correction in New England," he said, "where the hours of labor are so long, the hours for meals so short, and the ventilation so much neglected." The female operatives themselves complained of their "enslavement," and struck occasionally as they did in Lowell in 1834, without success. The "peaceable, industrious, hardworking men and women" of the same mills petitioned the Massachusetts legislature, asking relief from the evils already come upon us, by toiling from thirteen to fourteen hours per day, confined in unhealthy apartments, exposed to the poisonous contagion of air, vegetable, animal and mineral properties, debarred from proper *Physical* exercise, time for *Mental* discipline and *Mastication* cruelly limited; and thereby hastening us on through pain, disease and privation, down to a premature grave.

By this time the more attractive aspects of the Lowell-Waltham system were diminishing. Immigrants willing to work for lower pay were replacing the more refined girls; the flower boxes, literary magazines, and French studies were relics of the past; the early paternalists of the textile industry were leaving the scene to capitalists and absentee stockholders, who viewed their factory hands much as did one Fall River owner:

I regard my work-people just as I regard my machinery. So long as they can do my work for what I choose to pay them, I keep them, getting out of them all I can. What they do or how they fare outside my walls, I don't know nor do I consider it my business to know.

Factory working hours might range from eleven to fifteen, depending upon the length of the daylight hours. Wages, both money and real, are difficult to determine due to a lack of information for the pre-1860 period and because of many qualifications that must be made, but they were generally low. The employment of women and children added to the family's income, but at the same time were factors in depressing wages. Rhode Island mill operators advertised for entire families, and often only the employment of several members of a family assured survival. In 1820, 45 per cent of the workers in the Massachusetts cotton mills and 55 per cent of those in Rhode Island were children; by 1831 the percentages had dropped to 21 and 41 respectively. In the eyes of many, child labor was a positive good: idleness was ungodly; by working, children would not only contribute to the family livelihood, but would also receive a moral and vocational education and grow up industrious and prepared to meet the realistic problems of life. Veterans of the child labor force sometimes assumed responsible positions at an early age. One fifteen-year-old boy set up and superintended a mill in Rhode Island, while the superintendent of the Pawtucket Thread Company in 1826 was only nineteen years old, but had nearly a dozen years of experience behind him.

As time passed, female employees declined proportionately. In the early 1830's, women had made up nearly four fifths of the Massachusetts mill force and in 1860 still provided 60 per cent of the labor in such fields as cotton textiles, men's clothing, and boots and shoes, but at this time accounted for only about 20 per cent of the total factory labor supply. With children, they were invariably paid on a lower scale than men. A breakdown of wages reported by a New Jersey manufacturer in 1828 showed male employees receiving $3.90 a week, women, $2.375, and children (under fourteen), $1.375.

Real wages rose 39 per cent and money wages 23 per cent between 1820 and 1860, while the cost of living dipped slightly. But real wages failed to rise as rapidly as production and skilled workers usually benefitted less than unskilled ones. Real wages were further lowered when workers were forced to accept depreciated paper money or payment in kind or in orders requiring purchase from company stores. How much it cost an average family to live depended upon local conditions and the standard of living involved. In 1851 Horace Greeley's New York *Tribune* published a minimum budget for a family of five which totaled $10.37 a week at a time when Pennsylvania coal miners were receiving under $7.00 a week and textile operators in Massachusetts $2.50. Obviously the level of living in some of the squalid industrial towns was no better than among the New York poor, where six people per room was average and where, according to the 1850 census, 18,500 families lived in 8,141 cellars.

While we know little of non-industrial workers of the pre-Civil War era—domestic help, farm hands, manual laborers, teamsters, and countless others not so directly affected by the coming of the factory system—it was the skilled craftsman particularly, and to a much lesser extent a few of the factory workers, who first reacted to changing conditions by attempting to maintain or better their positions through organization. Such a narrow-based effort brought relatively few reforms but set the stage for broader, more pervasive movements as the budding industrial society unfolded.

X

A TRANSITIONAL WAR

LONG BEFORE 1861, while the nation was in a state of economic flux, the seeds were being sown for the mighty sectional struggle which momentarily tore the Union asunder, pitted brother against brother in four years of bloody fighting, and left behind scars which even time has not fully healed. Because he understands too little of human behavior and lacks standards by which to measure the significance of individual contributing factors, the historian will never know with certainty and preciseness exactly why this great holocaust came about. Recognizing multiple causation, he must determine his emphasis according to the examination of fragmentary evidence and the dictates of his conscience.

Among other interpretations—state rights versus nationalism, slavery as a moral issue, majority rule and minority rights, the work of extremist agitators, and blundering politicians, for example—that of economic sectionalism has found wide acceptance, especially as developed by Louis Hacker and by Charles and Mary Beard. No observer, impartial or otherwise, could have viewed the United States in the mid-nineteenth century without recognizing greatly divergent economic patterns between the North and the South. Both regions were predominantly agricultural, but Northern agriculture was more diversified, and in the North a growing emphasis was being placed on an industry and commerce based on a system of free wage labor. The Southern economy was based on a single staple crop, to the neglect of transportation, industry, and finance. The South, says one writer, was, economically speaking, "a fabric of cotton." "Cotton was map-maker, trouble-maker, history-maker."

Southerners had long believed themselves exploited by the North, particularly the Northeast, which dominated manufacturing, shipping, and credit. The indictment of Hinton R. Helper in his book *The Impending Crisis* was not palatable to the South, but it accurately pointed up that section's dependence by 1857:

> In one way or another we are more or less subservient to the North every day of our lives. In infancy we are swaddled in Northern muslin; in childhood we are humored with Northern gewgaws; in youth we are instructed out of Northern books; at the age of maturity we sow our "wild oats" on Northern soil; in middle life we exhaust our wealth, energies and talents in the dishonorable vocation of entailing our dependence on our children and on our children's children, and, to the neglect of our interests and the interests of those around us, in giving aid and succor to every department of Northern power; in the decline of life we remedy our eye-sight with Northern spectacles, and support our infirmities with Northern canes; in old age we are drugged with Northern physic; and, finally, when we die, our inanimate bodies, shrouded in Northern cambric, are stretched upon the bier, borne to the grave in a Northern carriage, entombed with a Northern spade, and memorized with a Northern slab!

Each section had decided economic interests to protect through government. A consumer of imported manufactured goods, the South, after cotton culture made serious inroads, traditionally opposed the tariff, federally financed internal improvements, a homestead bill, and a Pacific railroad except by a Southern route. For years, despite the dynamic expansion of the North and her obvious victory in the battle of the census returns, Southern politicians, by give and take and by combination with Western agrarians, had exerted strong influence in the nation's capital. Gradually, however, North-South ties by water would be superseded by East-West links—turnpikes, canals, and finally railroads— binding the important Northwestern states closely to the industrial, commercial Northeast. There would come a time, as in the election of 1860, when political parties would take on a sectional flavor, and this only increased the gnawing fear of Southerners that Northern economic interests were free to stifle the South.

Southerners had seen their power declining, their institutions under attack, and their interests in jeopardy much earlier and had fallen back on various devices in efforts to maintain a political balance—a "strict" construction of the Constitution and a vigorous defense of states' rights—even to the extreme of nullification. Sectional differences had brought crisis after crisis, and apart from the effort of South Carolina to nullify the tariff in 1832, they revolved around the question of slavery.

Slavery, of course, was an integral part of the Southern agricultural system and was but one facet of fundamental economic and social differences between North and South. Missouri's petition for admission as a slave state in 1819 first made the expansion of slavery a major issue, for it involved the political equilibrium in the Senate. The Compromise which settled it was viewed by Jefferson as "a reprieve only, not a final sentence," and the acquiring of additional territory in the Mexican War threatened to disrupt the arrangement until adjusted by the Compromise of 1850. Meanwhile, one of the moral reform movements sweeping the North in the thirties, abolitionism, became a significant political force and its vigorous indictment of the South's peculiar institution pushed Southern leaders to a defense of slavery as a "positive good" and to violence against its critics. Moderates arranged the sectional adjustments in 1820, 1833, and 1850, but after each settlement another crisis soon developed. The final one began in 1854 with the Kansas-Nebraska Act, which reopened the question of slavery extension in those two territories. Out of it came bloodshed in Kansas, the formation of the Republican Party, and the election of Abraham Lincoln in 1860 on a platform committed to oppose the extension of slavery, favoring a higher tariff, internal improvements, and a homestead law. Lincoln's election was the signal for secession by the Deep South and with opponents of compromise in control in both sections, war came in April, 1861.

Walter Millis has called the Civil War a "transitional war," a war which came at a time when industrialism was beginning to transform the economy of the North; a war which for the first time in American history required a major commitment of resources for a sustained period of time; a war in which strategy was changed somewhat by new devices, especially railroads, telegraphs, ironclad steamers, and centralized procurement of troops by conscription.

In this greatest of all American wars up to 1941, the North at the outset held obvious advantages. Her twenty-three states outnumbered the eleven Confederate states in population, 22 million to 9 million; she had 66 per cent of the railroad mileage, 81 per cent of the factories, and 75 per cent of the wealth. Most of the navy and merchant marine was in the hands of the Union at the war's beginning, enabling a blockade, which though never fully effective, did sorely limit Southern commerce abroad. The North outclassed the South not only in industry, transportation, and population, but also in available arms and equipment, vital raw materials, financial resources, and in productive capacity.

The cost of a large-scale war over a four-year period was staggering. Actual expenditures, property ruined or destroyed, and the destruction of slavery ran into billions of dollars. Even the direct expense of prosecuting the war, huge by nineteenth century standards, would require the utmost ingenuity to sustain. Both governments used variations of the same devices—taxation, loans, and paper money—to finance their operations. Those of the North are of more importance, not only because they were more successful, but because some of them would be retained as part of the nation's fiscal structure long after the cannon were silent.

Roughly 20 per cent of the direct war cost of the Union was met by taxation, which, including the tariff, brought in some $667 million. With the Southerners withdrawn from Congress, the tariff was boosted upward to an average levy of around 47 per cent; such laws, poorly drawn without much thought, would for thirty years remain the basis of the American protective system. In addition, a series of war taxes on manufacturing, sales, stamps, and occupations was used, along with an income tax, moderate at first, but increasing by the war's end to 5 per cent on incomes between $600 and $5000 and 10 per cent on those above that. Borrowing brought in over three times as much revenue for the North as all other sources. As a result of a number of loans bearing at least five different rates of interest and maturing at nineteen different times, the national debt by 1866 totaled $2.8 billion. Most of these loans were floated through private banking agents, the best known of which was Jay Cooke, who mass-financed $400 million worth of government bonds, at no mean profit to himself.

Add to this the issuance of paper money. Beginning in 1862, when tax receipts were slow and bonds were not selling, the federal government authorized the issue of $150 million in paper greenbacks based solely on "the credit of the United States" and considered legal tender for all debts except the tariff and the interest on government bonds. Subsequently the total rose to $450 million, most of which was still outstanding at the war's end. In addition, some $20 million of fractional currency was issued. Unbacked paper was an easy answer to financing but its value declined, sometimes as low as twenty-nine cents on the dollar, and the corresponding inflation raised the cost of living. Butter went from twenty cents a pound early in 1860 to fifty-five cents early in 1865; coal doubled in price; coffee tripled. Wages did not keep pace with rising prices, and the common man suffered and bore part of the cost of the war effort through depreciated currency. In addition, after the passage of the National Banking Act of 1863, some national bank notes were in circulation, but these were unimportant to the war effort, although the National Banking Act itself would be the bulwark of the banking structure until 1913.

The Confederacy also utilized taxation, loans, and the issue of paper money. She attempted, quite unsuccessfully, an export tax on cotton, but levied no tariff on imports. She put a direct tax on property and gave the individual states the option of paying a stipulated sum to the central government and raising the funds as they saw fit. By 1863, license fees and an income tax were included and soon a tax in kind was put on agricultural products. But the Southern tax program started late, the section's economy was in turmoil, administration was hampered by states' rights sentiment, with the result that taxation brought in relatively little—a total of only $207 million.

Not much more successful was the Confederacy's attempts to obtain loans, partly because the government issued bonds in such huge amounts that faith in the ability to repay was shaken. Unique, but not effective, were the so-called produce loans, with subscribers depositing certain commodities with the government in exchange for bonds. Equally disappointing were the efforts to borrow abroad by pledging cotton as security for future delivery. Small loans totaling about $2.5 million were obtained from the Erlangers in France, but loans in general were disillusioning.

Paper money actually financed most of the Southern war effort. How much was issued even the Confederate government did not know: estimates run to $1 billion and sometimes to $2 billion. Depreciation was prompt and complete as prices shot skyward. Southern currency was worth two cents on the dollar at the end of the war and scarce goods brought fabulous prices: salt went from eighty cents a bushel in 1861 to $30 by the end of 1862; a drink of whiskey cost $5 in 1864; and by early 1865 flour brought $1,200 a barrel in paper money. Federal greenbacks, brought in by invading Union soldiers, circulated at a much higher value in the South than did Confederate currency.

Economically the North fared much better than the South, although struck by a sharp recession in 1861–62 because of shaky bank reserves and the general uncertainties. But after the initial setback, the Northern economy expanded as its resources were mobilized for war. Through the greater use of machinery agricultural production increased, the Northern wheat crop of 1863 totaling 191 million bushels as compared with 142 million in 1859. Wheat exports in 1862 and 1863 were triple the value of that of any prewar year, and domestic wool production more than doubled between 1860 and 1865. The war accentuated the Northern trend toward commercial agriculture, while in the South, by cutting off the markets for staples, it resulted in a move in the opposite direction, toward self-sufficiency in foodstuffs.

Northern industries for the most part continued to expand, although some, like the textile manufacturers, were hurt. Freight haulage reached new heights, factory expansion featured laborsaving machinery, and war industries produced more than one millionaire and lay the basis for more than one post-Appomattox business empire. However, as Thomas Cochran points out, the Civil War probably did not give a real fillip to industrial growth; that growth was well under way prior to the conflict and statistical evidence seems to indicate that rate of growth was not as great during the war as in the periods before and after.

The Confederacy fared less well economically. Lacking the resources, the capital, and the skilled technicians for industrial production, the South encountered extreme difficulty in gearing its agricultural economy to a war effort. The government itself took over production of some essentials such as munitions, salt, and whiskey, but the Southern story in general was one of shortage, sacrifice, and suffering. The Confederacy had counted upon England's need for cotton to break the blockade for that commodity, but British textile manufacturers had an oversupply of cotton at the war's outset, and by the time the shortage was felt, the war involved the larger question of freeing the slaves, some cotton was trickling through from the North, a few new sources were opening up, and the outcome was already apparent. Besides, bad wheat crops from 1860 to 1862 had forced England to import heavily from the North, so that King Cotton diplomacy simply collapsed.

> They smoke me with powder and stain me with blood,
> And smear me all over with water and mud.
> I am therefore determined to vacate the field.
> To some other monarch my kingdom I yield,
> And proclaim to the world, from this stone by the oak,
> That *Cotton is fallen and the King is "flat broke."*

XI

THE RAILROAD ERA

NOT INAPPROPRIATELY, the half century between the Civil War and World War I is often referred to as the Railroad Era. The railroad greatly overshadowed all other means of internal transportation in this period and it was the key—at once both cause and effect—to many of the remarkable changes that took place in the economy. It speeded up distribution and contributed to specialization in both manufacturing and agriculture, a transformation which made a division of labor easier; it increased the mobility of labor and capital and created new investment outlets; it permitted a rapid expansion of the farmers' west in the era up to 1890, and at the same time, because of international transportation links, it put the farmer into global competition; because it made possible competition between products from different regions, it contributed to industrial efforts to reduce operating costs and to increase productivity, sending real wages and the general standard of living upward; it contributed also to a growing tendency toward urbanization. Truly, the economy was said to have been undergoing "railroadization."

Several main trends were apparent. The rail network expanded greatly, creating a great national system. At the same time, important technological advances were being made, and new modes of financing were being used, some of which were questionable, to

151

say the least. Combination and consolidation characterized the industry, and, in reaction, regulation came piecemeal, first at the state, then at the national level.

Railroad mileage more than tripled between 1860 and 1880 and doubled in the next twenty years, growing from slightly over 35,000 (mostly east of the Mississippi) in 1865, to 387,208 miles by World War I—greater than all of Europe combined. Between 1865 and the panic of 1873, some 30,000 miles were built, much of it in the East and on the Lake Plains. Building picked up again slowly, with a great deal of promotional construction, until a recession caused a slump in 1884. Construction boomed again by the late 1880's and an all-time high of 12,876 miles was added in 1887. The depression of 1893, labeled a "railroad panic" by some economists, brought a sharp cutback, with only a moderate rate of expansion thereafter. Indeed, the record high for railroads in receivership came between 1893 and 1898, when almost 200 railroads, involving 67,000 miles of line, went into receiver's hands, among them the Baltimore and Ohio, the Erie, the Union Pacific and the Northern Pacific. By World War I roughly half the trackage would be west of the Mississippi, although the proportion of mileage to population was heaviest in Eastern states—New Jersey, Massachusetts, Pennsylvania, Ohio, Illinois, and Indiana, in that order. More freight and more passengers were also carried in the East, and by the turn of the century the framework of the national rail system was well established; soon it would be filled out and consolidated.

The volume of rail traffic also expanded and investments increased sharply. Between 1882 and 1914 the number of passengers carried increased 357 per cent, the amount of freight rose seven times, and the number of locomotives more than tripled. Railroad investments expanded fourfold between 1876 and 1914, when they made up about one tenth of the nation's total wealth. At the same times, rates were dropping. Although they rose in the 1860–65 period, they declined precipitously in the mid-seventies, then more gradually to the turn of the century when they tended to level off.

Interest in the 1860's centered upon a transcontinental line. The idea of a railroad to the Pacific went back to the 1840's, when

RAILROAD MILEAGE, EQUIPMENT, FREIGHT, AND PASSENGER SERVICE,
1865–1914*

Year	Mileage	Number of locomotives	Freight (million ton miles)	Passengers carried (1,000)
1865	35,085	—	—	—
1870	52,922	—	—	—
1875	74,096	—	—	—
1880	115,647	17,949	—	—
1885	160,506	25,662	—	351,428
1890	208,152	31,812	76.21	520,439
1895	233,276	35,699	85.23	507,421
1900	258,784	37,663	141.60	576,831
1905	306,797	48,357	186.46	738,835
1910	351,767	60,019	255.02	971,683
1914	387,208	67,012	288.64	1,063,249

* *Historical Statistics of the United States, Colonial Times to 1957,*
pp. 427, 428, 430, 431.

Asa Whitney, a New Yorker interested in the China trade, had
sought to convince Congress of the desirability of such an enterprise. Five government surveys between 1853 and 1855 had
investigated possible routes running from the Missouri River in the
North to the thirty-second parallel in the South, and the Kansas-
Nebraska Act had been passed in 1854, granting the idea of
popular sovereignty in exchange for the more central route. But
sectional differences prevented Congressional action authorizing
the construction of any line until 1862, after the South had
withdrawn.

In that year Congress chartered the Union Pacific Railroad
Company to build westward from Omaha and the Central Pacific
Railroad Company to build eastward from Sacramento. Both
were to receive liberal land grants and direct loans. The war
hampered construction, but activity picked up smartly after 1866.
Gangs of sweating, cursing Irishmen and Civil War veterans built
the Union Pacific with one hand and fought off hostile Indians
with the other. A Philadelphia editor described the actual process
of track laying as he witnessed it in 1868:

Track-laying on the Union Pacific is a science. . . . A light car,
drawn by a single horse, gallops up to the front with its load of

rails. Two men seize the end of the rail and start forward, the rest of the gang taking hold by twos, until it is clear of the car. They come forward at a run. At the word of command the rail is dropped in its place, right side up with care, while the same process goes on at the other side of the car. Less than thirty seconds to a rail for each gang, and so four rails go down to the minute! . . . The moment the car is empty it is tipped over on the side of the track to let the next loaded car pass it, and then it is tipped back again, and it is a sight to see it go flying back for another load, propelled by a horse at full gallop at the end of sixty or eighty feet of rope, ridden by a young Jehu, who drives furiously. Close behind the first gang come the gaugers, spikers, and bolters, and a lively time they make of it. It is a grand Anvil Chorus that those sturdy sledges are playing across the plains. It is in triple time, three strokes to a spike. There are ten spikes to a rail, four hundred rails to a mile, eighteen hundred miles to San Francisco. . . . Twenty-one million times are those sledges to be swung— twenty-one million times are they to come down with their sharp punctuation, before the great work of modern America is complete!

Actually, those who built the Union Pacific had the easier part of the task. The level Platte Valley in Nebraska made construction simple—except for the scarcity of timber for crossties (2,630 per mile of track); even crossing the Rockies was not difficult compared with the task of crossing the Sierra Nevadas with their core of granite and their high passes covered with forty to fifty feet of snow in the winter. Here the Central Pacific force of pig-tailed Chinese coolies ("They built the great wall of China, didn't they?") inched their way forward, hand-blasting tunnels, laying track under long snowsheds ("railroading in a barn," the old-timers called it), and pushed out across the hot deserts of Nevada and Utah to meet the Union Pacific at Promontory Point, May 10, 1869. There, 1,086 miles west of the Missouri River and 680 miles east of Sacramento, East and West were wedded with steel bands and the entire nation celebrated.

With the trail thus blazed, four other transcontinentals would be completed before the end of the century. The Northern Pacific, defunct when Jay Cooke failed in 1873 but revived under Henry Villard, was pushed to completion between Lake Superior and Puget Sound in 1883. The next year, the Southern Pacific linked

New Orleans with San Francisco, and the Atchison, Topeka and Santa Fe connected Kansas City and Los Angeles. Nine years later, one-eyed James J. Hill completed his Great Northern, without federal land subsidy, between Duluth and Seattle, over a route generally north of his rival, the Northern Pacific.

Less spectacular, perhaps, but an important part of what was happening, was expansion east of the Mississippi, where trunk lines were being built and feeders and spurs being run to tap new resources and industries. Cities and states vied vigorously to attract railroads and the railroads themselves drove competing lines into growing urban areas. Especially did they seek entrance into New York City in the East and Chicago or St. Louis in the West: by 1875 four major lines connected the Atlantic Coast with Chicago—the New York Central, the Pennsylvania, the Baltimore and Ohio, and the Grand Trunk. Many a line was built as a promotional or speculative venture; more than one was run paralleling another for its nuisance value and sale to its competitor. At the same time, empires were being built and numerous piecemeal lines integrated into unified systems. The South was slow in responding to the railroad era, but after the early 1880's, using Northern capital, its construction advanced rapidly.

The great expansion of construction created large new markets for iron and steel and the expansion of these industries in turn helped other facets of the economy—coal, iron ore, Great Lakes shipping, and rolling stock. More manpower and more capital went into railroad building and operation after the Civil War than into any other single industry, although the rate of growth leveled off somewhat in the latter part of the century. The railroad industry acted in this era much as the automotive industry would in the twentieth century. A sharp setback to the industry, a drop in construction, might have implications for a broad sector of the economy.

In the expansion and the creation of an integrated network of railroads, advances in technology and in operational methods played a significant part. Locomotives and rolling stock improved and grew heavier and more substantial: steel replaced iron in locomotive construction, boilers were larger, frames longer, driving wheels more numerous. The four driving wheels of the Civil War era gave way to the six commonly used in passenger service and eight or ten for freight. The average axle load of the new coal-burning expansion-cylinder locomotives increased from 20,000 pounds in 1868 to about 70,000 by the 1920's, and pulling power multiplied ten times over. The sleeping car and the refrigerator car came into their own, and the steel frame, then the all-steel body, made for greater durability and safety. Coal cars of the 1870's were of twelve-ton capacity; by 1905, fifty tons was common, and subsequent models held one hundred tons.

Speed accelerated accordingly. In 1893 the New York Central's famous engine "999" hit 112 miles per hour, a record which by 1905 had been raised to 127 miles per hour. Faster, heavier trains called for better rails and roadbeds and for additional safety devices. Block signals came into use in the early seventies; the automatic coupler (1871) speeded up operation while reducing risk; automatic air brakes, perfected by George Westinghouse through a series of patents between 1868 and 1907, were another safety factor without which the long trains of the era could not have been handled.

Uniformity of gauges was slow in coming. There were still at least twenty-three different gauges in 1871, but the standard width—4 feet, 8½ inches—predominated. Gradually abandoning efforts to use hoists, double tracks, or variable wheels, most companies adopted the standard width in the 1880's. Unified procedures for handling bills of lading were added, and plans worked out for the exchange of rolling stock on a per diem basis. In 1883 the establishment of four separate time belts abolished nearly one hundred different local times, made for a standard time system, and paved the way for regularized time tables. Rate and traffic agreements were made, sometimes the result of consolidation, sometimes independently.

Many of the common techniques for financing railroads had been worked out before the Civil War. Now they were refined, new twists added, and old ones sometimes perverted. Capital came from various sources, governmental and private. In addition to indirect aid in the form of the remission of the tariff on imported rails until the domestic steel industry could meet demands, the federal government gave a direct subsidy in the form of land grants. The Union Pacific and the Central Pacific had originally received ten sections of land for each mile of track built and the amount was later doubled. In addition, these two concerns received government loans—$48,000 a mile in mountain terrain, $32,000 in hilly, $16,000 in flat. Most Western railroads received land grants until the practice was discontinued in 1871, and after forfeitures were counted, about 137 million acres—an area larger than France or Germany—passed into railroad hands. Individual states added another 55 million acres.

Since many of the Western lines ran from "nowhere in particular to no place at all," into thinly populated country ahead of both civilization and demand, they were either built for the profit to be made from promotion or construction or their backers believed that demand could be created. Thus most of the land-grant railroads, from the Illinois Central on, maintained land departments which attempted to settle farmers along their route and were actively engaged in recruiting European immigrants.

Along with their land grants, states often paid survey expenses, provided tax exemptions, and subscribed to railroad stock. Towns and counties did likewise, frequently floating bond issues to support railroad securities or even donating land or money so as not to be bypassed, as was Ft. Benton, Montana, when it refused to contribute to Hill's Great Northern. Of the utmost importance, both in magnitude and in the provision of working capital, were private investments, both domestic and foreign. These might be made indirectly through the purchase of government bond issues on behalf of railroads, or directly through the purchase of railway securities themselves. Statistics indicate that American railroad capital stock and bonded indebtedness totaled $1.1 billion in 1860, had risen to $10.1 billion by 1890, and twice that by 1914, although because of the prevalence of stock watering and the sale of securities at discount, the actual investment was undoubtedly less. The great majority of stock was in American hands: foreign ownership, mainly German and English, ran from about 12 per cent of American rail securities outstanding at the time of the Civil War to approximately 25 per cent for the 1900–1910 era.

In many instances, financing was notoriously unsound. A common practice was to employ separate concerns, owned and controlled by railroad directors, to handle construction contracts, with the actual work passed on to legitimate builders after extracting a large profit. Thus the Credit Mobilier, the most infamous example, made an estimated $40 to $50 million in building the Union Pacific line. Nor was it uncommon for railroad directors to control the companies that maintained the lines, built and owned bridges and ferries, or sold coal and other supplies.

Stock watering was a common pastime. Large amounts of stock were sold without any increase in physical plant and valuation, often leaving legitimate investors with a shoddily built road—the proverbial two streaks of rust and a right of way—with little chance of dividends because of a huge overcapitalization. Too frequently "plungers" and looters manipulated railroad stock to their own advantage and cast off the broken hulk when through. Typical of this group in the 1860's and 1870's was the unlikely triumvirate of Daniel Drew, Jay Gould, and James Fisk. Bucolic "Uncle Daniel" Drew, for many years treasurer of the Erie Railroad and a leading bear on Wall Street, was described by Charles Francis Adams, Jr., as "Shrewd, unscrupulous, and very illiterate —a strange combination of superstition and faithlessness, of daring and timidity." But he was successful.

> He toiled not, neither did he spin,
> But how he raked the dollars in!*

Diminutive Jay Gould was "an uncommonly fine and unscrupulous intriguer," skilled in stock manipulation and indifferent to public opinion. The flamboyant "Jubilee Jim" Fisk, said Adams, was "not yet forty years of age and had the instincts of fourteen." All three men played fast and loose with the Erie, to its detriment. Gould and Fisk managed to block Cornelius Vanderbilt in his drive to acquire control of the road, mainly by printing an endless run of stock which prevented the Commodore from acquiring a controlling interest. At the end of the fight, the Erie was left pillaged and decrepit. Its common stock never paid an earned dividend until World War II.

Men like Drew, Gould, and Fisk were primarily destroyers.

* From "Clipper Ships and Captains" by Stephen Vincent Benét.

By contrast, men like James J. Hill, William H. Vanderbilt, and Edward H. Harriman built empires through conservative financing, improved service, and increased physical valuation and left behind them as monuments railroad systems in good operating condition. Yet they were men who stood solidly behind Vanderbilt's classic and oft-quoted "public be damned" attitude. "The railroads are not run for the benefit of the dear public," said Vanderbilt in 1882. "That cry is all nonsense. They were built for men who invest their money and expect to get a fair percentage on the same." Toward this end some flexibility of conscience was permitted in an era of business standards and social responsibility lax by modern criteria. Railroad leaders learned of necessity to protect themselves, even if this meant the judicious issue of free passes to public men, the occasional bribing of juries or legislatures, and the maintenance of powerful lobbies.

Competition was fierce at times and legitimate railroad operators had their hands full. Investments in road and terminal facilities were large and fixed; operating expenses did not increase in proportion to the traffic carried. It cost very little more to run a full train than one half-full and the greater the traffic the lower the per unit fixed cost. Hence bitter rate wars ensued as railroads sought to capture business from their rivals. During a freight rate war in the early 1870's, hauling charges on grain between Chicago and New York fell from sixty cents a hundredweight in December, 1873, to thirty cents by March, 1875. In a passenger rate war in 1887 fares on the Santa Fe Railroad reportedly fell from $100 to $8 between Kansas City and Los Angeles before being resolved. In such cases, either one competitor would be driven out or a truce would be arranged, with competition disappearing in either event. When rate agreements failed, pools were common until forbidden: competing railroads might agree on noncompetitive rates; they might divide business on a percentage or geographic basis, or perhaps according to the type of trade. Under pressure, they granted rebates to large shippers in competitive areas and sought to make up the difference by boosting rates in regions where no competition existed.

One result of competition was the absorption of weaker companies and the formation of large rail empires. Largely at the insistence of his son William, Cornelius Vanderbilt consolidated several small lines in New York, linked them to the New York Central, bought out some of his competitors, and by the time of his death had pushed the line all the way to Chicago, amassing a fortune of $100 million in the process. Not only that, the Vanderbilts had vastly upgraded the nearly one thousand miles of route with heavy rails and new rolling stock, and their improved service reduced running time by half. By 1915, the system would own and operate nearly 14,500 miles of track. After 1900, empires were frequently built through control of already existing systems. Edward H. Harriman, one of the great railroad geniuses, put together the Illinois Central, the Union Pacific, and the Southern Pacific to form a vast working rectangle touching Chicago, New Orleans, San Diego, and Portland, Oregon.

In the great era of bankruptcy and reorganization (1893–98) stronger lines sometimes invested in weaker ones and brought them under their control. The House of Morgan often marketed securities for reorganized concerns, and in order to insure wise use of the money to be raised, put a man on the board of directors or managed a voting trust which gave an even stronger voice over a period of years. Morgan and Company also acquired stock outright in a number of rail concerns. By 1906 the Pennsylvania Railroad, which it controlled, owned nearly one half of the preferred and over one third of the common stock of the Baltimore and Ohio, and Morgan men sat on both boards.

Railroad consolidation and other methods of reducing competition elicited little sympathy from farmers and small businessmen, who took the lead in the sixties and seventies in demanding regulation in the public interest. Western and Middle Western farmers especially believed, and with good cause, that the railroads, like other middlemen, were bleeding them white. Freight rates rose progressively in Western regions, increasing in 1877 from ninety-five cents a ton-mile east of Chicago to $1.32 between Chicago and the Missouri River, and to $4.80 beyond. That traffic moved one direction at harvest time and that side traffic was lacking farther west did not convince the farmer. Let the railroads explain why lines paralleling the Great Lakes raised their rates in winter when water competition was still. Let them explain why Dakota farmers were charged for shipping their wheat all the way to Chicago, though it went only to the mills in St. Paul, four hundred miles short of the Windy City. What about the grain elevator monopolies held by railroads in many areas and the unwillingness to load railroad cars directly or to run spurs to competing elevators? Farmers and small businessmen both complained about special tax concessions granted on railroad property, and they were incensed at higher rates charged between intermediate points where there was no competition than between large cities, where several lines competed. They resented pools and were not strong enough to pressure rebates from the carriers. Meanwhile, large businesses received preferential rates. The New York legislature in 1880 found that in an eighteen month period Standard Oil had received rebates totaling $10 million, the amount based in part on the company's own shipments and in part on those of its rivals.

Farmers and small businessmen, therefore, headed the drive to bring some semblance of government regulation to the railroad industry, and were soon joined by such groups as the Civil Service League and the Anti-Monopoly League in working for better government and in linking railroads to political corruption. Even railroad management itself was not averse to some form of regulation, in part to forestall more effective controls, in part in the hope of eliminating rebates and rate wars, and at the same time improving public relations.

The first efforts at regulation came with the Granger laws in a number of Midwestern states late in the 1860's and early in the 1870's, setting maximum rates to be charged by railroads, grain elevators, and warehouses on the grounds that such enterprises were essentially public in nature. The carriers challenged the laws in the courts, arguing that the exclusive power to regulate commerce was vested in Congress and that the states in limiting rates were depriving a person (i.e., corporation) "of life, liberty, or property without due process of law," in violation of the Fourteenth Amendment. In 1877 the Supreme Court held in the case of *Munn v. Illinois* that when property was used in a certain way it became cloaked with the public interest, subject to regulation for the common good. Rate-fixing was thus legal, but was a legislative, rather than a judicial function, and in the absence of Congressional action, a state might exercise its powers over interstate commerce. However, a decade or so later, in the Wabash case and others, the Supreme Court held that regulation involving transit of goods across state lines could only be done by federal and not state action.

Even before this, because state regulatory laws proved useless, numerous proposals had been introduced in Congress for national action, but none was forthcoming until 1887, after the Wabash decision and publication of the Cullum Report (1886) showed a clear need for restraints and prompted the passage of the Interstate Commerce Act. This law forbade rebates, pooling agreements, and discriminatory charges. Rates must be "just and reasonable," and must be published in advance with written notice of increases. The Interstate Commerce Commission was created, but was granted only vague, limited powers, with little or no enforcement authority. Enforcement, in effect, lay in the hands of the courts, which further weakened the Commission by its decisions, denying it the power to set rates, and in the years between 1897 and 1906 deciding sixteen out of seventeen cases against it. Still, despite the vagueness of its wording and the damaging interpretations of the courts, the Interstate Commerce Act was important as a beginning—a foundation upon which subsequent regulatory legislation could be built as the climate of opinion changed in the twentieth century.

A reform-conscious public soon demanded stronger regulation and progressive leaders and their supporters in Congress acted to tighten the laws. Under pressure from Theodore Roosevelt, the Elkins Anti-Rebate Act of 1903 was written into the statute books, providing heavy fines not only for the railroads that gave rebates, but also for shippers who accepted them. The law was applied with some vigor: Judge Kenesaw Mountain Landis fined Standard Oil over $29 million on 1,462 counts in 1907, but a higher court reversed the decision. In 1906, again under Roosevelt's prodding, and over the objection of a railroad representative from Pennsylvania that it would mean complete government ownership within ten years, Congress passed the Hepburn Act, which for the first time gave the Interstate Commerce Commission some degree of effectiveness. Express companies, sleeping car companies, and pipelines were brought under its jurisdiction, and the Commission was given the right, upon complaints, to set aside existing rates and establish new maximums, while the railroads set out to prove that their proposed rates were not unfair. With the burden of proof on the carriers, cases no longer lingered in the courts for years; they were handled much more quickly, and in general rates were revised downward. But the Commission could not initiate rate changes, it could only block unreasonable increases; and due to the wording of the law, it was still unable to prevent short haul–long haul abuses, until the Mann-Elkins Act of 1910 reworded the original phraseology to plug the gap. The Mann-Elkins Act also brought telephone and telegraph companies under the Commission's authority and permitted it to initiate investigations instead of waiting for complaints.

The same law required safety appliances for railroads and subsequent legislation limited railroad ownership of water carriers through the Panama Canal (1912), sought to outlaw any Credit Mobilier type of operation (1914), authorized the Commission to determine the fair value of railroad property in an effort to determine "just and reasonable" rates (1913), and provided an eight-hour day for railway employees engaged in interstate commerce. Moreover, the courts were more sympathetic, especially in the 1906–14 era and their interpretations gave the Commission greater leeway, even over intrastate commerce where it directly affected commerce across state lines. But the period after World War I would see a reversal; a conservative court would do little; the Commission would be packed with railroad men; and during the decade of the twenties, regulation would be lax.

Railroads dominated the American transportation system by the turn of the century, but urban transportation was undergoing significant change, the automobile was on the brink of instituting another far-reaching revolution, and Great Lakes traffic was flourishing and expanding.

City transportation was in transition as urban demand far outstripped supply. Horse-drawn streetcars had reached their peak in the 1880's and even in 1890 dominated nearly 70 per cent of the track. By 1902 horse cars had almost vanished, then accounting for 1.1 per cent, while electricity powered over 97 per cent. The street-railway boom reached its peak in the World War I era, though it left behind a legacy of manipulation and political corruption. Elevated trains and subways alike served major cities, and electric interurban railways linked independent communities, hauling freight, express, and mail, as well as passengers. But neither the interurbans nor the street railways were destined to dominate their fields long. The coming of the automobile spelled rapid doom for the interurbans and as early as 1914 motorbuses were beginning to provide intense city competition.

The automobile was a worthy competitor which burst upon the scene with a swift and spectacular rate of adoption. Four motorcars had been registered in 1895; by 1916, when production for the first time topped a million, there were over 3.5 million on the roads, and the Ford Motor Company was manufacturing about half of the annual output. A born tinkerer, Henry Ford had already been associated with several abortive efforts to manufacture automobiles when he organized the company in 1903, at a time when the financing of the new gas buggies was sometimes difficult and when insurance men swore they would never insure "a gasoline can on wheels." After half a dozen years of experimentation and building moderate priced cars, Ford decided that Americans would not buy a new automobile every year and that a cheap, simple, sturdy machine—a "universal car"—was the answer. In 1909 he announced his Model T, a standardized product with the same chassis for all and available "in any color so long as it was black." Mass producing on an assembly line basis, Ford turned out 808,590 vehicles in 1917 and eventually put some 15 million of the Model T's on American highways, at prices which at one point fell to $290, until competition from General Motor's Chevrolet in 1927 forced abandonment of the immortal Tin Lizzie in favor of the Model A.

Production costs dropped and automobiles in general improved. Auto registration fees had commenced in New York in 1904 and a motor fuel tax was first levied by Oregon fifteen years later. But little state highway aid was yet forthcoming, though the stage was being set for a later era in which federal and state governments would share the function of building and maintaining improved roads.

Traffic on inland waterways, apart from the Great Lakes, decreased sharply in the "Railroad Era." Railroads often ruined competing canals in rate wars and were not particularly interested in those—about one third of the total mileage by 1909—which came under their control. The Erie Canal, which in 1880 handled about 18 per cent of the traffic between Buffalo and New York City, by 1906 hauled only about 3 per cent. In 1880 at least 63 per cent of the cotton coming into New Orleans came by river; thirty years later this had dropped to 10 per cent. Only the Ohio River maintained its commerce without substantial loss.

But Great Lakes commerce improved steadily. Large lake steamers could haul long distance more cheaply than railroads: wheat went by lake and canal to New York for 4.42 cents a bushel in 1900, while railroads charged 9.98 cents. Eastbound cargoes consisted mainly of iron ore from the Mesabi Range and wheat, much of it from the breadbasket of Canada, with coal being the major westbound cargo. Competition was bitter and active, as independents vied with vessels owned by railroad or steel companies. By 1910 the Great Lakes fleet was larger than the ocean fleet of any foreign nation except Germany and Great Britain.

Communications expanded and improved also. Western Union after 1866 came to control a continental monopoly on the telegraph, which increasingly became important to businessmen of all kinds. Rates dropped somewhat and technological advances made it possible to send many messages simultaneously over the same wire. Emperor Dom Pedro's classic remark on the telephone in 1876—"My God, it talks!"—gave no hint of the importance the new instrument would assume in subsequent years. It was introduced into all major cities in the 1880's and lines were open between Boston and New York in 1884 and were extended to Washington in 1885, Chicago in 1892, and San Francisco by 1915. By the turn of the century over 400,000 telephones were in use and their rates were gradually being reduced from the peak of as much as $200 a year in the 1890's.

Postal service improved and revenues increased from a mere $8.5 million in 1860 to $288 million in 1914, although only five times in this period did the Post Office Department show a surplus.

The adoption of the penny post card (1873) and the two-cent letter rate (1883) lowered rates to the public and other improvements expanded postal services, adding free city delivery (1863), postal money orders (1864), special delivery (1885), rural free delivery (1896), postal savings (1910), and parcel post (1912).

The number of daily newspapers increased from 574 in 1870 to 2,600 by 1910, with the total circulation expanding more than eight times in the same period. Improvements such as the web printing press, cheaper newsprint made from wood pulp, and Mergenthaler's linotype machine speeded up production and reduced costs, making mass circulation possible. "Yis, sir," said Mr. Dooley, "th' hand that rocks th' fountain pen is th' hand that rules th' wurruld." Increasingly news was gathered by news services, especially United Press (1907) and the earlier Associated Press, with heavy dependence on telephone, telegraph, and international cable. The emergence of newspaper chains only added to this tendency toward standardization. Another noticeable trend by the turn of the century was "yellow journalism," the lurid sensationalism of the circulation-seeking papers of Joseph Pulitzer and William Randolph Hearst. "A Hearst newspaper," said one contemporary critic, "is like a screaming woman running down the street with her throat cut."

To the American economy, the revolution taking place in transportation—notably the remarkable growth of the railroad network, together with the development of the telegraph and steamship—was probably one of the most basic forces for change in the era from the 1850's to World War I. Upon it were based the rapid transformations which affected population shifts, industry, commerce, finance, and agriculture.

XII

THE LAST FRONTIER

IN 1860 about one seventh of the nation's population of 31.4 million was west of the Mississippi River. Only the first tier of states beyond the river, plus Texas, Oregon, and California, had been admitted to the Union. Except for Mormon Utah, most of the remainder had been bypassed when the frontier jumped across to the Pacific Coast, mainly in the forties. Much of the area had been set aside to the Indians "forever," or it was undesirable. The Great Plains, that dry, treeless region east of the Rockies and roughly west of the ninety-eighth meridian went down in many a geography book as the "Great American Desert."

Yet between 1860 and 1900 the vast trans-Mississippi regions were filled in at a pace unsurpassed in American history. In motion at the same time were three separate frontiers, moving from different directions and squeezing the Indian into oblivion. The miner's frontier, fluid and unpredictable, might drift in any direction whenever attracted by hope of precious metal. The cattleman's frontier pushed north over dusty trails from Texas to meet the rail lines thrust out across the plains. The farmer's frontier moved generally from east to west, fencing and plowing the lush buffalo grass as it came. And the transcontinental railroad, often in advance of settlement, brought settlers and troops in ever increasing numbers. By 1890 the Director of the Census could re-

167

port that the country's "unsettled area has been so broken into by isolated bodies of settlement that there can hardly be said to be a frontier line." By 1910 there were 23.7 million people living beyond the Mississippi, almost a quarter of the nation's total population, and the value of farm property there more than equaled that east of the river.

The history of the mineral West falls into at least four distinct periods. The first, 1848–58, was the era of golden California—an era of trial and error apprenticeship—with accent upon simple placer techniques—panning, sluicing, the use of the long tom—requiring relatively little capital investment but considerable outlay of labor, much of it wasted. The second period, 1858–68, brought an extension of placer mining to other parts of the Far West, with spectacular rushes in almost every state and territory. The rush to Pike's Peak, Kansas Territory, in 1859, attracted thousands and left dozens of mining camps dotting the Rockies. Rich discoveries occurred on the Snake and Salmon rivers in what later became Idaho in 1860 and 1861, and in Montana the following year. In California this period brought the beginning of deep-level quartz mining and the further stabilizing of hydraulicking. Moreover, large scale deep-level activity was getting underway in Nevada. There, along the route to California, prospectors seeking gold had been plagued by a heavy blue substance clogging their equipment. Eventually, when assayed, it proved rich in silver, and the rush was on to Virginia City, site of the fabulous Comstock Lode, where large joint-stock companies soon came to dominate. Deeper in Nevada, at such camps as Austin and Eureka, miners were frustratingly exposed to complex ores in formations which often decreased in richness with depth. The third era, 1869–79 belonged mainly to the incredible Comstock, from which was extracted some $340 million in silver between 1860 and 1890, and where engineering advances speeded up the exploitative processes, but wild speculation often hindered them. Elsewhere, except for California, Utah, and perhaps the Black Hills, Western mining fell into decay or failed to prosper due to a lack of capital, improved transportation, or new methods of handling refractory ores. The year 1879 opened yet another era, the fourth one, in which Colorado replaced the Comstock Lode in pre-eminence, thanks to the discovery of rich silver-lead ore at Leadville and the adaption of European techniques to reduce them. Soon vast new deposits would be opened in the Coeur d'Alene country of Idaho and at Cripple Creek in Colorado. Copper would come to dominate Butte, Montana (once described as "an island of easy money completely surrounded by whiskey"), as it would Arizona, New Mexico, and Utah. The growing emphasis on base metals and on Eastern financing indicated that Western mining was being integrated into the national economy.

Within this framework, mining camps went through a remarkably similar pattern of experience. After greatly exaggerated rumors of a rich strike leaked out, a rush was on and the mining camp erupted spontaneously, without civic planning. Virginia City, Nevada, was thus described in 1860:

> Frame shanties, pitched together as if by accident; tents of canvas, of blankets, of brush, of potato-sacks and old shirts, with empty whiskey barrels for chimneys; smoking hovels of mud and stone; coyote holes in the mountain-side forcibly seized by men; pits and shafts with smoke issuing from every crevice; piles of goods and rubbish on craggy points, in the hollows, on the rocks, in the mud, in the snow, everywhere, scattered broadcast in pell-mell confusion, as if the clouds had suddenly burst overhead and rained down the dregs of all the flimsy, rickety, filthy little hovels and rubbish of merchandise that had ever undergone the process of evaporation from the earth since the days of Noah.

It was a diverse and ofttimes cosmopolitan crowd that came pouring in, a mobile population quickly attracted elsewhere by the next rumors of discovery. Many were old California miners, and as they moved from one mining frontier to another they carried with them ideas and institutions, so that the rest of the mining West owed much to California not only in transfer of methods, but also of mining codes and their interpretation.

If a camp had worthwhile minerals, placer deposits and veins near the surface would be exploited rapidly. Then would come a day when these simple techniques no longer sufficed. As placer mining played out and deep-level mining became necessary, capital and more sophisticated techniques were required. Tunneling, driving shafts, hoisting equipment, and smelting apparatus to separate complex ores all required money, and as companies came in the day of the individual miner was over. But in most camps when this transition was being made, wild experiments in refining processes proved almost as wasteful as the speculative mania so common in Western camps. A few made fortunes; some went from rags to riches; but most of those who prospered were capitalists rather than the original owners. Alvah Gould in the early sixties sold his half interest in the Gould and Curry Mine on the Comstock Lode for $450 and went shouting down the street that he had "got away with the Californians." Years later he was running a peanut stand in Reno; meanwhile, the Gould and Curry had turned out $9 million for her new owners in two years.

The mineral West made important contributions. The precious metal it injected into the monetary system probably tempered the depressions of 1873 and 1893 by expanding the money supply somewhat when the banking structure was too inflexible to do so. It made copper available just when electricity was coming into widespread use for communications and power. It brought large numbers through Indian country, hastening the final clash with the red man. It meant opportunity to bankers, merchants, railroads, and farmers, and to numerous auxiliary industries. "It takes a mine to run a mine," goes an old saying. In 1872 one Nevada mining company spent $28,000 for chemicals, $74,000 for quicksilver, $23,000 for blasting powder, $11,000 for candles, and $67,000 for timbers; five years later, another concern was spending $22,000 annually for ice to cool the lower levels of its mine. Litigation was another ancillary industry: in five years the twelve leading mines of the Comstock engaged in a total of 245 lawsuits, consuming 10 per cent of the total product of the Lode. The sale of mining machinery was important in itself; it and financing made San Francisco the most important mining center in the West, while Denver to a lesser degree served the same function in the intermountain region.

Meanwhile, following the Civil War, an extensive cattle frontier was developing on the Great Plains. Destruction of the buffalo and a gradual shrinking of Indian lands left lush grazing lands free under a lenient federal land policy; east-west rail lines pushed through to provide the necessary link with expanding urban markets. Cattlemen discovered that the tough, mean longhorn cattle that roamed the Texas grasslands by the thousands were worth ten times as much on such markets in Northern and Eastern cities. Their problem then was to join a $5 steer with a $50 market and they solved it by driving the animals north to meet the rail lines reaching out across Kansas and Nebraska. Between 1867, when Joseph McCoy built his shipping yards at Abilene, and 1880, an estimated 4 million cattle reached Kansas shipping points and were hauled to Eastern markets. They came up on long drives, 2,500 or 3,000 head strong, over one of the standard routes—the Chisholm Trail, the Western Trail, or the Goodnight-Loving Trail—terminating in some wild and woolly cow town like Abilene, Dodge City, or Ogallalla.

Farther north, in Colorado, Wyoming, Montana, and the Dakotas, a separate range cattle industry had arisen and soon the long drives pushed from Texas to the northern ranges, where cattle might increase in value from $5 to $8 a year at a cost of about $1 a head. No large investment was necessary: 160 acres of homestead land could form a nucleus for a small "spread," and the free public domain could be used for grazing. During the great cattle boom of the early 1880's, Midwestern cattle—"pilgrims"—were brought in to stock these ranges, and considerable English and, especially, Scottish capital was invested.

However, in the mid-1880's came a decline and a modification of the industry. With better railroad facilities to Texas, and with state legislative restrictions to keep out the dread Texas fever, the long drives dwindled. Clashes with sheepmen and farmers may also have contributed to the difficulties, much to the delight of twentieth-century movie scenario writers. Moreover, the Northern ranges became overstocked, and the government began to enforce its land laws, depriving ranchers of grazing land. Then came dry summers and the exceptionally severe winters of 1885–86 and 1886–87. The Eastern-bred "pilgrims" were unable to survive as had the old Texas longhorns and some outfits lost as much as 80 per cent of their cattle, with those that survived in poor condition, their gaunt bones, according to one historian, "resembling the insides of gothic cathedrals." Under pressure from creditors many dumped their cattle on the market at low prices, at the same time when Midwestern farmers were selling heavily because a dry cycle had momentarily boosted corn prices. Many cattle companies went bankrupt, and the day of the open range, dependent upon free use of the public domain, was at an end. Now cattlemen realized that herds must be restricted in size, stocked with picked animals; grazing lands must be fenced and adequate winter food grown or purchased.

At the same time, plodding unromantically across the Great Plains came the farmer's last frontier. This region running from about the ninety-eighth meridian to the Rockies, relatively flat, treeless, with from fifteen to twenty-five inches of rainfall annually, insufficient for normal agricultural activity, has been described perceptively by Walter P. Webb in his classic, *The Great Plains:* "East of the Mississippi civilization stood on three legs— land, water, and timber; west of the Mississippi not one but two of these legs were withdrawn—water and timber—and civilization was left on one leg—land." Whatever its deficiencies, whatever its characteristics, by 1900 the Great Plains had filled in, its settlement being part of a great agricultural expansion which doubled the area of occupied land in the United States. The rising cost of land in the East and free or cheaper land in the West speeded the process, as did the general optimism of the farmer that agriculture was basic to the economy and that prices would eventually rise come what may. Moreover, in the 1860–1900 era men found answers to many of the problems which had prompted pioneers to bypass the plains region for so long.

By the Homestead Act of 1862, the federal government would give any citizen, or one who had declared his intent, 160 acres of land in the West if he were tough enough to live on it and improve it for five years. Between January 1, 1863, when Daniel Freeman, a Union soldier home on leave, filed the first application on land near Nebraska City, and 1900, some 80 million acres of the public domain would be registered as having been taken up under the Homestead Act. That does not mean that the trans-Mississippi was settled primarily by homesteaders on free government farms. Far from it. Millions of acres were at the same time passing from the federal government's hands into those of nonsettlers. Grants to railroads reached 137 million acres by 1871; those to road and canal companies, 3 million acres. Prior to 1889, in violation of the spirit of the Homestead Law, speculators purchased at least 100 million acres from the government; likewise, until 1887, land made available when Indian reservations were reduced went to speculators in large blocks—at least another 100 million acres. Much of the land scrip awarded veterans of all wars down to 1856 passed into speculative hands and was reclaimed in the post-Civil War era. By the Morrill Act of 1862 and others like it, states received additional millions of acres, much of it in the West, which was sold to speculators. In other words, although settlers eventually bought much of this land, they paid more for it, and only about one acre in ten was taken up directly by homesteaders prior to 1890. The Homestead Act may have advertised the West, but it was not the magic formula it has often been made out to be.

During part of the period, government lands, even forest and mineral, were not classified, and the land laws in general—drawn up by legislators conditioned to a humid, forested area—paid too little attention to the geographic realities of the situation. Such laws as the Timber Culture Act (1873), granting 160 acres for the planting and growing of a specified amount of timber, or the Desert Land Act of 1877, permitting cheap purchase of 640 acres in any of eight Western states and territories in exchange for irrigating part of it within three years, were patently absurd and manifestly unworkable in a semiarid region. Meanwhile, Congress refused to break with tradition and ignored informed recommendations like those of Major John Wesley Powell for an abandonment of the rectangular survey system, which made for easy monopolization of water, and for a distinction between size of land units to be used for irrigated farming (80 acres) and for grazing (2,560 acres).

The period from 1865 to 1890 was notorious for its general corruption and Western lands were no exception. Speculators evaded and abused the laws, sometimes building empires by fraudulent entry or by having employees make entries under various statutes. Technically it was possible for one person to take up as much as 1,280 acres in this fashion. Land Commissioner William A. J. Sparks investigated land irregularities, restricted the purchase to bona fide settlers, and restored some 41 million acres of illegally entered land to the public domain in the middle 1880's before pressure from Western congressmen brought his resignation. But he succeeded in bringing the need of reform to the fore and Congress in 1891 repealed pre-emption, the Timber Culture Act and the Desert Land Act, in addition to outlawing sale of government land by auction.

Still, from one source or another, relatively cheap land was available and served as a magnet to draw westward thousands of genuine settlers. Once there, these people had to adjust to their new environment. If adequate rainfall was lacking, they had to shepherd what moisture there was carefully. The coming of cheaper, more efficient windmills in the 1870's and 1880's made the task easier, but wells simply could not produce water beyond the immediate needs of humans and livestock. Government reclamation and irrigation projects were not forthcoming until the end of the century, although in the early 1890's Congress did underwrite a strange attempt at rainmaking by aerial explosions. So, water not being available for the growing of standard crops by time-honored methods, men sought out crops like hard spring and winter wheat that would grow with a minimum of moisture, doing most of their growing during the damp season. Through the Morrill Act (1862) setting up land-grant colleges, and the Hatch Act (1887) for agricultural experiment stations, the federal government aided in the development of new strains to withstand dry conditions better. Even cultivation methods had to be modified, and the age-old technique of dry farming, earlier used in the United States by the Mormons in Utah, now became universal on the Great Plains. It involved allowing a portion of the land to lie idle part of the time, deep plowing just before the winter rains and snows, sparse planting and frequent cultivation to keep down the weeds, and stirring the topsoil so that a fine dust was formed to maintain a capillary action to draw up moisture to the plants' root system. The yield thus produced, however, was not comparable to that produced by normal methods or by irrigation, a wheat crop of ten to fifteen bushels an acre being normal.

Lacking timber for fencing, the prairie settler experimented with growing hedges, especially Osage Orange, but with little success; only after 1874 when J. F. Glidden of DeKalb, Illinois, put a workable barbed wire on the market at reasonable cost was this problem solved. For fuel, the settler burned anything available—buffalo chips, twisted sunflower stalks, even corn on the cob when prices were down. Hay and grass were frequently used, twisted into solid sticks, or "cats," for specially designed hay-burning stoves. He constructed his house of "Kansas Brick" or "Nebraska Marble"—sod, a cheap, easily accessible material not without its disadvantages. As the old folk ballad ran:

> My house is constructed of natural soil,
> The walls are erected according to Hoyle;
> The roof has no pitch but is level and plain,
> And I never get wet till it happens to rain.

Farming on the plains was a struggle with the raw elements. Searing summer heat might leave crops parched and wilted; hail might batter ripe grain to the ground, and winter blizzards might paralyze isolated farms for weeks at a time. Dust storms sometimes blackened the sky and prairie fires lit up the night and burned over thousands of acres. Chinchbugs left corn dry and curled, and invasions of grasshoppers ravaged the land, leaving "nothing but the mortgage." Pleuropneumonia destroyed live-stock by the hundreds and black rust ruined wheat almost over-night. Farm prices were generally low and farm life on the plains had about it an aura of loneliness and isolation that almost defies description. So, not unsurprisingly, many a sodbuster family moved on or returned East, chanting such ditties as

> Fifty miles to water
> One hundred miles to wood,
> To hell with this damn country
> I'm heading home for good.

But vast numbers stuck it out, not necessarily by choice, sometimes to better days, sometimes not. And by 1900 the "sod house frontier" was no more. Branch railroad lines would lower transportation costs on fuel and building materials; the development of local coal mines and brickyards would help ease shortages. Taken together as the "last frontier," and greatly hastened by expansion of the railroads, this late nineteenth-century movement of farmers, cattlemen, and miners brought to a close the great westward migration that had been a part of American development since the beginning, and which, in one way or another, exerted profound influence in the shaping of American life and institutions.

XIII

AGRICULTURE IN AN INDUSTRIALIZING SOCIETY

THE PERIOD after the Civil War accelerated many of the trends in agriculture which had been evident before. Industrialization and urbanization created metropolitan centers to be fed and clothed, foreign markets expanded steadily, and the growth of a national transportation network, closely integrated with an international one, gave American farm products easy access to these markets, thus hastening the shift from self-sufficient to commercial farming, just at the time the public domain was being thrown open for exploitation. Regional specialization continued even more sharply than before, and the farm domain more than doubled in size by the time of the World War, thanks in part to transportation growth. But at the same time, these developments in transportation brought the American farmer into competition with the rest of the world and were instrumental in the falling of farm prices, which in turn led to agrarian protest.

In the half century between 1860 and 1910, 471 million acres, including grazing land, an area almost as large as France, Germany, and Italy combined, was added to American agriculture, as the farmer took up more land than his forebears had done in the previous 250 years. Cultivated land rose from 163 million acres in 1860 to 347 million in 1910, while the value of land, imple-

177

ments, livestock, and improvements went from $8 billion to $42 billion. The average farm was becoming smaller, however, dropping from 199 acres in 1860 to 134 acres by 1880, remaining fairly constant until about 1910, then increasing somewhat.

FARMS, LAND IN FARMS, AND VALUE OF FARM PROPERTY, 1850–1914*

Year	Number of Farms (1,000)	Land in Farms (1,000 acres)	Value of Farm Property† (millions of dollars)	Average Value per Acre (dollars)
1850	1,449	293,534	3,270	11.14
1860	2,044	407,179	6,642	16.32
1870	2,660	407,723	7,441	18.26
1880	4,009	536,064	10,193	19.02
1890	4,565	623,207	13,273	21.31
1900	5,737	838,583	16,603	19.81
1910	6,406	878,792	34,793	39.59
1914	6,447	909,627	39,579	43.51

* Historical Statistics of the United States, Colonial Times to 1957, p. 278.
† Farmland and buildings.

In absolute numbers, farm population and income expanded: the number of people went from 19 million to 32 million between 1860 and 1910, and their income increased fourfold. But in relative terms, the per cent of American population on farms fell from about 60 to 35, while income dropped from 31 to 22 per cent of the national total in the same period. After World War I population on farms would decline in absolute terms also.

The trend toward regional specialization continued. More than ever, New England and the Middle Atlantic states found competition with the West and Midwest in the production of staple crops impossible, and the emphasis was placed more on producing goods for nearby urban markets—dairy products, poultry, fruit, and vegetables. In New England farm abandonments were common.

The North Central states, ranging from Ohio on the east, as far west as Kansas and Nebraska, and as far north as the Dakotas, had become the nation's chief producer of grain and livestock. Corn, with Illinois and Iowa regarded as the heart of the Corn Belt, continued to be the leading crop, 85 per cent of it being used to feed livestock. Wheat was second among the cereals and was more important for the export trade, about one third of the crop being shipped abroad by 1900. By 1910 the North Central states were producing about three fourths of the nation's wheat. On the Great Plains cattle had at first predominated, until wheat began to make serious inroads, but even at peak, the Great Plains did not handle more than 30 per cent of the country's cattle; the bulk of the nation's beef (and pork as well) was being produced by a feeder industry on farms farther east, mainly in the Corn Belt.

In the Far West, California became more important as a producer of wheat and livestock, and grew almost all of the lemons in the country and 75 per cent of the oranges. In Washington by 1900, thanks to the rolling Palouse country, wheat was the state's most important crop, though after World War I apples took the lead.

In the South the old staples were still predominant, but emphasis was now on tenant farming, share-cropping, and the crop-lien system. Under the ordinary tenant-farm arrangement, the tenant furnished everything except the land, and paid for its use in cash or with part of the crop. Under the share-crop arrangement, the share-cropper furnished only the labor, while the owner of the land provided not only the ground, but house, seed, fertilizer and implements as well, with the crop being divided, usually fifty-fifty, or sometimes with the lion's share going to the land owner. Under the crop-lien system, the local capitalist— often the storekeeper—extended credit to the small farmer and took a mortgage on his future crop, furnishing seed, food, clothing, and equipment until the harvest came in, at which time he sold the crop and settled the account, usually leaving little, if any, money for the farmer's pocket.

Despite such arrangements, Southern production increased steadily between 1866 and World War I and the number of farms went from 672,000 to 3 million between 1860 and 1910, the average size decreasing from 335 acres to 114. Cotton remained the most important cash crop, although not until 1878 was the old prewar record of 4.5 million bales equalled. But in 1916, a particularly prolific year, over 16 million bales were produced.

Cotton by the turn of the century accounted for about a third of the value of all Southern crops and just over a tenth of those of the nation. Overproduction and low-grade cotton held prices low: at its nadir it was 4.59 cents a pound (1894); it never rose above ten cents between 1882 and 1902, nor did it go as high as fourteen cents until World War I. Mississippi was the heaviest producer until superseded by Texas in 1890. Louisiana remained the leading sugar and rice producer, while Kentucky was first in tobacco, followed by Tennessee and North Carolina. Considerable subsistence corn and livestock were grown and specialty crops were developed in some sections—apples in Virginia, peaches in Georgia, grapefruit in Florida, and peanuts in many areas.

Noticeable was the failure of the South to keep pace with mechanization. With tenant, share-crop, and crop-lien systems prevailing, capital was not available for mechanical improvements. Thus in 1910, when the value of farm machinery and implements per acre of farm land was ninety-two cents in the East North Central region, nearly twice that in the West North Central states, in Georgia the figure was seventy-eight cents. Not until World War II was a practical mechanical cotton picker perfected, and, even though it could pick a bale in three hours, as opposed to eighty-six hours for hand labor, its cost was prohibitive to the average farmer.

Elsewhere, thanks to the application of science and technology, relatively fewer farmers produced more. Especially in the West and Middle West did mechanization provide the base for modern, commercialized agriculture. The ordinary reaper, already harvesting 70 per cent of the wheat in the Midwest in 1860, gave way to the improved Marsh harvester in the 1870's, and this was superseded in the next decade by the twine binder, which automatically bound the sheaves as they were cut. Large-scale farms adopted the combine, which accomplished both reaping and threshing in one operation, harvesting from twenty to fifty acres a day, and was drawn by twenty to forty horses. Steam power, while too expensive for the average farmer, made great inroads after 1870, especially on combines and threshers and for plowing on the vast "bonanza" farms of the plains and Far West. By 1910 an estimated 70,000 steam threshers were in use, but already the gasoline tractor was making its appearance as the ultimate replacement for the belching, smoking steam monster. Gang plows, sulky plows, disc harrows, spring-tooth harrows, seed drills, and corn binders were all widely used by the turn of the century.

New milling processes made possible the use of hard spring wheat and threw open the expanses of Minnesota and the Dakotas to the grain farmer. Constant search and experimentation provided new strains of crops to thrive on the semiarid plains— Kaffir corn, Sudan grass, Crimean wheat, for example. More than ever the agricultural press boosted scientific farming, and the federal government gave substantial support through the Morrill Act and the Hatch Act. A separate Department of Agriculture was established in 1862 and raised to cabinet status in 1889. The Smith-Lever Act (1914) created a system of county agents and sought to foster cooperation between state and national government for the benefit of improved farming. More than one railroad and agricultural-implement manufacturer furthered scientific farming and maintained their own agricultural development departments.

Dry farming techniques, of course, had made the Great Plains usable, but little irrigation, save by the Mormons and a few other Western cooperative colonies, was attempted prior to the 1890's, although by 1910 some 14.4 million acres of irrigated land would be under cultivation. Only when the government was willing to foot the bills were such projects undertaken.

Expansion, specialization, mechanization, and better crops and techniques spelled increased production, both in total yield and per man hour. Between 1830 and 1900 the time required to prepare the ground and sow one bushel of wheat had dropped from more than half an hour to two minutes; where it had taken about thirty-nine man hours to grow and harvest forty bushels of corn in 1855, with machinery it took about fifteen by the mid-1890's. One farm worker in the 1820's could produce food for 4.5 people; in 1920 he could produce for ten. If such efficiency made farm tasks less onerous, helped raise the rural standard of living, and released farm hands to work in the cities, it would make it increasingly difficult for the man with little or no capital to enter the field, and it would help stimulate overproduction. The old fear of the Malthusians that population would outrun the food supply—that people would reproduce faster than pigs, so to speak—was being replaced with the realization that the food supply in the United States was actually outstripping population. This would be part of a perplexing dilemma besetting American agriculture, part of a combination of circumstances creating a "farm problem" of considerable magnitude beginning late in the nineteenth century.

Most farmers had completed the shift to commercial farming: the farm, in effect, became a factory without a roof, and the average farmer became a part of the capitalistic world, producing his wheat or his pork or his cotton for Chicago, New York, or London. But unlike his industrial brethren, he had no means of controlling the price of his wares. Individualistic and unorganized, he could not enter into pooling arrangements to regulate price or production; with a few exceptions, he had no benefits from a protective tariff, which only pushed the cost of consumers' goods higher; he found it almost impossible to create a demand for a staple commodity through advertising. Convinced that his was the true basis of the economy, the farmer produced blindly more and more goods for world markets, competing not only with his fellow Americans, but also with farmers from Russia, India, Canada, Australia, and Argentina. The value of his crop was set elsewhere and depended on factors beyond his control. If crops were good the world over, the price sagged and he was faced with ruin. But if war closed the Russian ports or if natural disaster —drought, locusts, or black rust—devastated the fields of his competitors, then prices held up, interest on the mortgage might be paid, and prosperity prevailed for another year.

Prices varied considerably, but in general rising production costs and periodic overproduction kept them low, especially between 1869 and 1900. Between 1869 and 1915 inclusive—forty-seven years—there were but nine years when the price of wheat averaged over one dollar a bushel, only twelve when corn went over fifty cents a bushel, and only seventeen when cotton went above ten cents a pound. Per capita farm income ranged consistently below the national average: in 1890, making up about

43 per cent of the gainfully employed, farmers received 18 per cent of the income of the country. Noticeably better times would prevail from 1897 to the end of World War I, but throughout the last thirty years of the nineteenth century the farmers' lot was generally neither an easy nor a profitable one.

VALUE OF FARM MACHINERY AND EQUIPMENT, 1850–1918*

Year	Value (millions of dollars)
1850	152
1860	246
1870	271
1880	406
1890	494
1900	750
1910	1,266
1914	1,719
1918	2,965

* *Historical Statistics of the United States, Colonial Times to 1957,* p. 285.

To compete, a farmer had to mechanize, which required greater capital. Where $1,500 would have established a 220-acre farm in Ohio or Indiana in 1835, probably $10,000 would be required in 1900. As a result, tenant farming increased, even outside the South. In 1880, 25.6 per cent of all American farms were operated by tenants; by 1890, 28.4 per cent; and by 1910, 37 per cent. Even in the period of depressed farm prices, land values continued to rise, increasing from an average of $16.30 per acre in 1860 to $21.30 in 1890, and $39.60 twenty years later. This fact enabled the farmer to plunge into debt and survive. By 1890 the farm debt ran to about $1,200 per farm; by 1900, fully one third of all farms were mortgaged, with interest rates ranging from 10 to 40 per cent. That the mortgage occupied a prominent place in the farmer's life is indicated by a contemporary song:

> We worked through spring and winter—
> Through summer and through fall,
> But the mortgage worked the hardest—

And the steadiest of them all.
The weevil and the cut worm—
They went as well as came;
But the mortgage stayed forever,
Eating hearty all the same.

The farmer believed that he was being exploited "by men who sit in their offices and behind their bank counters and farm the farmers." In the farmer's mind there was no doubt that production costs could be cut if the middlemen—those "heartless monopolies and soulless corporations"—who took part of his legitimate profit could be curbed. Wheat selling in New York for $1.25 a bushel in 1869 brought the Minnesota grower only two thirds of that; Iowa farmers later burned their corn in their stoves because at twenty-five cents a bushel it was cheaper than coal, yet on the Eastern seaboard corn retailed for one dollar a bushel. Honest labor did not receive the just fruits of its toil. As another popular song put it,

The farmer is the man, the farmer is the man,
Lives on credit till the fall;
Then they take him by the hand, and they lead him
    from the land.
And the middleman's the one who gets it all.

More specifically, the machinery trusts, the Beef Trust, warehousemen, grain buyers, and railroads invoked agrarian wrath, especially the railroads with their pools, rebates, rate discrimination, elevator monopolies, and bountiful land grants. No doubt the American farmer was exploited by these groups and he centered his attack on them because they were tangible and assailable. In so doing, however, he simplified his problems, ignoring the implications of his basically new role as a mass producer in world competition.

In addition to his economic troubles, which he never fully understood, the farmer also encountered difficulties of a more physical nature. Recklessly, he often shot dice with Mother Nature and lost. Wasteful, like the rest of society in his day, he mined his soil ruthlessly, destroying any timber that might exist, cultivating staple crops year in and year out, virtually inviting the ravages of drought, erosion, or flood in areas already poorly equipped for intensive cultivation. On the Great Plains he had to cope with extremes in both summer and winter and wherever he was he might have to combat insects or disease of an infinite variety.

In a social sense, the farmer had his problems, too. There was a time when farmers had been regarded as "the chosen people of God." "God made the country and man made the town," said the earlier romanticists, steeped in the Jeffersonian agrarian tradition. But increasingly the growing cities, with their superior educational, recreational, and cultural facilities, their business and professional opportunities, offered a social prestige that farm life could no longer match. Almost from the beginning there had been a rift between the city and the country, but with time the gap widened and more than ever the city dweller came to regard his country cousin as an inferior being—a rube, a hick, a bumpkin —an attitude naturally resented by the farmer, whose life was dull and monotonous by urban standards.

Nor could his other problems be divorced completely from the political, since most of the farmer's proposed solutions required legislation at the state or national level. Yet farmers in general were losing political power. Those in the South seldom cooperated at the polls with those of the West or Midwest, and increasingly the major parties came to reflect urban, railroad, banking, and industrial interests. Unable to control either major party, farmers turned to organizations of their own, not always political in character, and sought to improve their lot by joint action.

One of the first such groups, the Grange, or Patrons of Husbandry, made a lasting imprint. Begun in 1867, it had an estimated membership of about 1.5 million by 1874 but soon fell back to about half of that. In theory the Grange was not a political party, but in practice it exerted considerable political influence, especially in Minnesota, Iowa, Illinois, and Wisconsin, where it held the balance of power between the evenly matched Republicans and Democrats, and was successful in pushing through the so-called Granger laws of the late 1860's and early 1870's regulating railroad, warehouse, and grain elevator rates.

Among their other activities, the Grangers sought to eliminate the middleman by founding their own co-operatives, elevators, packing plants, insurance companies, and even experimenting with the manufacture of farm machinery. Unfortunately, while these enterprises did perhaps give the farmer a better appreciation of the role of the middleman, inadequate capital, inexperienced management, and cutthroat competition doomed many of them to failure, though many still survive. In the end, probably the greatest contribution of the Grange was social: it brought people together at regular meetings and helped break down the isolation and monotony of farm life.

As the Granger movement waned somewhat in the late 1870's, disgruntled farmers would make several significant efforts to join hands with urban workers in new political parties designed to solve mutual problems. Invariably, since the farmer was a debtor, the desire for an inflated currency to raise prices would play a leading role in these third-party movements. In the late sixties and early seventies the farmers had fought for continuation in circulation of the $450 million in greenbacks issued during the Civil War and to prevent their being backed with specie, but in the end settled for compromises which did little to bring about the desired inflation.

It was this paper money controversy, especially its last phase, which gave birth to the Independent National, or Greenback, Party in 1876, a party whose platform by 1880 reflected the typical agrarian complaints. It denounced the contracting of the number of greenbacks and deprecated the small amount of silver in circulation; it condemned the waste of public lands and demanded that they be reserved for bona fide settlers only; it called for woman suffrage, a graduated income tax, government regulation of interstate commerce, suppression of Chinese immigration, shorter working hours, and the creation of a federal bureau of labor. The Greenbackers netted but 1 per cent of the total vote in 1876 and about 3 per cent four years later, but succeeded in electing a number of congressmen, despite a brief upsurge in farm prices in 1880. In 1884, when the party combined with the Anti-Monopolists to support Benjamin Butler of Massachusetts on a platform calling for strong control of corporations, it drew even less farm support.

Out of a number of small local organizations created in the South and prairie West during the 1880's emerged two major farm groups: the National Farmer's Alliance (the Northern Alliance), founded by Milton George; and the Farmers' Alliance and Industrial Union (the Southern Alliance). Not political parties, the Alliances early decided upon political action to improve the farmers' lot. Under various party labels they won complete or partial control of legislatures in a dozen states, elected six governors, three U.S. senators, and about fifty representatives in the election of 1890, and were instrumental in forming the People's, or Populist, Party in the following year. In 1892 the Populists waged a remarkably effective campaign for a first-time effort, running the old Greenback campaigner James B. Weaver for the presidency and winning over a million popular votes—9 per cent of the total—and twenty-two electoral votes.

The Populist platform, written by the versatile and talented Ignatius Donnelly of Minnesota, called for sweeping reforms, many of them reflecting the special plight of the farm element. Strict governmental economy, a land policy restricted to actual settlers, establishment of postal savings banks, and government ownership of railroads, telegraph, and telephone facilities were advocated. A graduated income tax, the Australian secret ballot, and the initiative and referendum were suggested, along with a one-term limitation for the President and Vice-President. To attract labor, the platform urged shorter working hours, an end to contract labor, and denounced the Pinkerton detectives for their role in strikebreaking. Again, the desire for inflation was apparent in the call for currency reform. The amount of money in circulation should be increased to not less than $50 per capita, a substantial jump from the $22.67 per capita in circulation in 1890. Next the party demanded "free and unlimited coinage of silver and gold at a ratio of 16 to 1," a plank, which if met, would inject a cheaper metal into the monetary system, since silver was at the time worth but 67.5 cents for the 371.25 grains that went into a silver dollar.

Led by colorful leaders like Mary Elizabeth Lease of Kansas, mother of four who denounced government "of Wall Street, by Wall Street, and for Wall Street," and urged Kansans to "raise less corn and more hell," or like Ben Tillman of South Carolina, who promised his constituents he would take his pitchfork to Washington and prod that "old bag of beef," Grover Cleveland, in his "fat old ribs," the Populist Party made such an auspicious beginning that the Democratic Party in 1896 soundly endorsed the principle of free silver and in addition borrowed some of the less extreme planks as its own. It was the magnetic Silver Tongued Orator, William Jennings Bryan, who then carried the agrarian banner:

> Prairie avenger, mountain lion,
> Bryan, Bryan, Bryan, Bryan,
> Gigantic troubadour, speaking like a siege gun,
> Smashing Plymouth Rock with his boulders from the West.*

But at the end of a dramatic campaign which centered on the issue of free silver, the Republican conservative, William McKinley, easily defeated the young Nebraskan, who carried only the mining states and those where staple farming and low prices predominated. Returning prosperity and rising prices of farm goods undoubtedly hurt the Democratic cause and bore out the ancient witticism, "When corn is $1 a bushel, the farmer is a radical; when it's $1.50 a bushel, he is a progressive; and when it's $2 a bushel, he is a conservative."

Many writers have tended to view the Populist Revolt and especially the election of 1896 as the triumph of industrialism over a last-ditch attempt of the farmers to beat it back. Probably a more realistic view is to see the movement not as the last great stand of the farmers, but as one of the first great responses to the problems created by the new industrial capitalism. New reform impulses of the twentieth century wrote into law many of the Greenback-Populist planks, but the agrarians called attention to the problems and helped prepare the ground.

After 1897 the American farmer enjoyed a score of the most prosperous years he had ever experienced. New land entries were slowing down, crop production remained fairly stable, while

---

* From "Bryan, Bryan, Bryan, Bryan" by Vachel Lindsay.

industry expanded at a more rapid rate than agriculture and could absorb farm products without leaving a surplus. Supply and demand stood in fair balance and the farmer prospered. The artificial stimulus of World War I, with demands for food for the war effort, pushed prices to new heights, land values soared, and American agriculture flourished as never before.

XIV

THE GROWTH OF INDUSTRIAL
CAPITALISM

JUST AS THE GROWTH of national and international transportation networks facilitated the rapid expansion of American agriculture after the Civil War, so also did these developments make possible the rise of the factory system at an unprecedented pace. High volume production, the offspring of the factory system, became possible as technology advanced, and especially as swift, large-scale movements of raw materials and finished goods became feasible. Transportation networks were welding hinterlands and growing cities together; corporate endeavor and techniques for the transfer of securities were replacing old modes of property ownership and control; mechanization of factory production was revolutionizing the relationship between labor and management. If Southern planters, and indeed sometimes their commercial associates, had sought to stay this onrushing tide, the outcome of the Civil War effectively removed Southern objections and left the way open for unchecked business advance. It was in this post-Appomattox era that the progress of the industrial, transportational, and agricultural revolutions were greatly accelerated and industrial capitalism became the most dominant single factor in shaping American life and thought. It would produce more goods cheaply, create new methods of business organization and con-

190

solidation and bring to the top a new group of financial and industrial wizards whose power would be political as well; it would redistribute population in a quickening urban pattern, and leave its imprint on social and cultural life as well as economic; it would raise the standards of living for millions, yet at the same time would create labor problems and evoke the rise of more powerful labor unions and even government intervention on behalf of the public welfare.

Industrial growth was uneven but impressive. Between 1860 and 1914 the number of industrial plants nearly doubled, the

GROWTH OF AMERICAN MANUFACTURING, 1860–1914*

	1860†	1914
Number of factories	140,433‡	268,450§
Number of workers	1,311,246	7,036,247
Value of goods produced	$1,885,861,676	$24,246,434,724
Value added by manufacture	$854,256,584	$9,878,345,893

* From Eighth Census, *Manufactures of the United States in 1860,* p. 742; *Abstract of the Fourteenth Census of the United States* (1920), p. 916.

† Year ending June 1.

‡ Includes hand and neighborhood industries.

§ Excludes hand and neighborhood industries.

industrial labor force increased fivefold, the value of goods produced increased twelve times, and the value added by manufacture, a more significant indication, was multiplied by eleven. By the beginning of the twentieth century, American manufacturing production had outstripped that of Great Britain and Germany combined, with a noticeable change in the ratio between manufacturing and agriculture. In the decade 1869–79, 14 per cent of the national income had come from manufacturing and 21 from agriculture; by the 1890's the balance was about equal, but by the 1919–29 period, manufacturing was producing 22 per cent of the national income, twice as much as agriculture. By 1950 the ratio would be four to one.

This great expansion of industrial capitalism came in the face of severe depressions in 1873, 1893, and to a lesser extent 1907, and it was nurtured by the continuation and extension of the same fortuitous circumstances that had attended its initial growth before the Civil War. The important natural resources were easily accessible: in 1860 the federal government still held title to more than one half the total area of the country—over a billion acres. A benevolent government, controlled by friends of business, it was ready to sell its holdings for a song, give them away or let them pass by occupation. Moreover, it was a government which generally subscribed to the idea of laissez faire. Government's responsibility was to protect property rights, but not to hamper the normal competitive processes of a natural economy. Its high tariff policy provided protection not only through infancy but into robust manhood; its direct aid to railroads by land grants, loans, and priority to American materials were positive benefits; its unwillingness to exert effective regulatory controls, except when public pressure was so great it could no longer be ignored, was a more negative benefit.

Larger amounts of capital were now available, some from fortunes amassed during the Civil War, some from maritime commerce as Britain came to dominate that field more and more, some from foreign investors, especially English, Dutch, and German, but most from increasing corporate savings and reinvestment of the profits from expanding domestic industry. Labor was always in short supply, but became more abundant than ever before as population multiplied itself nearly three times between 1860 and 1910, jumping from 31.4 million to 92 million. By the next census, urban dwellers would outnumber rural. Much of this increase came from high birth rates and a steadily lengthening life span, but much also was the result of immigration from the Old World. In the forty years after 1860 nearly 14 million immigrants arrived, many of them poor, unskilled, and illiterate, and tending to congregate in the industrial cities and squalid mining towns where their labor was needed.

Population growth meant also broadening markets, which expanded even more as living standards and purchasing power slowly rose and as a rapidly spreading rail network facilitated distribution on a national level. By the end of the century, the United States had 39.4 per cent of the world's railroad mileage, a vital factor in specialization of manufacturing and agriculture, in

POPULATION OF THE UNITED STATES, 1860–1910*

Year	Total Population	Rural Population	Urban Population	Population per Square Mile
1860	31,443,321	25,226,803	6,216,716	10.6
1870	39,818,449	28,656,010	9,902,361	13.4
1880	50,155,783	36,026,048	14,129,735	16.9
1890	62,947,714	40,841,449	22,106,265	21.2
1900	75,994,575	45,834,654	30,159,921	25.6
1910	91,972,266	49,973,334	41,998,932	31.0

* *Historical Statistics of the United States, Colonial Times to 1957,* pp. 8, 14.

localization of production, and in the exchange of raw materials and finished goods in a nation where resources and population were widely dispersed. Without an excellent system of rail and lake carriers it would have been impossible, as Andrew Carnegie pointed out with some amazement, to bring iron ore some 900 miles from the Mesabi range in Minnesota to Pittsburgh, with new mass production techniques smelt it with Pennsylvania coke, mixed with lime from Kentucky and manganese from Virginia, to produce a steel that could be offered to the consumer for a penny a pound.

American inventive and administrative ingenuity met the challenges of the new era, making possible a revolution in technology and in the amassing and organizing of capital without which industrial capitalism would have been greatly retarded. New processes, laborsaving machinery, and mass production underlay the new industrial order and the increasing use of the corporate form reduced risk and encouraged small investors, though it also opened the way to speculation. Beyond the corporation itself— one of the dominant features of the period—developed an even more elaborate structure, combination being made relatively easy through lenient general laws of incorporation and ingenious devices by which vast industrial empires were built.

But men, not corporations, built such empires and guided the industrial machine, and the business leaders of the era were at once contributors to and products of their age. Some have called them Robber Barons and likened them to the freebooters of the

Spanish Main. Vernon L. Parrington refers to them as "ruthless, predatory, capable; single-minded men; rogues and rascals often, but never feeble, never hindered by petty scruple, never given to puling or whining—the raw materials of a race of capitalistic buccaneers." Others have viewed them more charitably as Industrial Statesmen, regarding them in the light of the accepted ideals and moral standards of their own day. Allan Nevins, for example, stresses the changing business ethics of John D. Rockefeller's era and believes the constructive aspects of entrepreneurial leadership in the long run more important than the destructive. Whatever they were, whether Robber Barons or Industrial Statesmen, the business leaders of the new era were capable organizers of men and material; they were masters of the administrative arts who saw the wastes and imperfections of the competitive system, and who pushed themselves to the top with ruthlessness and imagination. Their moral standards varied and in the tradition of their time, their ideas of social responsibility were somewhat limited, or certainly obscured, by their unqualified acceptance of laissez faire. Political connections were not regarded as unethical: gifts of stock or outright bribery could even be defended as means to an end. Control of government, such as Montana by Anaconda Copper or California by the Southern Pacific, was taken for granted; it was said that Standard Oil did everything to the legislature of Ohio except refine it. H. O. Havemeyer, head of the gigantic sugar trust, frankly admitted in 1899 a commonly accepted idea: "Business is not a philanthropy. . . . I do not care two cents for your ethics. I don't know enough of them to apply them. . . . As a business proposition it is right to get all out of a business that you possibly can." In the public mind, never before nor since had the businessman stood on such a high pedestal. The Senate was so filled with railroad and industrial tycoons— George Hearst, Mark Hanna, Chauncey Depew, Simon Guggenheim, to name but a few—as to be called the Millionaire's Club.

Some, like the pious Daniel Drew, sad-eyed Jay Gould, and genial Jim Fisk ("all solid brass"), were primarily speculators who exploited businesses for their own ends and left behind corporate wreckage, but most were essentially builders who prospered by making magnificent production records and who passed on to their heirs plants of vastly increased value. They ranged from salty old Cornelius Vanderbilt, who never read a book until the age of seventy, but who left an empire in railroading to his son William H. Vanderbilt, no mean businessman himself, to precocious Edward H. Harriman, boy wonder of the stock market, who ultimately controlled thousands of miles of rail lines in the West. Outstanding were the princely J. P. Morgan, a man of good education and strong emotions, whose embarrassingly red nose, as he put it, "was part of the American business structure"; slender, soft-voiced Andrew Mellon, a giant in many fields, including aluminum; diminutive Andrew Carnegie, a superb judge of men and builder of the organization which became the nucleus of gigantic United States Steel; John D. Rockefeller, the best known of all, a man of piety and patience who hated waste and disorder and who was creator and guiding light of the great Standard Oil empire. Many lesser known figures often stood in the shadows of the giants, but were important parts of industrial development. Henry Clay Frick, Captain Bill Jones, and young Charlie Schwab were to Carnegie as were Henry R. Rogers, Henry Flagler, and John Archbold to Rockefeller, for one of the uncanny abilities of the captains of industry was the selection of extremely competent subordinates, subordinates who would themselves inevitably go to the top.

Such men, like the public in general, subscribed to a loose-jointed, multisided philosophy, the Gospel of Wealth, which saw riches as a hallmark of success, an evidence of Divine blessing. Hard work, thrift, self-reliance, and initiative invariably brought success, while conversely, poverty sprang mainly from intemperance, laziness, speculation, or other weaknesses of character or ability. The doctrine of Darwinian evolution was taken over and tailored to fit the industrial era. Was not life, corporate and individual, a struggle for existence? And didn't the fit survive— Carnegie, Rockefeller, Vanderbilt, and the others? It was a Rockefeller who said that the giant American Beauty rose could be produced "only by sacrificing the early buds that grew around it." Survival of the fittest, especially by clawing their way upward by their own volition, implied leadership by this natural aristocracy chosen in the hard school of competition; it implied laissez faire, for regulation of railroad rates or government relief in time of depression would be in effect to take from the wealthy and give to the poor, who by right ought to fall by the wayside. Thus the better specimens of the human race evolved and the public benefited with cheaper prices as the more inefficient competitors were weeded out. Moreover, the Gospel of Wealth carried with it a stewardship responsibility perhaps sometimes guilt inspired, an obligation to contribute to socially useful causes, whereby the fit would be enabled to improve their own status. Thus Carnegie built a total of 2,811 public libraries, Philip Armour donated the money for the Armour Institute in Chicago where ambitious young men could train for technical work in night school. Even "Coal Oil" Johnny Rockefeller considered his contributions to the University of Chicago the best investment of his life. The Gospel of Wealth assumed that the poor would accept the guidance of those who rose to the top, but overlooked two possibilities, both of which by the early twentieth century had become reality: that those who did not prosper might appeal to political action to equalize taxation, restrict business practices, or otherwise gain aid; and that the poor might raise up leaders out of their own ranks, organize and challenge industrial power. By 1900, through legislation and by labor unions, industrial government was being strongly disputed.

If one obvious characteristic of industrial enterprise after the Civil War was unprecedented growth, another was specialization. Climate, supply of labor and capital, proximity to markets, sources of power, and raw materials all helped determine where manufacturing might be located and what products might be emphasized. Between 1850 and 1890, while the center of population moved 243 miles westward, the center of manufacturing moved 225 miles in the same direction. New England declined, relatively speaking, though not in total values; her contribution to the over-all value of manufacturing in the country dropped from 27 per cent in 1850 to 14.4 per cent in 1900, but she remained the most important producer of textiles and shoes. The Middle Atlantic states, especially New York, New Jersey, and Pennsylvania, produced about 38 per cent of the total in 1900, with emphasis on chemicals, clothing, furniture, and iron and steel, but declined to about 33 per cent by 1914. Meanwhile, the East North Central states—Ohio, Indiana, Illinois, Wisconsin, and Michigan—were making rapid industrial progress and by 1914 were turning out 27 per cent of the nation's manufactured goods. Iron and steel were important, and this region led the country in meat, liquor, implements, railroad equipment, and automobiles, with 62 per cent of the latter being produced by Michigan alone.

In the South, a lack of capital together with a strong agricultural tradition hindered industry and its role in the manufacturing economy declined from 9.9 per cent in 1850 to 6.3 per cent in 1880. Then it began to pick up momentum as cotton textile mills began to shift nearer the source of raw materials and cheaper labor, so that by 1890 the number of spindles in the South was roughly seven times that of 1860. By 1927, 52 per cent of the nation's spindlage was located in the South. Exploitation of the Chattanooga and Birmingham iron ore deposits began in the 1880's; lumbering, phosphates, tobacco products, and subsequently cottonseed by-products brought more industrial development and in 1901 the famous Lucas gusher at Spindletop, Texas, ushered in a new era for that state and especially for Oklahoma and Louisiana. But despite rapid strides, the South continued to lag behind the Northeast and the Midwest: in 1910, with 32 per cent of the nation's population, the sixteen Southern states produced but 12.8 per cent of the value of goods manufactured.

Another outstanding characteristic was mechanization, which was vital to the trend in manufacturing that grew in importance as the nineteenth century passed—mass production. Writing for the *Encyclopaedia Britannica* in 1926, Henry Ford defined mass production as "the focussing upon a manufacturing project of the principles of power, accuracy, economy, system, continuity, and speed. . . . And the normal result is a productive organisation that delivers in quantities a useful commodity of standard material, workmanship and design at minimum cost." Mass production in its early form tended to be obscured by the dominance of small scale industry, but after 1900 it became more general and its evolution more spectacular. Guns, watches, and clocks were the products first identified with mass production, even before 1860; among other early leaders after the Civil War were sewing machines, bicycles, agricultural machinery, typewriters, steel, and by World War I, automobiles.

Mass production was made possible by diverse factors. In the first analysis, of course, it was not possible without mass consumption—without markets for the additional goods it produced. It was dependent, certainly, on the progress of technology and invention, and particularly upon the development of the machine-tool industry. Evolving before the Civil War, usually from early gun shops, which were also machine shops, the machine-tool industry expanded remarkably. An English observer commented in 1885: "The tools and processes which we are inclined to consider unusual are the commonplaces of American shops, and the determination to do nothing by hand which can be done by machinery is the chief characteristic." By 1900 a machine-tool industry apart from manufacturing had developed. The turret lathe, developed after mid-nineteenth century, was by this time automatic, as was gear cutting, and jigs and fixtures attached to machines eliminated much hand finishing. The adoption of a standard system for threads for bolts, nuts, and screws after the 1860's and of Brown and Sharpe's micrometer caliper (1867), which gave accuracy to one-thousandth of an inch, represented significant advance. Above all, machine tools were important because they speeded up operation and produced standardized goods, often by multiple drilling or the punching of numerous parts simultaneously. Such equipment increased production many fold: hand weaving required over 5,600 hours of labor to manufacture 500 yards of cotton cloth; machinery by 1900 reduced this to a mere fifty-two hours. At the same time, Owen's bottle-making machine virtually eliminated the skilled glass blower, and the largest farm implement factory in the country, located in Chicago, was turning out 200,000 machines of all kinds per year, even using an early example of an assembly line—"a little railway"—to convey parts and materials.

The machine-tool industry and manufacturing in general were highly dependent upon the availability of cheap, improved steel, for this era has been aptly labeled the Age of Steel, and the role of this metal in the industrial transformation was truly revolutionary. Steel production was up from under 20,000 long tons in 1867 to 7.1 million by 1897 and 31.3 million by 1913, as the United States became the world's leading producer. New fields provided the basis of the great new industry—the Birmingham-Chattanooga deposits in the 1880's; the Marquette, Menominee, Gogebic, and Vermillion ranges of the Lake Superior region in the 1870's and 1880's; and the most important of all, the giant Mesabi range in Minnesota in the 1890's, which could be stripped with new techniques and equipment such as the steam shovel. Moreover, the Bessemer-Kelly process lowered refining costs and made possible the large scale production of steel; the Siemens-Martin open-hearth process which gradually replaced it allowed closer control and resulted in a superior product. Coke supplanted charcoal and anthracite for smelting and in the late 1870's two Englishmen solved the problem of handling phosphorous ores with a special limestone lining in the hearth. Soon chemical advances and electric furnaces made it much easier to produce the special high carbon steel used for machine tools or the other alloys containing molybdenum, tungsten, or tantalum used in modern industries.

GROWTH OF STEEL PRODUCTION, 1860–1914*

	1860	1914
Number of factories	13	427
Number of workers	748	274,162
Value of goods produced	$1,778,240	$918,664,565
Value added by manufacture	$973,068	$327,838,873
Number of tons produced (2240 lbs)	11,838	23,403,957

* From Eighth Census, *Manufactures of the United States in 1860,* p. 741; *Census of Manufactures* (1914), II, p. 218.

The availability of power was another prerequisite to mass production. Water power was still cheaper than steam in 1880, but steam had more mobility and rapidly forged ahead for industrial use until the early twentieth century, when electricity began to make serious inroads, accounting for 73 per cent of industrial power by 1925. Unlike steel, in which most important innovations came from abroad, the electrical field was developed primarily by

Americans. Charles F. Brush devised an electric arc light for street use and Thomas Edison made many contributions, especially a satisfactory incandescent lamp and developments in electrified railways, but Edison placed his faith in direct current, which proved difficult to transmit. George Westinghouse brought a group of engineers together, bought up various patent rights, and put together an alternating current system, cutting transmission costs by sending high voltage current over a small wire, then using transformers at the end to lower the voltage to a safe, usable level. Westinghouse received the contract to light up the 1893 Columbian Exposition in Chicago and the result made a tremendous impression on the public.

Meanwhile the Westinghouse group was working with an induction polyphase motor, the invention of a Hungarian immigrant engineer, Nikola Tesla, which when perfected proved the key to successful application of electricity to industry and transportation. By the turn of the century both Westinghouse and the Edison group (General Electric) were using the steam turbine to generate current at central stations and by 1902, 1.5 billion kilowatts were being produced for industrial use. Industrial advantages of the new "white coal" were great. Once transmission problems were solved, industry could establish itself anywhere without reference to coal or water power sources. Electricity was clean, relatively cheap, and extremely versatile. It added new electrolytic processes of vast importance to the chemical and metal industries, and was essential to the development of the automobile, telephone, radio, and television; from it came improved photography, high-speed printing, and the phonograph and movie industry.

Mass production depended partly upon managerial as well as mechanical improvements. With huge investments in new machines, industrialists sought the most economical and efficient use of their facilities. Overhead costs remained much the same regardless of output, hence a large volume output and low cost unit production were desirable. Toward this end disciples of "scientific management," of whom the best known spokesman was Frederick W. Taylor, established planning departments, streamlined time and work methods, and rearranged machinery and job organization. Out of this would come "continuous-flow production," as Henry Ford called it—an assembly line system with power-driven conveyors delivering parts to factory workers. Taylor especially gave wide publicity to scientific management concepts and in 1911 Louis Brandeis, arguing a railroad rate case before the Interstate Commerce Commission, suggested that railroad companies by using such methods could economize and not have to raise rates.

Science more and more became a handmaiden of industry. Such men as George Eastman and Thomas Edison had conducted research in photography and electricity, but now industrial research became deliberate and planned, with emphasis on the trained man, especially the "chemist," a loose term describing almost any scientist. More institutions joined Yale University and Harvard University in providing technological training: Columbia School of Mines was founded in 1864; M.I.T. three years before; and the other land-grant colleges emphasized engineering as well as agriculture. By the end of the century 147 institutions of higher learning offered technical education, almost 45 per cent of them supported partly or wholly by state or federal government. Pennsylvania's Wharton School of Finance was endowed in 1881; the Graduate School of Business at Harvard in 1908; and dozens of universities built programs around "scientific management" of business enterprise.

Before 1880 the cotton textile industry was often used as a prime example of modernization and mechanization; by the 1890's steel was often taken as a model; and by 1914 the automobile industry, particularly as exemplified by Henry Ford, was the most frequently used illustration of advanced technology and scientific management. Ford was not the inventor of the automobile nor was he the first manufacturer. But he led the way in mass-producing a relatively cheap, durable, standardized motor vehicle that made his name an American byword. Ford early called in a specialist in manufacturing procedures, who brought in new machines, relocated the old, and reorganized operations in an orderly sequence similar to the line production of the steel industry. Turning out most of its own parts, the Ford Motor Company in 1913 produced 168,000 automobiles, one third of the industry's output, and could assemble a Model T in about 12.5 hours. Early in the next year, the idea of a moving assembly line was borrowed from the meat packers: now final assembly took only ninety-three minutes and production nearly doubled. But perfect timing was necessary: a breakdown or work suspension could cripple the entire plant. Moreover, while efficient, these changes left the factory crowded. Every foot of floor space, explained Ford, carried the same overhead cost. Furthermore, a tightly disciplined operation, with each workman specializing in a single detailed job as the work moved by at a predetermined speed, left little opportunity for personal contact between workers.

No less dramatic than the new technology and management was the increased use of the corporate form of business. Limited liability reduced risk; the use of preferred stock with prior claim on dividends and assets in case of dissolution and the issue of interest-bearing mortgage bonds with interest and principal due at a specified time gave additional security. On the other hand, the corporate form made it possible for speculators to use, or misuse, other people's money in dubious enterprises and it separated ownership and management with the effect that often neither was willing to accept social responsibility. Profits were more important than the welfare of workers or of communities.

Using reorganization of manufacturing processes to include interchangeable parts, minute specialization, and assembly line production, the corporation might cut costs if its factory worked at full or near full capacity. But such increased productivity made for intense competition as the result of which weaker competitors were often absorbed or eliminated, with the survivors being consolidated into larger and larger business units. Thus consolidation was another of the major trends in the industrial world after the Civil War.

Consolidation had obvious advantages for the manufacturer. Working with greater efficiency, large units could reduce competition, concentrate production in the most efficient plants, and maintain lower unit costs by operating at full capacity. The elimination of competing brands cut advertising costs and permitted emphasizing the more successful products. Large corporations could better put pressure on railroads for rate concessions and were assumed to have an advantage in international trade. They could better utilize byproducts, and a single unified management meant a reduction of office and sales force, with specialization of managerial talent. Horizontal combinations, dominating all of a particular industry, such as the manufacture of sugar or baseballs, meant control of production and prices; vertical combinations, with control of raw materials, transportation, manufacturing, marketing, and financing of a single product, meant far greater independence than enjoyed by an ordinary concern. In steel and oil, where combinations were both vertical and horizontal, corporations were in effect sovereign entities.

But as a House of Representatives Industrial Commission pointed out in 1900, consolidation was not without its evils. It reduced employment, led to the bankrupting of small concerns through the use of unfair methods, and often meant higher prices and careless service for the consumer. Large combinations were more susceptible to overcapitalization, speculation, and manipulation by shrewd promoters. Moreover, the Commission thought that the rise of large combinations reduced independent businessmen into being hired subordinates, thus "in reality sapping the courage and power of initiative of perhaps the most active and influential men in the community." The more specialized decision-making required within the large organization bred bureaucracy and threatened "inertia resulting from our great size," contended Alfred Sloan, president of General Motors, as he later commented upon a trend still prevalent in the middle of the twentieth century.

Probably an inevitable consequence of American capitalism, consolidation had become a dominant characteristic of industry and transportation by the turn of the century. By 1900 eight powerful groups controlled 108,464 miles of railroads, considerably more than the independents. Between 1859 and 1900 the value of manufactured goods increased eight times, while the number of factories rose by only 50 per cent. Steel production was up nearly a thousandfold between 1860 and 1905, but the number of producers dropped by two-thirds; the number of agricultural implement manufacturers was cut in half between 1880 and 1890. By 1905, out of a total of 216,000 industrial establishments, about 24,000 or roughly 11 per cent controlled 81 per cent of the capital, 72 per cent of the wage earners, and 79 per cent of the value of products manufactured.

Consolidation might be achieved by any one or a combination of devices. The Bell Telephone companies and the United Shoe Machinery Company owed their early advantages to control of patents and the same was later true in the aluminum industry. Pools of various kinds were common after the early 1870's and were in general merely gentlemen's agreements among competitors to maintain price levels by common consent, to control production, to allot territory for marketing, or even to divide profits. But they were unenforceable—"ropes of sand," Rockefeller called them—and were outlawed by the Interstate Commerce Act of 1887 and by the Sherman Antitrust Act of 1890 and by subsequent court rulings, though in actual practice they still occasionally persisted.

Much more important was the new form of organization, the trust, in a narrow, formal sense, of which the first of significance was the Standard Oil Company (1882), which came to control from 90 to 95 per cent of all oil refined. Under the trust arrangement, competing concerns joined hands by turning over their securities and power to a board of trustees of a new concern, shareholders receiving certificates of trust in exchange. In the 1880's cottonseed oil, lead, whiskey, and sugar were among the fields which came to be dominated by such combinations. Of the sugar trust, controlling practically all refining in the United States, Judge Barrett of the New York Supreme Court said:

It can close every refinery at will, close some and open others, limit the purchase of raw material, artificially limit the production of refined sugar, enhance the price to enrich themselves and their associates at the public expense, and depress the price when necessary to crush out and impoverish a foolhardy rival.

Because of antitrust legislation at both the state and national level after 1890, the trust as known in the 1880's gave way to the holding company, a concern formed expressly to control a number of existing corporations, the stock in these simply being exchanged for stock in the holding company. John Moody, in his

Masters of Capital (1904), listed 318 industrial combinations, representing a consolidation of nearly 5,300 plants, of which 236 (with five sixths of the total capital of over $7 billion) had been incorporated as holding companies since the beginning of 1898, 170 of them in New Jersey, where incorporation laws were conveniently lax. Among them were the Pennsylvania Railroad, American Bell Telephone, International Harvester, Standard Oil of New Jersey, and the greatest of all, United States Steel, a combination of eleven constituent companies with 170 subsidiary concerns. By this time the term "trust" came to mean any combination, even with a holding company organization. Outright merger, interlocking directorates, and the establishment of a community of interest were other forms of consolidation, but the holding company was and still is the most significant type of organization.

Combination often produced both monopoly and opposition, though size alone was no guarantee of profit, as shareholders of J. P. Morgan's United States Shipbuilding Company and the International Mercantile Marine Company sadly learned. By 1890, in reaction to the trend, at least fourteen states had constitutional prohibitions against monopoly or restraint of trade and thirteen had enacted antitrust laws. But disinterest and an inability or unwillingness to enforce these provisions threw the question into the lap of Congress, which, after remarkably little discussion, passed the Sherman Antitrust Act in 1890. This was to pay lip service to the idea of control demanded by a sizable segment of the public—labor, small businessmen, farmers, reformers—clamoring through third party movements like the Greenback, the Anti-Monopolist, and various local agrarian "potato-bug" parties of the 1880's.

The Sherman Antitrust Act declared illegal any "combination in the form of trust or otherwise, or conspiracy in restraint of trade," and prescribed penalties for violation of these prohibitions. But the law was ambiguous: it failed to define trust or what was meant by "restraint of trade," leaving the courts to interpret. Its vagueness, the laxity of enforcement, and adverse decisions of the Supreme Court all rendered the law ineffective. Down to 1901 the federal government had instituted but eighteen suits under it, with practically no success. In the classic case involving the American Sugar Refining Company, the court held that sugar refining was not commerce in a strict constitutional sense and that because the concern held control of 98 per cent of sugar refining in the United States that did not in itself necessarily constitute restraint of trade. That the law was not working was indicated by the fact that of the 318 industrial trusts cited by Moody in 1904, all but twenty-three had been formed after the passage of the Sherman Act. Indeed, the period 1897–1904 was the heyday of trust formation.

Early in the twentieth century new voices of protest arose as young reformers, the Muckrakers, widely publicized the malpractices of big business and called for a cleansing of the Augean stables. Through periodicals and in novels and nonfiction, such writers as Lincoln Steffens, Ida Tarbell, Thomas W. Lawson, Frank Norris, and Upton Sinclair exposed the practices of the trusts, the railroads, and the stock market, and showed the links between business and corrupt politics. As the godfathers of widespread reform pressure under the name of Progressivism, the Muckrakers kept the question of control of the trusts before the public in the first decade or so of the twentieth century.

Theodore Roosevelt indicated some tendency to wield his "big stick" against business combinations, though believing them inevitable and generally desirable, a position which brought comment from Mr. Dooley: "Th' trusts, says he, are heejous monsthers built up be th' inlightened intherprise iv th' men who have done so much to advance progress in our beloved counthry," he says. "On wan hand I wud stamp thim undher fut; on th' other hand not so fast." Roosevelt prevailed upon Congress to create a Bureau of Corporations to probe and publicize the activities of certain types of business concerns, and in his administation forty-four antitrust suits were brought, the most notable being the Northern Securities case. The $400 million Northern Securities Corporation was a compromise bringing together the Northern Pacific, Great Northern, and Burlington railroads after a long struggle for control between James J. Hill and J. P. Morgan on one side, and E. H. Harriman, aided by Kuhn, Loeb & Company, on the other. When the case had finally wound its tortuous way

through the courts, the Supreme Court (1904) called the Northern Securities Corporation a combination acting in restraint of
trade and ordered it dissolved. As Roosevelt's trust busting continued, the Beef Trust, the Fertilizer Trust, and the American
Tobacco Company were all ordered disbanded, but invariably the
constituent companies thus created continued to work in unison.
Standard Oil, for example, though ordered broken down, continued to exist and even to expand through corporations chartered
in various states. Eventually Roosevelt came to distinguish between "good" trusts showing concern for public welfare and
"bad" trusts which ignored all except selfish ends, and by 1911
the Supreme Court was making the same distinction as it followed the "rule of reason."

Roosevelt's hand-picked successor, William Howard Taft, in
four years in office brought almost twice as many antitrust suits
as his predecessor had brought in seven and a half years. The
most important, those against United States Steel and International Harvester, were not upheld by the Supreme Court, but
the campaign exerted a salutary effect. In addition, the Pujo
Committee exposed the existence of a "Money Trust" and recom-
mended change in the currency and banking structure.

By the time of the election of 1912, the Progressive movement
was at its peak and all three major candidates, Taft, Roosevelt,
and Woodrow Wilson, took stands in favor of action to curb
business combinations. Roosevelt and the Bull Moose Progressives advocated control by an administrative commission; Taft
urged stricter enforcement of the antitrust laws; Wilson demanded
a "New Freedom" which by regulation would restore competition
to the business world. "I am for big business, and I am against
the trusts," said the former Princeton professor. "Any man who
can survive by his brains, any man who can put the others out of
the business by making the thing cheaper to the consumer at the
same time that he is increasing its intrinsic value and quality, I
take off my hat to." But free competition must prevail.

Once elected, Wilson exerted real leadership and much of his
New Freedom program, though somewhat modified, was enacted
into law. Along with the first real lowering of the tariff since before the Civil War and the establishment of the Federal Reserve

System, the program included several measures designed to make national policing of trust activities more effective. The Federal Trade Commission (1913) replaced the old Bureau of Corporations and had expanded powers to ferret out illegal or harmful business practices and to initiate action against them. Congress passed the Clayton Act, designed to supplement the Sherman Act and to hit the ever-popular holding company. It was watered down from its original version, having been reduced, according to a senator from Missouri, from "a raging lion with a mouth full of teeth" to "a tabby cat with soft gums, a plaintive mew, and an anemic appearance," but despite this, it broadened and strengthened the existing statutes. It prohibited practices that tended to lessen competition, create monopoly, or bring about undesirable price discrimination; it restricted various types of holding companies and interlocking directorates, if monopolistic practices were involved; and it conferred rights on labor by exempting unions and farm organizations from antitrust prosecution, specifically sanctioning strikes and peaceful picketing, and prohibiting the use of court injunctions in labor disputes, except where "irreparable injury" was caused to property.

World War I tended to divert attention. Big business seemed less wicked and the trust issue faded from the headlines. Corporations on the whole were inclined to obey the Federal Trade Commission, and the courts more and more adhered to the "rule of reason," punishing those actually guilty of unreasonable restraint of trade. But in the postwar decade, supervision was for all practical purposes mild or nonexistent. The principle of regulation was always hovering in the background, however, as the notion persisted that the competitive system did not, in itself, provide adequate safeguards for the entire community.

XV

LABOR IN AN INDUSTRIALIZING
SOCIETY

OUT OF CONSOLIDATION and its abuses came an adverse public reaction and a movement for government regulation; out of the bigness, the impersonality, and the lack of responsibility of the corporation came a reaction of labor, and a significant movement for unionization. National unions came into existence after the Civil War and for the first time survived the vicissitudes of depression and gave evidence of playing some significant role in political and economic life. That is not to say that organized labor was yet a potent force. Even by 1920 only about 15 per cent of the almost 31 million nonagricultural workers in the country were organized.

American labor after the Civil War was faced with a set of circumstances which gave incentive to organization, yet at the same time made organization increasingly difficult. Manufacturers might best meet pressure for low prices by reducing their unit cost of production, primarily through increased mechanization. Machines might replace semiskilled workers, thus reducing labor costs. Many machines required but brief training to operate. According to Henry Ford, in 1922, 43 per cent of the jobs in his automobile factory required only one day of training; only 15 per cent required as much as one month of training. Skilled

209

workers, as in the prewar era, fearful of lower standards or of replacement by less skilled under a minute division of labor, took the lead in labor organization.

The impersonality of the great corporation, submerging the bargaining power of the individual, helped bring forth the rise of labor unions. At the same time, because of their size and their strength, the great corporations were in a position to resist labor organization on better than even terms. At their disposal were funds for closing factories and starving workers into submission or for actively combating strikes for long periods, importing strike breakers or the Pinkerton detectives to "protect property." Corporations could well afford to hire topflight lawyers to fight their disputes through the courts or to control or even purchase both newspapers and politicians. Until the 1930's, labor, except for railroad workers, was least successful in organizing in those industries dominated by the large corporations—oil, coal, automobiles, and iron and steel.

A nationwide transportation network tended to make labor more mobile and to reduce labor standards to the lowest common denominator by moving cheap labor from the South or from Europe into the North. At the same time, strikes, particularly against railroads, often carried national implications and elicited a hostile public opinion. Imbued with the Gospel of Wealth idea, a broad segment of the public believed that competition brought progress and that labor organizations were alien and contrary to the American way of life. "We are not opposed to good unionism, if such exists anywhere," said one leader of the National Association of Manufacturers. "The American brand of unionism, however, is un-American, illegal and indecent." A minority of radical, militant agitators, who believed in anarchism and openly advocated the violent overthrow of government and the "bloated plutocrats," cast all of labor in a bad light and literally invited criticism.

Another influence was immigration. In the 317 years from 1607 to 1924 an estimated 50 million people, mainly Europeans, migrated to the United States. Before the 1880's most came from northern and western Europe—England, Ireland, France, Germany, and the Scandinavian countries; subsequently a significant shift took place, with the newcomers coming in increasing numbers from eastern, central, and southern Europe, where conditions were worse than in other parts of the continent. In the 1880's Italians, Slovaks, Croats, Magyars, Greeks, and Poles made up 19 per cent of all entries into the United States; by the 1900–1910 decade, they constituted 66 per cent of the total.

This so-called "new immigration," usually Catholic or Jewish in religion, Mediterranean and Slavic in culture, often illiterate and poor, unskilled but eager to work, settled in the industrial areas to form part of the growing labor pool so essential to the expansion of the national economy. By their very presence these newcomers caused criticism. Native Americans complained that the strain was being watered down, that immigrants pushed crime rates upward and contributed to corrupt politics. The antiforeign American Protective Association gained considerable strength in the 1890's, and poet Thomas Bailey Aldrich asked the rhetorical question,

> O Liberty, White Goddess! Is it well
> To leave the gates unguarded?

The workingman in particular resented the influx of unskilled competition willing to work for low wages. Furthermore, the "new immigrants" often clung tenaciously to their traditions, including antagonisms brought from the old country: Poles hated the Germans and the feeling was returned; Magyars detested the Slavs, and the Slavs despised the Croats. Employers were able to capitalize on these feelings and certainly labor organizers found themselves hard put to reconcile these differences and to obtain co-operation from diverse ethnic groups.

It is not surprising, therefore, that organized labor was one of the most important influences working for the restriction of immigration. Such restriction came slowly and piecemeal, first barring prostitutes, paupers, and other undesirables; then in 1882 excluding Chinese laborers. By 1917 there was a literacy requirement and by 1921 came widespread prejudice and the first severe limitations, as the door swung shut to all but a trickle, comparatively speaking.

It was in this setting of changing patterns of immigration, an ofttimes unfavorable public opinion, and of the increasingly mechanized large corporation, that organized labor moved forward, its course hampered or altered by adverse winds. Many unions rose and fell, but the most important were a handful of national organizations, a few of which survived.

One of the first was the National Labor Union, founded in 1866 by William Sylvis, an iron molder. Insisting that his union would not "be bought with gold, scared by a loud noise nor whipped with the traces of falsehood and willful misrepresentations of the most corrupt newspapers on the face of the earth," Sylvis built its membership to a peak of 600,000 in 1868, mainly in the building trades, machine shops, and foundries. The National Labor Union displayed an interest in greenbacks, housing reform, an eight-hour day, and enforcement of the apprenticeship system, but unfortunately ventured into politics in 1872, endorsing as a third party the erratic Horace Greeley, candidate of the liberal Republicans and Democrats. That, plus the panic and depression of 1873, spelled disaster and the organization failed to survive.

Contemporary with it was the Knights of Labor, established in 1869 by Uriah Stephens, a Philadelphia garment cutter who had once trained for the Baptist ministry. Originally a secret, ritualistic mutual protection society, the Knights limped along for more than a decade, then suddenly began to thrive, despite such opposition as that of Allan Pinkerton, who called it "an amalgamation of the Molly Maguires and the Commune." In 1878 a humanitarian middle-class reformer, Terence V. Powderly, became Grand Master Workman, as the head was called, and soon the organization abandoned its secrecy and began to increase its membership, which reached about 100,000 in 1885, then blossomed forth sensationally to an estimated 700,000 in 1886, although Powderly later commented that "at least four hundred thousand came in from curiosity and caused more damage than good."

The secret of rapid growth may have been linked to the winning of a strike against one of Jay Gould's railroads, but was more likely connected with the eight-hour day movement then sweeping the country. Ordinarily the Knight's leaders put little faith in strikes, stressing instead "agitation, education and organization." Broadly based, the union welcomed all workers, regardless of sex, degree of skill, or type of work, excepting only bankers, lawyers, stockbrokers, liquor dealers, professional gamblers, and, for a time, physicians. Some locals were organized by shops, some by departments, some by industries, but above the local level, organization was on a geographic basis. Among its other desires, the Knights stood for the eight-hour day, equal pay for women, abolition of child labor, greenbacks, postal savings banks, and an income tax. It was particularly interested in the co-operative movement as a means of banishing "that curse of modern civilization—wage slavery," a theme which ran through many of the union's songs.

> Lo from Labor's sons and daughters,
> In the depths of misery
> Like the rush of many waters,
> Comes the cry "We will be free!"
> Comes the cry "We will be free!"

If the rise of the Knights of Labor was meteoric, its demise was equally rapid. The failure of the group's co-operative ventures brought disillusionment; Powderly's leadership was not able to hold together the diverse groups making up membership; the Knights entered into strikes quite unprepared and their resort to violence on several occasions brought them into public disfavor; the eight-hour movement collapsed and membership began to fall off while the *coup de grâce* was the Haymarket Riot in Chicago (May, 1886), for which conservatives unfairly blamed the Knights, while radicals within the union condemned Powderly for not pursuing a more vigorous course.

No doubt a sizable number of Knights, particularly skilled workers, turned to another relatively new group, the American Federation of Labor, which had been formed in 1881, but reorganized in 1886 as the A. F. of L. Its founder was Samuel Gompers, a colorful Jewish cigar maker who had been born in a London tenement house and who would be elected president of the A. F. of L. every year but one between 1886 and 1924. Its membership grew slowly, reaching some 200,000 by 1889, over 2 million by 1910, and twice that by the end of World War I.

It was a loose "union of unions," mostly national, organized mainly on craft lines, though in later years industrial unions would be common among its affiliates. Under Gompers and men like his fellow cigar maker Adolph Strasser, the A. F. of L. adopted a down-to-earth approach, ignoring long-range social reforms in favor of more immediate gains—higher wages, shorter hours, better working conditions, the closed shop, and death, sickness, and unemployment benefits. "We are all practical men," said the hardheaded Strasser before a Senate committee in 1883. "We have no ultimate ends. We are going on from day to day. We are fighting only for immediate objects—objects that can be realized in a few years." Basically nonpolitical, the union supported whichever candidates seemed most likely to aid it. Aggressive, it levied dues on its members, built large strike funds, and relied heavily on the strike and the boycott, though not neglecting the legislative approach. For many years it was more interested in skilled than unskilled workers and it traditionally shied away from co-operatives. By 1900 it was strong in the bituminous coal fields, but found organization extremely difficult in the anthracite fields, where the owners were consolidated and, as one of them put it, regarded anthracite mining "as a business, and not a religious, sentimental or academic proposition." Only the intervention of President Theodore Roosevelt brought anything like recognition, and the union experienced even greater difficulty in the coalfields of Colorado and West Virginia and made almost no inroads in oil and steel.

To these other early unions might be added the Industrial Workers of the World, a militantly radical organization opposed by the more conservative labor groups like the A. F. of L. Founded in 1905, the I.W.W. demanded "one big industrial union" to "take possession of the earth and the machinery of production and abolish the wage system." With never more than about 60,000 members, the Wobblies, as they were called, were strongest among unskilled workers in textiles and in Western mines, oil fields, lumber camps, and canneries. Especially under the crude and aggressive "Big Bill" Haywood, they kept before

GROWTH IN MEMBERSHIP OF THE AMERICAN FEDERATION OF
LABOR, 1897–1917*

Year	Membership (1,000)	Year	Membership (1,000)
1897	265	1907	1,539
1898	278	1908	1,587
1899	349	1909	1,483
1900	548	1910	1,562
1901	788	1911	1,762
1902	1,024	1912	1,770
1903	1,466	1913	1,996
1904	1,676	1914	2,021
1905	1,494	1915	1,946
1906	1,454	1916	2,073
		1917	2,371

* *Historical Statistics of the United States, Colonial Times to 1957*, p. 97.

them the idea of the class struggle, urged the use of the general strike, and frequently resorted to violence. For the more indirect approach of other reformers, particularly religious, they had no patience, as one of the best known songs in their famous *Little Red Song Book* indicates with considerable irony:

> You will eat, bye and bye
> In that glorious land above the sky (way on high)
> Work and pray, live on hay,
> You'll get pie in the sky when you die (that's no lie).

Internal dissent and opposition to World War I brought the downfall of the I.W.W., and many of its members were subsequently absorbed in the Communist Party. The I.W.W. no doubt did much to harm the entire labor movement in the eyes of the public, but in another sense the Wobblies had a salutary effect: they called attention to the need of doing something for the unskilled workers, with the result that the A. F. of L. would soon adjust its policies accordingly.

Of the major national unions here mentioned, the most conservative, the A. F. of L., survived and grew in importance, though fought by employers individually or through antiunion combinations like the National Association of Manufacturers (1895), and though experiencing serious strike setbacks throughout the period.

Of the more than 35,000 strikes between 1881 and 1905, a few stand out as being particularly significant. Especially bitter were the mass walkouts on numerous railroads throughout the country in 1877, with rioting in Chicago, St. Paul, Omaha, and San Francisco, and in Pittsburgh, where troops clashed with the strikers and a mob fired the roundhouse and burned 104 locomotives and more than 500 coaches and box cars. Another particularly bitter strike came in the summer of 1882 on the New York Central system, where freight handlers demanded an increase in pay from seventeen to twenty cents an hour, only to be defeated by strikebreakers brought in by the railroad.

> There's Field, Jay Gould, and Vanderbilt, their millions
> they did save
> By paying starvation wages and working men like slaves;
> They hum round honest labor as the bee does round the
> flower,
> And suck the sweetness of your toil for seventeen cents an
> hour.

Probably two of the most important strikes, both of them lost by labor, occurred in the 1890's. One, the Homestead Strike at the Carnegie Steel Company on the outskirts of Pittsburgh, came ostensibly over failure to agree on a wage scale after the introduction of new laborsaving machinery, but actually because of the determination of Carnegie's manager, Henry Clay Frick, to break the power of the Amalgamated Association of Iron and Steel Workers. Pinkerton detectives, 300 strong, were hired to protect the plant and in the pitched battle that followed, ten persons were killed. At Frick's request, the Governor sent in the militia, which enabled the company to hire strikebreakers and maintain them until the union gave in. The power of the Amalgamated was broken in the only major concern in which it had a foothold, and for the next forty years the steel industry would be able to prevent the organization of its labor.

The second significant strike of the same era came in Chicago in 1894, in part the aftermath of depression. Workers of the Pullman Palace Car Company struck after wage cuts and discharges had taken place without a corresponding reduction of rents in the company village of Pullman. The American Railway Union under Eugene Debs took sympathetic action and refused to handle trains which included Pullman cars. The boycott ultimately spread to twenty-seven states, but strike activity centered in Chicago, where there was disorder and property destruction and where a federal circuit judge issued an injunction under the Sherman Act to restrain union officials from hampering the flow of interstate commerce. Debs spent six months in prison for contempt and the Supreme Court upheld his conviction, though on grounds broader than those of the Sherman Act. Moreover, President Cleveland was persuaded to send federal troops to maintain order, over the protest of Illinois Governor John Peter Altgeld, who complained bitterly and with good cause of this unnecessary infringement on state sovereignty. As a result of the court order and federal intervention, both the strike and the union were broken and for the next forty years organized labor would battle against the use of the injunction as a weapon of capital in labor-management disputes.

Eugene Debs was not the only labor leader to run afoul of the Sherman Antitrust Act, a law originally directed against capitalistic monopoly, but sometimes construed to include unions as well. The most notorious example involved 197 members of the United Hatters of North America who were assessed damages totaling $240,000 in 1908, on the grounds that their nationwide boycott of a hat manufacturer in Danbury, Connecticut, constituted conspiracy in restraint of trade. In the Clayton Antitrust Act of 1914, Congress exempted labor unions insisting that "the labor of a human being is not a commodity or article of commerce." At the same time, it limited the use of the injunction in labor disputes "unless necessary to prevent irreparable injury to property, or to a property right." During the Wilson administration, these stipulations were helpful, but with the coming of the reactionary 1920's it was obvious that the Clayton Law was not the "Magna Carta" for labor that Gompers first thought it was.

Both union and nonunion workers made gains during the period. The average work day in industry dropped from eleven hours in 1860 to ten in 1890 and nine in 1914, though it varied from industry to industry. Real wages rose, especially before

1890, with a slower gain or leveling off after that date, but productivity rose even more rapidly.

In addition, labor benefited from social legislation, especially in the reform era of the early twentieth century. As early as 1885, under the prodding of the Knights of Labor, Congress had prohibited the importation of contract labor. By 1892 an eight-hour day for federal employees went into effect, and in 1916 by Congressional action it became standard for all interstate railroad workers. A separate Department of Labor was created in 1913, and twice Congress attempted to prohibit child labor, once in 1916 under the cloak of regulating commerce and again in 1919 in the guise of taxation, only to have both attempts declared unconstitutional by the Supreme Court. A constitutional amendment barring child labor was subsequently proposed but never ratified, in part because many states had eliminated the worst abuses, in part because compulsory school attendance laws served the same purpose, and in part because after 1938 the Court would reverse its decision.

In general, prior to World War I social legislation affecting labor came through state action rather than federal, and was based on the police powers of the Constitution giving the right to protect the morals, health, safety, and welfare of the people. Still, conservative courts often nullified such legislation as violating the due process clause of the Fourteenth Amendment, although in time the courts would assume a more liberal position. The progressive reformers, particularly, were concerned with efforts to protect the weak and to improve working conditions. Thus they led the movement for abolition of child labor, shorter working hours for women, equal pay for equal work, liability and compensation laws in case of accidents, and elimination of slums and sweatshops. In some areas considerable success was achieved; in others very little.

State laws setting minimum age limits for workers were enacted by every state except one by 1914, but many were wholly ineffective. A few states prior to 1900 had limited the hours women might work to sixty per week, and the movement spread rapidly in the next few years. Although invalidating a New York law limiting labor in bakeries to ten hours a day (*Lochner v. New*

York, 1905), the Supreme Court in 1908 upheld an Oregon statute which prescribed the ten-hour day for women only (*Mueller v. Oregon*), the majority opinion contending as follows:

That woman's physical structure and the performance of maternal functions place her at a disadvantage in the struggle for subsistence is obvious. This is especially true when the burdens of motherhood are placed upon her. Even when they are not, by abundant testimony of the medical fraternity continuance for a long time on her feet at work, repeating this from day to day, tends to injurious effects upon the body, and, as healthy mothers are essential to vigorous offspring, the physical well-being of women becomes an object of public interest and care in order to preserve the strength and vigor of the race.

By 1917 thirty-nine states would have laws regulating women's work hours; in addition, many precluded women from certain occupations—coal mining, foundry work, track work on railroads, and saloonkeeper, for example.

Equal pay laws for women were enacted in a few Western states as early as 1878, but they almost invariably dealt only with the teaching profession; not until 1919 was a really comprehensive equal pay law passed (in Michigan) and that, like those of sixteen other states which subsequently adopted them, would prove difficult to enforce. By the turn of the century, roughly half the states had factory inspection laws to help safeguard the health and safety of employees. Beginning with Wisconsin, states began to enact workmen's compensation laws to indemnify workers injured on the job, thus overturning the old theory under common law that the employer was responsible only when negligence could definitely be proved. Now it was assumed that both industry and society as a whole had a responsibility in this regard.

Still, such gains were piecemeal and came only after agitation and frequently after long court battles. If labor unions by 1914 were definitely established and if social legislation was likewise being more commonly accepted, the day of "Big Labor" was not yet at hand, and the role of government would tend to lessen after World War I until the coming of the New Deal in the 1930's.

XVI

SHIFTING PATTERNS OF TRADE
AND COMMERCE

WITH THE ADVENT of a highly technological and specialized manufacturing and a growing maturity of the American economy, the system of distribution also matured and grew steadily more complex as the gap between producer and consumer widened. Domestic trade was increasing at a more rapid rate than foreign and the process of distribution consistently increased in relative importance. In 1870, 6 per cent of the labor force was engaged in distribution; in 1910, 9.3 per cent, and 37 per cent of the retail price of goods was distributing cost.

On one hand, the period between the Civil War and World War I was characterized by a strong trend toward specialization in both wholesaling and retailing that went along with the growing urbanization of the era; on the other, the period gave rise to an increasing number of middlemen—jobbers, commission agents, salesmen, and advertising experts—and to the growth of large-scale retailers—department stores, chain stores, and mail-order houses, sometimes powerful enough to influence or even eliminate wholesalers. Giant new industries like Standard Oil, for example, often built their own marketing structures, bypassing middlemen in the process.

Whereas the general store, even in 1914 a basic distributing point for the rural market, operated on a credit basis, the urban oriented department store frequently sold only for cash. Pioneers such as Macy's and Stewarts in New York, John Wanamaker in Philadelphia, and Marshall Field in Chicago could offer lower prices due to large-scale operation and direct purchases from manufacturers in many cases. By 1910 department store sales ran to nearly $700 million annually; by 1919 to about $2.5 billion.

Beginning with George Gilman's Great American Tea Company in 1858, subsequently reorganized in 1869 as the Great Atlantic & Pacific Tea Company, the chain store joined the department store as an ever-expanding phenomenon. By 1911 the A & P had 400 stores and ten years later 4,500. F. W. Woolworth had opened his first permanent "Five and Ten Cent Store" in Lancaster, Pennsylvania, in 1879; thirty-three years later the Woolworth chain included 602 stores, with sales of over $50 million. Meanwhile, competitors, beginning with the Kresge chain (1897), began to crop up throughout the country and the chain idea spread into the drug, food, and clothing fields. Volume business and bulk purchases direct from producers may have been keys to success, as Woolworth's advertising insisted, but privately in 1892 Woolworth added another explanation: "We must have cheap help or we cannot sell cheap goods." By 1919 total chain-store sales reached $3 billion annually and the figure continued to rise.

Another innovation was the mail order house. The first of significance was Aaron Montgomery Ward's Original Grange Supply House, opened in Chicago in 1872 to meet the needs of the Grangers, who were complaining about parasitic middlemen. Ward prospered and by the 1890's had built up an annual business of more than $1 million. By then his chief competitor, Sears, Roebuck and Company, also in Chicago, was coming up fast, with gross sales of over $400,000 in 1894. Rural free delivery after 1896 and the inauguration of government parcel post service in 1913 would do much to boost mail order business to a total of over half a billion dollars by 1919. Moreover, the coming of the automobile undercut the general store by facilitating excursions to town, where opportunities for both shopping and diversion were superior. By the middle twenties mail order houses were opening retail outlets in smaller cities and larger towns to capture a share of the expanding urban market, and this in turn helped speed the demise of the general merchandiser.

By 1919 department, chain, and mail order stores together accounted for 13 per cent of total retail sales and were obviously an important factor in the economy. They helped bring about the one-price system, which John Wanamaker had been using since the 1860's; they adopted the practice of guaranteeing goods and of refunding money to dissatisfied customers. More and more the large retailer came to shift some of his services on to the manufacturer who now did more processing and packaging of products like coffee, sugar, bacon, and cereals which previously had come in bulk. In addition, by self-service the consumer took over some of the retailer's responsibility in exchange for lower prices. Banks and finance companies gradually took over the credit function, whereas both retailers and wholesalers had undertaken this themselves previously.

Cheaper, more rapid transportation facilitated the distribution process, as did such innovations as commercial refrigeration, the typewriter, the cash register, and the adding machine. Thanks to communications and transportation improvements, advertising tended to become national in scope. In the 1860's the public became aware of Dr. Lyon's tooth powder tablets; as early as 1895, they knew that Ivory soap was 99 44/100 % pure; and that children cried for Fletcher's Castoria. Patent medicines were the largest single advertisers, and Lydia Pinkham's famous vegetable compound was the best known, although Peruna, Davis' Celebrated Painkiller, and Hostetter's Vinegar Stomach Bitters were publicized from coast to coast.

Before an adverse reaction set in momentarily in the 1890's, thousands of gaudy advertisements were carried by sandwichmen or plastered on billboards or barns. In the late 1870's full-page department store advertisements began to appear in metropolitan newspapers and were regularly run in the late 1880's, when periodicals also became important in this respect. The cost of advertisements in newspapers and magazines combined had been less than $10 million in 1867, but totaled almost $100 million by 1900, and five times that by 1919 as advertising came to be the most important source of revenue for these publications. Advertising would blossom forth in the twentieth century, using techniques which shocked the Muckrakers and the Progressive reformers, who, with such laws as the Pure Food and Drug Act of 1906, tried to legislate truth into the profession.

Apart from a few state restrictions, such as high taxes on margarine and out of state liquors to protect local products, or bans on importation of fruit to prevent the introduction of insects and plant diseases, the United States constituted a free trade area, uninhibited by major barriers to the flow of commerce. With mass production of goods, installment buying already being used, and advertising to stimulate desires, the prosperous future of American business seemed assured by the time of World War I.

With industrial growth, improved transportation, better credit and banking facilities, and extension of settlement into new regions, foreign commerce continued to expand as before the Civil War. The annual average of combined exports and imports in the immediate pre-Sumter years was slightly over $670 million; by 1914 it totaled more than $4 billion. Only Britain and Germany had a higher foreign trade. In terms of dollar value, exports rose at a slightly higher rate than did imports. In general, before 1875, imports outweighed exports. Only fifteen of the eighty-six years from 1790 to 1875 returned a favorable balance of trade, while only three of the eighty-seven years between 1876 and 1962 had an unfavorable balance. But until World War I, the United States continued to be a debtor nation. The merchant marine was declining and freight and insurance charges had to be deducted from the favorable balance, along with the money spent by travelers, sent home by immigrants, or paid in interest and dividends to foreign investors. Gold made up the ultimate deficit. Foreign investment in the United States rose from an estimated $1.4 billion in 1869 to $6.7 billion by the middle of 1914, over half by this later date in railroads. American investments abroad increased from about $80 million in 1869 to some $684.5 million by 1897; then began a remarkable expansion to more than $3.5 billion in 1914. Largely because of the coming of the war and the growth of the merchant marine, the United States emerged a creditor nation.

The transformation of foreign trade continued. In 1870, 79.4 per cent of American exports were agricultural products; by 1913

TABLE OF U.S. MERCHANDISE IMPORTS, BY ECONOMIC CLASSES, 1860–1918
(in Millions of Dollars)*

Year	Total	Crude materials	Crude foodstuffs	Manufactured foodstuffs	Semimanufactures	Finished manufactures
1860	354	40	46	60	35	172
1865	239	30	35	48	30	96
1870	436	57	54	96	56	174
1875	533	89	90	113	63	178
1880	668	142	100	118	111	197
1885	578	120	93	103	78	183
1890	789	180	128	133	117	231
1895	732	188	141	107	96	200
1900	850	282	98	133	134	203
1905	1,118	396	146	145	178	252
1910	1,557	578	145	182	285	368
1914	1,894	650	248	228	319	449
1918	3,031	1,234	346	397	650	405

* Historical Statistics of the United States, Colonial Times to 1957, pp. 544–45.

VALUE OF U.S. MERCHANDISE EXPORTS, BY ECONOMIC CLASSES, 1860–1918
(in Millions of Dollars)*

Year	Total	Crude materials	Crude foodstuffs	Manufactured foodstuffs	Semimanu- factures	Finished manufactures
1860	316	217	12	39	13	36
1865	137	34	14	48	11	30
1870	377	214	42	51	14	56
1875	499	208	79	110	27	75
1880	824	243	266	193	29	93
1885	727	251	123	202	39	111
1890	845	309	132	225	46	133
1895	793	269	99	219	62	144
1900	1,371	340	226	320	153	332
1905	1,492	479	118	283	210	402
1910	1,710	574	110	259	268	499
1914	2,330	800	137	293	374	725
1918	6,048	972	547	1,406	1,053	2,069

* Historical Statistics of the United States, Colonial Times to 1957, pp. 544–45.

FOREIGN TRADE TOTALS, 1860–1918*
(in Millions of Dollars) †

Year	Exports	Imports
1860	400	362
1865	234	249
1870	451	462
1875	606	554
1880	853	761
1885	784	621
1890	910	823
1895	921	789
1900	1,499	930
1905	1,660	1,199
1910	1,919	1,646
1914	2,532	1,991
1918	6,443	3,165

* Includes merchandise, gold, and silver.
† *Historical Statistics of the United States, Colonial Times to 1957,* pp. 537–38.

only 46 per cent fell in that category. Manufactured and semi-manufactured goods became increasingly important, rising from 30 per cent, by value, just prior to the Civil War, to almost 60 per cent by the eve of World War I. Cotton still remained the most important single export, and wheat was also prominent, especially before 1900, but gradually a variety of manufactured goods, especially petroleum products, locomotives, and industrial machines, rose on the export scale.

On the other hand, if the export of agricultural products declined relatively and manufactures and semimanufactures increased, the converse was true with regard to imports. In the immediate pre-Civil War era, finished manufactures had made up 48 per cent of American imports, with cotton and woolen textiles being most important; by 1914 finished manufactures comprised only 22 per cent of American imports. Meanwhile, imports of raw materials grew in the same period, from 12 per cent to 35 per cent. By World War I, four of the first five imports were agricultural—hides, coffee, sugar, and raw silk.

As before, Europe, and Britain in particular, made up the most important trade area, but other regions were taking a larger share. In 1860, 75 per cent of American exports went to Europe and

61 per cent of her imports came from there; by 1914 the percentages had dropped to 63 for exports and 44 for imports. Great Britain remained the best customer, both in imports and exports, but Canada now came second on the list, followed by Germany, France, and Cuba. As a producer of crude materials, Asia was becoming more a part of the trade pattern, contributing about 16.5 per cent of our imports by 1900.

The coasting trade thrived and was still restricted to American vessels, but the ocean-going merchant marine declined after the Civil War. By 1914 it was still the world's third largest merchant fleet, but about six sevenths of it was on the Great Lakes or engaged in coastwise trade. It went from a peak registered tonnage for foreign trade of 2.5 million in 1861 to a nadir of 726,213 tons in 1898, then rose slowly to 1 million by 1914, when it carried less than 10 per cent of American trade abroad. The federal government gave aid through improvement of waterways and harbors and by favoring American ships on tonnage fees and the coasting trade monopoly. But federal subsidy was unimportant; indeed by forbidding American registry to foreign-built vessels prior to 1914, the government in effect forced Americans to buy their ships at home, at prices that were from 20 to 25 per cent higher than abroad. A slowness in shifting to steam and to iron hulls was a drawback, as were higher construction and operating costs, and the competition of industry, domestic transportation, and agriculture for capital. The margin of profit was so slim that when Congress passed the La Follette Seamen's Act of 1915, prescribing better working and living conditions for sailors in the merchant marine, shippers insisted that the extra expense would scuttle the industry. It was the war in Europe and the elimination of competition from the German merchant fleet and from much of the Allied fleet that brought prosperity and expansion.

Through the tariff, which remained protective, the federal government exerted some influence over commerce in the 1860–1914 era. The level of the tariff, pushed up during the Civil War, did not decline appreciably, apart from a few reductions of a temporary nature resulting from the Liberal Republican agitation of the early 1870's. A mounting treasury surplus helped bring the creation of a tariff commission in 1882, but the result of its recommendations —the so-called Mongrel Tariff of 1883—kept general levels high and was, as a contemporary put it, "a mere bending of the top and branches to the wind of public opinion to save the trunk of the protective system."

Neither political party took a firm stand on the tariff question until 1887, when Grover Cleveland labeled it "a vicious, inequitable, and illogical source of unnecessary taxation," which boosted consumer's prices. The Senate thought otherwise and the tariff became a leading issue in the election of 1888, with high tariff men arguing for the continuing protection of infant American industry and of the American wage level and standard of living, further beclouding the issue by assuring Irish-American voters that a vote for Cleveland was a vote for perfidious Britain, the leading free-trade nation. Cleveland's defeat was taken as an approval of the protective principle, and Congress, after considerable log-rolling, enacted the McKinley Tariff of 1890, which pushed levels to a new all-time high, averaging over 49 per cent, though it also sought to reduce the Treasury surplus and to stimulate domestic sugar production by removing the duty on sugar and paying a bounty on that produced at home.

Four years later, after Cleveland had been returned to office and with Democrats in control of both houses, the Wilson-Gorman Tariff became law without the signature of the President, who called it "party perfidy and party dishonor," but thought it better than no revision at all. The new law dropped rates to an average of 41.3 per cent, and in addition contained a 2 per cent tax on personal incomes, a provision which Joseph Choate, lawyer and later diplomat, labeled "Communist, socialistic," and which the Supreme Court in 1895 declared unconstitutional (*Pollock v. Farmer's Loan and Trust Company*).

Meanwhile, during the depression which began in 1893, customs receipts for the first time dipped below those from internal revenue (1894). A period of treasury deficits for the first time since the Civil War gave Congress arguments for the replacement in 1897 of the Wilson-Gorman Act with the Dingley Tariff, which boosted rates almost to the old McKinley levels and which came in time to take part of the credit, according to the protectionists, for the return of prosperity.

In the progressive reform era of the early twentieth century, the tariff, the "mother of trusts," was being tied to the dominance of big business and blamed for high consumer prices and the retaliatory closing of foreign markets to American farm goods. Politicians in both parties sought to exploit this unrest. William Howard Taft, running on the Republican ticket in 1908, called for a downward modification of customs rates, but the Senate, with multimillionaire industrialist Nelson W. Aldrich leading the way, amended the reform bill beyond recognition. Duties were decreased on unimportant items, according to Mr. Dooley, facetiously, including kelp, lifeboats, marshmallows, stilts, turtles, and curling irons. "The new tariff bill," said Mr. Dooley, "puts these familyar commodyties within the reach iv all." When Taft not only signed the Payne-Aldrich bill, but praised it, the Progressive wing of the Republican Party felt betrayed, and the tariff was one of the issues helping split the party, making possible the election of a Democrat in 1912.

That Democrat, Woodrow Wilson, quickly urged a lower tariff as part of his New Freedom program. A high tariff, he reiterated, unjustly raised prices, fostered business monopoly, and made the government a tool of business interests. Under his urging, after he had castigated protectionist lobbyists, Congress in 1913 responded with the Underwood-Simmons Tariff, which reduced rates on the average of about 12 per cent and put many new items on the free list. By no means free trade, this was the first real lowering of the tariff since the Civil War. To offset the loss of revenue, the Underwood-Simmons Act provided for an income tax (legal under the Sixteenth Amendment, effective February 25, 1913), starting at 1 per cent on $3,000 a year and gradually rising to a maximum of 6 per cent on $500,000 or more. Experts considered this one of the best balanced tariff laws ever passed, but the coming of World War I disrupted normal trade patterns and left little opportunity to gauge its effectiveness, for with the return to "normalcy" in the 1920's, tariff rates were pushed upward again.

Few tariffs were scientifically determined in this period; they were based on the emergency legislation of the Civil War and were the results of political log-rolling and the maneuvering of lobby groups. There was occasional reciprocity, as with Hawaii in 1875 and Cuba in 1903 (both involving the admission of duty-free sugar), but no real consistency or planning until the end of the era. By 1900 American industry had obviously come of age and most industries were beyond the need of protection. The high tariff was in effect a form of subsidy paid industry by the American consumer. Yet despite the tariff's high level, foreign commerce flourished and it is doubtful if the tariff had much effect before World War I in curtailing trade activity.

XVII

MONEY AND BANKING IN AN
INDUSTRIALIZING ECONOMY

As THE NATION'S ECONOMY expanded and matured, the monetary and banking systems were subject to stresses and strains and to periodic modification. The years from 1873 to 1896 were generally years of deflative trends and of protracted and often bitter struggles between those who desired inflation through cheaper money and those who preferred hard money and deflation. Under the National Banking Act passed during the Civil War, banking assumed a more conservative nature than before, and proved too inflexible for the rapidly growing economy. The widening role of the investment banker and the broader use of demand deposits available by checking were also trends in the era ending with the passage of the Federal Reserve Act (1913), which not only made the money and banking structure more versatile, but also put a greater degree of control in the hands of federal agencies.

The Civil War, like other wars, was a period of inflation, followed by a difficult though not especially painful readjustment, after which came falling prices with general prosperity punctuated by depressions in 1873, 1884, and again in 1893. From the early 1870's to 1896 the era was generally one of deflation, in which factory production increased swiftly and the living cost index fell from 102 to 74, while workers' real wages rose almost three

times. Money in circulation increased by about 50 per cent, but
not nearly as rapidly as industrial production. After 1896 rapidly
growing urban markets broadened the demand for both farm and
manufactured goods and so were instrumental in bringing rising
prices. Tariff rates and revenues remained high and built up a
Treasury surplus and whittled the national debt from $2.75 billion
at the end of the war down to just under $1 billion by 1893.

In addition to the interest-bearing debt, the federal government
had issued some $450 million in greenbacks, unsupported by gold
or silver, during the war. Under Johnson, Secretary of the Treasury McCulloch had reduced the amount in circulation somewhat
and had succeeded in raising their value from sixty-four to
seventy-one cents before being halted by Congress. McCulloch
also sought to resume specie payment, that is, to make the greenbacks redeemable on demand in gold or silver at par.

But one element of society argued that low prices were the
result of an inadequate currency and believed that the greenbacks
—the "people's money"—provided an opportunity to inflate the
currency and drive prices upward. These inflationists, or "soft
money" men, drew the bulk of their support from the farmers—
the most conspicuous of the debtors—a relatively few businessmen, and perhaps some workers interested in the co-operative
movement. Wholesale prices, being more sensitive than retail,
dropped first; hence the farmer, who sold to wholesalers and
bought from retailers, was usually hit sooner and harder by deflation than others. On the other hand, creditors, most businessmen,
and wage earners (certainly those with fixed incomes) stood by
"hard money" and opposed any inflationary effort.

The inflationists urged that even more greenbacks be issued
and supported the Ohio Idea—that holders of Civil War bonds be
paid off in greenback currency then (1868) worth only 70 per
cent of par, unless otherwise specified on their bonds. On both
counts—expansion and paying part of the debt with depreciated
currency—the inflationists were unsuccessful, but the struggle
continued.

Touched off by the crash of the banking house of Jay Cooke
and Company in the autumn of 1873, the nation was plunged into
a severe depression. Among numerous basic causes of this de-

pression might be noted the inelasticity of the banking system; the feverish building of railroads in Western areas, which because of heavy overcapitalization and speculation could not pay dividends; a tax structure penalizing lower income groups, thus limiting consumption; and a heavy specie drain as foreign investors began to liquidate their American holdings. In the face of the depression, railroad construction came to a halt, farm prices plunged even lower, steel production was cut in half, and the soft money men stepped up their drive, now seeking, unsuccessfully, to prevent the resumption of specie payment. Congress in 1875 authorized the redemption of greenbacks in gold beginning in 1879 and subsequently set the amount to remain in circulation at $346.7 million. Despite dire predictions that redemption would bring a catastrophic run on the Treasury's gold supply, no such run occurred; the greenback came back up to its full value even before 1879, after which it remained co-equal to gold and silver.

Forced to accept a one-sided compromise, soft money advocates next turned to the political arena, where the Greenback Party, as mentioned earlier, picked up momentum in the late 1870's and early 1880's, but then withered away, though entering a candidate in each presidential election from 1876 down to 1960. Stymied on the greenback issue, the inflationists shifted their emphasis from paper money to demands for an injection of more silver into the monetary system. By 1866, the workings of Gresham's Law had driven the silver dollar from circulation. The amount of gold in a gold dollar and the amount of silver in a silver dollar were established in a definite ratio set by Congress, but due to a heavier supply of gold on the market, silver prices remained relatively high. With each silver dollar containing $1.036 worth of silver at market value, silver bullion was not brought to the mint for coinage but was sold instead on the open market. Congress, recognizing a situation which had prevailed for years, in 1873 simply dropped the standard silver dollar from the lists of coins minted. But almost immediately the situation changed: the amount of silver bullion on the open market increased greatly with the discovery of vast new deposits in Nevada and when a number of European nations abandoned silver as a monetary standard. Silver prices began to drop: by 1876 only ninety cents worth of the metal would theoretically go into a silver dollar; by 1894 only forty-nine cents.

Now the mineral interests and the inflationists began demands for the coinage of silver dollars in unlimited amounts at the old ratio of approximately sixteen to one. The mineral industry would obviously be aided and a cheaper money would result. The congressional action of 1873 dropping the coinage of the silver dollar was denounced as a conspiracy, the "Crime of '73"; the bill had been "written by a Jewish banker and backed up by British capital"; it was part of a diabolical scheme by "the syndicated, monopolistic, domineering, plutocratic tyranny of Wall Street, and the rule and ruin policy of its foreign connected, across-the-water bosses."

Instead of repeal of the Crime of '73 to permit unlimited coinage of silver, Congress compromised, first with the Bland-Allison Act (1878) providing for the minting of from $2 million to $4 million worth of silver into dollars each month. Over a twelve-year period, a total of $378,166,000 dollars were thus coined, and Congress in 1886 permitted the issue of silver certificates based on the Bland-Allison dollars. But this was limited coinage and the silver advocates never relaxed their pressure as silver prices continued downward. Another compromise was affected in 1890 in the Sherman Silver Purchase Act, the bastard offspring of support by the silverites for the McKinley Tariff in exchange for the backing of the protectionists in Congress. The Sherman Act authorized the purchase and coinage of 4.5 million ounces of silver per month and the issue of notes against this amount to be redeemable in either silver or gold. In the three years in which it was in effect, the law doubled the amount of silver purchased under the Bland-Allison Act, but silver prices continued their downward spiral.

But the Sherman Silver Act contributed to a fiscal crisis. Since the greenbacks and the treasury notes of 1890 were redeemable in gold, a substantial gold reserve had to be maintained. But immediately the gold, the more highly valued of the two metals, began to drain out of the Treasury. Foreign investors sold their American securities for gold and the fall of Baring Brothers, the great British investment house, only accentuated the trend. Private hoarding at home at the same time reduced tax receipts. The run eased off momentarily, but in 1892 commenced again, with an unprecedented flow reducing the Treasury's gold reserve to below $100 million (regarded as the safe minimum) for the first time since 1879.

Meanwhile, the failure of two business giants, the Philadelphia and Reading Railroad Company and the National Cordage Company, touched off an ever-widening spiral of financial ruin: in 1893 alone, over 15,000 commercial houses, 600 banks and other fiscal institutions, and more than 50 railroads had gone under. Before the ensuing depression was over, a quarter of the nation's railroad mileage was in bankruptcy, unemployment had risen to the staggering total of 4 million, and "industrial armies" were carrying their grievances to Washington. Blaming the Sherman Silver Purchase Act for continuing drain of reserves, President Cleveland called Congress into special session and secured the repeal of the measure, much to the distress of his agrarian backers, but the flow continued. In desperation, the government sold four bond issues—a total of $262 million—for gold in order to build up reserves. But to acquire gold to buy bonds, purchasers simply redeemed treasury notes or greenbacks, drawing further on the reserves. The government, forbidden by law from retiring the greenbacks, paid out paper money to meet its obligations, making currency available for bond purchasers to commence the cycle anew. Even when investment banker J. Pierpont Morgan was persuaded to buy $65 million in bonds, bringing half the gold from overseas, the drain was not completely halted, although the transaction netted Morgan $7 million and prompted hostile critics to damn even louder the linkage of big business and government. But Morgan's action undoubtedly helped, and by early 1896, when the last of the four loans was subscribed, the gold crisis was over.

That autumn, the Democrats, led by William Jennings Bryan, adopted the money plank of the Populists and made free silver the major campaign issue, but were unsuccessful, as returning prosperity tempered somewhat the attitude of the American voter. Farm prices improved as the Indian wheat crop failed, new gold discoveries in the Klondike and better methods of processing and recovering that precious metal brought general price rises, and the silverites no longer presented a serious challenge. Indeed, in 1900 the United States went officially on the gold standard, at the same time replacing the 1890 treasury notes with silver dollars and authorizing the Treasury Department to float short-term bond issues to maintain an adequate gold reserve, if necessary. While vestiges of the battle between supporters of soft money and of hard lingered, the issue was fought out and settled by the turn of the century.

The basis of the nation's banking system throughout the period was the National Banking Act of 1863, amended in 1864, a wartime measure designed in part to provide a means of marketing government bonds and in part to help control a helter-skelter issue of notes by local banks. Under the law, banks might become "national" banks by meeting the charter requirements of the federal government. Each was to have a minimum capital of from $50,000 to $200,000, depending upon the size of the city in which they were located. Each was required to invest a third of its capital or $30,000 (whichever was larger) in government bonds, which were then deposited with the Comptroller of Currency and the bank permitted to issue national bank notes equal to as much as 90 per cent of the current value of its deposited bonds. Reserve requirements were set by law but varying amounts of reserves were permitted to be deposited in other national banks in larger cities.

Since there were provisions for federal supervision and inspection, state banks were slow to join, even when a 2 per cent tax was levied on state bank notes, but a 10 per cent tax in the spring of 1865 brought a host of joiners and eliminated the fluctuating state bank currency that had been such a bane before. State banks declined momentarily, but gradually increased in number until 1892, when there were as many state as national banks, although the assets of the latter remained considerably larger. By 1914, 17,542 state banks had total assets almost equal to those of the then 7,525 national banks, but not until the 1920's would assets be equal for any sustained length of time.

State banks survived and even increased for several reasons. Until 1900 the fairly high capitalization requirements of the National Banking Act prevented the establishment of national banks in small communities. Moreover, national banks were prevented by law from making loans against real estate, hence were not particularly helpful to the farmers in the South and West. Banks chartered under state law, while unable to issue notes, could take in savings, discount paper, or make loans on land. In addition, demand deposits were becoming increasingly important, a fact on which the Secretary of the Treasury commented in 1867: "In all the cities and towns throughout the country, checks upon credits in banks, and bills of exchange, have largely taken the place of bank notes. Not a fiftieth part of the business of large cities is transacted by the actual use of money."

This practice, although less in the West and South than elsewhere, had spread widely by 1890 even to rural areas. Bank loans no longer had to be in notes, but could be in the form of deposit, on which the customer could draw by check. Hence the state banks could do a thriving business without the necessity of handling bank notes, and demand deposits helped somewhat to offset the limited amount of currency in circulation.

Admittedly the banking structure had its weaknesses. To a considerable extent it neglected the farmers and the import-export trade. The note supply based on government bonds was too rigid, although by buying or selling bonds a national bank might contract or expand the supply of notes. But since the federal government was continually retiring its national debt, the amount in bonds, and therefore in national bank notes, decreased from time to time, though the presence of silver certificates and demand deposits somewhat mitigated the effect of this. Moreover, there was a pyramiding of reserves, with national banks in small towns depositing part of their reserves in banks in cities where interest was higher and city banks in turn depositing part of their reserves in banks in New York City, which meant that by 1910 a mere half a dozen New York banks held almost three quarters of all national bank reserves. These New York banks put the funds out on short-term call loans for use on the stock market. The system was inflexible, as emergency need for reserves required the calling in of reserves all along the line, with great pressure on the call-money market. In the absence of any central co-ordinating agency to ease pressure on individual banks in time of crisis, sometimes informal co-operation, as by membership in the New York Clearing House, proved helpful. Or sometimes, as in the panic of 1907, an important leader—in this case J. P. Morgan—took the helm to steer not only his own, but other interests as well, through dangerous waters. But the system was unwieldy, unpredictable, and haphazard.

The federal government modified the system slightly from time to time. In 1900 the minimum capital requirements for national banks were lowered from $50,000 to $25,000, a change which brought a substantial increase both in the number of national banks and the number of failures. The country had weathered the abrupt but localized "rich man's panic" in 1903, which caused U. S. Steel to pass its dividends, and which brought about numerous business casualties, but four years later it experienced another which was more severe. The San Francisco earthquake, as well as the investigations by bearded Charles Evans Hughes, had shaken the insurance business; foreign credit was disrupted, and when a $52 million New York street railway concern and the $34 million Westinghouse Electric Company failed in the fall of 1907, it was obvious that credit was strained to the breaking point. Businessmen liked to lay the blame for the panic that followed on Theodore Roosevelt and his trust-busting activities. But the government took action by issuing Panama Canal bonds and depositing surplus to reassure the banking world, and J. P. Morgan and a committee from the New York Clearing House created a relief fund to aid specified insolvent banks, and the panic passed.

The "Roosevelt Panic," as financiers dubbed it, brought public demands for reform which were partially met by temporary measures in 1908. By the Aldrich-Vreeland Act, five or more banks might pool their assets in case of distress and receive emergency currency, backed by the government. An effort was made to expand currency by permitting national banks to deposit state, city, or county bonds, as well as federal, against which the Secretary of the Treasury could issue notes. The law also created a National Monetary Commission to review the banking structure. Under ultraconservative Nelson Aldrich of Rhode Island, the Commission made an exhaustive study, analyzing some twenty-seven weaknesses, but Congress refused to act upon its recommendation.

Meanwhile, Representative Arsène Pujo of Louisiana and a subcommittee of the House Committee on Banking and Currency were investigating banking abuses, and in 1913 released a report which deplored the "vast and growing concentration of control of money and credit in the hands of a comparatively few men." Through interlocking directorates, a handful of banking firms, including J. P. Morgan and Company, constituted a "Money Trust," said the report, controlling at least $22.3 billion in resources. Morgan was particularly significant, not merely because of the vast influence he wielded, but also as an example of the investment banker, a figure of vital importance on the American scene. With no power to issue money or create deposits, the investment banker served as an intermediary to bring investors together with businessmen in need of financing. He aided corporations and undertook to sell their securities for them or sometimes purchased securities and resold to the public at a profit. He also became a promoter, and played a key role in reorganization, as Louis Brandeis put it, "adding the duties of undertaker to those of midwife." In time, as the Pujo Committee pointed out, investment banking houses came to control commercial banks, trust companies, and insurance concerns and were able to use funds from these sources for their own operations.

Given the tenor of the Pujo and Aldrich reports and the nature of the Progressive movement in general, it is not surprising that the administration of Woodrow Wilson put the revamping of the banking structure well up on its list of priorities. Aldrich had advocated creation of a highly centralized system—in effect a powerful third Bank of the United States—controlled by spokesmen of the banking interests, but the Bryan wing of the Democratic Party recoiled in horror, fearful of even more concentration of power in the "Money Trust." The Federal Reserve Act (the Owen-Glass Act) which was passed late in 1913 provided something of a compromise between the two extremes.

The Federal Reserve System it created was to be superimposed upon the National Banking structure. National banks must join and state banks might if they chose. The country was divided into twelve districts, each with a Federal Reserve Bank owned by member banks, with a network of interlinking pipelines through which the flow of currency and credit could be speeded to areas in financial distress. On top sat the Federal Reserve Board, made up of the Secretary of the Treasury and the Comptroller of Currency, ex officio, and five additional members to be selected by the President with the consent of the Senate.

The Federal Reserve district banks did not deal with the public: they were banker's banks. After 1917 member banks were required to keep their legal reserves (which varied with capitalization) at the district level. A new currency, the Federal Reserve note, printed by the United States, was backed by at least 40 per cent gold and the remainder in commercial paper, and the amount of money in circulation could be increased by rediscounting commercial paper. By raising the discount rate in times of inflation, Federal Reserve banks could discourage lending; by lowering the rate the opposite effect might be had. In addition, controls might be exerted by means of pumping reserves into the system through the purchase of government securities on the market or by withdrawing reserves by selling securities.

Although many bankers were skeptical and believed the new law smacked of socialism, the Federal Reserve System by establishing some over-all coordinating unit, creating a more elastic currency, and requiring centralized reserves with some element of control, especially at the district level, represented a distinct advance. The Federal Reserve machinery would see the nation through the war years, but was not able to cope with the unrestrained money market of the 1920's. But it marked a vast improvement over the loose conditions that had existed at the beginning of the era.

XVIII

ECONOMIC IMPERIALISM AND
WORLD WAR I

AFTER THE LATE 1890's the flowering of American manufacturing and the expansion of trade and commerce overseas was accompanied by new imperialistic aspirations on the part of the United States. A major world force in the 1870's and 1880's, imperialism led nations to extend control outside their own boundaries. Closely allied with the Industrial Revolution, late nineteenth-century imperialism sought cheap, vital raw materials, markets for stepped-up production of manufactured goods, and outlets for the investment of capital amassed in industry, transportation, and trade. It was influenced also by other motives—missionary, philanthropic, and the search for coaling stations in this new era of steam navies. Britain, Germany, and France—all industrial nations—competed in a mad scramble for world territory, partitioning the Black Continent of Africa and joining with Japan and Russia to carve out spheres of influence in the Far East.

Even with these examples before her, the United States remained preoccupied with internal affairs until late in the century, only then joining in the race. Business interests had not been enthusiastic about the Spanish-American War in 1898, but once the brief war was over the mood began to change. The United States emerged with a two-ocean empire: to previous holdings

241

in the Pacific were added Guam and the Philippines and soon Hawaii; in the Caribbean she acquired Puerto Rico and what amounted to a protectorate over Cuba, newly freed from Spain. To be sure, anti-imperialists, aided by farm interests fearing sugar and tobacco competition and labor groups apprehensive of cheap labor, fought annexation of the Philippines vigorously, but a sizable segment of the business world was now convinced that acquisition of the islands would open a line of rapid trade expansion into the Far East. "Hands across th' sea," sneered Mr. Dooley, "an into 'tuther fellers pocket." But the bulk of the American people, with President McKinley leading the way, saw no alternative but to take in the "Little Brown Brothers," to uplift and civilize them, even though it meant waging a two-year war against the Filipinos themselves.

With colonies secured in two oceans came the desire for a canal to link them. Once rights in Panama had been secured by devious methods and the construction of a canal commenced, American diplomacy in the Caribbean would be geared toward protection of the waterway and the expansion of business investments in Latin America. It was Theodore Roosevelt who interpreted the Monroe Doctrine to mean assumption by the United States of the role of policeman in the Western Hemisphere to maintain stable governments and economies and prevent European intervention which might pose a threat to the canal lifeline. Said Roosevelt, shortly before the United States concluded an agreement to take over customs houses of the Dominican Republic and supervise collection of the duties to assure payment of foreign debts:

> Chronic wrongdoing, or an impotence which results in a general loosening of the ties of civilized society, may in America, as elsewhere, ultimately require intervention by some civilized nation, and in the Western Hemisphere the adherence of the United States to the Monroe Doctrine may force the United States, however reluctantly, in flagrant cases of such wrongdoing or impotence, to the exercise of an international police power.

Believing "necessity the mother of intervention," Roosevelt sent troops repeatedly to bolster friendly Caribbean governments or to protect property, and the policy would be continued through subsequent administrations down to that of Herbert Hoover. Not only Cuba, but also Haiti, the Dominican Republic, Nicaragua, and even Mexico heard the tramp of marching American marines.

Soon the Roosevelt corollary was buttressed with the two-sided concept of "Dollar Diplomacy," as employed by William Howard Taft, who sought to replace European investments in Latin America and the Far East with American, on the assumption that American dollars invested abroad would bring economic control and political influence overseas, and that foreign policy should be used to protect those dollars. Dollar Diplomacy proved unsuccessful in China, but more effective in Latin America, where American capital was invested freely. By the late 1920's more than $1 billion had been invested in public utilities, mines, sugar, and railroads in Cuba alone; by World War I about $90 million had gone into Central America, about a third in fruits and a third in railways. In South America, Chilean copper mining was most important, and in Mexico, American holdings by 1914 had reached $850 million, three times as much as British investments in that country. Strong man Porfirio Diaz had thrown Mexico wide open to American capital in 1876 and it poured into mines, oil, ranches, and railroads, despite the confusion of the Mexican Revolution from 1910 to 1917, which brought property destruction and pressure for armed intervention, twice forthcoming.

Economic imperialism had its shortcomings. The Philippines did not prove lucrative as a market or as an entry to other Asian markets; an "open door," as it turned out, could not be enforced short of war. Intervention and Dollar Diplomacy won few friends in Latin America. In time, with support from American manufacturers interested in amicable relations and an assured supply of raw materials, the federal government began to backtrack, granting the Filipinos their ultimate independence and substituting the Good Neighbor policy for blatant military intervention in the Caribbean.

In the meantime, the United States was being drawn into World War I, and for the first time since 1865—except for minor clashes like the Indian campaigns and the brief war against Spain—the American economy would feel the pressure of wartime demands. When the European powder keg exploded in the summer of 1914,

President Wilson urged Americans to be "impartial in thought as well as in action," an admonishment which time proved impossible to follow, as various influences worked to break down neutrality. Along with such forces as superior Allied propaganda, German diplomatic blunders and ineptness, and American idealism were several with economic implications.

After a brief financial crisis as European investors sought to convert American securities into cash, American production shot upward, and exports to Europe jumped from $1.5 billion in 1913 to $3.8 billion in 1916. Iron production doubled between 1914 and 1917, output of coal was up 20 per cent, copper 80 per cent, and manufactures 30 per cent. The wholesale price index went up 22 per cent and consumer prices 11 per cent from 1913 to 1916. While American exports to Europe were rising, imports from that source fell from $900 million to $633 million in the same period. Desperately needing foodstuffs, manufactured goods, and munitions, Europe made up part of her deficit with gold shipped from South Africa, American securities liquidated by Europeans, and immigrant remittances, but nonetheless was forced to borrow from private sources in the United States. From June, 1914, to April, 1917, these private loans totaled about $3 billion, of which only $40 million had gone to Germany, while France received $640 million and Britain, with J. P. Morgan and Company serving as purchasing agent, received some $1.3 billion.

Trade, too, tended to favor Britain and France. When isolationists and German-Americans sought to halt the flow of goods to the Allies, Secretary of State William Jennings Bryan announced that "The markets of this country are open upon equal terms to all the world, to every nation, belligerent or neutral." In theory this was true; in practice it was not feasible. Despite the U-boat menace, the Allies had swept the German merchant fleet from the seas, leaving Germany unable to take advantage of American markets. Only one German ship, the submarine *Deutschland,* arrived in the United States for purposes of trade during the war, and its presence, if anything, symbolized the helplessness of Germany on the high seas and her almost nonexistent direct trade with the United States.

In short, the bulk of American trade and private loans (there were no government loans before the United States' entry into the war) went primarily to the Allied powers and this economic bond undoubtedly helped pull the United States into the war on the Allied side. Responsible historians, however, have long since discarded the extreme position of the Nye Committee Report in the 1930's that the United States had been drawn into the struggle in 1917 primarily by propagandists, profiteers, munitions makers, and Wall Street bankers.

More important, and linked to the economic aspects in a number of ways, was the violation of neutral rights by belligerent powers on the high seas. In an effort to throttle the German economy, Britain blockaded the whole of the North Sea, redefined contraband of war to include many new items, blacklisted American firms suspected of dealing with the enemy, leisurely searched neutral United States vessels hauled into English ports, censored neutral mail, and even on occasion flew the Stars and Stripes to evade U-boats. If these violations of neutrality confiscated cargo and tied up shipping, those of the Germans involved a loss of life, as unrestricted submarine warfare menaced passengers on both American ships and on those of other countries. It was this factor more than any other which was most powerful in breaking down the American neutral position.

When the United States entered the war in the spring of 1917, it was undertaking its first all-out mobilization of manpower and resources; it was becoming part of a global conflict in which the Industrial Revolution was being recruited to fight. Manpower, of course, was important, for Russia had collapsed on the Eastern Front and the full weight of the German army was being thrown against the Western Front, where the war had bogged down in trenches and in barbed wire entanglements. Selective Service created an army: by November, 1918, two million American troops were abroad and an equal number under arms at home.

But this was but one aspect of modern war. "It is not an army we must train for war," said President Wilson in 1917, "it is a nation." Total mobilization demanded that the entire economy be subordinated to the struggle. Laissez faire, already on the decline, went into mothballs for the duration, as Congress handed over broad, almost blanket, emergency powers to the President.

Under a Council of National Defense, consisting of the secretaries of War, Navy, Interior, Commerce, Agriculture, and Labor, and an advisory body of experts, numerous specialized boards were created and empowered to deal with various sectors of the economy.

One such agency, for example, was the War Industries Board, established in 1917 to co-ordinate industrial needs and production. It did not function effectively at first, and the conversion of industry to a wartime basis moved much too slowly. No American-built tank or airplane saw battle; most of the artillery used by the A.E.F. was French or British; and British Prime Minister David Lloyd George was disappointed that "the organization behind the lines was not worthy of the reputation which American businessmen have won for smartness, promptitude, and efficiency." However, after the War Industries Board was reorganized early in 1918 and put under millionaire Bernard M. Baruch, who was given greatly expanded powers, production rose sharply. Directly responsible to the President, Baruch controlled priorities of transportation and raw materials, fixed prices of finished goods, regulated the labor requirement, standardized operations, and reduced waste.

Other agencies sought to expedite the working of the transportation system, both domestic and transatlantic. Recognizing the inadequacy of the merchant marine, Congress had created the United States Shipping Board in 1916. When the war came, this was expanded and soon reorganized to include a subsidiary, the Emergency Fleet Corporation, which constructed ships, while the United States Shipping Board supervised shipbuilding in general, along with training of merchant mariners and the operation of government vessels. German ships stranded in American ports were taken over, as were all steel vessels then being built, and all other ships of 2,500 tons or more. Accent was on rapid construction. There was some experimentation of shipbuilding with prefabricated parts and with concrete, but though shipyard capacity increased tremendously, most American troops went overseas in British vessels and most of the new ship constructions were not completed until after the armistice.

The country's railroad network proved too shaky and inefficient to meet wartime demands without drastic controls. Rolling stock and equipment were inadequate and outdated and had not been replaced due to rising costs and demands for higher wages. The thirty-odd rail systems, no two of them organized alike, were so un-co-ordinated and ineffective that late in 1917, after a careful survey by the Interstate Commerce Commission, President Wilson brought them all under federal supervision. Wilson's son-in-law, Secretary of the Treasury William Gibbs McAdoo, became Director General of Railroads and subsequently the telegraph and telephone lines were put under the Postmaster General and marine cables and radio under the Navy. McAdoo directed and controlled the railroads, but operation was left in company hands under company executives. Government rail losses totaled some $200 million in two years, in part because of the rate of compensation to the owners, in part because of rising costs and the poor condition of the lines, and in part because of a failure to boost rates until late. When the lines were ultimately returned to private ownership, the rail companies, perhaps forgetting the condition of their equipment in 1917, charged that their property had been allowed to run down, an allegation the government stoutly resisted. Certainly there is no question but that government control improved transportation: equipment was standardized, routing and traffic control reformed, duplication of passenger service eliminated, and the handling of troops and supplies greatly facilitated.

To conserve critical materials and release others for wartime uses, Americans were called upon to tighten their belts. Faced with a shortage both of coal and of ships to carry it, the Fuel Administration under Harry Garfield, son of the assassinated President, sought to stimulate coal mining, and also to reduce noncritical consumption. Ultimately, in April, 1919, coal was rationed. Daylight saving time was introduced (March, 1918) to conserve power and Americans experienced "gasless" Sundays, "heatless" Mondays, and "lightless" Tuesday and Thursday nights. Food was even more a pressing problem. The American ambassador in London informed Wilson in April, 1917, that the British had on hand a food supply sufficient to last only six or eight weeks. This may well have been exaggeration, but European

Allies leaned heavily upon the United States for an increased supply of foodstuffs, and Wilson appointed Herbert Hoover to mobilize food production and eliminate waste. Hoover, millionaire mining engineer and promoter already well known for his administering of Belgian relief after 1914, prompted voluntary sacrifices—the growing of war gardens, wheatless Mondays, meatless Tuesdays, and porkless Thursdays—and he was also empowered to control the storage and distribution of foodstuffs, some of which, like sugar, wheat, butter, and meat, were closely regulated. Producers, manufacturers, distributors, and retailers of food products were licensed. Some prices were fixed either directly or, in the case of grain, through the U.S. Grain Corporation, which made all purchases of grain and flour, not only for the federal government, but for the Red Cross, Belgian relief, and the Allies as well. Such a campaign paid dividends: during the first year of the war, the per capita consumption of wheat in the United States dropped from 5.3 bushels to 4.1 bushels and by 1919 the amount of food shipped to the Allies had almost tripled. Without it, Allied survival was questionable.

Labor prospered and for the first time received equal recognition with business. Samuel Gompers of the A. F. of L. had been included as a member of the Advisory Council. With immigration sharply reduced by the war and with some 4 million men withdrawn for the armed forces, labor was in short supply, although at least a million women stepped into the breach. Money wages rose and union membership increased from 2.8 million in 1916 to 4.1 million in 1919. Organized labor in general co-operated. "This is labor's war," said Gompers, as the A. F. of L. called for an informal truce for the duration. There were still strikes, usually short and uncritical, and various governmental agencies handled such disputes somewhat haphazardly until early 1918 when a centralized War Labor Board took over the task, relying mainly on public opinion to enforce its decisions. At the same time, a War Labor Policies Board determined the general policy toward labor in matters of wages, working hours, and conditions. Organized labor made some gains, especially the right of workers to join a union of their choice and not to be discharged for union activities. Real wages in general did not rise appreciably, except in manufacturing, so labor benefitted little in the long run. When the Socialists were seriously weakened and the I.W.W. all but demolished by their antiwar stand, the labor movement lost much of the vigorous left-wing elements which conducted an aggressive militant fight for improvements. And in the end, intolerance, in large part engendered by wartime animosities, would do more harm to labor than to any other class.

As World War I indicated, modern warfare is tremendously expensive. During the nineteen months it officially participated, the United States spent some $33 billion on the war effort, including $9.5 billion for loans to Allied and friendly nations—approximately ten times as much as in the entire Civil War. Emphasis had been put on mobilization of manpower and the economy with all possible speed, and undoubtedly the war might have been less expensive. "Damn it all, the business of an army is to win the war, not to quibble around with a lot of cheap buying," snapped Charles G. Dawes, first Director of the Bureau of the Budget. "Hell and Maria, we weren't trying to keep a set of books, we were trying to win the war!"

About two thirds of the direct cost of the war was paid by current taxation, the remainder by loans. The tariff played no major role in raising funds, but many old taxes were increased and new ones added on liquor, tobacco, public utilities, luxuries, and amusements. Income taxes, both personal and corporate, rose substantially and an estate tax was introduced. Individual income taxes, which ranged from 6 to 63 per cent, brought in almost $68 million in 1916 and more than $180 million in 1917; corporate income taxes jumped in total intake from $57 million to $207 million, not counting excess profits taxes. Undoubtedly higher taxes bore the brunt of the war's direct cost and also aided in curbing inflation. Bond issues and war savings stamp sales accounted for approximately $22.5 billion, and included four Liberty Loan drives, the first in early 1917, and one Victory Loan issue in March, 1919, after the war was completed. With interest rates varying from 3.5 to 4.5 per cent, these five bond issues pushed the gross national debt to a peak of $26.6 billion by August, 1919.

Despite heavy investment in war bonds and increased taxation, inflation persisted. To this, the influx of gold from abroad also contributed. Using government bonds as backing, Federal Reserve banks expanded circulation of Federal Reserve notes about six times between 1916 and 1919, while credit expanded even more. Purchasing power was boosted further when the Treasury anticipated receipts from bond issues and sold short-term certificates of indebtedness to banks. Most business prospered, as production rose sharply to a peak in 1917, then leveled off. Farm income doubled between 1914 and 1919, as fewer men pushed crop yields upward with little change in the number of farms. New fortunes were created and a growing segment of the public through the purchase of war bonds became familiar with securities—subtle preparation for widespread investment in the decade of the twenties. More than before, companies financed expansion from their own resources, not from investment bankers. When German imports of dyes, medicines, and industrial chemicals were cut off early in the war, domestic production of these coal-tar products soon revolutionized the coke industry. Subsequently, when German patents were confiscated and passed into the hands of private American firms, the chemical and dye industries received a tremendous advantage.

World War I also accentuated the country's new role as a creditor nation. Not only were American exports far greater than her imports, but her investments overseas had doubled between 1914 and 1919, while foreign holdings in the United States dropped from $7.2 billion to $3.3 billion. During the early part of the conflict the United States had slipped into new markets in Latin America and in Asia. However, the liquidation of European investments in the United States and the economic dislocation in Europe during the war and after would preclude any satisfactory balance in international trade.

Another product of the war was a brief acquaintance with a planned and managed economy. Temporary though it was, it provided at least some experience for later governmental controls. Here a number of future New Dealers would get their baptism under fire; here were direct antecedents for agencies created during World War II.

XIX

THE GREAT ILLUSION

WHEN WORLD WAR I ENDED, most Americans were enjoying unprecedented prosperity. In the midst of a business civilization dominated by high productivity and expansion in many fields and with new emphasis on advertising, installment buying, and industrial combination, the United States experienced a return to what Warren Harding in 1920 buoyantly called "normalcy." The force of the Progressive movement was now blunted, not only by the war, but also by the conservative reaction that followed. Frustrated Progressives, no longer the old evangelical reformers of the prewar era, still sought social and economic improvement through legislation, but for the most part their efforts were consistently thwarted by conservatives, to the distress of the farmer and many wage earners.

Reconversion to a peacetime economy came with little real planning. With a rapid return to normalcy in mind, the government set about demobilization of manpower and resources immediately. Two days after the signing of the Armistice, the War Industries Board began to remove price controls. War contracts were quickly terminated and government wartime agencies themselves disbanded. Federal spending continued for some time in the form of payments to returning veterans, settlement of cancelled contracts, loans to Allied powers, and subsidization of shipbuilding. A number of industries, such as automobiles and

251

building construction, previously held back by the war, now flourished vigorously to meet pent-up demands. Demobilization and reconversion brought some unemployment, but the immediate dislocation was brief and temporary.

In mid-1921, however, as government spending and loans dropped and recession-torn Europe was unable to purchase American goods, this postwar boom collapsed. Both imports and exports in 1922 fell to half the 1920 level. Farm prices dropped and net farm income was cut nearly in half in 1921 over the previous year. The number of unemployed in all fields rose from slightly over half a million in 1920 to nearly 4.75 million a year later. Some 505 bank suspensions occurred in 1921, most involving state and rural banks of small capital unaffiliated with the Federal Reserve System.

However, while the rest of the world suffered, the American economy recovered rapidly. By the end of 1922 deflation had run its course. Unemployment dwindled again and for most sectors of business, but not agriculture, prosperity was the keynote of the remainder of the decade. Population rose about 12 per cent, but production nearly doubled. Moreover, with the acceleration of the tendency toward greater technology and scientific management techniques, productivity per worker went up 60 per cent from 1921 to 1929, and national income rose by at least $20 billion, while value added by manufacturing—that is, the value of finished goods less the value of raw materials consumed in their production—almost doubled.

New industries boomed and old ones were revitalized. The war-stimulated chemical industry now grew in geometric proportions, as major concerns like Du Pont and Union Carbide branched out into such fields as plastics, paints, artificial fabrics, and metal alloys. Chemical and electrical advances made possible the cracking of petroleum and more efficient processes for iron and copper refining. One of the great thriving new industries was the manufacture of automobiles, now back from the war effort. The industry had produced 573,039 motor vehicles in 1914; it turned out 5.4 million in 1929, a figure which compares favorably to the 5.7 million produced in 1953, an excellent year. By 1925, with his amazing assembly line, Henry Ford was able to roll out one of his Model T's every ten seconds. By the end of the decade, total automobile registration was 26.5 million—one for every five persons as compared with the ratio of one to forty-three in England or one to 325 in Italy.

The great increase in automobiles had social and economic implications far beyond the impact on the industry itself. Directly or indirectly, the industry provided some 4 million jobs by 1929. It was the leading consumer of steel, rubber, glass, lead, and petroleum products. It promoted construction of roads from the city on up to the interstate level, with municipal, county, state, and federal funds all involved. In addition to creating employment in the building and improving of roads, the automobile was also responsible for the hundreds of gasoline stations, hotdog stands, and motels which came to depend upon highway traffic for their livelihood. Beyond that, not only did the automobile help break down family solidarity and transfer courting from the parlor to the front seat, it did much to break down rural isolationism and to increase mobility. It had much to do with the mushroom growth of the suburbs, it tied urban areas more closely together, and it generally hastened the tempo of life.

Electrical development also made giant strides in the twenties. Production of kilowatt hours rose 100 per cent between 1922 and 1929, with about half of this increase being used in industry, which was probably about 75 per cent electrified by 1929. Moreover, beginning November 2, 1920, when station KDKA began regular broadcasting at Pittsburgh, radio commenced a spectacular commercial rise. The National Broadcasting Company was formed in 1926, the Columbia Broadcasting Company a year later. In the same year (1927) the Federal Radio Commission was created to license and assign wave lengths, and by 1930, 40 per cent of American families—over 12 million—owned radios.

Building construction boomed, at least until the middle twenties. The war had temporarily halted construction and now new waves of migration from the country to the city and from the city to the suburb created new demands. City skylines changed radically, that of New York, for example, featuring magnificent new skyscrapers, the tallest and most spectacular of which was the 102-story Empire State Building completed in 1931. Not only office buildings, but homes, schools, and industrial plants were rushed to completion as real estate prices skyrocketed in urban areas, though farm lands dropped. Unfortunately, real estate and stock market speculations were often closely related, for real estate operators used their paper profits to secure funds for market speculation. The high point of the building boom was reached in 1925, after which it tapered off, falling from $5 billion to $3 billion by 1929. Nowhere did it exist more dramatically and more extremely than in Florida, where the country saw it at its flamboyant worst. Lavish advertising focused attention on the "Riviera of America" and investors purchased land with abandon, driving prices upward phenomenally. One promoter even hired William Jennings Bryan to declaim on the advantages of Florida from a raft in a lagoon, but even the Great Commoner could not have staved off disaster after 1926. By that time the boom had lost its momentum, new buyers were scarce, and old ones were defaulting on their installment payments at an alarming rate. And then, says Frederick Lewis Allen, "Just as it began to be clear that a wholesale deflation was inevitable, two hurricanes showed what a Soothing Tropic Wind could do when it got a running start from the West Indies." Jerry-built developments were ruined, banks failed, cities that had overtaxed themselves eventually defaulted on their debts, and hundreds of individual speculators lost heavily.

But this was the age of business. Installment buying surged upward, and when consumer purchases lagged, high-pressure advertising techniques created demand. It seemed to many as if the economy could be explained in one simple formula: mass production plus installment buying plus advertising equals prosperity, now and forever. Advertising, a $1.5 billion industry in 1926, relentlessly sought to increase sales by new consumer approaches. President Coolidge in 1926 thought advertising "the most potent influence in adopting and changing the habits and modes of life, affecting what we eat, what we wear, and the work and play of the whole nation." It increasingly emphasized human social desires and planned obsolescence rather than well-made products, and the twenties was the era of unabashed testimonials from politicians, social leaders, and other prominent personages. "I believe in sleep," said Guglielmo Marconi for the Simmons Mattress Company; ". . . sleep," echoed H. G. Wells, "I cannot do without it." New stress was put on salesmanship. It was the president of Kraft Cheese Company who commented in 1929, "I do not suppose anyone else ever planned a cheese business to live through the ages. After we are gone, there will be Kraft salesmen trekking the veldt of Africa, braving the snows of Siberia and battling the superstitions of Mongolia—all earnestly striving to increase sales." Advertising and sales techniques created the desire for goods, but did not create buying power as such nor redistribute national income. With increased installment buying, more and more of the national income went for interest charges rather than additional consumer's goods.

Probably never before nor since have businessmen been held in such high esteem. Had not Calvin Coolidge set the tone with his pithy "the business of the United States is business"? Business ethics and methods permeated the pattern of American life, even the churches reflecting the influence. Bruce Barton's best seller *The Man Nobody Knows* (1925) rated Christ as a businessman par excellence: "He picked up twelve men from the bottom ranks of business and forged them into an organization that conquered the world." Revealing chapter headings included "The Executive," "His Advertisements" (the parables), and "The Founder of Modern Business."

Businesses in the twenties were concerned about consumer relations and deliberately sought to create a favorable public image. Gone now was the "public be damned" attitude of earlier captains of industry. "It matters not how much capital you may have, how fair the rates may be, how favorable the conditions," wrote Samuel Insull, the public-utilities empire builder, "if you haven't behind you a sympathetic public opinion, you are bound to fail." Many concerns established "public relations counsels"; through trade associations they not only lobbied effectively in government and promoted the collection and distribution of all types of business information, they also did much to improve (and distort) their own image before the public. The Chamber of Commerce of the United States, formed in 1912 to "reflect the views of American business," was particularly important in this respect. Nor did national concerns neglect their relationships at the grass-roots level. Knowing full well the importance of influencing prominent local citizens who might help shape public sentiment, companies scattered their bank deposits about the country in thousands of local banks and spent millions of dollars for memberships in organizations ranging from chambers of commerce to farm groups and church societies.

Reminiscent of the 1897–1904 era, business consolidation revived, especially in utilities and financial institutions, and government viewed the trend sympathetically. By 1929, 1 per cent of the banks controlled nearly half the banking resources of the country and 70 per cent of the nation's electric power was turned out by ten holding companies. Many concerns expanded into by-product fields or achieved vertical integration. Chain stores multiplied their own units from 29,000 in 1918 to 160,000 by 1929 and branched out in other directions. By 1930, for example, the gigantic holding company Drug, Inc., owned 10,000 Rexall drugstores, over 700 Liggett Stores, plus the West Coast Owl chain and major drug producers like Vicks, Bayer Aspirin, and Bristol-Myers.

The most popular form of consolidation was through the holding company, many of which were formed "with water in their veins and a gleam of monopoly in their eye" (*Fortune*). From them, speculators and promoters reaped much profit, and when large empires were created, stock was widely owned and a relatively small block meant control; more numerous shareholders also meant more potential customers for a producing company. Large corporations grew more rapidly than small ones, and no field was so heavily concentrated as the electric power industry, where holding company pyramided on holding company, sometimes five and six deep. The most notorious was the fantastically complex structure created by Samuel Insull, president of Commonwealth Edison, in which control of $1 at the top level controlled $1,750 at the bottom. Later, after the Insull empire had toppled in what has been called "the largest corporate failure in American business history," Owen D. Young, himself a top corporation lawyer and board chairman of General Electric, admitted that it was "impossible for any man to grasp the situation of that vast structure. . . . It was so set up that you could not possibly get an accounting system which would not mislead even the officers themselves."

Nor was there any real regulation of such concerns. The federal government from Harding through Hoover operated on the principle that civilization and profits went hand in hand. "Never before, here or anywhere else, has a government been so completely fused with business," said the *Wall Street Journal*. Businessmen overshadowed all other groups and Republican Party spokesmen attributed prosperity to lower taxes, higher tariffs, balanced budgets, and free enterprise, despite the fact that the tariff, particularly, now undoubtedly worked to limit expansion of markets.

Antitrust laws were largely ignored and the several government agencies concerned with transportation, industry, and finance were packed with men sympathetic to business interests. Under a chairman who previously called the agency "a publicity bureau to spread socialistic propaganda," the Federal Trade Commission was turned over to business representatives; the Tariff Commission was put into the hands of protectionists; while the Interstate Commerce Commission was placed under control of railroad spokesmen. The Supreme Court, in a conservative frame of mind, gave decisions favorable to business, while interpreting away many of the guarantees accorded labor during and just prior to the war. The Department of Commerce under Herbert Hoover provided an increasing amount of information of all kinds for businessmen at government expense. Secretary of the Treasury Andrew Mellon, who resigned directorships in sixty corporations (total capital $2 billion) to avoid conflict of interest, led the move to lower taxes all along the line, with the result particularly beneficial to the upper income brackets.

The government disposed of its wartime merchant fleet to private concerns at bargain prices, then subsidized these concerns with lucrative mail contracts and loaned funds for construction of more vessels to encourage American competition with European carriers. Passing over the labor-supported Plumb Plan, which would have had the national government purchase and operate the railroads, the rail lines were handed back to their original owners by the Transportation Act of 1920 (Esch-Cummins Act), which theoretically broadened the powers of the Interstate Commerce Commission, created a revolving fund from railroad profits to be used as loans for weaker lines, and sanctioned consolidation under the Commission's supervision. But few of the provisions proved workable and most were subsequently abandoned or modified drastically.

In general, railroads faced increasing troubles in the twenties. Prices were rising and they were confronted with the need for new investments in equipment and rolling stock. Freight revenues were up slightly, but passenger traffic was down 30 per cent due to automobile and bus competition. The better railroads met such competition by acquiring their own bus systems, by streamlining and air conditioning their trains, and improving schedules and service, and prospered as never before; the poorer ones, not well situated or managed, were hard put to survive. Air competition was not yet significant, although airplanes made a sudden advance between 1929 and 1931 with rapid improvements in safety and equipment and with subsidies for carrying the mail.

In spite of a generally prosperous, bustling appearance, all sectors of the economy did not share good times. Agriculture recovered from the 1921–22 recession gradually through 1926, then slumped again. Farm population dropped more than a million during the twenties, the number of farms decreased by 158,000, and the average value per acre fell more than one third. Farm tenancy rose from 38.1 per cent to 42.4 per cent, and while net farm income by 1929 was back almost to where it had been in 1920, farm prices did not keep pace with prices in general. Thus the farmer lacked purchasing power consistent with other parts of the economy and was in no position to acquire his share of the automobiles, bathtubs, and radios being produced in ever-increasing numbers.

Many farmers had expanded operations and bought additional machinery during the war years; mechanization, especially in the form of the gasoline tractor, continued on into the twenties, when the use of such equipment increased ten times over 1918. The war had encouraged the cultivation of a single crop, and adjustment was difficult when markets became glutted. Freight rates remained high as did local real estate taxes, and farm prices

FARM INCOME AND PARITY RATIO, 1919–33*

Year	Realized net income of farm operators (millions of dollars)	Ratio of prices received by farmers to prices paid by farmers†
1919	9,494	110
1920	7,070	99
1921	3,887	80
1922	4,401	87
1923	5,073	89
1924	5,300	89
1925	6,333	95
1926	5,900	91
1927	5,854	88
1928	5,826	91
1929	6,264	92
1930	4,523	83
1931	2,886	67
1932	1,928	58
1933	2,767	64

* *Historical Statistics of the United States, Colonial Times to 1957,* p. 283.

† Based on an index of prices received and paid by farmers (1910–14 = 100); included also are taxes, interest, and wage rates.

dropped more rapidly than retail prices or wages. Moreover, the American tariff policy of the twenties, because of retaliation, was detrimental to farm interests. An emergency tariff act in 1921 and the Fordney-McCumber Tariff of the following year pushed rates upward and authorized the President to adjust them as much as 50 per cent if he saw fit. Both Harding, who once called for a tariff that would "help the struggling industries of Europe to get on their feet," and Coolidge made such adjustments and thirty-two out of the thirty-seven times the rates went upward. The high tariff policy brought recriminations against American farm products, and since reparations payments and debt payments were linked to their ability to trade, European nations found their commerce throttled and could not meet their obligations.

As in the earlier period of the "Agrarian Crusade," the American farmer sought redress in the twenties through government action. One movement was the Nonpartisan League, originally organized in North Dakota in 1915 to control state and local government. It elected a governor of the state and soon spread through the wheat belt, furthering what economist Thorstein Veblen called "agrarian syndicalism," establishing state banks, elevators, flour mills, coal mines, and other enterprises before it declined in the early twenties. At the national level, primarily through the Farm Bloc, organized in 1921 by a group of Western and Southern senators, legislation was from time to time enacted for the benefit of agriculture. Included were laws to regulate the rates and activities of meat packers to preserve competition among them, to put grain exchanges under the eye of the Secretary of Agriculture, and to exempt farm co-operatives from the antitrust laws and define the conditions under which they might engage in interstate commerce. The Agricultural Credits Act of 1923 had created a dozen Intermediate Credit Banks to make loans to groups of farmers, but on a limited scale. Other legislation extended the work of the Federal Farm Loan Act of 1916 (which remained ineffective) and established a Division of Co-operative Marketing in the Department of Agriculture. But none of these measures did much to restore farm buying power, and farmers constantly called for more radical plans.

Among those urging government action to support farm prices was George Peek, an executive of the Moline Illinois Plow Company who had served on the War Industries Board. "You can't sell a plow to a busted customer," said Peek practically. It was Peek who proposed a system, which with some modification was embodied in the McNary-Haugen bills. The federal government would purchase specified farm commodities at prices designed to give the grower a fair return, then would sell the surplus abroad for what it would bring, making up the loss with an "equalization fee" levied on all of that particular commodity sold by the producer. Both Harding and Coolidge fought the McNary-Haugen plan and Coolidge twice vetoed such bills as wasteful, ineffective, and expensive, though he offered no alternative of his own. The plan itself may not have worked in the 1920's, even if adopted, since the American farmer has not since been receptive to production controls, but the wide publicity it received may have contributed to preparing the public mind for government agricultural programs accepted in the thirties.

Some of the more militant farm spokesmen preferred the export debenture plan urged by Charles L. Stewart of the University of Illinois as early as 1924 and subsequently endorsed by the National Grange. This would have established a bounty for agricultural exports. For each bushel of wheat shipped abroad, for example, the exporter would receive a fee paid in transferable Treasury debentures amounting to about half the existing duty on wheat. Such debentures could then be sold at discount to importers who could use them to pay tariff charges on goods brought in. Thus receipts from the protective tariff would directly aid the farmer. Others supported the proposal of Senator George Norris of Nebraska, suggesting government purchase of farm surpluses, to be stored in federal elevators and warehouses, and carried abroad by United States ships for sale. The Norris plan never got beyond a Senate committee and the export-debenture scheme was blocked by the opposition of President Hoover, who put his faith in the protective tariff and in the Agricultural Marketing Act of 1929, which provided loans to co-operatives to improve marketing procedures. Despite pressure from the Farm Bloc, farm legislation of the twenties, when forthcoming at all, proved limited, inadequate, and often unworkable.

Neither did organized labor, on the whole, fare well in this period. Bitter strikes were lost in the immediate postwar years, as in the case of the Boston police strike of 1919 which made Governor Calvin Coolidge a hero for his proclamation that there was "no right to strike against the public safety by anybody, anywhere, any time." An acrimonious steel strike failed the same year, and strikes by coal miners and railroad shopmen in 1922 were broken when the federal government intervened. The courts weakened the safeguards provided by the Clayton Act, declaring the secondary boycott illegal and sanctioning easy use of the injunction against unions. Labor leadership was not up to its earlier standards. William Green, who succeeded Samuel Gompers in 1925, was capable but less dynamic. Gone were many of the radicals who kept more conservative leaders on their toes, but enough remained to provide whipping boys for the public and to bring labor into disrepute during the excesses of the Great Red Scare. Skilled workers proved noticeably unprogressive and labor found it difficult to organize in the automotive industry as well as in Southern textile mills.

Moreover, business took a more positive approach. Using the labor spy aggressively, concerns now established the "company union," which was docile and more easily controlled. Businessmen stepped up antiunion publicity, depicting labor leaders as "designing pirates" exploiting the mass of workingmen for their own personal benefit. Through trade groups, open-shop associations, and other agencies, business circulated far and wide its American Plan, a way of thinking which emphasized the inherent "un-Americanism" of collective bargaining and the closed shop. Through the application of "welfare capitalism," business often took the initiative from union leaders and through the establishment of their own cafeterias, medical programs, pension plans, vacation and profit-sharing programs developed an *esprit de corps* among employees not easily broken. The net result was that union membership fell from 5 million in 1920 to 3.6 million in 1929.

One gain for which labor had agitated for decades was achieved: immigration was drastically restricted, an accomplishment symptomatic of the general intolerance of the era. Beginning in 1921, an immigration quota was established, the limit in any year not to exceed 3 per cent of each nationality in the United States according to the census of 1910. Subsequent amendment in 1924 reduced this to 2 per cent based on the census of 1890, a change which would provide larger quotas for countries in Northern and Western Europe at the expense of Eastern and Southern Europeans, and discriminating against Jews and Italians especially. Canadians and Mexicans were exempted; Japanese and Chinese debarred completely. In 1927 the system was revised on the basis of the national origins of those already in the United States, and the total quota set at a mere 150,000 annually, a startling contrast with the peak year 1907, when nearly 1.3 million migrants entered the country.

The majority of Americans saw the twenties as years of plenty and of accelerated productivity. There was a renewed concentration of business and a substantial return by government to laissez faire. Fresh emphasis was put on advertising and installment buying as new industries flourished, some like the automobile mak-

UNEMPLOYMENT, 1919–33 (Annual Averages)*

Year	Number of unemployed (thousands)	Percentage of civilian labor force
1919	950	2.3
1920	1,670	4.0
1921	5,010	11.9
1922	3,220	7.6
1923	1,380	3.2
1924	2,440	5.5
1925	1,800	4.0
1926	880	1.9
1927	1,890	4.1
1928	2,080	4.4
1929	1,550	3.2
1930	4,340	8.7
1931	8,020	15.9
1932	12,060	23.6
1933	12,830	24.9

* *Historical Statistics of the United States, Colonial Times to 1957*, p. 73.

ing a profound impact on American life. That agriculture, organized labor, and a handful of industries did not share the good things of the postwar decade was largely ignored.

XX

THE GREAT DEPRESSION

FROM ALL SIDES in the 1920's, Americans were being assured of the triumph of prosperity and the eradication of want. Herbert Hoover accepted the nomination of the Republican Party in 1928 optimistically predicting that "we shall soon, with the help of God, be in sight of the day when poverty will be banished from this nation." John Raskob, vice-president of General Motors and chairman of the Democratic National Committee, outlined a simple investment plan whereby a man could invest $15 a month and accumulate $80,000 over twenty years. "In my opinion," he said early in 1929, "the wealth of the country is bound to increase at a very rapid rate. . . . I am firm in my belief that anyone not only can be rich, but ought to be rich." Leading economists like Irving Fisher of Yale talked about the "permanently high plateau of prosperity" and the "golden age" ushered in by the twenties.

From time to time rumblings on the stock market (1927, mid-1929) prompted voices of caution, as the New York *Times* and men like Thorstein Veblen and Roger Babson predicted an inevitable fall. Bernard Baruch dumped many of his stocks and bought United States bonds in the winter of 1928, but did not publicize the fact. Around him, the American public went its way, smug, complacent, its optimism reflected in one of the hit tunes of the day, "My God, How the Money Rolls In":

My sister she works in the laundry,
My father makes bootlegger gin,
My mother she takes in washing,
My God! How the money rolls in!

The American people, said Al Smith, former Governor of New York, "never carry an umbrella. They prepare to walk in eternal sunshine."

Then suddenly, beginning in October, 1929, the sun no longer shone: from seeming prosperity, the nation was plunged to the depths of the worst depression in its history. Beginning with a crashing stock market, an ever-widening spiral of disaster swept into its vortex speculators, bankers, industrialists, wage earners, and farmers. The gross national product (the total production of the economy) was nearly a third less in 1933 than in 1929; personal income was almost cut in half in the same period; 85,000 businesses, with total liabilities of $4.5 billion, failed; and between October 1, 1929, and August 31, 1932, 4,835 banks went under, their deposits aggregating nearly $3.3 billion. Dividends fell off 56.6 per cent, wages dropped 60 per cent, and industrial production was down 47, per cent in 1932 over 1929. The issue of domestic securities by American corporations fell in 1932 to a mere one twenty-fourth of the 1929 figure. Imports were cut almost to one third and exports to about one half. Farm prices and land values plunged: wheat fell from $1.036 a bushel to $.38; cotton from nearly seventeen cents a pound to six and a half cents. By the end of 1932 the automobile industry was running at 20 per cent of its 1929 output and steel plants were at 12 per cent. An estimated 13 million were unemployed by 1933, and those who retained jobs took substantial wage cuts: in April, 1931, 50 per cent of all Ford employees were working only three days a week and even the immortal Babe Ruth took a salary reduction the following year.

Marriages declined, reaching the lowest rate (7.9 per 1,000 in 1932) in modern American times, while the birth rate fell more than two full points, from 18.8 to 16.6 per 1,000 between 1929 and 1933. The annual rate of increase in admissions to state hospitals for the insane was up alarmingly, and the Missouri Pacific Railroad noted a heavy increase in transients trespassing

GROSS NATIONAL PRODUCT, PERSONAL INCOME, AND
UNEMPLOYMENT, 1928–39*

Year	Gross national product (bil. dol. 1929 prices)	Personal income (bil. dol. current prices)	Unemployment (1,000)	(Per cent of civilian labor force)
1928	98.5	79.8	2,080	4.4
1929	104.4	85.8	1,550	3.2
1930	95.1	76.9	4,340	8.7
1931	89.5	65.7	8,020	15.9
1932	76.4	50.1	12,060	23.6
1933	74.2	47.2	12,830	24.9
1934	80.8	53.6	11,340	21.7
1935	91.4	60.2	10,610	20.1
1936	100.9	68.5	9,030	16.9
1937	109.1	73.9	7,700	14.3
1938	103.2	68.6	10,390	19.0
1939	111.0	72.9	9,480	17.2

* Historical Statistics of the United States, Colonial Times to 1957, pp. 73, 139.

on its freight trains. By early 1930, when the Federal Council of Churches designated April 27 as Unemployment Sunday, the dislocation was obviously more than temporary. By Christmas, the sidewalks of major cities were crowded with unfortunates hawking apples at five cents apiece, under a scheme proposed by the International Apple Shippers' Association. Breadlines and soup kitchens were swamped; privation and hunger stalked the streets; and the song "My God, How the Money Rolls In" was replaced by another—"Brother, Can You Spare a Dime?"

What had gone wrong? Why was there "poverty in the midst of plenty," to use the phrase of Carlyle, with starvation in the cities and farm products in the Midwest worth too little to pay for shipping? At least one segment of the public, urged on by political partisans, was willing to make Herbert Hoover or emaciated Andrew Mellon the scapegoat (empty freight cars became "Hoover Pullmans" and the shanty towns along city outskirts, "Hoovervilles"). But to lay the blame upon the shoulders of one man or even two is a naïve and misleading approach to a terribly complex set of problems upon which economists and historians are not yet in full accord, even among their respective disciplines, except to agree that the holocaust was the product of a number of intricate and unmeasurable factors.

STOCK MARKET ACTIVITIES, 1920–39*

Year	Index of common stocks (1941–43 = 10)	Volume of sales on N.Y. Stock Exchange (millions)
1920	7.98	227
1921	6.86	173
1922	8.41	259
1923	8.57	236
1924	9.05	282
1925	11.15	454
1926	12.59	451
1927	15.34	577
1928	19.95	920
1929	26.02	1,125
1930	21.03	810
1931	13.66	577
1932	6.93	425
1933	8.96	655
1934	9.84	324
1935	10.60	382
1936	15.47	496
1937	15.41	409
1938	11.49	297
1939	12.06	262

* *Historical Statistics of the United States, Colonial Times to 1957,* pp. 651, 659.

The factor which triggered the Depression was the Great Bull Market and its crash in the fall of 1929, although without other basic weaknesses the economy might not have reacted as it did. Through most of the twenties, but especially after 1927, the stock market boomed; the number of stockbrokers rose from 29,609 in 1920 to 70,950 nine years later; between 1923 and 1928 the volume of sales on the New York Stock Exchange leaped from 236 million shares to 1,125 million; days of 5 million share transactions were not uncommon in 1929. U.S. Steel rose from 87 in mid-1923 to 261¾ at the peak in September, 1929, while A. T. & T. climbed from 122 to 304. The average price of common stock was 280 per cent higher in 1929 than five years earlier, and trading had increased almost 400 per cent.

Perhaps fewer than a million people actually invested on the markets, but millions more followed the daily quotations and thrilled to the rags to riches investment stories that went the rounds. Frederick Lewis Allen later described the fascination that the Great Bull Market had for business-idolizing Americans:

> The rich man's chauffeur drove with his ears laid back to catch the news of an impending move in Bethlehem Steel; he held fifty shares himself on a twenty-point margin. The window-cleaner at the broker's office paused to watch the ticker, for he was thinking of converting his laboriously accumulated savings into a few shares of Simmons. Edward Lefevre told of a broker's valet who made nearly a quarter of a million on the market, of a trained nurse who cleaned up thirty thousand following the tips given her by grateful patients; and of a Wyoming cattleman, thirty miles from the nearest railroad, who bought and sold a thousand shares a day—getting his market returns by radio and telephoning his orders to the nearest large town to be transmitted to New York by telegram.

New stocks and bonds were brought onto the market in seemingly endless numbers. The holding company, which Franklin Roosevelt later called a "ninety-six-inch dog being wagged by a four-inch tail" (because its power was grossly disproportionate to its size and capital) stood two or perhaps three deep above the level of operating companies and shares from all could be marketed. A relatively new device, the investment trust, increased in popularity in 1929, multiplying at the rate of one each business day, having assets of over $8 billion, and marketing an estimated $3 billion worth of securities. Pyramided like holding companies, the investment trust rested theoretically on the desirability of diversified holdings and reliance on experts; in practice, however, many were highly speculative, flimsily erected by promoters, or even set up by parent concerns to push their own stock.

Perhaps 90 per cent of the market transactions in the late twenties were purely speculative. Moreover, the whole boom was based on credit, which at times became overextended. Most buying was done "on the margin," the buyer advancing his "margin" (cash amounting to from 20 to 40 per cent of the purchase price of the shares) and borrowing the rest from a broker, who in turn acquired call money from a bank. The stock thus purchased was put up as collateral against the loan. Interest rates on call money ran as high as 12 per cent by the end of 1928 and in a crisis might rise as high as 20 per cent. But call loans were considered safe because of the cash margin and the security against them, and New York banks found it profitable indeed to borrow from the Federal Reserve banks at 5 per cent and relend on the call market at 12. Call loans rose from $1.6 billion in 1923 to over $8 billion in the summer of 1929.

The Federal Reserve Board, "a body of startling incompetence," in the words of John Kenneth Galbraith, failed to make effective use of the instruments of control available to it and certainly made no effort to gain additional powers. Although the Board boosted the rediscount rate at least twice in 1929 and from time to time sought to sell securities to shrink the available market funds, these attempts were too limited to have any appreciable effect. Again and again the Board urged banks to refrain from borrowing Federal Reserve money for speculative loans, but to no avail: when a crisis arose in March, 1929, for example, the National City Bank of New York offered $25 million in call money—a direct slap in the Board's face. The Board took the position that it had no control over call money offered by foreign banks or nonbanking corporations like Standard Oil of New Jersey, and it was not disposed to ask Congress for authority to set margin requirements, even when a proposal to this effect might have brought a decline of trading, or, thinks Galbraith, even "a robust denunciation of speculators and speculation by someone in high authority and a warning that the market was too high would almost certainly have broken the spell." President Coolidge left office in 1929 believing the economy "absolutely sound" and stocks "cheap at any price." Herbert Hoover gave nominal support to the Federal Reserve Board, urged the press to condemn speculation and the New York Stock Exchange to do something about it, but his position was anything but forceful.

Even in the boom era of 1927–29, the market fluctuated severely. The "Hoover Bull Market," which began with the election of the Great Engineer in November, 1928, lasted about a month. After the British raised their bank rate in an effort to cut the flow of gold to the United States, sharp declines came in February and March of 1929. In September came the beginning of the end. First came the "Babson break," which followed a prediction by Roger Babson of a crash "sooner or later." With Babson denounced, the market rallied but commenced a downward trend. Confidence was further shaken by the collapse of the amazing Hatry financial empire in England and the refusal of Massachusetts to permit the Edison Company of Boston to split its stock. Another rate raise by the Bank of England helped stop the flow of gold onto the market and these events brought falling stock prices and what Irving Fisher called a "shaking out of the lunatic fringe." On October 23 came "a perfect Niagara of liquidation," with nearly 13 million shares sold in a single day as margins were exhausted or about to be exhausted. At this point a group of powerful New York bankers headed by Morgan's senior partner, Thomas Lamont, pooled their resources to bolster the market. "There has been a little distress selling on the Stock Exchange due to the technical condition of the market," explained Lamont. With this group buying above current prices, the market rallied momentarily, but Black Tuesday, October 29, brought the "slaughter of the innocents" and a frantic dumping of over 16 million shares. The Big Bull Market was over; depression was on its way. *Variety* summed it all up on October 30: "Wall Street Lays an Egg." By mid-November, when order was finally restored, averages for fifty leading stocks and for twenty-five leading industrials had been cut in half. Bottom was reached in July, 1933, by which time five sixths of the September, 1929, paper value—or about $74 billion—had evaporated.

The market crash shattered business confidence, ruined investors, toppled holding companies and investment trusts, and wiped out important sources of long-term capital, at the same time causing a sharp cutback in consumer demand. As credit collapsed, demand based on it fell off. This in turn meant a slowing up of production and the laying off of men, lower wages, salaries, and dividends, and increased unemployment. Lower income and higher unemployment, in turn, further depressed demand and thus further lowered income and added to unemployment as the spiral widened and deepened. Even the well-to-do were hard hit —a group which controlled a large portion of consumer income and who now became ultracautious in terms of investments. The collapse crushed confidence in lending and made borrowing impossible. Foreign loans halted and other nations managed to achieve a balance of trade mainly by curtailing their purchase of American goods, particularly cotton, wheat, and tobacco.

Even before the crash there had been indications that all was not well with the economy. Indeed, there had been internal weaknesses through much of the 1920's, as a number of "sick" industries had not shared the general prosperity. Coal over-expanded during the war years and, forced to compete with oil and hydroelectric power, fell on difficult days, bituminous coal miners in 1929 receiving but $.68 per hour, compared with $.845 in 1923. Cotton and woolen textiles faced ever-increasing competition from rayon and Japanese silk. New England cotton mills had to meet the rivalry of Southern factories operating with lower transportation and labor costs. Building construction had fallen off after 1925, and certainly agriculture was in distress during most of the decade.

After reaching a peak in June, 1929, indices of industrial and factory production started downward and steel output declined. Payrolls, department store sales, and freight car loadings all dropped in October, even before Black Tuesday, for reasons which are not clear. Perhaps it was a matter of industrial output momentarily outstripping consumer and investment demands; possibly it was a more fundamental dislocation connected with the relative lag of wages and prices behind productivity per worker. Public appetites were by no means sated, but a poor distribution of income somewhat reduced the amount available for consumer goods. Five per cent of the population received roughly one quarter of all personal income, leaving the other 95 per cent to share about 75 per cent of the income. With more money than it could spend for luxuries, the upper 5 per cent invested a heavy portion of their income either in speculation or in expansion of capital goods designed to produce more consumer goods. Had a larger share of profits gone into salaries and wages, the purchasing power of a broad segment of population would have been raised for consumer buying, which is usually more stable than luxury spending and investment.

At least temporary technological unemployment existed and the growth of the labor force did not keep pace with over-all expansion of population or capital equipment. Laborsaving machinery put men out of work for the time being, though in the long run probably more were employed. The average number of unemployed for the 1921–29 period was slightly over 1.7 million per year. But the introduction of new machines turned out more goods per man without being paralleled with shorter hours, higher wages, or appreciably increased buying power.

Nor was the banking system without its defects, despite the improvements of the Federal Reserve Act. State and private banks outnumbered national banks more than two to one throughout the twenties, and frequently suffered from limited capital, inadequate regulation, mediocre management, and excessive optimism. A local problem, such as a crop failure, might bring down an independent bank and start runs on others with a dominoing effect. Between 1921 and 1929 a total of 5,055 banks suspended operation, most of them nonmembers of the Federal Reserve System. Others, especially in New York, contributed to the speculative mania, their officers sometimes using depositors' money for market operations or speculating in the bank's own stock.

With government the tool of business, regulation in the twenties proved a burlesque. Business stubbornly opposed effective legislation for the relief of agriculture and neither the Federal Reserve Board nor any other agency made more than an anemic effort to curb speculation or undesirable practices of any sort.

World conditions also contributed. Pools sometimes pegged prices artificially high (coffee in Brazil, sugar in Cuba, wool in Australia), with the effect of stimulating overproduction. The shifting of gold to France and the United States deranged international finances from time to time. European nations must either increase their exports, decrease their imports, or default on their debts to the United States. Impoverished by the war and a long depression of their own, they were prevented from raising their exports by high American tariffs, while the United States insisted on payment of its war debts, which could only be done if private loans abroad continued. Moreover, nationalist strivings for self-sufficiency brought a multitude of tariff barriers and a disruption of normal trade within Europe.

As the Depression deepened following the first shock of the crash, official and unofficial optimism prevailed on the surface. President Hoover assured the public that prosperity was "just around the corner," but privately had reservations. "Forward America, Nothing Can Stop U.S.," screamed the billboards. Businessmen added their expressions of confidence, to the distaste of Will Rogers, who thought less optimism and more action in order. "Passed the Potter's Field yesterday," he wrote, "and they were burying two staunch old Republicans, both of whom died of starvation, and the man in charge told me their last words were, 'I still think America fundamentally sound.' "

The situation was too critical for any but positive action, but no one agreed on the kind of action. Railroads thought higher railroad rates would start all business on the way to recovery. Farmers believed federal price supports the answer, though a militant minority believed the farmer should neither buy nor sell until prices rose. Old W. H. "Coin" Harvey came back into the limelight with talk of free silver at a ratio of sixteen to one. In California gaunt Dr. Francis Townsend built a strong following for his old-age pension plan and Upton Sinclair pushed E.P.I.C. (End Poverty in California), a proposal for a barter-based economy for the unemployed. In Louisiana, "Kingfish" Huey Long urged his "share the wealth plan," complete with a leveling of all salaries, and refrigerators and college educations for all who wanted them. The Technocrats, followers of Howard Scott, advocated a government run by technicians—engineers and economists—with the value of all goods to be determined by the amount of energy that went into their manufacture. Many a young idealist came to believe that the entire capitalistic system should be junked in favor of communism.

These, of course, were radical ideas, incompatible with the tenor of the Hoover administration. A humanitarian and a self-made man, Hoover put deep faith in the industrial machine and was hesitant to interfere with natural economic laws. "Economic de-

pression cannot be cured by legislative action or executive pro-
nouncement," he said. "Economic wounds must be healed by the
action of the cells of the economic body—the producers and consumers themselves." In a series of conferences late in 1929, he
urged industrial leaders, railroad owners, construction men, and
others ("those who have much and lost little," Senator Hiram
Johnson called them) to maintain full employment and wages,
even reducing hours to put more men to work. But with business
activity decreasing, such urgings were in vain. A staunch advocate
of "rugged individualism," Hoover found the idea of federal
relief distasteful and delegated that function to private and state
agencies.

The Red Cross, Salvation Army, Y.M.C.A., and other organizations did what they could. The American Legion led a drive to
find a million jobs on a six-hour-day work program; Milwaukee
sought three days work a week for its 10,000 unemployed; Detroit
attempted to induce the automotive industry to rotate jobs and
hire more men. But as time passed, private and local agencies
were overwhelmed by sheer numbers. In Akron, for example, in
the entire year 1929, the Family Service Society had been called
upon to deal with 257 needy cases; in the next two years it had to
cope with 5,000 each month. Contributions and tax collections
dwindled, limiting the state role, and more and more eyes turned
toward the nation's capital.

Convinced that a government dole would weaken the national
fiber, President Hoover stood firm against demands for direct
relief and public works, but after supporting slight income tax
cuts and furnishing federal funds to feed livestock in areas devastated by drought and duststorms in 1930, he worked out a compromise between direct aid and a strict laissez faire position. The
national government would aid financial institutions—banks, railroads, credit agencies—believing that if economic health could
be restored at the top level, the benefits would percolate down
to those at the bottom.

To the Agricultural Marketing Act, already passed to help
stabilize farm products, Hoover added a Cotton Stabilization and
a Grain Stabilization Corporation to buy and hold farm surpluses
against rising prices. But both programs were so limited and so

ineffective that the only discernible result was the loss of $148 million of the taxpayers' money. Federal Home Loan Banks were created to discount home mortgages to banks, insurance companies, and other credit agencies, and the capital of the Federal Land Banks was increased to provide more loans to rural credit organizations and hence to farmers. Hoover stepped up public works, spending some $2.5 billion on improving roads, harbors, buildings, and dams, the most notable of which was Hoover Dam on the Colorado River. He permitted 40 million bushels of surplus wheat and some raw cotton (made into clothing) to go to the unemployed through the Red Cross, but vetoed the Garner-Wagner direct relief bill in 1932. In the same year Congress created the Reconstruction Finance Corporation, although Hoover had previously opposed it and had sought unsuccessfully a voluntary union among leading banks for some of the same purposes. The RFC was patterned after and headed by the director of the War Finance Corporation, created in 1918. It was capitalized at $500 million, could borrow three times that much, and was permitted to lend to banks, insurance companies, building and loan associations, and (with the approval of the Interstate Commerce Commission) to railroad companies. Its lending power increased to $1.8 billion, this "millionaire's dole," as Fiorello LaGuardia called it, was soon allowed to loan to states and municipalities for relief and public works projects.

At the same time, in order to protect against the fear that withdrawal of gold from circulation might take the country off the gold standard, the Glass-Steagall Act (1932) eased pressure by making more securities eligible for Federal Reserve discounting. Congress the year before had authorized loans of up to 50 per cent on veterans' bonus certificates of 1924 and some $1.7 billion was paid out of the Treasury on that account, much to Hoover's distress. Demanding the other 50 per cent, veterans marched on Washington, eleven thousand strong, but their demonstration and encampment was broken up with loss of life by the army, under Douglas MacArthur, acting on Presidential order.

Hoover supported and refused to veto the Smoot-Hawley Tariff of 1930, with rates so high the law was called "a declaration of war against the whole of the civilized world," and protests were forthcoming from thirty-four nations and 1,028 members of the American Economic Association. As time indicated, the new rates brought discrimination from abroad and helped paralyze world trade. On the other hand, in the following year, Hoover attempted to bolster the European economy by calling a year's moratorium on the payment of debts owed to the United States— debts closely linked to commerce.

The old chestnut that the Great Engineer quickly drained, ditched, and damned the country is neither true nor fair. Hoover reaped the whirlwind sown throughout the twenties, but his administration had taken more responsibility in this depression than any previous President's in a similar circumstance. His efforts, however, were too limited, too indirect, and often too late. Despite the rise of the national debt from $16.2 billion in 1930 to $22.5 billion in 1933 as a result of deficit financing, conditions improved but little.

XXI

THE NEW DEAL YEARS

ON THE EVE of the election of 1932, the election which swept Franklin D. Roosevelt and the Democratic Party into office, the incumbent, Herbert Hoover, had already foreseen the outcome. "I'll tell you what the trouble is," he said privately. "We are opposed by six million unemployed, ten thousand bonus marchers, and ten-cent corn." His figures may not have been accurate, but his reasoning was correct. The Depression, of course, had been the central issue of the campaign, with Hoover stressing its foreign causes and emphasizing the need for a high tariff and for the retention of the gold standard ("the dollar should ring true on every counter in the world"). Roosevelt, on the other hand, had underlined the domestic bases of the Depression, had promised to balance the budget, and had managed to appeal to a widely divergent backing with a pledge of a "new deal for the American people," especially "the forgotten man at the bottom of the economic pyramid."

Following the election came a four-month interregnum before the President-elect and the new Congress took office in March. During this period of uncertainty, while the economy plunged even lower, the outgoing administration sought to commit Roosevelt to its own policies—a balanced budget, no substantial borrowing, and no tinkering with the currency—but the Hyde Park aristocrat refused to bind his hands in this fashion.

277

Once described by Walter Lippmann as "a pleasant man who, without any important qualifications for the office, would very much like to be President," Roosevelt exuded confidence and leadership. His inaugural address, delivered at a time when the national income had been halved, when nearly a quarter of the labor force was unemployed, when farm prices were at rock bottom, and when bank failures had reached an alarming level, underscored the need for optimism and action. "The only thing we have to fear is fear itself," said Roosevelt. "Our greatest primary task is to put people to work." Farmers' purchasing power must be raised, industry and transportation pulled out of the doldrums, banking stabilized and, along with credit and investment, more closely supervised, "an adequate but sound currency" assured, foreclosures halted, and attention in general devoted "to putting our own national house in order and making income balance outgo."

Gathering around him a Cabinet devoid of important party leaders, plus a coterie of "Brain Trusters," mainly economics and law professors from Columbia and Chicago, Roosevelt assumed the Presidency in March, 1933, and immediately called Congress into special session. Between March 9 and June 16—that famous "Hundred Days"—Congress would write into law many of the fundamentals of Roosevelt's New Deal program. The former Governor of New York entered the White House with no carefully prepared, well thought-out plan of action. Described by Eric Goldman as "the most complete devotee of playing by ear the White House had ever known," Roosevelt was willing to experiment, and, as he told the public in one of his early fireside chats, he "had no expectation of making a hit every time I come to bat." Thus the New Deal, a program involving a vast body of domestic legislation between 1933 and 1938, was often unplanned, unsystematic, and at times contradictory. Its short-range goals were relief for the needy and immediate recovery; its ultimate aims were more permanent recovery and reform of abuses to prevent a recurrence of depression disaster. Frankly recognizing the responsibility of national government to act on behalf of the welfare of the individual in time of distress, the New Deal was not in itself revolutionary. Through economic planning in certain areas it speeded up the decline of laissez faire that had been in progress for decades. Unconsciously perhaps, the New Deal drew something from Populism, Progressivism, the experience in World War I, and even from Herbert Hoover's cautious use of agencies like the RFC.

Roosevelt's first action came in the field of banking, where between 1930 and 1932 a total of 4,377 banks, their deposits aggregating nearly $3 billion, had failed. In early 1933, state after state began to proclaim banking holidays, until by Inauguration Day, at least seventeen had done so. When New York and Illinois quickly followed, Hoover admitted that we "were at the end of our string." Roosevelt quickly proclaimed a national bank holiday to give time for preparation of an emergency banking bill before Congress convened on March 9. Passing over extreme plans like Rexford Tugwell's to have the postal savings system assume the deposit and demand functions of banks or that of a few old Progressives for a truly nationalized banking structure, Secretary of Treasury Woodin worked closely with prominent bankers to prepare the Emergency Banking Bill, which was ready within seventy-two hours, and became law the same day it was introduced into Congress.

It approved Roosevelt's action in temporarily suspending bank operations, and it provided a plan for reviewing, licensing, and reopening closed banks if they could meet certain requirements. Reopening commenced March 13, and about half completed the process in a few days; the others did so more gradually and only about 5 per cent remained closed permanently. The new banking law also gave the Secretary of Treasury the power to call in gold and gold certificates, and it authorized the issue of more Federal Reserve notes in an effort to expand currency and help restore confidence.

Additional legislation followed, both for banking recovery and for reform. The second Glass-Steagall Act (June, 1933) authorized the creation of a Federal Deposit Insurance Corporation to guarantee deposits up to $2,500 (raised to $5,000 in 1934, and $10,000 in 1950); it separated commercial and investment banking functions to prevent bank speculation with deposits; and it enlarged the power of the Federal Reserve Banks to curb credit expansion by member banks. Two years later (1935) Congress centralized more authority in the Federal Reserve Board (its members were now called governors) and enhanced its power over credit.

Meanwhile, by cutting veterans' pensions, reducing federal salaries up to 15 per cent, and reorganizing governmental agencies, the new administration reduced operating costs by perhaps a quarter of a billion dollars, before the economy was submerged in a flood of deficit spending. Seeking a "managed currency," Roosevelt moved away from the gold standard cautiously, first prohibiting, by executive order, the export of gold except for "legitimate and normal business requirements," then ordering all gold turned into the banks to be turned over to the Federal Reserve System. Next Congress rejected clauses in contracts requiring gold payment and was upheld by the courts, amid howls of anguish from all sides at this abrogation of the gold standard. Next, in an attempt to raise prices and deflate the dollar in foreign exchange to increase exports, Roosevelt pegged the price of gold at $35 an ounce, progressively devaluing the dollar to 59.06 cents of its former gold value. The title of gold was vested in the U.S. Treasury and Federal Reserve notes were made lawful money. Although narrowly defeating a free silver bill, Congress did authorize the purchase and minting of domestic silver at a rate higher than market price in an effort to produce inflation. Seemingly the devaluation of the dollar (the "baloney dollar," Al Smith called it) helped bring prices up, but since heavy federal spending was pumping millions of dollars into the economy at the same time, it is difficult to evaluate its true impact.

Reform of the stock exchange mechanism was a foregone conclusion, especially after the Senate Banking and Currency Committee headed by Ferdinand Pecora revealed startling examples of fraud, deceit, and manipulation by speculators, brokers, and even bankers of supposedly impeccable reputation, completely shattering the Wall Street idol of the twenties. Early in 1933 the Securities Act was passed to force truthful representation of stock and bond issues. When this proved inadequate, it was supplemented a year later by the Securities and Exchange Act, which established new controls. Officers, directors, and large shareholders were required to report all transactions in securities of their own company. A new agency, the Securities and Exchange Commission, was created with broad authority to prescribe rules for trading, with the power to set margins (shared with the Federal Reserve Board) and responsibility for the general policing of market activities. Under the first Securities and Exchange Chairman, Joseph P. Kennedy, father of the late President Kennedy, these measures represented an improvement but were gingerly applied. Only in 1937, after the indictment of Richard Whitney, former president of the New York Exchange, on charges of using clients' securities for speculation, was the Commission reorganized under William O. Douglas as a highly effective body.

Congress also moved to eliminate some of the abuses attending the pyramiding of holding companies, particularly in the utilities field. By the Public Utility Holding Company Act (1935), holding companies were limited to two stories or to a "single integrated public-utility system, and to such other businesses as are reasonably incidental, or economically necessary or appropriate." Rates were to be reasonable, financial records open to inspection, and such concerns were required to register with the Securities and Exchange Commission and were held responsible for statements made while promoting their securities.

One of the most urgent concerns was that of relief for the 12 million to 15 million unemployed. Early in the Hundred Days, Congress created the Federal Emergency Relief Administration, which provided some $3 billion for states and cities, ostensibly on a matching basis though in the end the federal government contributed over 70 per cent. At first, the FERA gave direct relief, but increasingly its administrator, spindly Harry Hopkins, emphasized a work program, and by the end of its life in 1935, the agency had about half of its beneficiaries on work relief.

To meet the exigencies of the winter of 1933–34, the Civil Works Administration was established to work directly from Washington through regional sub-offices. By January it was employing on emergency jobs about 4.3 million unemployed, many of them drawn from the rolls of the FERA. By the time it was absorbed by the FERA a few months later, the CWA had expended $900 million, mainly on road improvements, erosion control, and repairs to parks, playgrounds, and schools.

By 1935, partly because widespread unemployment continued and partly to offset support for pie-in-the-sky schemes proposed by such radicals as Huey Long, Dr. Townsend, and Father Coughlin, the administration stepped up its relief programs, putting them on a more "permanent" basis, and emphasizing more and more the morale-building character of work relief over direct relief, which Roosevelt called "a narcotic, a subtle destroyer of the human spirit." Thus when Congress established the Works Progress Administration (later the Work Projects Administration), direct relief was given over to state and local agencies, while the new WPA undertook to put people to work.

Headed by Harry Hopkins, a social worker by background and by inclination who operated on the basic principle that "hunger is not debatable," the WPA sought to find work for which the individual was best suited. Much construction was done: prior to its liquidation in 1942, the WPA built 664,000 miles of new roads, 122,000 public buildings (libraries, schools, hospitals, courthouses), over 500 airports, including the $40 million North Beach Airport for New York City, more than 100,000 bridges and viaducts, not to mention countless improvements in parks, sewage plants, and water purification systems or the extensive dental and health work accomplished in nearly every community in the land. Before 1941 it maintained nearly 1,500 nursery schools and served some 600 million hot lunches to school children. Through various branches it provided employment for more professional skills. A Federal Writers' Project employed over 6,000 writers at peak, among them promising young men like Richard Wright and Vardis Fisher; a Federal Music Project gave employment to musicians and entertainment to the public; so did a Federal Theatre Project until condemned by the Dies Committee in 1939 as being Red-tinged. A Federal Art Project aided struggling artists, and government support went to Gutzon Borglum for completing his monumental Mt. Rushmore sculpture. Late in 1938, some 3.2 million were on WPA payrolls and during its lifespan of almost eight years it provided jobs for nearly 9 million people. It spent about $10.5 billion of federal funds, plus another $7.7 billion contributed through state and local agencies, and despite the sneers of critics who labeled much of the work "boondoggling" and who insisted that the initials stood for "We Play Around," millions of the unemployed were kept alive at wages of from $40 to $95 a month, while the nation and taxpayers benefited.

Another agency, the Public Works Administration, was not primarily a relief organization, but it did provide employment. Created in 1933 by the National Industrial Recovery Act, the PWA sought to stimulate industry with a program of federal spending for heavy construction, which would at once inspire orders for lumber, steel, cement, and other materials and put men to work directly and indirectly. Under Harold Ickes, free-swinging "Secretary of Things in General" (Secretary of the Interior), the PWA spent nearly $6 billion in its lifetime on over 34,000 projects, ranging from the construction of the Triborough Bridge in New York City to Grand Coulee Dam on the Columbia. By working day and night it completed Hoover Dam more than two years ahead of schedule, it built huge TVA projects, improved harbors, cleared slums, built roads and even warships. Unlike Hopkins, who was primarily concerned with putting the maximum number of unemployed to work regardless of careful planning or a direct return to the taxpayer, Ickes was more inclined to think in terms of the finished product and infinite care and planning preceded actual beginnings.

For young people there were special relief programs, one of the most successful of which was the Civilian Conservation Corps created in 1933 to employ young men between the ages of seventeen and twenty-three. Semimilitary in organization, the CCC provided uniforms, food, housing, and medical care, plus $30 a month, of which $22 was sent home. Outdoor work of reforestation, swamp drainage, fire and flood control, and state and national park improvements quickly caught the public's imagination and the so-called "tree army" had great appeal despite its high per capita cost. Though it could take only a minority of those who applied (never more than 500,000 at any one time) it provided a haven for more than 2,750,000 and spent $2 billion before disbanding in 1942. Another program, the National Youth

Administration, an auxiliary of the WPA, provided part-time aid for high school and college students between 1935 and 1940. At jobs ranging from washing windows to operating movie projectors, high school students could earn about $6 a week, college undergraduates and graduate students slightly more. Undoubtedly the NYA was important in keeping college enrollments up after an initial fall of about 8 per cent prior to 1934.

Federal relief programs were not without their critics. Some attacked the basic idea of governmental aid of any kind; others were critical of the duplication, waste, expense, and lack of planning often so apparent; still others condemned relief measures as political means of swelling the administration's bandwagon in election years ("Nobody ever shoots Santa Claus," said Al Smith). Federal relief nevertheless provided urgently needed jobs, kept people alive, and even gave some sense of belonging. Not only had the government assumed responsibility for the prevention of starvation, it at the same time sought to inject additional purchasing power into the economy.

But work relief offered little security to those threatened with home loss through mortgage foreclosure. Foreclosures more than doubled between 1928 and 1933, when 252,400 families lost their homes. Recognizing the inadequacies of Hoover's Federal Home Loan Bank Act, Congress early in 1933 created the Home Owners' Loan Corporation, which in effect refinanced mortgages carried by those who would carry them no longer, usually setting lower payments over a longer term. The HOLC ultimately held about one sixth of the total urban mortgage debt in the country and undoubtedly did much to prevent a total collapse of the real estate market, and by enabling thousands to retain their homes helped consolidate middle-class support behind the New Deal program. Foreclosures did not halt, but they declined steadily after 1933, reaching the pre-Depression level by 1938.

Under the PWA, an Emergency Housing Division financed slum clearance and built more than 22,000 dwelling units by late 1937. Meanwhile, in 1934 the Federal Housing Authority had been established to help finance the purchase of homes, or their repair or expansion, and by the end of 1940 had underwritten loans totaling $1.3 billion on improvements for 3 million dwellings and nearly $3 billion for construction of 600,000 homes and more than 300 rental projects. By the Wagner-Steagall Act (1937) the United States Housing Authority was authorized to provide funds for local housing agencies for slum clearance, renovation, and new construction under federal supervision. The 200,000 family dwellings built under the USHA by 1941 were needed, but undoubtedly benefited the lower middle class more than the destitute.

Housing programs and relief from foreclosure meant improved living conditions and greater security for many, at the same time that other federal measures were attempting to assure the individual of security at a different but still personal level. In the United States old age assistance, health and unemployment insurance, and aid for the blind and dependent were traditionally matters to be handled by individual savings, private charities, and county homes. Now, especially under the energetic leadership of Frances Perkins, a talented and experienced social worker who had once been with Jane Addams at Hull House and who was Secretary of Labor, the administration fought for acceptance of the concept that the national government should assume such responsibilities. "As I see it," said Miss Perkins in 1934, "we shall have to establish in this country substantially all of the social insurance measures which the western European countries have set up in the last generation."

As enacted in 1935, Social Security legislation was a combined federal and state program, of which one part—old-age insurance—was administered by the national government and financed by a payroll tax on both employers and employees. Public aid for the blind, for crippled and orphaned children, for maternal and child welfare services, and for public health facilities was put on a matching basis, handled through local agencies, while unemployment compensation was left to the states, with a federal tax for this purpose adding strong incentive for creation of state programs.

Many, like Alfred P. Sloan of General Motors, condemned the very principle of Social Security, believing that the law would "undermine our national life by destroying initiative, discouraging thrift, and stifling individual responsibility"; some complained of the tax levy and the bookkeeping; and economists thought the tax too heavy and deflationary. Others believed the program was too limited, but in spite of the misgivings of a few, the principle of Social Security won broad acceptance and its coverage and benefits were soon extended to a larger and larger percentage of the American people.

Agriculture by 1933 had reached its lowest point in more than a decade of depression, and a bold, radical New Deal approach sought to restore the farmer's purchasing power to the level of the good years from 1909 to 1914. This was to be done by "planned scarcity," the establishment of "parity" prices, and at the same time by furthering mild inflation, reducing farm indebtedness, providing greater security against mortgage foreclosure, extending relief and rehabilitation for farmers on submarginal lands, and developing a conservation and land improvement program.

The key law was the Farm Relief and Inflation Act of 1933, better known as the Agricultural Adjustment Act, originally administered by George Peek. Under this law the federal government paid growers of basic crops such as corn, wheat, cotton, hogs, and tobacco for not growing these products, on the theory that the farmer would benefit directly from the government payment and indirectly from higher farm prices as the surplus was reduced. Financing would come from processing taxes levied on millers, ginners, meat packers, and others, who passed it on to the ultimate consumer. Off to a late start in 1933, the AAA reduced the cotton crop by over four million bales that year and half a million wheat farmers collected a total of $98 million for curbing production. Plowing under of part of the cotton crop and the destruction of six million pigs as the program got under way brought vehement criticism, although the animals were used for relief food wherever possible and industry was not condemned for cutting back its production in the same period. Only Americans, said Norman Thomas, could invent "bread lines knee deep in wheat."

In the autumn of the same year the Commodity Credit Corporation was created to make loans to farmers who agreed to participate in the 1934 crop reduction program, the commodity to be accepted as security and the loan made at above-market prices. If prices rose above the loan level, the grower could redeem his crop and sell it; if prices remained low, the crop remained in government hands, the loan was canceled and the Commodity Credit Corporation took the loss. Moreover, beginning in 1934, voluntary curbing of production began to give way to compulsion in the form of heavy taxes on surpluses produced by farmers who had agreed to a definite quota.

Early in 1936 the Supreme Court declared the AAA unconstitutional, holding that the processing tax was illegal and that agriculture was a local, not national concern. Congress responded immediately with the Soil Conservation and Domestic Allotment Act, financed from general funds, to pay farmers for not planting crops that depleted the soil rapidly—essentially the same crops farmers were paid not to produce under the AAA. In 1938, with a more receptive Supreme Court, the 104-page second Agricultural Adjustment Act retained the soil conservation features and added more, including Secretary of Agriculture Henry A. Wallace's "ever-normal granary" idea of storing surpluses in good times and releasing them in times of scarcity. Using the Commodity Credit Corporation, the Secretary of Agriculture was empowered to make loans on crops, as before, with loans based on a parity price determined by buying power in the 1909–14 period. Payments were still made to farmers who accepted acreage allotments, but growers themselves now voted approval or disapproval.

By 1940 at least 6 million farmers were under the program, which helped agriculture but had not eliminated surpluses or low prices. Cotton had risen from 6.52 cents a pound in 1932 to 12.36 cents in 1936, before dropping back to 8.6 cents the next year; wheat rose from a seasonal average of 38 cents a bushel in 1932 to $1.025 in 1935, but slumped back to 56 cents in 1938. Net farm income went from $1.8 billion in 1932 to $5.1 billion in 1936, but remained fairly constant till dropping off to $4.3 billion in the recession of 1938. And how much of the gain was the result of the AAA and how much was due to drought and the dust storms—the great "black blizzards"—that swept across the Great Plains in the mid-thirties, leaving a trail of withered crops and dying livestock in their wake, is impossible to say.

If farm income generally rose, the rise was not even. Truck gardeners, poultry farmers, and tenant farmers in the South suffered more than other groups and the more prosperous farmers seem to have benefited most, since farm income in the period varied directly with the degree of mechanization, according to the findings of the National Resources Committee in 1937. Farm tenancy had reached 42 per cent of all the farms operated in the depths of the Depression, but actually declined in the South as tenants were "tractored" off the land. "In '34," said one Oklahoman later, "I had I reckon four renters and I didn't make anything. I bought tractors on the money the government gave me and got shet o' my renters." The so-called "suitcase farmer," the small-town businessman who purchased a farm or two, then used a tractor to farm during part of the year, living in town the rest of the time, became increasingly common, especially in the wheatlands of western Kansas and Nebraska.

Early in his administration Roosevelt consolidated the various agricultural credit agencies into a new Farm Credit Administration to help scale down mortgage and interest payments. Through regional land banks, farmers were helped to refinance at lower rates over longer terms and occasionally received direct loans. The total farm mortgage debt was lower in 1934 than it had been since 1920, and it gradually decreased throughout the thirties, but foreclosures were high (39 per 1,000) in 1933, although they dropped to 20 per 1,000 for the year ending March 15, 1936. Through the Farm Security Administration (1937), loans were made to enable nonowners to purchase their own farms, to establish rural co-operatives, or to survive crop failure, though this program was too limited to meet all demands.

Meanwhile, the Rural Electrification Administration speeded the spread of electric power to the American farmstead and WPA labor often ran lines into farm homes, so that where only 9.5 per cent of farms had been electrified in 1930, 30.4 per cent were by 1940 and 90 per cent by 1944. The Taylor Grazing Act (1934) halted homesteading on the great ranges and established a controlled grazing district over 80 million acres, much of it nearly ruined from overstocking. TVA did much for rural conservation and land improvement, and federal agencies devoted considerable energy to reforestation in the Dust Bowl, and to the teaching of crop rotation, contour plowing, and other techniques of more scientific farming designed to conserve resources. At the same time farmers on submarginal lands were relocated.

More was done for the farmer in this period than in any previous era in history, but the results were never wholly satisfactory. Conservatives recoiled in terror. "We are on our way to Moscow," frowned Representative Joseph Martin of Massachusetts when the AAA became law. Production controls were not always effective, and promotion of better techniques, machinery, and relocation of farmers from poor lands seemed contradictory to the aim of reducing the surplus. Large-scale farmers became more conservative when prices rose and even those who accepted AAA payments frequently had misgivings about other government spending and the "coddling" of labor. The farm problem was obviously not eliminated under the New Deal, but for many it was alleviated somewhat.

In general, the industrial segment of the economy had not been suffering as long as had agriculture, but had plunged to the depths beginning in 1929 and was still flat on its back in 1933, when it became the object of an extensive New Deal effort to promote both recovery and reform, at the same time putting people back to work. Designed to further co-operation among industry, labor, and government, the National Industrial Recovery Act of 1933 was considered one of the most significant administration measures by Roosevelt, who commented when he signed it that history would probably record it "as the most important and far-reaching legislation ever enacted by the American Congress."

Based in part on the precedent of the trade associations of the 1920's, which Hoover had encouraged to adopt codes of fair practices, the NIRA sought self-regulation of industry under federal supervision. Industries were to work out codes of "fair competition," which, when accepted by the administration, were to have the force of law. Such codes regulated production and prices, set the hours of labor (usually at a forty-hour week), put a floor under wages, and generally abolished child labor. They usually clarified conditions of credit and discounts and attempted to eliminate undesirable competitive, advertising, and financial practices. Ultimately nearly eight hundred groups, employing over 22 million persons, drew up their own codes or organized under "blanket" codes established by the President.

The program was under General Hugh Johnson, a graduate of West Point as well as the War Industries Board, who has been described as "part cavalry officer, part veteran business man, part economic seer, part government administrator." Despite a strenuous effort by Johnson to sell the NIRA to the public, it soon became apparent that this was not the most successful of the New Deal enterprises. Some, like publisher William Randolph Hearst who called it "a measure of absolute state socialism," opposed it from the start; important concerns like Montgomery Ward and Company and the Ford Motor Company steadfastly refused to co-operate. If morale was lifted at first and men put to work under the PWA part of the program, too much rested on the necessity of voluntary sacrifices by labor and business and violations of codes were frequent and almost impossible to prevent. Many "chiselers," as they were called, displayed the NIRA blue eagle sticker with its slogan "We do our part," but made no effort to live up to their obligations. Southern mill owners agreed on reduced production but used the stretch-out and the speed-up to maintain high output levels without increasing their payrolls. Labor was disgruntled as a wave of strikes in 1934 and 1935 indicated, and a review board created in 1934 headed by Clarence Darrow concluded that the NIRA was actually fostering monopoly at the expense of the consumer and of small industry. Discouraged, Hugh Johnson resigned in a storm of criticism, or as he put it, "in a hail of dead cats."

Moreover, in 1935 the Supreme Court declared the law unconstitutional, holding that control of local business was not interstate commerce and that the code-making procedure was an illegal transfer of legislative power to the President. Roosevelt complained of this "horse and buggy" interpretation, but made no effort to have the NIRA re-enacted in different form as when the first AAA, a much less complex program, was invalidated. The NIRA was not working as hoped and in effect the Court decision rescued the administration from an embarrassing position. Parts of the program were salvaged, especially the provisions relating to labor and unfair competition, but an effort to set up a special code for the bituminous coal industry was nullified by the courts. After 1938 the administration turned to a rather selective trust-busting campaign, but monopolies in business remained.

If the complicated and ambitious NIRA must be deemed a failure, another federal experiment in the industrial realm, the Tennessee Valley Authority, was not. During the twenties, the electric power industry had expanded and undergone rapid consolidation, with high prices and with policies misleading to the public. At Muscle Shoals in the Tennessee River, the national government had built plants to produce nitrates during World War I and had retained the property in the postwar years, despite the efforts of Henry Ford to buy it, but did nothing to develop it until creation of the TVA in 1933. Then it was decided to develop the hydroelectric potential of the entire Tennessee River Valley, thereby putting thousands to work, while at the same time using federal power production as a yardstick by which to test the fairness of rates charged by private power concerns. Thus commenced a project which would ultimately construct more than thirty dams and which was concerned not only with production of power, but also with reforestation, flood control, prevention of soil erosion, development of recreational areas, and the manufacture of nitrogen products for fertilizers and explosives. TVA was a major experiment in regional planning and rehabilitation, and proved extremely successful.

TVA power, sold to private concerns for consumer distribution at fixed prices, averaged about half the cost of private power, and private utility companies were not slow in attacking this example of "creeping socialism in concrete," arguing that government competition with the $12 billion private utilities industry could only lead to what Herbert Hoover had called "degeneration." But the Supreme Court upheld the validity of TVA, and it continued to thrive, despite repeated protests. Probably the yardstick mechanism did not work too well, but the physical achievements of the undertaking were remarkable: along with nitrogen products and cheap electricity vital to the wartime production of explosives, aluminum, and atomic power, it eliminated damaging floods and made the Tennessee River navigable for more than

630 miles; it reduced water pollution, virtually eliminated malaria, and halted erosion while developing one of the country's outstanding recreation areas. Undoubtedly it did much to help raise the living standards of the 2.5 million people in the Valley. But Congress never repeated the experiment; never was it as "socialistic" as during the Hundred Days. Although it authorized the construction of such enterprises as Grand Coulee and Bonneville dams on the Columbia, these were not broad programs in the fashion of TVA.

The federal government extended its controls over transportation and communications. The Reconstruction Finance Corporation had given aid to railroads and between 1933 and 1936 a Federal Railroad Co-ordinator worked to harmonize activities of the railroad companies to cut fixed charges, eliminate waste and duplication, improve credit, and strengthen finances. By 1935 the power of the Interstate Commerce Commission had been extended over interstate bus and truck traffic, and a more powerful Federal Communications Commission had replaced the old Radio Commission, with broader jurisdiction over the airwaves, as well as telephone and telegraph systems. After a brief interlude when the army flew the mail, private carriers handled airmail, with supervision divided among the ICC, the Postmaster General, and the Secretary of Commerce, until consolidated under the new Civil Aeronautics Authority in 1938. Two years earlier a new United States Maritime Commission had superseded the old U.S. Shipping Board and Merchant Fleet Corporation and direct federal subsidies were now given, both for construction of ships and their operation. At the same time a Maritime Labor Board began to mediate labor disputes.

In general, the position of organized labor was strengthened in the New Deal era. In terms of purchasing power, minimum labor standards, and collective bargaining, substantial gains were made. The famous Section 7a of the NIRA stipulated that each industrial code should reserve the right of employees "to organize and bargain collectively through representatives of their own choosing," free from the "interference, restraint, or coercion" of employers. In addition to this sanction of government for collective bargaining, "yellow-dog" contracts forbidding union membership were outlawed and workers could not be forced to join a company union.

Not long after the NIRA was declared unconstitutional, Congress passed the National Labor Relations Act (the Wagner Act), a law referred to by one irate editor as "un-American to the core." It reasserted the principles of Section 7a and spelled out in more detail unfair practices against labor unions. Moreover, it established the National Labor Relations Board as successor to an earlier agency and gave it authority to recognize proper collective bargaining units and to generally enforce the law. Although under fire as unconstitutional (which it was not) and as helping lead to the closed shop (which it did), the Wagner Act reinforced labor, and the reasonably effective NLRB furthered the cause of industrial unionism by showing a tendency to favor industrial over craft organization.

After the NIRA, the federal government continued its efforts to improve working conditions, first by the limited Walsh-Healy Public Contracts Act of 1936, then by the more comprehensive Fair Labor Standards Act of 1938, which abolished child labor and put a floor under wages and a ceiling over hours for most workers involved in interstate commerce. Such laws, together with the old-age and unemployment insurance aspects of Social Security, gave evidence of a larger government role in restraining management, enlarging worker security, and promoting union growth.

The strengthening of collective bargaining by the Wagner Act had much to do with the rise in union membership, which climbed by nearly a million between 1933 and 1935, then shot up from 3.7 million to nearly 9 million in 1939, the largest share of this growth in the mass-producing industries organized by the new C.I.O. However, this was still only one sixth of the total labor force. At the same time, industry resisted what it called "collective bludgeoning," and fought tooth and nail to prevent labor organization. In two and a half years General Motors Corporation paid $994,855.58 to detective agencies for spy services, and Henry Ford became famous for his "service division," made up of secret agents and strikebreakers.

Labor was by this time divided, with more aggressive leaders like John L. Lewis and David Dubinsky favoring broad industrial organization rather than the traditional A. F. of L. craft basis. Out of such differences came a schism which led to the formation of the Congress of Industrial Organizations in 1936, which under the dynamic John L. Lewis quickly became a potent force. Taking the United Auto Workers under its wing in 1936, it conducted a series of sit-down strikes and brought both General Motors and Chrysler Corporation to their knees, although it was not until 1941 that Ford recognized the union.

> Across the board sat Henry Ford
> And his face was full of woe;
> Oh, he bit his nails and his face grew pale,
> But he talked with the C.I.O.

Next, in 1937 Lewis obtained recognition from U.S. Steel, theretofore an implacable foe of labor, without an actual strike, but "Little Steel" (Bethlehem, Inland, Republic, National, and Youngstown Sheet and Tube) fought a bloody series of strikes for four years before agreeing to bargain with the C.I.O. The recession of 1937–38 set back organized labor momentarily, but more than ever before it was playing a growing role in economic life. Soon federal controls would be turned in its direction as well.

PUBLIC DEBT OF THE FEDERAL GOVERNMENT, 1932–39*

Year	Gross Debt (1,000 dols.)	Per Capita (dols.)
1932	19,487,002	156.10
1933	22,538,673	179.48
1934	27,053,141	214.07
1935	28,700,893	225.55
1936	33,778,543	263.79
1937	36,424,614	282.75
1938	37,164,740	286.27
1939	40,439,532	308.98

* Historical Statistics of the United States, Colonial Times to 1957, p. 720.

The New Deal was a tremendously expensive program when figured in dollars and cents; it was partially paid for by increased taxation. In 1935, perhaps in part a response to Huey Long's "soak the rich" proposals, taxes were sharply raised, especially inheritance and gift taxes and levies on incomes over $50,000. A new graduated corporate income tax was dubbed by the NAM a measure "to penalize thrift and success," and the next year a tax on undistributed profits was added, to be abandoned in 1939. Falling primarily on the wealthier classes, such taxation not only provided revenue, but made profits available to increase buying power when pumped back into the economy by federal spending.

In the beginning, Roosevelt had attacked his predecessor for failing to balance the budget, but the national debt climbed from $22.5 billion in 1933 to $40.4 billion in 1939, exclusive of defense spending. How much the ideas of British economist John Maynard Keynes directly influenced the administration in its early years is difficult to say, but the Keynesian gospel became the bible of economists in the later thirties and had a profound impact on American thinking. Keynes contended that investment was of prime importance in economic expansion, and if private funds are not available the government should step in and sustain buying power through deficit spending. As paraphrased by Frances Perkins, Keynes once summarized his theory: "A dollar spent on relief by the government was a dollar given to the grocer, by the grocer to the wholesaler, and by the wholesaler to the farmer, in payment of supplies. With one dollar paid out for relief or public works or anything else, you have created four dollars' worth of national spending."

Deficit spending prevailed and the economy made progress after 1933. The Federal Reserve Board's Adjusted Index of Industrial Production, at a high of 125 in 1929, went from 59 in March, 1933, edging slowly upward by fits and starts, to 100 by late 1935, and was at 117 in August, 1937, when recession began a downward trend, plunging it to a low of 76 in May, 1938. This Roosevelt Depression, as critics labeled it, was precipitated by several factors, including labor troubles, a contraction of credit, an overstocking by businessmen anticipating coming inflation, business distrust of the New Deal, and a sharp cutback of federal spending as the administration made an effort to balance the budget. In this relapse Roosevelt promptly abandoned the budget-balancing attempt, stepped up spending for relief, housing, and public works, and even made a gesture toward government investment with the so-called lending-spending bill rejected by Congress in 1938. The economy turned upward once more.

The New Deal was and is controversial. Few of its commentators are able to view it with complete detachment and the vision of both supporters and detractors is often clouded by bias and sentimentality. Where its critics have cried "socialism," its defenders have pointed out the essential retention of the capitalistic framework. Historian Henry Steele Commager has gone so far as to call Roosevelt "the greatest conservative since Alexander Hamilton" for this reason. Where critics have condemned the expense, waste, duplication, and inefficiency of the New Deal, friends have emphasized the need for speed in sustaining the economy and insisted that "balancing the human budget" outweighed mere monetary considerations. To the charges that labor and the farmer were pampered and class antagonisms were stirred up against business, New Dealers expressed matters in different terminology: they spoke of the establishment of a better balance between business, labor, and agriculture and a more equitable distribution of income. To charges that the New Deal had not cured the Depression but had merely administered sedatives and that only World War II brought an end to unemployment and production problems, Roosevelt supporters cited comparative statistics to show marked improvements in the economy between 1933 and 1939. While not yet back to the 1929 level, farm income was up from $2.7 billion to $4.4 billion; farm prices averaged 77 per cent of parity rather than 55 per cent; real wages had risen 20 per cent; unemployment had been cut some 5 to 6 million, while the total labor force increased by about 3 million.

Both critics and defenders have to admit that the program was not always clearly thought out and that inherent contradictions were sometimes manifested within it, as in the case of the farm program. Nor could they deny that a bold approach had been taken in a time of crisis. It was an Englishman who commented near the end of Roosevelt's first term: "Mr. Roosevelt may have given the wrong answers to many of his problems. But he is at least the first President of modern America who has asked the right questions." Certainly the federal government had played no comparable role in any previous depression, and its action in this instance greatly accelerated the movement toward a mixed economy, part private, part government. Such an extension of federal authority not only brought a shift of power from Wall Street to Washington and made the United States government the largest single employer in the world, it also brought to the fore one of our most pressing domestic problems, the question of how far government may go in exerting control over the economy without curtailing individual freedoms. On this there is no concerted agreement, but the basic idea of an expanding role of government on behalf of public welfare has been accepted and continues to be extended.

XXII

WORLD WAR II

THROUGHOUT THE THIRTIES, while men sang the "WPA Blues," tightened their belts, and watched prices slowly inch their way upward, the world witnessed the breakdown of collective security, the repudiation of international law, and the remarkable rise of totalitarian powers disgruntled at World War I settlements and now seeking a place in the sun. It was fortunate indeed that by the end of the decade the economy had improved before the United States was called upon to meet the crucial external crises forced by the have-not nations, Italy, Japan, and Germany.

In the twenties and thirties the United States, like Britain and France, was playing a less vigorous role in foreign affairs and was endeavoring to follow a neutral course. It had failed to join the League of Nations and its unwillingness to co-operate helped scuttle the London Economic Conference in 1933. It had mildly protested Japanese aggression in Manchuria in 1931, and had piously refused to sell or transport munitions to either side when Mussolini's Italy invaded Ethiopia in 1935. A year later, the United States applied its neutrality to both sides in the bloody Spanish Civil War, despite aid from Germany and Italy to the Franco "rebels." In the "undeclared war" between Japan and China which began in 1937, American neutrality laws were not applied, because as revised that year, they provided that for a limited time, raw materials (including scrap iron, gasoline, and oil), but not munitions, could be sold to belligerents on a cash and carry basis. Japan, with a sizable merchant marine, would have benefited, while China, with a small fleet, would have been at a disadvantage.

Meanwhile, in Europe Nazi Germany had rearmed, reoccupied the Rhineland, and had incorporated Austria without firing a shot. In 1938 came Adolph Hitler's masterly annexation of the Sudetenland, with England and France abandoning Czechoslovakia, settling for what British Prime Minister Neville Chamberlain believed was "peace in our time." Mussolini soon seized Albania, the rest of Czechoslovakia was swallowed by Hitler. Next came a German war of nerves against the Poles, followed by the signing of commercial and nonaggression pacts with the Soviet Union in August, 1939, and the immediate invasion of Poland, which signaled the beginning of World War II.

Following the outbreak of war, after bitter and prolonged debate, Congress amended the neutrality laws to permit the sale of goods, even armaments, on a "cash and carry" basis, at the same time prohibiting American merchant ships from transporting such supplies and forbidding Americans to travel on belligerent vessels or into prescribed war zones. Theoretically, matériel of war would thus reach friends because of the superiority of the British and French navies, and the loss of American lives would be avoided.

President Roosevelt stepped up defense spending, requesting $1 billion in 1938 for naval and air expansion, and receiving an additional $552 million early the following year, but not until the "Phony War" phase ended and Nazi armies overran Western Europe in the spring and summer of 1940 was Congress jolted into more positive action. It now set aside $4 billion for a two-ocean navy, embarked on a program to build some 50,000 airplanes, stepped up funds for the Export-Import Bank's lending in Latin America, and by October, 1940, had appropriated nearly $18 billion for defense—half as much as the country had spent in World War I.

Neutrality was obviously being eroded. British warships were being repaired in American shipyards and modern planes were being sent to the Allies, despite restrictive laws that had to be circumvented. In September, 1940, fifty World War I-type destroyers were exchanged for bases on British possessions ranging from Trinidad and throughout the Caribbean and as far north as Newfoundland. Late the same year, when financial difficulties made it questionable whether England could continue to buy war materials on American terms, Roosevelt suggested Lend-Lease, as he put it, "to eliminate the dollar sign." Under this proposal the United States would make armaments available to the enemies of totalitarianism on almost any basis—on loan, on lease, by gift—with the equipment or its equivalent to be returned when the war was over. The Lend-Lease bill (No. 1776) precipitated one of the bitterest debates in congressional history. Senator Burton Wheeler of Montana, fearing a complete breakdown of neutrality, called it the "New Deal's Triple-A foreign policy—to plow under every fourth American boy." But despite stinging opposition, Lend-Lease became law in March, 1941, and, with public support generally behind it, the United States set out to make itself, in the words of the President, "the arsenal of democracy." Eventually the nation would funnel over $50 billion in arms, equipment, food, gasoline, and services into Allied countries, three fifths of it going to the British Commonwealth and one fifth to Russia. In return, by the end of the war reverse Lend-Lease in the form of raw materials, food, services, and quarters for American troops abroad had totaled about $9 billion.

In more than one sense Lend-Lease was significant: not only did it provide much-needed materials to Allies at crucial times, it helped gear American production to a war effort at least a year earlier than would otherwise have been possible. It helped pull England and the United States closer together and to break down neutrality further, for efforts to protect Lend-Lease goods on the Atlantic led to the torpedoing of several American destroyers by German "rattlesnakes of the sea," as Roosevelt called them. By late autumn of 1941 the United States was engaged in an actual but undeclared shooting war against Nazi submarines in the Atlantic.

In the meantime, taking advantage of each totalitarian move in Europe to better her own position in Asia, Japan had moved into southern China and Indochina, had subordinated Siam by treaty, and had protected her flanks with pacts with Italy, Germany, and the U.S.S.R. Late in 1940, having refrained until then for fear that Japan would invade the Dutch East Indies to obtain oil denied her elsewhere, the United States began a series of embargoes on goods to Japan, which in time halted the flow of essential war materials, including iron and gasoline. Japanese, as well as German and Italian, assets were frozen in this country, and Lend-Lease aid to China began in August, 1941, over the Burma Road. It was such economic pressure from the United States that prompted Japan to the bold and deliberate stroke at Pearl Harbor which brought American entry into the war in December, 1941.

Before Pearl Harbor some businessmen let their hatred of Roosevelt and the New Deal obscure the need for defense; others were not convinced that the United States would be drawn into the conflict; still others saw no reason to give up the fruits of returning consumer-goods prosperity. Some recalled the stigma attached by the Nye Committee to the "merchants of death" who produced munitions for World War I; others were afraid to move without adequate stockpiles of vital copper, rubber, and aluminum, and wanted guaranteed profits or a fast tax write-off on new plants. In order to hasten production, especially for Lend-Lease, the federal government permitted a five year tax write-off and, using funds from the Reconstruction Finance Corporation, built new defense plants for lease to private manufacturers. Thus by late 1940 a limited defense boom was under way, with shipyards and aircraft factories especially expanding.

Ignoring the pleas of Bernard Baruch for the establishment of a powerful World War I-type economic czar, Roosevelt had created a weak War Resources Board in 1939, but abandoned it quickly when it proved not only antilabor but anti-New Deal as well. After the fall of France other agencies had been established in an effort to increase and direct the flow of goods for national defense requirements. But because of great confusion and the lack of defined authority, none of these proved particularly effective, and not until January, 1942, after Pearl Harbor, did Roosevelt establish the War Production Board (headed by Donald Nelson of Sears, Roebuck & Co.), an agency of the type Bernard Baruch had long urged, which promptly absorbed the function of its predecessors and took upon itself the task of setting priorities, assigning raw materials, transportation, and a thousand other details. The War Production Board found that since Pearl Harbor too many plants were being built in some fields, that the armed forces were indiscriminately ordering goods, and that waste characterized the process of procurement and conversion. The WPB had the task of trying to handle both civilian and military allocation and found itself clashing incessantly with the armed services.

With growing complexity, a large part of the WPB work was taken over in October, 1942, by the Office of Economic Stabilization, soon reorganized as the Office of War Mobilization under the tireless James M. Byrnes, whose wide powers brought the informal title of the "assistant President," and who made the agency an effective one. Through it and the bewildering maze of boards and bureaus underneath it, the federal government in effect decided what was to be manufactured, by whom, for whom, when, and at what price. In 1944 it also was considering problems of reconversion to a civilian economy once the war was won.

Production problems were many. Despite coordination boards, interservice rivalries and considerable duplication persisted. German submarines limited shipping and Japanese conquests in Southeast Asia cut off critical supplies, necessitating, for example, the creation of an entire new synthetic rubber industry, headed by William Jeffers of the Union Pacific Railroad and operated by private industry backed by government capital. New sources of copper had to be developed in Africa and South America to meet increased demands. So important was this need that the Army furloughed some four thousand G.I.'s who were experienced copper miners. Oil and gasoline consumption soared at a time when the Allies were cut off from their normal sources of supply. American oil production was up about one third between 1939 and 1945, but shortage still persisted and to alleviate it rationing was instituted, new tankers were built, and the Big Inch and Little Inch pipelines were constructed to bring petroleum from the Texas fields to the Atlantic seaboard to avoid the sea-route danger from submarines.

Steel production nearly doubled between 1939 and 1944;

aluminum output increased almost six times in the same period as newcomers like Henry Kaiser and the Reynolds Company were encouraged to expand and to break the monopoly of the Aluminum Company of America. Production of magnesium increased 4,000 per cent, and in both of the light metals, power produced by TVA and by Grand Coulee Dam was instrumental in their manufacture.

Hermann Göring, head of the German Luftwaffe, once made the remark "Americans can't build planes, only electric ice-boxes and razor blades." Production of military aircraft in 1944 reached 95,000 and between 1940 and July, 1945, American factories turned out 300,317 planes. The same period saw the production of 72,000 naval ships of all kinds; 4,900 merchant vessels; 86,330 tanks; and 2,681,000 machine guns. By a year after Pearl Harbor, most production problems had been solved; by 1944 American production was twice that of Germany, Italy, and Japan combined, and some cutback of war goods was being made.

Civilian industry converted, sometimes completely: no automobiles were made for consumer purchase between 1942 and 1946, for example. Chrysler was building tanks; Packard, airplane engines; A. C. Spark Plug Company, machine guns; and Ford's Willow Run plant was the nation's largest producer of bombers. Roughly one third of all contracts went through ten major corporations; General Motors alone received $14 billion worth of wartime orders. Much of this was sub-contracted to smaller firms, but a host of small businesses failed during the war years. Consumer goods were not completely driven out by the war; far from it. At maximum effort, an estimated 42 per cent of America's gross national product was devoted to the war, as compared with from 50 to 55 per cent for England and 50 per cent for Germany by the latter part of the conflict. Thus the superior capacity of the United States was instrumental in beating the Axis.

And more than ever before, science and technology played a commanding role. New weapons such as the bazooka, the proximity fuse, and the long-range fighter plane were perfected in response to specific needs. Where German science was handicapped by the Nazi Party with personal and political intervention by Hitler, American science was given a blank check. The federal government was willing to gamble $2 billion on a number of different approaches to atomic fission, knowing that all might fail. Under the Office of Scientific Research and Development (1941), headed by Vannever Bush and James Conant, science went to war, but it was with government co-operation rather than control. Moreover, the atomic bomb was a joint enterprise, with British and Canadian contributions as well as American.

Transportation was geared to the emergency, but the government did not take over the railroads as in the previous war, although the Office of Defense Transportation (December, 1941) coordinated rail lines, airlines, trucking, and other forms of domestic transport. With aid from the ODT whose head, Ralph Budd, was a railroad man, the American rail network, despite run-down equipment and poor tracks, handled twice the traffic in 1944 as in 1939 with only a slight increase in the number of passenger cars, 2.5 per cent more locomotives, and 8 per cent more freight stock. While the War Shipping Administration controlled ship ownership and shipping, the United States Maritime Commission, originally created in 1936, was revitalized in mid-1941 and given the task of co-ordinating and facilitating ship construction. To offset a huge loss to German submarines (twelve million tons in 1942), the Commission by April, 1943, was turning out 140 vessels a month (1 million tons), many of these the cheap, rapidly-constructed, and slow freighter, the Liberty Ship. Using time-cutting welding and prefabrication techniques, such vessels were being built in an average of forty-two days in 1944 and Henry Kaiser once built one in fourteen days. In all, 271 of the Liberties, and 531 of the larger, faster Victory Ships were built, plus many tankers and other types. Unlike in World War I, most men and materials of war went abroad in American, not foreign, bottoms.

Agricultural production in 1944 was about 23 per cent over the 1939 level, though acreage under cultivation had increased only 6.5 per cent and the farm labor force had decreased by almost a million. Productivity per man hour was up 25 per cent and some $6 billion worth of food was sent to the Allies during the war. When the conflict started, Henry Wallace's "ever normal granary" contained a two-year supply of corn, wheat, and cotton, but high demands quickly eliminated the surpluses and brought a wave of prosperity for the American farmer. Net income almost tripled from 1939 to 1945, the value of farm implements and machinery doubled, while the farm mortgage debt fell by more than $2 billion.

In 1942 two federal agencies were created, one to co-ordinate food production, one for food distribution, and these in 1943 were consolidated into a single War Food Administration. Through the War Production Board farmers received allocation of equipment and generous draft exemptions were given. Moreover, agricultural pressure was successful in retaining the Depression subsidy plan, even though underproduction rather than overproduction now prevailed. Congress raised commodity price ceilings to 110 per cent of parity, over the protest of the President, who sought to hold prices down, but without subsidies, production incentive might have been limited due to the setting of retail meat prices by the Office of Price Administration, those prices eventually reaching back to the farm.

Labor, like agriculture, also benefited. The army of unemployed shriveled from 8.1 million in 1940 to 670,000 in 1944, and at peak (1943), the employed civilian work force totaled 54.5 million, of whom one third were women, despite a deduction of nearly 15 million for the armed forces. Urban population rose some 9 million between 1940 and 1946, and farm population fell. The Pacific Coast especially boomed, gaining one third in population during the war years. Negroes moving north for the first time cracked job barriers. Wages were up from $0.633 for the average hourly earning of production workers in manufacturing in 1939 to $1.023 five years later; the average weekly wage went from $23.86 to $44.39. Prices mounted, too, but under federal controls, and real wages rose by 50 per cent by 1944.

Under Paul V. McNutt, former Governor of Indiana, the War Manpower Commission (1942) allocated manpower for both civilian and military needs, but was hampered by the limitations of its head and by a lack of absolute authority, other than the threat of the draft, to force workers from nonessential to essential industries. Actually, the manpower shortage was not as serious a problem as the training of the unskilled, the high rate of turnover, and the relocation of a large part of the labor force in industrial centers where housing, transportation, and schools were inadequate. Adolescents found easy employment, as did retirees and housewives, as "Rosie, the Riveter" became not only a popular song but also a valuable contributor to the shipbuilding and aircraft industries.

In general, the position of organized labor was strengthened, both in terms of numbers and in public stature. Union membership was up nearly 65 per cent, increasing from almost 9 million in 1939 to 14.8 million in 1945. As the refrain from one of the United Autoworkers songs went,

> It's that UAW–CIO
> Makes the army roll and go,
> Turning out the jeeps and tanks,
> The airplanes every day;
> It's that UAW–CIO
> Makes the army roll and go,
> Puts wheels on the U.S.A.

When the war came the C.I.O., the A. F. of L., and the Railway Brotherhoods joined in a no-strike pledge, provided the cost of living could be held at a reasonable level, a pledge which with relatively few exceptions was kept. The earlier abortive National Defense Mediation Board was replaced early in 1942 with the War Labor Board, which was made up of representatives of labor, management, and the government, and which had strong powers not only to mediate disputes but also to stabilize wages by adjusting them to living costs according to the Little Steel formula, which in 1942 had permitted a regulated increase of 15 per cent in earnings.

There were numerous strikes, but only a comparatively few were crucial. In response Congress passed the Smith-Connelly Act of 1943, which required unions to wait thirty days before striking and gave the President the authority to seize and operate any war industry tied up by such action. Four times John L. Lewis' United Mine Workers struck, and twice the mines were taken over until wage adjustments brought the miners back. Public opinion castigated the strikers: "There are no strikes in foxholes," said the critics; to which labor could reply "there are no profits in foxholes, either," an oblique reference to the rise of corporate profits, after taxes, from $5 billion to nearly $10 billion between 1939 and 1944. But public spirit was probably more effective than the Smith-Connelly law; the percentage of total working time lost by stoppage remained remarkably low, and in general, labor supported the war effort, prospered, and grew strong.

World War II was expensive. For the fiscal years 1941 through 1945 federal expenditures totaled more than $321 billion, a sum roughly twice as large as all federal expenditures from 1789 to 1941 and ten times as great as American expenses in World War I. In 1944, the peak year, the war was costing the United States nearly $250 million a day. As in the previous war, taxation and borrowing underwrote the financing of the war effort. Taxes accounted for about 45 per cent, but Roosevelt believed that half the cost should be raised in this manner. Although Congress consistently dragged its heels, the minimum income tax rate was stepped up to 20 per cent and the maximum eventually reached 94 per cent, while excess profits taxes went to 90 per cent. New excise, luxury, transportation, and recreation taxes were levied, but almost three fourths of total tax revenue came from individual and corporate income taxes, and their high levels meant that few millionaires were created by the war. Tax collection was tightened up: about 28 million people paid income taxes in 1942; with the new withholding provision the figure went up to more than 40 million in 1943. Individual and corporate income taxes approximately doubled every year, with corporate taxes, surtaxes, and excess-profits taxes greater than individual income tax payments through 1943, but with the reverse true in 1944 and 1945.

With more than half the cost of the war financed by borrowing from individuals, banks, and other corporations, the public debt rose sharply from $40.4 billion (or $308.98 per capita) in 1939 to $258.7 billion (or $1,852.74 per capita) in 1945. Seven War Bond drives and one Victory Bond drive, plus payroll deduction plans, netted a total of about $100 billion from small investors and nonbanking concerns, while another $87.5 billion was borrowed from Federal Reserve and commercial banks. In spite of attempts to limit purchases of government securities by commercial banks, by 1946 such institutions owned about 40 per cent of the debt, nonbanking corporations 37 per cent, and individuals the remaining 23 per cent. This in itself represented a serious weakness in wartime financing, for taxes and loans were designed not only to furnish funds, but also to help curb inflation. When so heavily concentrated in banking hands, loan securities had an opposite effect, providing the base for expanding credit and money in circulation. Government borrowing was itself inflationary, but the Federal Reserve System dared not use its controls: if it resorted to open-market operations it might weaken the government bond market. Rather than curb bond sales, it worked to promote them, thus encouraging inflation, a trend already accentuated by scarcity of consumer goods, high buying power, and pressure of business, labor, and agriculture for greater profits.

Taxes and bond drives reduced purchasing power somewhat, and through the Office of Price Administration price controls and rationing functioned as devices to keep prices down as much as possible. Early in 1942 the OPA was granted authority to freeze rents and control the prices of consumer goods in defense areas, but farm prices were exempted until they reached 110 per cent of parity and wages and rents elsewhere rose until Congress finally overhauled the law to permit the freezing of wages, salaries, rents, and farm prices throughout the country. Administrator Leon Henderson resigned under fire at the end of 1942 and his successor, the amiable former senator Prentice Brown, proved ineffectual. A new enforcement agency, the Office of Economic Stabilization, created in October, 1942, was not able to keep wholesale and retail prices from creeping upward until April, 1943, when Roosevelt issued his "hold the line" order against increases and rolled back prices of meat, butter, and coffee by 10 per cent. Reorganized under the extremely competent Chester Bowles, the OPA then exerted a rigorous program of controls which limited the cost-of-living rise for the next two years to 1.4 per cent. Installment buying was sharply restricted and certain commodities were rationed, partly to hold living costs down and insure a fair supply for all, partly to reduce spending and curb inflation, and partly for psychological reasons, to bring home the impact of war to each individual. Sugar, coffee, meat, cigarettes, tires, and shoes all went on the ration list, and A-card holders were entitled to 1.5 gallons of gasoline per week as the national speed limit dropped to thirty-five miles per hour. Some black market activities flourished, yet war on the home front was not "blood, sweat and tears" and Americans never experienced the severe rationing endured by the British. But the fight against inflation bore fruit: the cost of living rose only about 29 per cent from 1939 to the end of the war as compared with a rise of 63 per cent during World War I. However, with the removal of controls in 1946 the climb was sudden and spectacular.

In an economic sense, the war meant many things to many people, but a few clear-cut trends are discernible. Prosperity and a rising standard of living was shared by a broad segment of the population, including labor and agriculture. The public debt grew, becoming for the first time greater than the private debt, but interest rates were held down and because new construction was impossible, states and municipalities reduced their obligations. Exports rose to a high of more than $14 billion in 1944, then fell back to about $10 billion in 1945, while imports rose steadily from $2.3 billion in 1939 to over $4 billion by 1945. American investment abroad rose from $12.3 billion in 1940 to $16.8 billion in 1945, and foreign investment in the United States also went up from $13.6 billion to $17.7 billion in the same period. At peak (1944), 42.3 per cent of the gross national product went into the war effort, but the indirect cost, apart from the impossibility of assessing the value of lives lost, would reach astronomical figures when veterans' benefits, debt interest, and rehabilitation assistance were considered. The war years, moreover, added, though not spectacularly, to the trend toward greater governmental control over the economy, while business recovered some of its luster lost in the Depression, and labor emerged with enhanced prestige.

XXIII

THE POSTWAR YEARS

THE POSTWAR ERA brought nominal conversion to a peacetime economy, although military expenditures would continue to make up a large and highly important percentage of the ever-expanding national budget. It was a period also characterized by inflation and an economy of abundance—an "affluent society," John Kenneth Galbraith called it; by a relatively moderate rate of economic growth when judged by earlier standards or by those of the Soviet Union; by periodic instability and recurring labor problems, including high unemployment; by a continuing farm surplus, despite federal subsidies; by a greatly accelerated technological advance and continuing growth of the supercorporation, a trend going back to the beginning of the century; by a retention and even an extension of the role of government in the economic sector; and, as the foreign aid programs indicated, an increasing economic awareness of the rest of the world.

The dismantling of the greatest industrial war machine the world had ever known came about quickly with relatively little dislocation. Unable to withstand pressure for an almost immediate readjustment, the federal government moved rapidly to demobilize the armed forces and to cancel contracts for war materials: by the middle of 1946 between 10 and 11 million men had been released from the armed services, nearly 3 million war

310

workers dismissed, and more than 300,000 government contracts cancelled. War plants were disposed of for a fraction of their value and early in 1946 the War Assets Administration was selling billions of dollars worth of surplus equipment, including the Big Inch pipeline, to private business. Manpower controls and most rationing were removed, but price and rent controls remained until late 1946, to the consternation of farmers and businessmen who insisted they were being deprived of profits justly due them. When controls were removed—except on rents in crucial areas—over the protest of President Truman, retail prices rose 32 per cent in a single year.

PERCENTAGE OF POPULATION LIVING IN RURAL AND
URBAN AREAS, 1910–60*

Year	Urban	Rural
1910	45.7	54.3
1920	51.2	48.8
1930	56.2	43.8
1940	56.5	43.5
1950	59.6	40.4
1960	63.0	37.0

* From U.S. Department of Commerce, *Statistical Abstract of the United States, 1962,* p. 21.

Demand for consumer goods ran well ahead of supply, as the wartime backlog of buying power was suddenly released and the American people settled down to what one federal official called "the pleasant predicament of having to learn to live fifty per cent better than they have ever lived before." Prices were inflated, but taxes were cut, employment more than held its own, and production climbed. Released veterans did not glut the labor market, as some had feared; servicemen's unemployment insurance—the "52-20 club"—helped ease the shock and millions of veterans took advantage of the G.I. Bill to finance a college education or to underwrite loans for homes or to set themselves up in agriculture or business.

But the rising cost of living bothered the wage earner, who now saw his overtime pay gone and his purchasing power dropping, while industry and the farmer (at least to 1948) made handsome profits. The United Auto Workers in 1945 sought as much take-home pay for a forty-hour week as had been received before V–J Day for forty-eight hours, and struck when this 30 per cent increase was not forthcoming. The steel industry saw 750,000 men walk out early in 1946 over a wage dispute, and the meat packing and electrical industries experienced similar disruptions. A nationwide rail strike was called off after forty-eight hours, just as the President went before Congress asking for power to "draft into the Armed Forces of the United States all workers who are on strike against their government." John L. Lewis took 400,000 United Mine Workers out of the soft-coal industry, despite a court injunction obtained by President Truman, who was accused by the president of the NAM of letting "the public freeze while his guts quiver." Truman seized the mines, the U.M.W. returned with increases, but were fined $3.5 million (later cut to $700,000), and Lewis was assessed $10,000. More than 4.5 million men went out on strike in 1946 and a record 116 million man-days were lost during the year.

Strikes did not cease: major walkouts occurred in the telephone industry and in coal in 1947; again in coal in the following year; in steel in 1949 and again in 1956; Chrysler Corporation was idled for 102 days by a strike in 1950. During the Korean conflict something of a temporary truce prevailed, though with many exceptions. Still, after 1946 there were fewer strikes and labor-management relations in many industries seemed more mature, more responsible, and less prone to extreme action by either side.

Since manufacturers could and did pass the cost on to the consumer, labor made substantial gains. Not only did money wages double and real wages increase 30 per cent from 1946 to 1958, but fringe benefits became increasingly significant. Vacation allowances, retirement pensions, and health insurance programs became common; coal miners received "portal to portal" pay; General Motors led the way in 1948 with an "escalator clause," providing for an automatic wage increase or decrease in keeping with the quarterly rise or fall of the price index of consumer goods. Unions stepped up their campaigns for a "guaranteed annual wage," especially in industries in which employment fluctuated seasonally, and in 1955 automobile workers received a modified guarantee and the steel workers at Continental Can and

American Can companies received the first real guarantee. American Motors in 1961 signed a U.A.W. contract providing for a profit-sharing plan for employees; and in 1963 New York electricians were on a twenty-five hour work week; and in the steel industry a plan for "sabbaticals" had been agreed upon.

While labor forged ahead, particularly in the immediate postwar years, public opinion reacted adversely to "Big Labor" and to labor "czars" like John L. Lewis of the United Mine Workers and James C. Petrillo of the Musician's Union. Conservatives demanded that labor be curbed and that the Wagner Act be modified to eliminate what they called "unfair" labor practices. With this prevailing mood and a Republican-controlled Congress elected in 1946, the controversial Taft-Hartley Law was passed in 1947, over the veto of Truman, who called it "a clear threat to the successful working of our democratic society," while George Meany of the A. F. of L. saw it as a "return to the medieval concept of master and servant."

In addition to enlarging the National Labor Relations Board, the Taft-Hartley Act prohibited the closed shop (under which only union labor could be hired), but permitted the union shop (under which hiring was not limited, but all new employees must then join the union), provided a majority of workers so voted and no state laws forbade it. It outlawed the secondary boycott, the practice of "featherbedding" (forced hiring of more men than are really needed), and the "check-off" (compelling the employer to withhold the worker's union dues to be turned over to the union). Unions were made liable for damages from jurisdictional disputes, leaders were required to take a non-communist oath, and broader freedom of antiunion expression guaranteed within union ranks. A sixty-day "cooling-off" period was to precede any strike, and unions were forbidden to contribute to political campaigns.

Despite labor complaints that collective bargaining would be demolished, organized labor was not hurt appreciably. Union membership rose to over 18 million, and in 1955 came the wedding of two unlikely partners, the C.I.O., stressing industrial organization, and the A. F. of L., emphasizing craft organization. Industry-wide bargaining was not halted and the NLRB which remained to enforce it, was filled with members not unsympathetic to labor's cause. Furthermore, the presence of a responsible new generation of "labor statesmen," like George Meany and Walter Reuther, mitigated the law's effect, and as time passed, the high tide of antiunion conservatism ebbed somewhat.

Ironically, Truman, who had vetoed the Taft-Hartley law and who was elected in 1948 with support of labor, twice used the injunction against the Mine Workers and in 1952 halted a steel strike by seizing the steel plants, an action which the Supreme Court refused to uphold, though it did affirm the use of the injunction to assert the supremacy of public over private interests in labor disputes. At the same time, a number of states enacted "right to work laws" to outlaw the union shop; yet in 1958, when such laws became issues in several state elections, several candidates supporting them, including Senate Minority Leader William Knowland, running for governor of California, were defeated.

By the middle fifties, congressional investigations had exposed corruption, misuse of union funds, and labor racketeering on the part of union officials, especially millionaire Dave Beck of the Teamsters, who ultimately went to prison. Also under fire was James Hoffa, Beck's successor. Out of these investigations, over the opposition of practically all of organized labor, came the Landrum-Griffin Act of 1959, to safeguard union members from their own leaders. Former criminals could not serve as union officials; nor former communists unless they had renounced the party at least five years before. All officers were to be bonded; detailed annual reports were to be published by the Secretary of Labor indicating the union's finances, loans, and all salaries over $10,000; and a "bill of rights" required periodic elections at various levels, with notice, the secret ballot, and safeguards for members to speak freely at union meetings.

In 1963, to avert a threatened rail strike, Congress enacted a compulsory arbitration law, with the approval of President Kennedy, who had made strong appeals to both labor and management in the fight against inflation. In 1962 Kennedy had persuaded labor leaders to minimize their demands in the steel industry, but when steel companies nevertheless boosted their prices, he forced a return to the old price level by a merciless use of publicity and by threatening to divert defense contracts and bring antitrust suits.

By 1961 population increases were adding nearly a million persons to the labor force each year and the total had risen to 71 million. The proportion of women workers increased to one in four in 1960 as compared with one in seven in 1870, and with broader Social Security and pension plans, workers over the age of sixty-five were being pushed out of the labor force. Increased emphasis on services rather than on production brought another shift in the employment pattern, with more workers now employed in services than in manufacturing. Accelerated technological advances, particularly automation, have increased the proportion of white-collar workers, precipitating a slight dip in actual union membership and a marked decline in the percentage of the total labor force belonging to unions, for white-collar workers have traditionally been less responsive to organization than others. Because of the threat posed by automation, unions have become more interested in job security than in wage increases. Except for periodic relapses, the average unemployment for the decade of the fifties was 4.6 per cent of the civilian labor force, as opposed to from 15 to 24 per cent during the Depression years. But nearly 5 million unemployed in boom times represents an anachronism of serious magnitude. In industries like textiles, automobiles, coal, and steel, "automation refugees" are increasingly a problem. The most common suggestion is retraining for new jobs, but in practice, such people are often reluctant to move. But adjustments must be made; the rate of economic growth must be stepped up or chronic unemployment may yet become endemic.

The postwar years have seen railroads playing a less important role in transportation than before, as automobiles, trucking, airlines, and even pipelines and new inland water routes have provided keen, sometimes almost overwhelming competition. Despite an investment of some $11 billion in the decade immediately after the war and the addition of 20,000 diesel-electric units, 585,000 new freight cars, plus improved tracks and centralized traffic control systems, the railroads steadily lost ground. Working capital dwindled from $1.6 billion in 1945 to $397 million in January, 1958; railroad employment fell from 1.4 million to

EMPLOYMENT AND UNEMPLOYMENT, 1946–62*

Year	Number, civilian labor force (thousands of persons)	Number of unemployed† (thousands of persons)	Unemployed as per cent of total civilian labor force†
1946	57,520	2,270	3.9
1947	60,168	2,356	3.9
1948	61,442	2,325	3.8
1949	62,105	3,682	5.9
1950	63,099	3,351	5.3
1951	62,884	2,099	3.3
1952	62,966	1,931	3.1
1953	63,815	1,870	2.9
1954	64,468	3,578	5.6
1955	65,847	2,903	4.4
1956	67,530	2,822	4.2
1957	67,946	2,936	4.3
1958	68,647	4,681	6.8
1959	69,394	3,813	5.5
1960	70,612	3,931	5.6
1961	71,603	4,806	6.7
1962‡	70,697	4,382	6.2

* From U.S. Department of Commerce, *Statistical Abstract of the United States, 1962,* p. 215.
† Annual figures are averages of monthly figures.
‡ March.

793,000 between 1945 and 1960; net income fluctuated from $960 million in 1955 to $473 million in 1960.

The plight of the railroads may stem from several factors. Railroad management has not always shown adequate vision and vigor in meeting competition. The companies insist that powerful unions have raised operating costs through such practices as featherbedding and the retention of antiquated wage-base formulas. Federal subsidies to airlines and, by highway construction, to trucking have strengthened competitors at the same time federal rate regulation has been too strict, they complain.

On the other hand, by the Transportation Act of 1955 the Interstate Commerce Commission has sought to ease the pressure on railroads, and the companies themselves have attempted to reduce costs through consolidation, but some major mergers, like the New York Central and the Pennsylvania, have been blocked by the federal government. Acting on the old adage, "If you can't lick 'em, join 'em," railroad lines have also gone into trucking and the bus business, or in the case of the Pennsylvania, hold stock in airlines. Many railroads in the 1950's went into "piggyback" service, transporting trucks long distances on flatcars for more rapid delivery, with truckers completing the local haul.

A good deal of freight traffic has been diverted to pipelines. By 1959 half a million miles of gas line and 205,000 miles of petroleum pipe lines existed, with 75 per cent of all crude oil transported by this means. Including fertilizer, coal, concrete, and other pulverized and liquified products, fully 20 per cent of all domestic freight is carried by pipeline.

Airlines greatly expanded since the war and cut deeply into railroad passenger trade. With the war creating experienced personnel and with federal subsidies for airmail and the financing of state and municipal airports, the number of airlines grew from twenty-three in 1939 to fifty-five in 1961. These directly employed three quarters of a million persons, with total payrolls of almost $1.5 billion; they served nearly 800 cities and carried more than 63 million passengers at an average of 6.18 cents a mile. Beginning in 1955, when Capital Airlines bought a fleet of British turboprop Viscounts, speed on normal runs had steadily accelerated until by 1960, with the latest pure-jet aircraft, coast-to-coast flight had become a matter of a mere five and a half hours.

In 1954, after Canada had threatened to go it alone, the United States agreed to co-operate in constructing the long-awaited St. Lawrence Seaway. Five years later, with American rail, power, and ocean port interests apprehensive and with the United States paying less than one third of the cost, the Seaway was opened, connecting Duluth with the Atlantic over 2,000 miles away and making mid-America accessible to ocean vessels of up to 10,000 tons. Chicago was now closer to Hamburg than was New Orleans; Cleveland was nearer to Europe than were the Atlantic coastal ports; and the steel, grain, and automobiles of the Great Lakes region now went directly abroad without transshipment.

The active ocean-going, nonlake merchant fleet numbered 597 (or 8.2 million tons) at the end of 1961, but carried only 10 per cent of the nation's commerce. Federal subsidies provided $98 million for new ship construction and $182 million for operational costs that same year, and private ship operators have called for laws curtailing the navy's Military Sea Transportation Service and requiring at least half of foreign aid cargo to be sent abroad in American vessels. Labor has also been critical, primarily over the so-called "runaway" ships, American owned, but not subject to union regulations because of their foreign registry.

INDEXES OF OUTPUT PER MAN-HOUR FOR SELECTED
INDUSTRIES, 1940–60*

Industry	1940	1950	1960
Coal mining	53.6	63.0	115.3
Railroad transportation	50.3	71.1	111.1
Flour milling	79.6	69.7	104.0
Paper and pulp	75.6	78.4	109.3
Petroleum refining	57.8	68.3	114.1
Synthetic fibers	18.1	51.9	114.6

* 1957–59 = 100. From U.S. Department of Commerce, *Statistical Abstract of the United States, 1962*, p. 229.

GENERATION OF ELECTRICITY, COMPARED WITH TOTAL ENERGY
CONSUMPTION FOR SELECTED YEARS, 1902–55*

Year	Electricity (million kilowatt hours)	Total energy consumed (trillion BTU's)
1902	5,969	8,715
1912	24,752	15,708
1920	56,559	19,768
1930	114,637	22,253
1940	179,907	23,877
1950	388,674	33,972
1955	629,010	39,729

* Adapted from Samuel H. Schurr and Bruce C. Netschert, *et al., Energy in the American Economy, 1850–1975* (Baltimore: The Johns Hopkins Press, 1960), p. 182.

Industry generally fared better than rail and ocean transportation. Buying power pent up during World War II, a substantial population boom (from 141 million in 1946 to 183 million by 1961), a rising standard of living, the impact of the Korean War with its heavy government expenditures, and much expansion investment to offset depletion during the war and Depression years all contributed to an era of industrial progress and prosperity. This great rise was punctuated, however, by recessions beginning in 1948, 1953, 1957, and again in 1960. Manufacturing firms grew in number, but a high turnover rate prevailed: in 1959, for example, 28,200 new concerns entered the field and 25,600 were discontinued, a rate of exits to entrants of 91 per cent. Production by 1959 was 2.5 times the 1929 volume: the amount of capital in manufacturing had doubled, and output had significantly outstripped labor and capital input.

In spite of high taxes and inflation, times were good and the standard of living rose. Although 398 people each made more than $1 million in 1961, more than in any year since 1929, wealth was more widely distributed than before the Depression and the middle class had broadened appreciably: 67 per cent of all families had an income of over $4,000. As opposed to 1929, when the top 5 per cent of families held one quarter of the income, by 1956 the upper 5 per cent received but 18 per cent, and labor now received 29 instead of 18 per cent. By 1960, 97 per cent of all families owned a refrigerator, four out of five owned television sets (of which there were more than telephones), three out of four had at least one automobile, and three out of five owned their own home. Over 55,000 private swimming pools were built in the single year 1957, and Saks Fifth Avenue was selling Mark II after-shower cologne at $2,500 a bottle and Nieman-Marcus in Dallas offered "his" and "hers" airplanes for $176,000. But these extremes by no means indicated that housing was adequate, that slums had been cleared, or that low incomes had been banished. But certainly prosperity was widespread, demands for consumer goods were strong, and Americans were better off materially than ever before in normal times.

By the early 1950's the Depression-born animus against business was being dissipated, and because of tax concessions, many small businessmen were organizing as corporations. Despite occasional recessions and rising foreign competition as industrial output per man-hour rose more rapidly in Germany, France, Italy, and Japan than in the United States, corporations now entered an era of relative security. Long-term labor contracts (two or three years), government underwriting of the economy in an emergency, and substantial and continuing defense spending all made for greater stability, although business failures remained high.

Industry continued to move West and South. Many corporations sought to diversify and entire areas, especially New England, followed the same course in trying to sustain economic growth. More postwar capital came from earnings rather than the sale of new securities, and a new professional managerial class more frequently steered an independent course of action, since shareholders became more numerous and more widely diffused, hence less able to exert pressure.

There was evidence of liberal concern at the growing rate of business consolidation—"creeping Charlie Wilsonism," a wag later called it. In 1946 the Department of Justice believed the problem "more serious and widespread than at any time since the passage of the Sherman Act." A study of the 1,001 largest manufacturing concerns in existence on the first day of 1951 indicates that 854 survived as of September 15, 1959, and that 138 of the 147 which disappeared were merged with other firms. Concerns with large assets have consistently shown a higher rate of return than smaller ones: in 1957 the two hundred largest manufacturing companies earned about one quarter of all corporate profits. Similarly, large firms have been most successful in obtaining lucrative cost-plus defense contracts. In 1959 twenty corporations received over half and one hundred concerns over 74 per cent of all prime military contracts, though much subcontract work was done by smaller firms. In addition to actual consolidation—by no means a new trend—some twelve thousand trade associations by the fifties regulated business practices and standards, often eliminating any real semblance of competition.

From time to time federal agencies have acted in attempts to break monopolistic combinations, but have obviously approached the problem gingerly. Proposed mergers between Bethlehem Steel and Youngstown Sheet and Tube, the New York Central and the Pennsylvania Railroads, and Eastern and American Airlines have been blocked. The Supreme Court in 1957 ruled that du Pont's 23 per cent interest in General Motors violated the antitrust laws and (1961) ordered that the interest be sold. In 1961 lower courts levied $2 million in fines on twenty-nine major electrical companies and brief jail sentences on a few of their top executives for criminal price-fixing and bid-rigging. Yet despite these and other decisions, the approach was one of moderation rather than of widespread trust-busting on a large scale.

Actually, while the early 1960's showed a greater tendency toward business mergers than any time since the 1920's, many of these were for purposes of diversification and growth. Often new industries, like electronics, found that problems of finance, management, and marketing soon replaced science and technology as prime factors in success, and as they matured, consolidations or sales to larger firms became prominent. Established concerns were eager to move into new product lines: Ford Motor Company's acquisition of Philco in 1961, for example, not only put Ford in direct competition with General Motors' Frigidaire brand of appliances, but also gave immediate entry into the field of electronics, a field which attracted numerous old-line firms, including General Mills, Bell & Howell, and Hammond Organ. Noticeable was the tendency for broad diversification within a single company. One illustration, Textron, a textile firm, had by the early sixties acquired half a dozen subsidiaries manufacturing electronic equipment, shoes, aircraft parts, fiberglass boats, optical equipment, and drugs.

Among mature industries regarded as indicators of the state of general economic health, automobile manufacturing represented a high degree of concentration. The replacement and rebuilding years immediately following the war had permitted Kaiser-Frazer to become the first real newcomer into the field since Chrysler in the late twenties. But the new entrant did not survive and the decade of the fifties opened with but nine automobile manufacturers and closed with only five. The Big Three—General Motors, Ford, and Chrysler—were consistently among the top half dozen or so of American corporations on the basis of assets and sales. Total automobile production reached an all-time high of 7.4 million in 1955, but leveled off at 5.9 million in 1956, and dropped even lower during the 1957–58 recession. "It is not the unemployed people who are causing the recession, but the employed people who refuse to buy," said a General Motors vice-president by way of explanation. The foreign car sales captured 12 per cent of the American market by 1959, when manufacturers reluctantly condescended to produce the lighter, cheaper, less flamboyant compact car, which within two years accounted for 36 per cent of sales. Yet the industry has continued to emphasize "planned obsolescence," with annual style changes and retooling, which cost nearly $2 billion in 1956. In 1961 the industry presented the public with a choice of 352 different models, more than ever before, as it sought to exploit the growing markets for specialized needs—sport cars, station wagons, second cars—and to take advantage of the American mania for "up-to-dateness."

PRODUCTION OF INGOTS AND STEEL FOR CASTINGS,
1946–60*

Year	Production (1,000 sht. tns.)	Per cent of capacity
1946	66,603	72.5
1947	84,894	93.0
1948	88,640	94.1
1949	77,978	81.1
1950	96,836	96.9
1951	105,200	100.9
1952	93,168	85.8
1953	111,610	94.9
1954	88,312	71.0
1955	117,036	93.0
1956	115,216	89.8
1957	112,715	84.5
1958	85,255	60.6
1959	93,446	63.3
1960	99,282	66.8

* From U.S. Department of Commerce, *Statistical Abstract of the United States, 1962*, p. 811.

Steel was a "feast or famine" industry, which either prospered or did poorly, its soundness being linked closely with the motor vehicle industry and to expansion of production in general. Although its growth rate lagged behind that of the gross national product, it steadily increased its capacity to 150 million short tons in 1960, but peak output (1955) reached only 117 million tons.

Production was down to nearly 97 million tons in 1961 when a slowdown in expansion occurred in major steel markets as competition rose from aluminum, plastics, and prestressed concrete and as the automotive field had a poor year. Whereas at the turn of the century the Pittsburgh area had produced half the nation's steel, by 1960 it produced only about one third, and a notable shift toward consolidation was apparent. Significant was the overwhelming use of the open-hearth process and the new oxygen furnaces which permitted Jones & Laughlin of Cleveland to pour 491 tons in an hour compared with 60 tons for a comparable sized open-hearth plant. Also of importance was the development of new processes for the use of low-grade taconite and the increase of iron ore imports from South America, the latter an indication that the United States, now also the world's leading importer of zinc, lead, and copper, was becoming a "have not" nation in many vital natural resources.

The most impressive growth since the war has come in such fields as utilities, aircraft, electronics, chemicals, and rubber and plastics. Especially spectacular has been the rise of electronics, which has been called the "multiple non-industry" because of so many military, industrial, and household applications. Vital to automation and to the guided missile programs, electronics spurted from forty-ninth place in importance in 1939 to fifth by 1956, a position it retained in 1960, with factory sales of $9.8 billion, behind only automobiles, steel, aircraft, and chemicals. Aircraft expansion was also closely tied to defense. Chemicals expanded into a host of subfields: industrial (including materials for the chemical industry itself), synthetic fibers to replace natural, synthetic rubber, detergents, high-concentration fertilizers, food additives, pesticides, and a booming drug market on which the public spent $3.3 billion in 1961, including $410 million for antibiotics and $350 million for vitamins.

One far-reaching characteristic of the period was an accelerated technological advance of a nature and a rate setting it apart from earlier eras. By early 1963 eleven revolutionary commercial nuclear power plants were in operation, eight more were under construction, and seven others planned. Several pilot plants had been built to convert seawater to fresh, but the relatively high expense did not yet promise relief for parched Western regions with fast-growing populations. Much more important in its immediate impact was automation, which, with high-speed, precision self-regulating devices, took over a growing number of production and service processes. The data processing industry had reached $1 billion by 1960, as International Business Machines still controlled 75 per cent of the market, but was meeting competition. Computers abolished many tedious jobs, helped analyze sales, and make economic forecasts. Without them, Merrill Lynch, Pierce, Fenner & Smith would be unable to handle their 18 per cent of the New York Stock Exchange volume and scientists could not follow the flight paths of space shots. Salami manufacturers have come to base their production on daily price fluctuation information compiled by computer and even Nevada gambling houses use such electronic devices to keep close tab on the performance of their slot machines. Automation and data processing equipment have been instrumental in the expansion of new industries, have completely reoriented production in certain fields, and have affected labor unions and the entire employment pattern.

GROSS NATIONAL PRODUCT (CONSTANT 1954 DOLLARS),
1950–61*

Year	Total GNP (billions of dollars)	Per capita GNP (dollars)	Federal government purchase of goods & services (billions of dollars)
1950	318.1	2,096	45.1
1955	392.7	2,376	73.2
1956	400.9	2,383	72.3
1957	408.6	2,386	75.5
1958	401.3	2,305	79.3
1959	428.4	2,419	80.1
1960	440.8	2,440	80.2
1961 (prel.)	448.8	2,444	85.5

* From U.S. Department of Commerce, *Statistical Abstract of the United States, 1962*, p. 314.

The new technology brought an emphasis on research and development, with total outlays for this purpose rising in the 1960–61 fiscal year to $14 billion, of which only 9 per cent was for basic research, a field once ridiculed by former General Motors head Charles Wilson as "an effort to find out why grass is green." Approximately twenty per cent of industrial research is applied, with an increasing share devoted to development. Through the fifties the federal government was the major source of research and development funds, although industry did between two thirds and three fourths of the work.

In general the rate of growth of the gross national product has been sluggish since the mid-fifties, and such industries as coal, steel, metal mining, textiles, and lumber have expanded output slowly. The rate of growth has been estimated at 4.31 per cent for the 1839–79 period, 3.72 per cent for 1879–1919, 4.7 per cent for 1921–29, and 2.9 per cent from 1950 to 1959, the latter less than half the rate of growth in the U.S.S.R. during the same period. This slowdown in some fields, the complex employment problems created by automation, and rising foreign competition through high productivity have all caused concern to government as well as business.

Strong consumer demands for both goods and services were elemental in the economy. Americans in general had greater leisure and were better able to meet basic wants, with the result that they placed more emphasis on services and nonessentials such as amusements, art, and tremendous Christmas buying. Or they succumbed to the lure of "progessive obsolescence," as a multitude of new styles and colors made them dissatisfied with appliances, automobiles, or other items in what one writer has termed a "gadget economy."

Personal income reached $384.4 billion in 1962, after taxes. Of this, $29 billion went into savings, maintaining an average slightly above the 7 per cent of disposable income which had persisted from the turn of the century. Of the remaining $355.4 billion, roughly three fourths went for food, clothing, housing, and transportation, the rest being divided among various categories for medical care, education, welfare and religion, foreign travel, recreation, and "personal business," such as bank service or interest on the consumer installment debt which absorbed almost $7 billion of income annually by 1962.

Retailing was undergoing noticeable change. Discount department stores, patterned somewhat after the food supermarkets, had

DISPOSABLE PERSONAL INCOME, 1962*

	Amount (millions)	Per Cent of Total
Food and tobacco	$ 91,974	25.9
Clothing, accessories, and jewelry	35,759	9.7
Personal care	6,213	1.7
Housing	46,595	13.2
Household operation	49,638	14.0
Medical care and death expenses	23,704	6.7
Personal business	22,115	6.3
Transportation	44,082	12.4
Recreation	21,555	6.2
Private education and research	5,208	1.5
Religion and welfare activities	5,140	1.5
Foreign travel and remittances, net	3,377	.9
TOTAL	$355,360	100.0

* From U.S. Department of Commerce, *Survey of Current Business* (July, 1963), pp. 14, 20.

EXPENDITURE OF DISPOSABLE PERSONAL INCOME, 1929, 1947, 1962*

	1929 (per cent)	1947 (per cent)	1962 (per cent)
Durable commodities	11.7	12.4	13.4
Nondurable commodities	47.7	56.5	45.5
Services	40.6	31.1	41.1

* From U.S. Department of Commerce, *Survey of Current Business* (July, 1963), p. 20; Stanford Research Institute, *Industrial Economics Handbook* (1963).

captured retail business estimated variously at from $10 billion to $25 billion by 1961, when some 1,500 to 1,900 of them were in operation. By aggressive promotion, reduced services, and convenient night hours, the discount houses were able to make a profit on volume sales at lower prices. Some manufacturers dumped surplus goods on them, undercutting other retailers who could not maintain fair trade prices. This, plus court decisions, seriously weakened the state fair trading laws which had been passed in the 1930's to prevent price competition among small retailers.

Small merchants found survival more difficult in the postwar business world, as chain stores and mail order houses grew and

GROWTH OF A & P STORES AND SALES, 1859–1961*

Year	No. of Stores	Sales (millions of dollars)	Year	No. of Stores	Sales (millions of dollars)
1859	1	—	1929	15,418	1,054
1880	100	—	1938	10,900	879
1900	200	—	1940	7,230	1,116
1910	372	—	1946	5,200	1,909
1914	991	—	1954	4,200	4,140
1919	4,224	195	1961	4,409	5,240

* Adapted from Godfrey M. Lebhar, *Chain Stores in America, 1859–1962*, 3rd ed. (New York: Chain Store Publishing Co., 1963), p. 33.

broadened their activities and as the rise of the supermarket and the shopping center accentuated the trend toward fewer but larger retail units. From 1929 to 1956 the volume of retail sales was up 400 per cent but the number of stores increased only 40 per cent. For every supermarket it opened after 1937, the A & P abandoned three neighborhood stores, reducing their total by 1961 from 14,700 to 4,400. In 1958, chain stores, with only 6.3 per cent of the total number of retail outlets in the country, were responsible for 26.7 per cent of the total sales. A & P and Sears, Roebuck & Company, the leading mail order house, both recorded $5 billion sales in 1961. Sears, Roebuck, like its competitors (which now include J. C. Penney Company), added a wide spectrum of products to its mail-order line, ranging from ringtail monkeys at $49.89 each to package tours and original works of art, but four fifths of its sales came from its 740 retail stores.

Since the war, suburban America has popularized the shopping center, and by 1960 some 4,000 of these, often ugly and unattractive, dominated by huge parking lots, but offering a variety of retail and service establishments, had swept the country at the expense of stores in central city areas. In 1930 downtown stores in Los Angeles commanded 88 per cent of metropolitan retail sales in that region; by 1959 only 19.6 per cent. By the end of 1961 an estimated one quarter of all American retail trade was done in the shopping center. Moreover, the drive-in, once limited largely to foods, pushed on to new frontiers. Americans on wheels need not leave their automobiles to view movies, post their letters, or deposit their money or their dry cleaning.

Pre-packaging of foods grew in importance. Frozen pastries, prepared dinners, and a wide selection of other foods needed only heating. Synthetics, like detergents or "wash and wear" fabrics, made deep inroads in traditional markets. Vending machines appeared in unlikely places with even more unlikely products, moving from candy, cigarettes, and chewing gum into hot foods and beverages (replacing entire cafeteria staffs), shoeshines, insurance, and laundry. Available twenty-four hours a day and presenting a minimal labor problem, the vending machine stands forth as a cold, efficient, impersonal symbol of American technological progress.

Advertising by 1962 had become a $15 billion a year industry as business sought to reduce the growing gap between capacity and sales. Advertisements then averaged 1,600 per person per day and 2.77 per cent of the national income was spent on them in 1959, an increase of nearly two and a half times over the 1947–49 period. Particularly evident in recent years has been the use of snob appeal and the status symbol in urging the public to "upgrade" itself through consumption ("They'll know you've *arrived* when you drive up in an Edsel"). Of special importance was the relatively new medium of television, which failed to live up to its potential as a cultural force (the chairman of the Federal Communications Commission called it a "vast wasteland" in 1961), but nevertheless became highly effective as an advertising medium and a major industry in itself. From around 10,000 sets in use in 1947, the number multiplied to 55.5 million by 1961, when more than 700 stations were in operation.

Agriculture displayed many of the same trends as before World War II. The amount of land in cultivation remained fairly constant, but the number of farms steadily decreased, from 5.9 million in 1945 to 3.8 million in 1961, and the average value of the land and buildings of each rose to $35,578. The family farm continued to decline, and in 1960 the top 9 per cent (in size and assets) of American farms produced as much as the bottom 91 per cent, although included in the Department of Agriculture's statistics are about 1.3 million spare-time farmers who receive

FARM IMPLEMENTS AND MACHINERY, 1940, 1950, AND 1960*

Item	1940	1950	1960
Total value (million dollars)	3,060	11,314	18,574
Number of tractors† (1000)	1,567	3,394	4,770
Number of motor trucks (1000)	1,047	2,207	3,110
Grain combines (1000)	190	714	1,065
Corn pickers (1000)	110	456	780
Farmers total expenditure for:			
Motor vehicles‡ (million dollars)	384	1,735	1,361
Machinery & equipment (million dollars)	241	1,279	1,178

* From U.S. Department of Commerce, *Statistical Abstract of the United States, 1962*, p. 639.
† Excludes garden tractors.
‡ Excludes family share of automobiles.

over 90 per cent of their income from other sources. More and more, large scale operations predominated. In certain fields of specialization, agrobusiness has replaced more traditional farm enterprise to a limited extent: meat packers, for example, frequently supply chicks and feed to poultry farmers, with a guaranteed return on each bird, the grower contracting to produce a stipulated number of fryers at periodic intervals, not for a free market but at known costs and prices.

Rural population continued to drop steadily and only 8.1 per cent of Americans lived on farms by 1961. But the standard of living rose, and despite a drop in agricultural employment, output of farm products climbed after the early fifties, and with a few brief declines, surpluses have continued to accumulate, even in the face of federal support programs. Farm prices failed to keep pace with consumer prices and the net income of farm operators averaged only $3,350 in 1956, compared with $3,250 for the unskilled worker, over $5,000 for the skilled or semi-skilled, and $10,750 for the self-employed businessman. Farm income in 1961 was exactly equal to the 1949 level, although the total national income had almost doubled in the same period. Farm indebtedness rose to $24.3 billion, about 12 per cent of the total value of assets by 1960. But the farm picture was spotty: large producers often prospered through increased production; small operators were not so fortunate.

Moreover, the continuance of federal support programs neither eliminated the surplus problem nor gave much help to the family farmer. Price supports had been retained after the war and when relief needs abroad had been met, surpluses began to build up. Congress showed a willingness to extend subsidies, retaining the basic principles of the New Deal farm program except for more flexible price supports based on the war years. In the 1952 campaign, Democrats attempted to capitalize on the then farm prosperity, attributing it to their own party's parity program:

> The farmer's farmin' every day,
> Makin' money, and that ain't hay!
> (Clap, clap)
> DON'T LET THEM TAKE IT AWAY!*

But the Eisenhower administration, despite a more conservative Secretary of Agriculture, Ezra Benson, made few significant changes: it suggested a lower scale for price supports, purchased $8 billion worth of surpluses, but lost $1.2 billion on them in two years through deterioration and sale overseas. Both parties took credit for passage of the "soil bank" in 1956, which removed land from cultivation for purposes of conservation. Unfortunately, the poorer land was taken out of crop use and better techniques raised the output on the remaining acres.

Government payments to the farmer had totaled $723 million in 1940; in 1961 they ran nearly $1.5 billion. In 1959 the stored surplus of farm commodities in federal hands had a value of nearly $9 billion and storage costs alone ran $1.5 million per day, even with the use of many government-owned merchant vessels for this purpose. Traditionally, farmers have not been satisfied with strict production controls and have rejected them, as the wheat growers did in 1963. With price floors sustained by the Department of Agriculture, large-scale farmers particularly have been able to reduce their acreage, but still produce more. Thus federal aid, designed to save the family farm, is most beneficial to the more prosperous commercial farmers, a small minority. Two of them, Producers' Rice Mill of Arkansas and the Delta and Pine Land Company of Mississippi, received more subsidies

* From the song by Robert Sour and Bernie Wayne.

in a single year than all the farmers in the state of Maryland. Flagrant abuses have appeared from time to time and spokesmen of both parties agree that the program has not achieved its purpose. They also agree that it is not politically expedient to discard it.

Experts consider agriculture a declining industry, the small farm an inefficient unit. Probably half the present number of farms could produce an adequate food supply and a series of "rural reconstruction" programs like the recent Rural Areas Development Plan have been suggested to infuse new life into communities dependent upon agriculture and to encourage farmers to move to town. Such "reverse homestead" laws, however, meet strong farm inertia; in addition, adequate funds for moving, housing, and retraining have not been available. Better utilization of crop surpluses is needed—for the indigent, especially—and long-range retirement of cropland. The irony is that for nearly half a century, only war seems to have solved the farm problem or, indeed, many other of our economic ailments.

The persistence of a federal agricultural program, even if not wholly successful, was an indication of the continuance of the basic New Deal premise that government must play a positive role on behalf of the general welfare. Shortly after the Japanese surrender in September, 1945, President Truman had set before Congress his own version of the New Deal, a multipoint program containing what he later called the Fair Deal. Included were expanded Social Security, higher minimum wages, a Fair Employment Practices Act, additional public housing and slum clearance, more TVA-type projects; federal aid to education, health insurance, and higher farm supports. Congress moved cautiously, many of its members refusing to accept "the corrupting idea that we can legislate prosperity, legislate equality, legislate opportunity," as Senator Taft of Ohio expressed it. But by the Employment Act of 1946, Congress committed the federal government to a general policy, authorizing the appointment of a Council of Economic Advisors to study the economy and make quarterly reports, with suggestions for actions necessary to maintain prosperity and a high level of employment.

Interpreting his election in 1948 as a mandate for his Fair Deal,

Truman pushed his program more vigorously, but at many vital points was blocked by a coalition of Republicans and conservative Democrats. An FEPA was defeated by a Southern filibuster; the American Medical Association raised $3 million to scuttle the health insurance program; and federal aid to education foundered on the question of whether or not it should go to parochial schools. On the other hand, Congress in 1949 did raise the minimum wage from forty cents to seventy-five cents an hour and the Housing Act of the same year provided for the construction of 810,000 low income housing units spread over a six-year period. Additional funds were forthcoming for TVA and for the Rural Electrification Administration and in 1950 Social Security benefits were extended to cover an additional 9.7 million beneficiaries.

The election of Dwight Eisenhower in 1952 brought a professed middle-of-the-roader to the White House, despite his apparent affinity for business interests and an original Cabinet made up of wealthy businessmen and the president of the United Association of Journeymen Plumbers and Steamfitters ("eight millionaires and a plumber"). The new administration abolished controls on wages and prices (linked to the Korean War), cut back federal employees, and trimmed budgets. Hoover's old RFC was permitted to die but was replaced by a Small Business Administration; offshore oil lands were handed over to the states; synthetic rubber plants to private concerns. But Social Security was extended to another 10 million people; minimum wages were raised to $1 an hour; and Congress voted 20,000 new housing units in 1954 and 45,000 the following year. Aid was voted for hospitals, rehabilitation centers, and urban renewal. Farm subsidies were continued, at slightly lower than Democrat desires; $2.5 billion worth of farm surpluses were released for foreign aid and school lunches; and the Reciprocal Trade Agreements Acts were renewed regularly. Eisenhower supported a $1.3 billion school aid bill in 1955, but got nothing; he supported measures for airport improvement, and got a highway bill in 1956 which would ultimately connect forty-two state capitals and 90 per cent of all cities over 50,000 population with at least four-lane superhighways. The Federal Education Act of 1958 set up a seven-year, $1 billion program of student loans and grants to improve teaching of sciences and languages. Eisenhower proposed a limited public health insurance program, but moved away from federal development of the Hell's Canyon power project in favor of private concerns. His administration moved to the right, but retained all the basic welfare programs of the previous twenty years, although his so-called dynamic conservatism provided more decentralization than pleased New Dealers and Fair Dealers.

Nor did the administration of the late John F. Kennedy depart from the accepted pattern. Kennedy attempted, but without complete success, to extend state welfare functions at a more rapid pace than his predecessor, but Congress often refused to vote funds for the purpose. In addition, Congress rejected his proposed program of federal aid for mass transit systems, and it spurned his Medicare plan for health insurance for older people under Social Security. On the other hand, Congress continued to support higher education, voted money for job retraining and vocational education and for county mental health centers, at the same time extending Social Security and raising minimum wage levels, specifically requiring equal pay for women.

Especially significant was the role of government in the economic dislocations of the postwar period. In each case, to one extent or another, the "automatic adjustors"—Keynesian spending through Social Security, farm supports, unemployment compensation, veterans' pensions and federal agencies for expanding or restricting credit—were brought to bear and undoubtedly helped mitigate recession. During the fourteen-month decline of 1948–49, industrial production fell off 10 per cent and unemployment rose to 3 million before readjustment set in and the Korean War brought increased federal spending and a return of prosperity as well as price and wage controls. Following the Korean armistice (July, 1953) and the dropping of controls, farm income began to decline and industrial output and unemployment figures followed the 1948–49 curve. Republicans blasted such "peddlers of gloom and doom" as Senator Paul Douglas of Illinois, but all agreed that government action must be taken to prevent another 1929. Credit was relaxed, taxes cut, Social Security and unemployment compensation stepped up, and the

President was willing to forgo a balanced budget for another year. By the summer of 1954 the Council of Economic Advisors could announce that the worst was over. A year later, steel was up to 95 per cent of capacity as compared with 65 during the trough of the cycle. When Eisenhower ran his second presidential race against Adlai Stevenson in 1956, the Republican Party could use the slogan, "Everything's booming but the guns," ignoring the plight of agriculture.

When Eisenhower proposed a budget of $71.8 billion, the largest in peacetime history to that date (1957), Secretary of the Treasury Humphrey predicted "a depression that will curl your hair" if it was not cut. Congress did trim $4.9 billion away, but the recession came anyway, although not necessarily because of Humphrey's clairvoyance. By late spring, 1958, industrial production was down nearly 15 per cent over the previous year and 5 million were unemployed. But again the "built-in stabilizers" cushioned the shock. Credit controls were relaxed and federal spending was stepped up for defense and public improvements. Unemployment-insurance payments were extended eight weeks. By fall, an upswing was clearly evident but recovery was slow and actually not complete until 1960.

Late that same year a fourth recession commenced, the mildest of the postwar crop. By February, 1961, when bottom was hit, production was off 7 per cent, and no real upsurge came until late fall, by which time unemployment had dropped from a peak 7 per cent to close to 6, and automobile sales and stock market activities were booming. The new President Kennedy consciously chose personal advisors from the "growth" school of economics —men who believed in a larger federal role in managing the economy and a more militant use of governmental power to achieve growth and full employment. The action of the Kennedy administration fell far short of the recommendations made by its advisors, but expenditures were quickly stepped up to increase private consumption, stimulate buying, and encourage expansion. The federal highway program was speeded up, and the minimum wage raised to $1.25; the depressed area redevelopment program was expanded to cover 675 "distressed" areas, and Congress authorized $4.9 billion for new public housing. Social Security was liberalized to include 3.6 million more people and unemployment compensation extended thirteen weeks. Never was there any question but that the federal government should act, even though it meant national deficits. Between 1954 and 1961 inclusive, there were but three years in which there were treasury surpluses, and the national debt continued to grow from $271.3 billion to $289 billion, which somewhat offset the government's efforts to limit inflation. By 1958 the dollar was worth about eighty cents compared with the 1947–49 dollar, though inflationary trends were more apparent in the average cost of services than of commodities. Currency and deposits increased, as did the net public and private debt, and tax rates, while lower than wartime levels, remained high, but loopholes in the form of low capital gains tax, exemption on state and municipal bonds, a 27.5 per cent depletion on resources, and deductible expense accounts tended to favor the wealthy.

Of the total budget dollar, in 1962 fifty-four cents came from individual income taxes, twenty-six cents from corporate income

PUBLIC DEBT OF THE FEDERAL GOVERNMENT, 1946–61*

Year	Total gross debt (millions of dollars)	Per capita debt (dollars)	Per cent of federal expenditures paid for debt interest
1946	269,422	1905.42	7.8
1947	258,286	1792.05	12.7
1948	252,292	1720.71	15.8
1949	252,770	1694.75	13.5
1950	257,357	1696.68	14.5
1951	255,222	1653.42	12.7
1952	259,105	1650.06	9.0
1953	266,071	1666.74	8.8
1954	271,260	1670.14	9.4
1955	274,374	1660.16	9.9
1956	272,751	1621.82	10.2
1957	270,527	1580.20	10.4
1958	276,343	1587.63	10.6
1959	284,706	1606.14	9.4
1960	286,331	1584.83	11.9
1961	288,971	1573.49	10.9

* From U.S. Department of Commerce, *Statistical Abstract of the United States, 1962*, p. 401.

taxes, twelve cents from excise taxes, and the remaining eight cents from miscellaneous sources. At the same time (1962), national defense absorbed sixty-two cents of each budget dollar, interest on the debt ten cents, veterans, agriculture, and health and welfare each six cents, while all other expenditures took ten cents. Thus the importance of defense spending even in peacetime looms large in the economy and is one of the vital factors maintaining or restoring economic health. Kennedy's "man on the moon" program, for example, promises not only scientific knowledge and strategic import, it will also ultimately pump some $40 billion into the economy.

Unlike in the 1920's, the United States after World War II made no attempt to retreat into a shell of semi-isolationism, but instead assumed broad responsibilities in helping Europe to its feet and in the emerging struggle against expanding Communism. Such responsibilities involved not only political, diplomatic, and occasionally military commitments as well, they quickly came to be rooted in programs of extensive economic support on a global scale.

Along with fifty-nine other nations, the United States became a party to the International Monetary Fund, an outgrowth of the Bretton Woods Conference in 1944, designed to stabilize exchange rates and remove trade obstacles. It joined and provided a third of the capital of the International Bank for Reconstruction and Development (better known as the World Bank), which guaranteed or gave direct loans for self-liquidating projects in underdeveloped countries throughout the world.

At the end of World War II, the United States was the only nation capable of supplying goods to war-torn Europe and to the underdeveloped nations, provided normal trade relations could be re-established. But, while the United States proved willing to expand her exports, she was not willing to step up her imports proportionately. Since American investments abroad soon outran foreign investments in the United States considerably, the over-all balance greatly favored the United States, and world gold supplies and invisible earnings were not sufficient to make up the difference. However, new modes combining military spending and

BALANCE OF INTERNATIONAL PAYMENTS, 1945, 1950, 1955, 1960
(in Millions of Dollars)*

Item	1945	1950	1955	1960
Export of goods and services	16,273	14,427	22,327	29,064
Import of goods and services	10,232	12,098	17,937	23,327
Balance on goods and services	6,041	2,329	4,391	5,738
Unilateral transfers, net (to foreign countries is–)	−7,113	−4,533	−4,811	−4,254
U.S. capital, net (outflow of funds is −)	−1,569	−1,421	−1,521	−4,965
Foreign capital, net (outflow of funds is −)	2,085	1,912	1,454	2,427
Gold sales (purchases are −)	548	1,743	41	1,702

* From U.S. Department of Commerce, *Statistical Abstract of the United States, 1962,* p. 858.

EXPORTS OF U.S. MERCHANDISE AND IMPORTS, BY
ECONOMIC CLASSES, 1950 AND 1960*

Item	1950		1960	
EXPORTS OF U.S. MERCHANDISE	Value (millions of dollars)	Per cent of exports	Value (millions of dollars)	Per cent of exports
Total	10,142	—	20,349	—
Crude materials	1,886	18.60	2,588	12.72
Crude foodstuffs	760	7.49	1,645	8.09
Manufactured foodstuffs	634	6.25	1,117	5.49
Semimanufactures	1,121	11.05	3,526	17.33
Finished manufactures	5,741	56.61	11,473	56.38

IMPORTS	Value	Per cent of imports	Value	Per cent of imports
Total	8,743	—	14,650	—
Crude materials	2,465	28.20	3,012	20.56
Crude foodstuffs	1,750	20.02	1,720	11.74
Manufactured foodstuffs	898	10.27	1,566	10.69
Semimanufactures	2,126	24.32	3,091	21.10
Finished manufactures	1,504	17.20	5,260	35.90

* From U.S. Department of Commerce, *Statistical Abstract of the United States, 1962,* p. 879.

foreign aid would be set up to transfer funds and at the same time to try and prevent the spread of communism into new areas.

Time brought shifting trade patterns, with increasing emphasis on the export of manufactured goods, the leaders in this respect by the middle 1950's being automobiles, industrial machinery, grain and grain products, chemicals, iron and steel, and electrical equipment, with raw cotton now reduced to ninth place. Where finished goods had made up about one third of all American exports in the early 1920's, they now made up almost two thirds. Raw materials and semimanufactures still dominated the import list, but the leading products of the eve of World War I—hides, coffee, sugar, raw silk, and crude rubber—gave way to nonferrous metals and ferroalloys, petroleum, coffee, paper and paper products, and sugar, indicating that the United States was consuming more and also depleting certain resources. Where in 1914 Europe had taken over 60 per cent of all American exports and had provided 44 per cent of the imports, by 1955 less than one third of our exports went to Europe and only about one quarter of our imports came from that source. Canada became the best American customer, taking one fifth of our exports and providing more goods than all of Europe, while Latin America became almost as important.

As a result of the General Agreements on Tariff and Trade, to which the United States was a party, tariff levels remained relatively low, running roughly 11 per cent of the value of imports, such cuts being made in this country under the Reciprocal Trade Agreement Acts of the 1930's, renewed periodically by Congress. A fluctuating volume of exports from time to time and rising labor and production costs raised doubts from numerous quarters as to the ability of the United States to compete on world markets, but a record $19.6 billion in exports in 1960 allayed such fears, at least momentarily.

But new problems remained. With the European Common Market countries booming in the late fifties, American business sought to tap these rich markets and in so doing in three years after 1959 established over eight hundred branches overseas, such investments in 1961 alone totaling over $700 million. These outlays, along with foreign aid payments, imports, expenditures by American troops and tourists abroad, and remittances by immigrants to the old country upset international balances. American exports did not increase in 1958 and 1959, and United States gold stocks fell to $17 billion, a twenty-two-year low. President Eisenhower sought to cut expenditures abroad by reducing the duty-free allowance for American tourists and by preventing overseas residence of dependents of American military personnel, an order subsequently revoked by President Kennedy. Faced with the prospect of intense competition from the Common Market, many American business and government leaders recognized the need for industrial modernization and full capacity production, rather than at 17 per cent below capacity as in 1961. Some also recognized the need for co-operation among government, labor, and business, although President Kennedy's bid for "new and bold authority" to cut tariffs in response to Common Market competition and for federal aid to industries harmed by imports encouraged by a low tariff was not immediately granted.

At the end of World War II Americans felt an obligation to aid Europe, where it was, as Herbert Hoover expressed it, "now 11:59 on the clock of starvation." Lend-Lease came to a halt, but primarily through the United Nations Relief and Rehabilitation Administration, financed mainly by the United States, an additional $4 billion had been poured into European aid between V-E Day and the spring of 1947, while direct relief was also provided by the privately operated CARE program and through army organizations in both Japan and Germany. By 1947 the federal government had spent over $11 billion in Western Europe alone and had in addition made available funds through the Export-Import Bank, bolstered the British economy with a loan of $3.8 billion, and granted aid to the Philippine Islands, which became independent in 1946.

While such programs were doubtless imperative, they were too limited to promote full rehabilitation by themselves. And, moreover, as the Russian Bear extended its influence, a new justification was added to the American philosophy of aid abroad. Faced with a vacuum left by Britain's decision to withdraw troops from Greece, and realizing the need to bolster both Greece and Turkey against the possibilities of a Communist coup, President Truman in March, 1947, suggested a $400 million aid program to "contain" Communist aggression. Said Truman:

I believe that it must be the policy of the United States to support free peoples who are resisting attempted subjugation by armed minorities or by outside pressures. . . . I believe that our help should be primarily through economic and financial aid which is essential to economic stability and orderly political processes.

Congressional acceptance of the limited Truman Doctrine for Greece and Turkey helped pave the way for more extensive foreign aid programs for other areas of the world. At Harvard University in June, 1947, Secretary of State George Marshall invited European nations to draw up a joint program for economic recovery, to be submitted to the United States, who would, if Conpress approved, implement it with funds for mutual assistance. A sixteen-nation group proceeded to do so, and Congress, impressed with the Communist coup in Czechoslovakia in 1948 at the very time the proposal was being debated in Washington, responded quickly to the need for economic aid to contain further Red expansion.

With Congressional authority, the Economic Cooperation Administration was established under Paul Hoffman, former Studebaker president, and $4 billion set aside to get the program underway. Within four years $12 billion had been channeled through ECA, with remarkable effects in bolstering European economic growth. Beginning in 1951 the functions of ECA were taken over by the Mutual Security Agency, emphasizing the increased importance of military aid, but the basic purpose of the program remained the same. By this time European industrial production was up 64 per cent and the standard of living was greatly improved, which in turn worked against the spread of Communism in such countries as Italy and France. Not all was sheer philanthrophy, however: healthy European economies meant healthy markets for American goods, although there were plenty of short-sighted critics at home who saw no practical advantage to the "Martial Plan" or "Operation Rathole," as they called it.

In his inaugural address of January, 1949, President Truman called for "a bold new program for making the benefits of our scientific advances and industrial progress available for the improvement and growth of underdeveloped areas." The poverty of people living in these regions, insisted Truman, "is a handicap and a threat both to them and to more prosperous areas." Thus did Truman set the stage for his Point Four program for technical assistance and capital investment for development, which the United Nations endorsed and which Congress translated into law in June, 1950. In the next three years $400 million would go into Point Four aid, sending technicians and training natives to fight disease and to increase food production, enlarging power and industrial facilities, and improving living conditions in some thirty-five countries, especially in Latin America, the Middle East, and Southeast Asia.

By the middle 1950's the U.S.S.R. was also using "economic and social collaboration as a means for jumping military as well as political barriers," according to Secretary of State John Foster Dulles, who urged that American foreign aid be kept high in order to counter Soviet assistance in such areas as Egypt, India, and Burma. Congress consistently reduced President Eisenhower's Mutual Security budget, but he supplemented it with Development Loan funds and with money loaned through the Export-Import Bank and the International Monetary Fund and through his Atoms for Peace project. President Kennedy in early 1961 suggested and Congress approved the Alliance for Progress, a ten-year program for growth and improvement in Latin America, except for Cuba, an omission which caused Ernesto Guevara to attack the plan as an "instrument of economic imperialism." But President Kennedy, though empowered by Congress to promise long-term aid for foreign development, remained dependent upon Congress for annual appropriations, hence aid programs lacked the long-range assurances they needed.

But by whatever name—whether Truman Doctrine, Marshall Plan, Point Four, or Alliance for Progress—foreign aid has become an integral part of American foreign policy, an aggressive and mutually beneficial arrangement, despite some shortcomings and an appeal from some European quarters for "trade, not aid." All together, between July 1, 1945, and June 30, 1962, the United States expended nearly $97.7 billion on foreign aid of all kinds, of which roughly two thirds was economic and one third military. Of this, nearly $45 billion went to Europe, over $22 billion to the

Far East; almost $18 billion to the Middle East and South Asia; some $7 billion to Latin America; and $1.8 billion to Africa. West Germany received $5 billion and Japan nearly $4 billion, together considerably more than all of Latin America, a fact which did not please our Latin neighbors.

By 1960, with almost 180 million people scattered in fifty states and the District of Columbia, the urban, industrial, and generally affluent United States stood as the world's foremost economic power. Especially after 1900, the various "revolutions" that began early in the previous century virtually transformed the national economy, bringing mass production and mass consumption of goods, rising standards of living, and a growing complexity not only of economic institutions but also of life in general.

A highly mobile and dynamic population, acquisitive in nature, adapted European techniques where applicable, then proceeded to reshape their economy in keeping with New World resources and environment. Expanding demands for cotton and other staples, the movement westward to help meet these demands, the widening and improving transportation network which tied together markets and raw materials and made possible a thriving commerce, and the slow and then more powerful surge of industrial growth were all based on technological advance—the key to lower production costs and cheaper goods.

But technological change brought complexity. To help supply credit and capital, commercial banking, a new and increasingly sophisticated institutional framework, appeared: savings banks, insurance companies, and in time investment banks would help provide the capital mobility required by business and agricultural expansion. As industrial capitalism began to grow more rapidly after the Civil War, new modes of business organization and administration accompanied technological improvements. Both consolidation and the scientific management of the early twentieth century sought to eliminate the waste of the competitive system and were instrumental to mass production.

Shifting trade patterns made the United States increasingly an importer of raw materials from non-European sources and an exporter of manufactured goods. Until after World War I, by which time the United States had achieved the status of a "creditor" nation, the prevailing high protective tariff probably did little to harm American foreign trade. On the domestic scene, the gradual growth of larger, more intricate wholesale and retail agencies was a dominant trend, as patterns of consumption changed along with those of production, distribution, and income. In a leisure-oriented society, consumer tastes have been unduly influenced, according to mid-twentieth century critics, by advertising and by the "waste makers"—the devisers of "planned obsolescence" who seek to sustain markets by producing new styles and colors each year to outmode old models overnight.

Obviously, the exceedingly complex phenomenon of economic development has left clouds on the horizon. The long-term plight of the American farmer, the problems of labor versus management, the displacement of human power by automation, the unsolved questions posed by mushrooming urban and suburban communities, the unfavorable balance of international payments of the late 1950's and early 1960's—all these are in their own way byproducts of the rise of industrial capitalism and of advancing technological change. And the challenges they pose are serious ones in modern America.

Moreover, another question of moment accentuated by developments since 1860 is the relationship of government to the economy. Except for the tariff and for direct and indirect encouragement to business and agriculture, the federal government played a minimal role until the late nineteenth century, when transportation and markets were clearly no longer local. By the time of World War I, railroads, banks, and business combinations were subject to regulation. If such controls were relaxed in the 1920's, Americans turned to Washington for stronger action when private enterprise seemed to falter during the dark days of the Depression.

In response to these demands, the New Deal era brought numerous programs of apparent permanency—Social Security, rural electrification, and farm subsidies, for example—and, above all, the basic concept that government should act on behalf of the public welfare in time of distress and without. The application of "automatic stabilizers" and fiscal weapons has been demonstrated repeatedly in the era since World War II, as security-conscious Americans have sought the assurance of maximum employment. In addition, the federal government, through its large-scale expenditures for defense, has helped to sustain the economy in good times as well as poor. In short, Big Labor came to offset Big Business, and Big Government counterbalanced both, as nineteenth-century laissez faire gave way grudgingly to a mixed economy, with growing demands for greater governmental participation.

Dwindling natural resources, vastly improved transportation and communications, and a common cause in two world wars and the Cold War have made the United States more of a part of an international structure than ever before—more than the Founding Fathers or the Captains of Industry could have imagined. For in the complexities of "growing up," the American economy in the twentieth century became ever more closely tied to overseas markets, investments, sources of raw materials, and ideological commitments.

BIBLIOGRAPHY

GENERAL AND SPECIAL SOURCES

Periodicals

Articles on the economic history of the United States appear from time to time in *The American Historical Review* and *The Mississppi Valley Historical Review*, but more regularly in the specialized journals *Agricultural History, Business History Review*, and *The Journal of Economic History*. The *American Economic Review*, the *Quarterly Journal of Economics*, and the *Journal of Political Economy* also contain many articles of historical significance. Indispensable to an understanding of American economic development in the twentieth century are the *Wall Street Journal* and *The New York Times*.

Government statistical sources

Exhaustive data are found in the Census Bureau's decennial *Census of the United States* and in its *Census of Manufactures*, now biennial. Detailed information for the more recent period is also available in the Federal Reserve Board's *Federal Reserve Bulletin;* the Department of Commerce's *Survey of Current Business;* and the *Monthly Labor Review*, published by the Bureau of Labor Statistics. Statistical materials from these and other sources are brought together conveniently in *Historical Statistics of the United States, Colonial Times to 1957* (1960), issued jointly by the Bureau of the Census and the Social Science Research Council. This may be supplemented by the annual *Statistical Abstract of the United States*, which contains more detailed and up-to-date figures.

345

General economic histories

Basic is the detailed multivolume *Economic History of the United States,* under the editorship of Henry David, Harold U. Faulkner, Louis M. Hacker, Curtis Nettels, and Fred A. Shannon. Of the ten volumes projected, eight are already published: Curtis P. Nettels, *The Emergence of a National Economy, 1775–1815* (1962); Paul W. Gates, *The Farmer's Age: Agriculture, 1815–1860* (1960); George R. Taylor, *The Transportation Revolution, 1815–1860* (1951); Fred A. Shannon, *The Farmer's Last Frontier: 1860–1897* (1945); Edward C. Kirkland, *Industry Comes of Age: Business, Labor, and Public Policy, 1860–1897* (1961); Harold U. Faulkner, *The Decline of Laissez Faire, 1897–1917* (1951); George Soule, *Prosperity Decade: From War to Depression, 1917–1929* (1947); and Broadus Mitchell, *Depression Decade: From New Era through New Deal, 1929–1941* (1947).

Excellent surveys of the field written by economists include: Herman E. Krooss, *American Economic Development* (1955); Chester W. Wright, *Economic History of the United States* (1941); and August C. Bolino, *The Development of the American Economy* (1961). Among the best written by historians are Arthur Bining, *The Rise of American Economic Life* (1955); Fred A. Shannon, *America's Economic Growth* (1951); Harold U. Faulkner, *American Economic History* (1960); and Edward C. Kirkland, *A History of American Economic Life* (1951). Occupying a more middle position between the two disciplines, either written jointly by historians and economists or by men teaching both fields, are: Donald L. Kemmerer and C. Clyde Jones, *American Economic History* (1958); Gilbert C. Fite and Jim E. Reese, *An Economic History of the United States* (1959); and George Soule and Vincent P. Carosso, *American Economic History* (1957). Two valuable multiauthor surveys are Harold F. Williamson, ed., *The Growth of the American Economy* (1944), written by both historians and economists; and Seymour Harris, ed., *American Economic History* (1961), done almost entirely by economists.

A popular history of business development is John Chamberlain, *The Enterprising Americans* (1963); much more significant is the provocative *The Age of Enterprise* (1943), by Thomas C. Cochran and William Miller, which emphasizes business enterprise in its social setting. Of a more theoretical nature is Joseph Dorfman's monumental *The Economic Mind in American Civilization, 1606–1933* (5 vols., 1946–1959). Note should also be made of an older general history which stresses economic forces and which is still stimulating, *The Rise of American Civilization* (2 vols., 1927), by Charles and Mary Beard.

Collections of readings on economic history

Older collections include Ernest L. Bogart and Charles M. Thompson, eds., *Readings in the Economic History of the United States* (1929); and Felix Flügel and Harold U. Faulkner, eds., *Readings in the Economic and Social History of the United States* (1929). More recent are N. S. B. Gras and Henrietta M. Larson, eds., *Casebook in American Business History* (1939); William Letwin, ed., *A Documentary History of American Economic Policy Since 1789* [to 1935] (1961); and Joseph T. Lambie and Richard V. Clemence, eds., *Economic Change in America* (1954), comprised of articles from recent journals.

Special sources and studies

The conditions of pre-American settlement are surveyed in Edward P. Cheyney, *European Background of American History: 1300–1600* (1904). A broad and original approach on the impact of world exploration and colonization on Europe is Walter P. Webb, *The Great Frontier* (1952). Curtis P. Nettels, *The Roots of American Civilization* (1938) covers the colonial period in detail and stresses economic aspects. Of interest for contemporary observations are John Smith, *The General History of Virginia, New England, and the Summer Islands* (1907); William Bradford, *Of Plymouth Plantation* (1952); and John Winthrop, *The History of New England, 1630–1649* (2 vols., 1959). On the coming of the Revolution, John C. Miller, *Origins of the American Revolution* (1943) is cogent, while the outcome is analyzed in J. Franklin Jameson, *The American Revolution Considered As a Social Movement* (1926), which is now being revised somewhat by recent historical research. For the period following the Revolution, compare the pessimistic *Critical Period* (1888), by John Fiske, with Merrill M. Jensen, *The New Nation: A History of the United States During the Confederation, 1781–1789* (1950), which takes a more positive view. Likewise, Charles Beard's classic, *An Economic Interpretation of the Constitution of the United States* (1913), should be read in the light of such recent critics as Robert E. Brown, *Charles Beard and the Constitution* (1956) and Forrest McDonald, *We The People* (1958).

For the period to 1865, Louis M. Hacker gives an astute interpretation based on the rise of capitalism, rather than the westward movement, in his *Triumph of American Capitalism* (1940). For the twentieth century, a fascinating source of detail on economic as well as social life is Mark Sullivan, *Our Times: The United States, 1900–1925* (6 vols., 1926–1935). Also pungent and interpretive is Frederick L. Allen, *The Big Change* (1952), on the first half of the same century. Excellent background on the 1920's is found in Allen's *Only Yesterday* (1931), while David A. Shannon, ed., *The Great Depression* (1961) is a collection of contemporary comments. John K. Galbraith, *The Affluent Society* (1958) is an economist's penetrating analysis of the modern scene, and Eric Goldman, *The Crucial Decade and After* (1961) is a broader treatment of the years since World War II. The 1950's get detailed discussion in Harold G. Vatter, *The U.S. Economy in the 1950's: An Economic History* (1963).

THE WESTWARD MOVEMENT

An excellent point of departure is George R. Taylor, ed., *The Turner Thesis Concerning the Role of the Frontier in American History* (1949, *Problems in American Civilization* series), which gives the germ of Turner's thesis and a sampling of its criticism. Standard surveys of the westward movement include Ray A. Billington, *Westward Expansion* (1960); Robert Riegel, *America Moves West* (1960); and Thomas D. Clark, *Frontier America* (1959). Also useful is Frederick Jackson Turner, *The Significance of Sections in American History* (1932); and Ralph H. Brown, *Historical Geography of the United States* (1948).

For the movement into the South, see Everett Dick, *The Dixie Frontier* (1948); and Emory Q. Hawk, *Economic History of the South* (1934). On the trans-Allegheny region, contemporary comments are to be found in Morris Birkbeck, *Notes on a Journey in America* (1818); Thomas Ashe, *Travels in America in 1806* (1808); and J. M. Peck, *A New Guide for Emigrants to the West* (1836). Beverly W. Bond, *The Civilization of the Old Northwest* (1934) and R. Carlyle Buley, *The Old Northwest* (2 vols., 1950) complement each other. Richard Wade's incisive *The Urban Frontier: The Rise of Western Cities, 1790–1830* (1959) pioneers in a long neglected field.

On the early history of the Far West, excellent coverage is given in Katherine Coman, *Economic Beginnings of the Far West* (2 vols., 1912); and Ray A. Billington, *The Far West Frontier* (1956, *New American Nation* series). Hiram Chittenden, *American Fur Trade of the Far West* (3 vols., 1902) is still the best work on the subject, though Paul C. Phillips and John W. Smurr, *The Fur Trade* [from colonial times] (2 vols., 1961) is broader and more recent. Kenneth W. Porter's *John Jacob Astor* (2 vols., 1931) is a thorough study of Astor's part in the fur trade as well as in many other business endeavors. The classic of the Santa Fe trade is Josiah Gregg, *Commerce of the Prairies* (2 vols., 1844). The Pacific Northwest is ably treated in Oscar O. Winther, *The Old Oregon Country* (1950); Utah in Leonard Arrington's fine *Great Basin Kingdom* (1959); and early California in John Caughey, *California* (1940).

A convenient survey of land policy is Roy Robbins, *Our Landed Heritage: The Public Domain, 1776–1936* (1942). Thomas Donaldson, *The Public Domain* (1884) is a compendium of undigested information of considerable value. A recent collection of essays from many authors, *The Public Lands* (1962), edited by Vernon Carstensen, is particularly valuable.

There is no good survey of the development of mining: Thomas A. Rickard, *A History of American Mining* (1932) is the best available, but has severe limitations. An excellent study of a more limited area is Grant Smith, *History of the Comstock Lode* (1943). William S. Greever ably brings together the story of the Western mining rushes between 1848 and 1900 in *The Bonanza West* (1963); and Rodman Paul, *Mining Frontiers of the Far West, 1848–1880* (1963), is a penetrating analysis of Western mining for the period it covers.

Older works are still the best surveys of the Western range cattle industry, especially Ernest S. Osgood, *The Day of the Cattleman* (1929) and Edward E. Dale, *The Range Cattle Industry* (1930), although later studies like Maurice Frink, *et al., When Grass Was King* (1956) and Lewis Atherton, *The Cattle Kings* (1961) have made substantial contributions to our understanding of financial and business aspects of the industry.

For the filling in of the agricultural West after the Civil War, Fred A. Shannon, *The Farmer's Last Frontier: 1860–1897* (1945) and Walter P. Webb's highly provocative *The Great Plains* (1931) are fundamental. Webb's attempts to relate geographic conditions to the development of institutions are criticized by Shannon and others in *Critiques of Research in the Social Sciences* (1940). *The Sod House Frontier* (1937), by Everett Dick, is both social and economic in content, and an excellent description of plains farm life is found in Howard Ruede, *Sod-House Days: Letters from a Kansas Homesteader, 1877–1878*, edited by John Ise (1937).

AGRICULTURE

Still the best brief summary is Everett E. Edwards, "American Agriculture—The First 300 Years," in United States Department of Agriculture Yearbook (1940). Joseph Schafer, The Social History of American Agriculture (1936) is by no means complete, but is precise and thoughtful. A fine modern collection of sources is in Wayne D. Rasmussen, ed., Readings in the History of American Agriculture (1960).

For the pre-Appomattox era, two good earlier histories are available: Lewis C. Gray, History of Agriculture in the Southern United States to 1860 (2 vols., 1933); and Percy W. Bidwell and John I. Falconer, History of Agriculture in the Northern United States, 1620–1860 (1925). More recently, a third excellent but less detailed study of much of the same period has been added, Paul W. Gates, The Farmer's Age, 1815–1860 (1960); and Fred A. Shannon, The Farmer's Last Frontier 1860–1897 (1945) carries the story on to the turn of the century.

An important work is Avery Craven, Soil Exhaustion as a Factor in the Agricultural History of Virginia and Maryland, 1606–1860 (1926). The best survey in its field is Rudolph A. Clemens, The American Livestock and Meat Industry (1923); more specialized are Paul C. Henlein, Cattle Kingdom in the Ohio Valley, 1783–1860 (1959); and John T. Schlebecker, Cattle Raising on the Plains, 1900–1961 (1963). Meyer Jacobstein, The American Tobacco Industry in the United States (1907); and J. Carlyle Sitterson, Sugar Country (1953) are the most thorough studies in their respective fields. On cotton, two works are outstanding: M. B. Hammond, The Cotton Industry (1897); and David L. Cohn, The Life and Times of King Cotton (1956).

The Peculiar Institution (1956), by Kenneth M. Stampp, has superseded Ulrich B. Phillips' American Negro Slavery (1918) as the standard work on slavery, although Phillips is still valuable for details of plantation life, especially his Life and Labor in the Old South (1929) and his Plantation and Frontier (2 vols., in John R. Commons, et al., A Documentary History of American Industrial Society (1958 reprint).

One aspect of agricultural technology is skillfully handled in Reynold M. Wik, Steam Power on the American Farm (1953). William Hutchinson's Cyrus Hall McCormick (2 vols., 1930, 1935) is much more than a biography of the inventor of the reaper. Some of the consequences of the new machines are considered in Leo Rogin, *The Introduction of Farm Machinery in Its Relation to the Productivity of Labor in the Agriculture of the United States during the Nineteenth Century* (1931). The "farm problem" of the late nineteenth century is dealt with in general fashion in Solon J. Buck, *The Granger Movement* (1913), and his *Agrarian Crusade* (1921); and in John D. Hicks, *The Populist Revolt* (1931). Prominent studies of the twentieth century "farm problem" include: Gilbert C. Fite, *George N. Peek and the Fight for Farm Parity* (1954); Theodore W. Schultz, *Agriculture in an Unstable Economy* (1945); and two objective volumes by Murray R. Benedict, *Farm Policies of the United States, 1790–1950* (1953) and *Can We Solve the Farm Problem?* (1955).

TRADE AND COMMERCE

One of the best general surveys of the field is Emory R. Johnson, *et al.*, *History of Domestic and Foreign Commerce in the United States* (2 vols., 1915). An incisive analysis of economic growth based on trade is Douglass C. North, *The Economic Growth of the United States, 1790–1860* (1961). Broad in approach and superb in execution is John G. B. Hutchins, *The American Maritime Industries and Public Policy, 1789–1914* (1941). Early trade with the Orient is covered by Foster Rhea Dulles in *The Old China Trade* (1930). Robert G. Albion, *The Rise of New York Port* (1939) is first rate for the 1815–1860 era, and Samuel Eliot Morison's *Maritime History of Massachusetts, 1783–1860* (1921), a much broader work than the title implies, is unsurpassed.

The ubiquitous peddler is the subject of Richardson Wright's delightful *Hawkers & Walkers in Early America* (1927). Lewis Atherton has made two careful studies of retailing, *The Pioneer Merchant in Mid-America* (1939), and *The Southern Country Store, 1800–1860* (1949); while in his *Pills, Petticoats and Plows* (1944), Thomas D. Clark considers many of the social aspects of the country store in the South. W. T. Baxter, *The House of Hancock* (1945) is a model history of an eighteenth-century Boston merchant house; and Stuart Bruchey and Robert Oliver, *Merchant of Baltimore, 1783–1819* (1956) is also important. Two especially good studies of merchant capitalism in the Pacific Northwest and the Southwest are respectively Arthur L. Throckmorton, *Oregon Argonauts* (1961), and William J. Parish, *The Charles Ilfeld Company* (1961). Among numerous histories of individual department or mail order stores, two of the most scholarly are Ralph Hower, *History of Macy's of New York, 1858–1919* (1943); and Robert W. Twyman, *History of Marshall Field & Co., 1852–1916* (1954). A popular and critical commentary on modern advertising, written with considerable historical background, is Joseph J. Seldin, *The Golden Fleece* (1963).

TRANSPORTATION

Much information is found in Seymour Dunbar's popular and detailed *History of Travel in America* (4 vols., 1915); and in Balthasar H. Meyer, ed., *History of Transportation in the United States before 1860* (1917); but the best survey of the period before the Civil War is George R. Taylor, *The Transportation Revolution, 1815–1860* (1951). An admirable book of a more specialized nature is Joseph A. Durrenberger, *Turnpikes: A Study of the Toll Road Movement in the Middle Atlantic States and Maryland* (1931). See also *The National Road* (1948), by Philip D. Jordan. Alvin F. Harlow, *Old Towpaths* (1926) is popular, but remains the best general treatment of the canal era.

On sailing vessels, Robert G. Albion, *Square-Riggers on Schedule: The New York Sailing Packets to England, France, and the Cotton Ports* (1938), and Carl C. Cutler, *Greyhounds of the Sea: The Story of the American Clipper Ship* (1930), are both colorful and reliable. Less impressive is John H. Morrison, *History of Steam Navigation* (1903). A popular description of steamboating on the Great Lakes is Walter Havighurst, *The Long Ships Passing* (1942). Interesting information on river traffic is found in Zadok Cramer, *The Navigator* (1814 and other years); in Leland Baldwin, *The Keelboat Age on Western Waters* (1941); and in Louis C. Hunter, *Steamboats on the Western Rivers* (1949), the latter an exceptional economic and technological study.

John W. Starr, Jr., *One Hundred Years of American Railroading* (1928), and Stewart Holbrook, *The Story of American Railroads* (1947), are surveys; Charles F. Adams, Jr., *Railroads: Their Origin and Problems* (1878) is a contemporary analysis. Two fine sectional studies are available in Edward C. Kirkland, *Men, Cities and Transportation* (2 vols., 1948), dealing with nineteenth-century New England; and Robert E. Riegel, *The Story of Western Railroads* (1926), on the transcontinental lines. Federal land grants to railroads are considered at length in L. H. Haney, *A Congressional History of Railways in the United States* [to 1887] (2 vols., 1908, 1910); and among many excellent histories of individual lines, Paul Gates, *The Illinois Central Railroad and Its Colonization Work* (1934) pioneered in a detailed explanation of the disposition of such lands by the companies.

Henry Adams and Charles Francis Adams, Jr., have written the classic description of financial manipulation of rail securities in *Chapters of Erie and Other Essays* (1886); William Z. Ripley, *Railroads: Finance and Organization* (1915) is more general and more scholarly. *The American Railroad Network, 1861–1890* (1956) by George R. Taylor and Irene D. Neu pulls together the threads that made individual lines work as an integrated system.

Apart from biographies of many important railroad men, several studies attempt to assess these men as groups. Among them are Thomas C. Cochran, *Railroad Leaders, 1845–1890: The Business Mind in Action* (1953); and Julius Grodinsky, *Transcontinental Railway Strategy, 1869–1893: A Study of Businessmen* (1962).

On the coming of the telegraph, the best book is Robert L. Thompson, *Wiring a Continent* (1947); while J. A. Miller, *Fares, Please* (1941) is an excellent survey of street railways. *The Automobile Industry* (1941), by E. D. Kennedy, is a general work; and now standard on Henry Ford and the Ford Motor Company is *Ford* (3 vols., 1954–1963), by Allan Nevins and Frank E. Hill. For air transportation, see Henry L. Smith, *Airways: The History of Commercial Aviation in the United States* (1942).

INDUSTRY AND MANUFACTURING

The most comprehensive survey to 1928 is Victor S. Clark, *History of Manufactures in the United States* (3 vols., 1929). Rolla M. Tryon, *Household Manufactures in the United States, 1640–1860* (1917) depicts nonfactory enterprise. Among the better histories of individual industries are: Melvin T. Copeland, *The Cotton Manufacturing Industry of the United States* (1923); Arthur H. Cole, *The American Wool Manufacture* (2 vols., 1926); Blanche E. Hazard, *The Organization of the Boot and Shoe Industry in Massachusetts Before 1875* (1921); and Joseph G. Butler, Jr., *Fifty Years of Iron and Steel* (1922). Also outstanding are John Rae, *American Automobile Manufactures* (1959); and Harold C. Passer, *The Electrical Manufacturers, 1875–1900* (1953). The early development of the petroleum industry is best covered by Paul H. Giddens, *The Birth of the Oil Industry* (1938); and the reader should compare Ida M. Tarbell's polemical *History of the Standard Oil Company* (2 vols.,

1904); with such recent examples of scholarship as Ralph W. Hidy and Muriel E. Hidy, *History of Standard Oil Company (New Jersey)*: *Pioneering in Big Business, 1882–1911* (1955).

John Oliver's *History of American Technology* (1956) is general but not always reliable. Allan Nevins and Jeannette Mirsky, *The World of Eli Whitney* (1952); and Matthew Josephson, *Edison* (1961) are competent portrayals of the great inventors of different eras. Two volumes dealing with technological advance are Roy T. Bramson, *Highlights in the History of American Mass Production* (1945); and Siegfried Giedion, *Mechanization Takes Command* (1948). Arthur F. Burns, *Production Trends in the United States since 1870* (1934); and George H. Evans, Jr., *Business Incorporations in the United States, 1800–1943* (1948) both use broad statistical bases. For an early account of business consolidation, written in the era of the Muckrakers, see John Moody, *The Truth About the Trusts* (1904). A more recent analysis of concentration is David E. Lilienthal, *Big Business, A New Era* (1953).

Industrial leaders are dealt with harshly in Gustavus Myers, *History of the Great American Fortunes* (3 vols., 1911); and in Matthew Josephson, *Robber Barons* (1934), both highly influential works. More objective, but by no means complimentary, is Frederick L. Allen's, *The Great Pierpont Morgan,* a fine portrait in words. Typical of the tendency of many modern scholars to view industrial and financial giants against the environment in which their subjects lived and to judge by standards of their subject's period are Allan Nevins, *Study in Power: John D. Rockefeller, Industrialist and Philanthropist* (2 vols., 1953); and Forrest McDonald, *Insull* (1962). *Men in Business* (1952), edited by William Miller, brings together essays by several authors who generalize about business leaders as a group; while in *Dream and Thought in the Business Community, 1860–1900* (1956), Edward C. Kirkland analyzes the thinking of businessmen on social issues of their day.

LABOR

Two useful one-volume surveys of labor history are Foster Rhea Dulles, *Labor in America* (1949); and Joseph G. Rayback, *A History of American Labor* (1959). John R. Commons, *et al., History of Labour in the United States* (4 vols., 1918–1935) is helpful; and Norman Ware, *The Labor Movement in the United States, 1860–1895* (1929) is particularly perceptive.

The best study of indentured servants is Abbott E. Smith, *Colonists in Bondage: White Servitude and Convict Labor in America, 1607–1776* (1947). A delightful and reliable book is Hannah Josephson's *The Golden Threads, New England Mill Girls and Magnates* (1949). Edith Abbott, *Women in Industry* (1910) is broader. General information on the relation of immigration and labor is found in Marcus L. Hansen, *The Atlantic Migration, 1607–1860* (1940); and Carl Wittke, *We Who Built America* (1939).

Still good is Selig Perlman, *A History of Trade Unionism in the United States* (1922). Lewis L. Lorwin, *The American Federation of Labor* (1933) and P. F. Brissenden, *The I.W.W., A Study in American Syndicalism* (1920) are the best on these unions. Early labor leaders have written interesting accounts, especially Samuel Gompers, *Seventy Years of Life and Labor* (2 vols., 1925); and Terence V. Powderly, *The Path I Trod* (1940). *The Bending Cross: Debs* (1949) is a sympathetic biography by Ray Ginger.

The foremost study of real wages is Paul H. Douglas, *Real Wages in the United States, 1890–1926* (1930). Labor since the New Deal is considered in Katherine Lumpkin, ed., *Labor in Postwar America* (1949); and Harry A. Millis and Emily Brown, *From the Wagner Act to Taft-Hartley* (1950).

MONEY, BANKING, AND FINANCE

A time-honored survey is Davis R. Dewey, *Financial History of the United States* (8th ed., 1922). Also valuable is J. Lawrence Laughlin, *The History of Bimetallism in the United States* (1896). *Robert Morris, Revolutionary Financier* (1954), by Clarence L. Ver Steeg, is an able work, really a history of Revolutionary War financing; just as E. P. Oberholtzer, *Jay Cooke, Financier of the Civil War* (2 vols., 1907) is much broader than the life of one man.

On banking, the outstanding study is Bray Hammond's prize-winning *Banks and Politics in America, from the Revolution to the Civil War* (1957). On the second Bank of the United States, Arthur P. Schlesinger, Jr., *The Age of Jackson* (1945); and Ralph C. H. Catterall, *The Second Bank of the United States* (1903) are both somewhat partisan but useful. Paul M. Warburg, *The Federal Reserve System* (2 vols., 1930) is long and detailed but spiced with personal experiences. The best short appraisal of American banking is found in Ross Robertson, *History of the American Economy* (1955).

Taxation is broadly treated in Sidney Ratner, *American Taxation: Its History As a Social Force in Democracy* (1942). Frank W. Taussig, *The Tariff History of the United States* (8th ed., 1931) is old, dull, but sound. The best single volume on investments in and from the United States is Cleona Lewis, *America's Stake in International Investments* (1938).

GOVERNMENT AND PUBLIC POLICY

Oscar Handlin and Mary F. Handlin, *Commonwealth: A Study of the Role of Government in the American Economy: Massachusetts, 1774–1861* (1947) is pertinent. Alexander Hamilton's concept of the function of government in economic matters becomes clear in Louis Hacker, *Alexander Hamilton in the American Tradition* (1957); and Broadus Mitchell, *Alexander Hamilton* (2 vols., 1957, 1962). Aid to transportation is analyzed by Carter Goodrich, *Government Promotion of American Canals and Railroads, 1800–1890* (1959). Sidney Fine, *Laissez Faire and the General-Welfare State: A Study of Conflict in American Thought, 1865–1901* (1956) is objective, and more theoretical.

Literature is abundant on the expanding role of government since the Great Depression. In *The Great Crash—1929* (1955), John K. Galbraith discusses at length the inability, or the unwillingness, of federal agencies to use controls which might have averted disaster. For the 1930's, Broadus Mitchell, *Depression Decade: From New Era through New Deal, 1929–1941* (1947); and Dixon Wecter, *The Age of the Great Depression* (1948) are invaluable. The multivolume works of Arthur M. Schlesinger, Jr., *The Age of Roosevelt* (4 vols., 1957–1962); and Frank Freidel, *Franklin D. Roosevelt* (3 vols., 1952–1956) are essential to an understanding of the New Deal. Excellent shorter coverage is given in Basil Rauch, *The History of the New Deal, 1933–1938* (1944); and William E. Leuchtenburg, *Franklin D. Roosevelt and the New Deal, 1932–1941* (1963, New American Nation series). Robert Sherwood, *Roosevelt and Hopkins* (2 vols., 1948) covers a multitude of problems, foreign and domestic; and useful commentaries by others who played important roles in planning or administering the New Deal program include David E. Lilienthal, *TVA; Democracy on the March* (1944); Hugh S. Johnson, *The Blue Eagle from Egg to Earth* (1935); and Raymond Moley, *After Seven Years* (1939). The presidential point of view for the Fair Deal years is reflected in Harry S Truman, *Memoirs* (2 vols., 1956); while Richard Rovere, *The Eisenhower Years* (1956) is a general appraisal of the first Eisenhower administration. Wilfred Lewis, Jr., *Federal Fiscal Policy in the Postwar Recessions* (1962) is an analysis by an economist of government action taken in the 1948–1962 era.

For authoritative discussions of economic mobilization and controls in World War I, see Bernard M. Baruch, *American Industry in the War* (1941); and H. J. Tobin and Percy W. Bidwell, *Mobilizing Civilian America* (1940). For World War II, material on the same subjects is available in John R. Craf, *A Survey of the American Economy, 1940–1946* (1947); Eliot Janeway, *The Struggle for Survival* (1951); and the U.S. War Production Board, *Industrial Mobilization for War* (1947). Postwar foreign aid is dealt in Willard H. Thorp, *Trade, Aid, or What?* (1954); and Redvers Opie and William A. Adams, Jr., *American Foreign Assistance* (1953).

INDEX